© 2018 Graham Jones
1st Edition
Cover Designed by James Weston
Picture research Graham Jones
ISBN: 9780-9928062-1-7
Order No. PMO105

Exclusive Distributors Music Sales Limited,
14/15 Berners Street, London, W1T 3LJ.

Published by Proper Music Publishing Limited,
1-5 Applegarth Drive, Questor, Dartford, Kent, DA1 1AG.

ery effort has been made to trace the copyright holders of the photographs
in this book but one or two were unreachable.
We would be grateful if the photographers concerned would contact us.

Design Aleph Studio

A catalogue record for this book is available from the British Library.
Visit Omnibus Press on the web at www.omnibuspress.com

The views expressed in this book are of Graham Jones
and not necessarily of Proper Music.

THE VINYL REVIVAL AND THE SHOPS THAT MADE IT HAPPEN

Contents

Side 2

THE SHOPS THAT MADE IT HAPPEN - The Vinyl Guide to UK Record Shops

Foreword by David Sinclair

I was talking to my brother, John, the other day. After a period of upheaval, he recently moved away from London. The first thing he did when he got installed in his new place was to pick up a vintage music system with a turntable and unpack the collection of vinyl albums he's been carting around, unopened and unplayed, for the last 25 years.

The records date back to the 1970s and before. Had he been tempted to get rid of them? "Never," John said. "They are things of beauty. And they evoke too many memories." We got talking about that and he reminded me of the first record he ever bought, "Tap Turns on the Water", a single by C.C.S. which reached No.5 in the UK chart in 1971. He recalled queueing up to buy it (can you imagine?) at an HMV shop in Union Street in Glasgow. Years later, at the same shop, he was amused to hear the big, middle-aged woman in front of him ask for "I Love a Feel". Without missing a beat, the youthful assistant pulled out "I Feel Love" by Donna Summer.

John is part of the vinyl revival – and he doesn't even know it, yet. Ironically, what got him back into vinyl, was listening to playlists that he and a bunch of his friends started circulating on Spotify - greatest songs of the 1970s, the 1980s, the 1990s, that sort of thing. Suddenly, he was gripped by the desire to listen again to these magnificent musical creations the way they were intended to be heard.

It is not only people of my brother's generation who are embracing the format. Jos, 27, who plays bass in my band the DS4, has a growing collection of vinyl LPs. "For me the sound of vinyl is just so cool," Jos says. "It immediately makes me think of all those hip acts in the 1990s who used scratchy old records to sample stuff from, like Beck and Moby and the hip hop guys. Buying an LP from Rough Trade West or one of the market stalls in Portobello Road is making a serious commitment to listening to that music. It makes listening to music a stand-alone experience rather than a background noise while you're travelling on the tube. Vinyl had pretty much gone when I was a kid, so getting an album puts me in touch with the deep musical values of an era I never lived through."

My daughter, Faith, 28, uses the picture sleeves of her 7 and 12-inch singles as artwork in her flat. When her favourite band, Alexisonfire broke up, she bought the anniversary, limited-edition, white-vinyl version of their album, *Crisis*. She could get somewhere between £70 and £140 for that now, according to Discogs.

At the same time as the pendulum of personal taste has swung decisively back in favour of a format that was thought to be in terminal decline, there has been a revolution in that part of the retail sector that embodies the spirit of the vinyl revival: the independent record shops. When I took the DS4 to play an in-store gig at Sound Knowledge in Marlborough, we were knocked out by the beauty of the shop, the range of stock and the professionalism of the staff. Sound knowledge, indeed.

Over the years we have played Record Store Day events all round the South of England – from David's Music in Letchworth, where we set up and played a set among the racks, to Badlands Records in Cheltenham where they hired the nearby nightclub Subtone for a full-scale gig. In every case, we found these shops were doing far more than selling records. They are a social and commercial hub for the musical communities of their towns.

If there is one man who saw all this coming, and who did about as much as anyone to bring it about, it is Graham Jones. A legend in the world of music retailing and a hustler supreme, Graham has devoted his time, energy, and considerable marketing expertise to the cause of supporting, promoting and celebrating independent record shops. His influential book *Last Shop Standing: Whatever Happened to Record Shops?* which started out as an obituary, turned into a catalyst for the rebirth of an entire retail sector. Since then, his evangelism has led him to embrace the vinyl revival, which has been the instrument by which the record shops have earned themselves such an auspicious reprieve.

The Vinyl Revival and the Shops that Made it Happen is the latest chapter in a love story that Graham has been living through his whole life. His passion for the shops, and the stories of the people who own and run them, spills from the pages as he treks across the counties, countries and several islands of the UK, leaving no stone unturned in his search for the latest news from the retail frontline and another batch of groan-aloud gags from behind the counter.

The old Radio 1 Roadshow character Smiley Miley has got nothing on Graham, and I doubt there is a more widely-travelled person in the UK music distribution sector. His latest book distils all that hard-earned wit and wisdom into an indispensable guide to the state of the nation's record shops. He is the man who moved the needle.

About this book

This book tells the story of the vinyl revival through the eyes of those who made it happen: the owners and staff of the record shops who take part in Record Store Day. Without Record Store Day, I am convinced that we would have fewer record shops now than we had a decade ago.

The book includes a few record shops that do not participate in this annual celebration, for reasons which are explained, and I have also included a few quirky record shops that, although off the beaten path, are well worth making the effort to visit.

There is another book to be written on the brilliant second-hand record shops and many wonderful vinyl market traders throughout the UK. However, my expertise is on record shops which sell new vinyl, as these are the retail outlets I visit as part of my day job as a sales representative for Proper Music. These are the shops of which I can offer a personal view.

This book tells the stories behind many much-loved record shops so that when you visit them you will feel like you already know the characters behind the counter. It is perfect for vinyl fans to keep with them on their travels around the country. If you are thinking of opening a record shop there is plenty of advice to help you fulfil that dream.

To appreciate the rise and re-birth of the independent record shop it is important to understand the reasons behind its fall, and that is where the story begins.

Introduction

2018 is my thirty-second year of travelling around the UK working as a sales representative selling new CDs, vinyl, cassettes and, in my early days, 8 track cartridges to independent record stores. I witnessed their number decline from more than 2,200 when I had started in the 1980s to just 269 by 2009.

To highlight the situation, I wrote the book *Last Shop Standing: Whatever Happened to Record Shops?* It told the story of the decline of the independent record shop. At the time independent record shops were closing at an average of ten a month yet nobody seemed to notice them vanishing from the high street. Even worse, nobody seemed to care. There was plenty of media coverage about the disappearing pub trade but nothing about the declining numbers of record shops. Maybe the media enjoy a drink more than a good tune, I pondered. Armed with my trusty voice recorder I toured the UK, calling on the 50 record shops that I felt would be among the Last Shops Standing, with the aim of recording their stories and bringing them some much-needed publicity.

As I set out on my journey I was convinced that I was writing the obituary of the record shop. It felt like I was recording history for future generations who would learn what a fantastic experience it had been to shop at these magical places and to understand why they had closed. I was aware that in the early part of the 20th century our high streets contained stamp shops, coin shops and candlestick makers, but who talks about them anymore? They had become forgotten retailers. I did not want record shops to vanish from our minds, as for decades they have helped define our youth and our musical tastes. It was important they did not go the same way as the candlestick makers.

At each shop I visited, I would take the owner to the pub (doing my one-man campaign to keep our pubs going). I would ask them how they had started and how the industry had changed over the years. I was keen to learn why they were still going while hundreds of others had closed their doors. It soon became clear to me that these shop owners were a breed apart. No record shop owner was in it for the money. They were simply passionate music fans who loved what they did and received enormous satisfaction from introducing their customers to new music.

To them it was a labour of love, or as Barry Everard from Record Collector in Sheffield termed it "a calling". When I mentioned the word "holiday" to them it was something they did not seem to recognise. If they did take a break it was almost always to a music festival or camping somewhere like Bognor Regis, as opposed to the beach in Barbados.

It soon became apparent that these shop owners had some great stories to tell. I laughed at some of the capers they got up to and some of the mad characters that paid them a visit. I became educated about the dodgy dealings and shenanigans the music industry got up to by hyping their records up the charts. I admired the tenacity these shops showed in keeping going while operating on a profoundly un-level playing field.

Record shops had brought so much joy to my life both as a youth growing up on Merseyside touring the record shops of the area each Saturday to build up my own vinyl collection, and through my work at HMV Liverpool. Since 1985, my job has involved selling directly to the independent record shops. Major record companies such as Sony, Universal and Warner Music would have numerous reps covering the country. Throughout my career, I have worked for the smaller distributors and often my area has been the whole of the UK.

Watching record shops close one by one, I felt obliged to do something about it. I was convinced that if I could inform the public of what was going on in the world of record retailing then maybe I could embarrass the industry into supporting the record shops and encourage the public to check them out and give them some much needed support.

As a first-time author, my expectations for *Last Shop Standing: Whatever Happened to Record Shops?* were extremely low. I had figured out that if each of the 50 record stores I had written about bought 10 copies then I might cover my costs. I had taken a somewhat economical approach to compiling the book, taking the budget option of asking my 15-year-old son Ben if he would do the first edit and then enlisting my next-door neighbour (a retired teacher) to do the second. A friend of mine from football practice, James Weston, offered to do the sleeve if I bought him a pint down the pub.

Most of the photos were taken on a digital camera I bought in the Argos sale, reduced from £69 to £49. This truly was a book on a budget.

To my amazement the book took off, even spawning a film, as I discovered there were thousands of music fans out there just like me. They loved their record shops and they were concerned about the record shops vanishing from their towns.

The final chapter of Last Shop Standing was titled "Hope."

I believed there was a future for the record shop if it could garner public support and capitalise on the developing interest in vinyl.

The start of Record Store Day in 2008 would become the catalyst for the vinyl revival as it was also giving shops some positive media coverage, a change from the usual reports of another record shop closing.

What happened next was beyond my wildest dreams. A comeback of Lazarus proportions has resulted in more than 100 record shops opening since 2009. Many have been launched by young, enthusiastic music fans who have embraced vinyl and vastly changed the record shop model.

Although I repeatedly updated *Last Shop Standing*, the changes in the music industry in recent years have been monumental. The time is now right to tell the story of the vinyl revival and the contribution made to it by independent record shops.

THE VINYL REVIVAL - From Carnage to Comeback

Chapter 1

Reasons for the decline of the independent record shop

The music business has changed virtually beyond recognition since the introduction of file-sharing and downloading in the 1990s. Technology changed the relationship between recorded music and physical product which inevitably changed the retail model for distributing recorded music. At the beginning of the 1990s if you wanted to buy music then it involved a trip to the record shop to purchase your chosen music either on vinyl, cassette or video. By the end of the decade, sales of vinyl were in freefall, cassettes were in decline, DVDs had replaced video, and CD had become the must-have music format.

The CD revolution initially gave independent record shops a boost, as the CD took up little space in a shop. But the format was quickly embraced by everybody from supermarkets and mail-order sellers to garage forecourts. With so many of their competitors now selling their core product, the CD became a contributing factor in the decline of record shops. But there were many other factors, some of them completely unrelated to technology, that hastened the wave of closures that engulfed the independent record shops.

The killer tax loophole
Nothing contributed more to the destruction of record shops in the UK than an EU tax exemption originally intended to save money. This loophole became known as the silent killer of record shops. Low Value Consignment Relief (LVCR) is an exemption from VAT on goods below a certain value threshold imported into the European Union. At the highest point in its history, this value was set at £18 which covered pretty much every CD and DVD. The purpose of the exemption was to save money by avoiding the complicated and costly process of collecting tax on "low value" packages. In practice, it was used by the Channel Islands mail order industry (which was outside the EU) to avoid paying VAT and, instead of saving money, this completely legal loophole cost the UK well over one billion pounds over 10 years.

This is how it worked:
A customer would search the internet to find the cheapest price to purchase a CD. As a Channel Islands-based internet retailer did not have to charge VAT on items under £18, their advertised products would always be cheaper than those of any retailer based in the UK who did have to charge VAT. More often than not, this price advantage ensured that the Channel Islands-based retailers obtained a UK customer's order at the expense

of a UK record shop or mail order company.

The Channel Islands-based internet retailer would order the CD from the UK record company which would ship the CD out to the Channel Islands. The CD would then be posted back in to the UK to the customer in a jiffy bag. No VAT was due because of LVCR being applied.

Can you imagine the feeling of despair throughout UK record shops as potential customers would come in to the shop and comment that the title they were interested in purchasing was cheaper online?

It was not long before this practice started having a huge impact on high street record shops and UK-based internet sellers alike, all of whom found themselves trading at a 17.5% (and later 20%) disadvantage. As virtually every CD in the UK retailed at a price below £18, this tax break proved to be devastating for the UK music retail trade. The UK government's failure to tackle the issue resulted in hundreds of record shop closures.

If you ever bought multiple CDs via a Channel Islands internet retailer, did you ever wonder why they were dispatched to you in separate jiffy bags? That was to keep the price below £18 and therefore avoid paying VAT. If multiple CDs were dispatched in the same jiffy bag the value would likely be above £18 ensuring the retailer would be liable for VAT.

LVCR should have been removed from Channel Islands mail order goods as soon as the Government became aware that it was being used to undermine UK high street retail. Unfortunately, HMRC and the UK Government made it clear that they had no plans to end the Channel Islands' use of LVCR. Due to the rapid growth of a company called Play.com (the first retailer to use the LVCR exemption to sell CDs) by the end of 2004 many UK companies were soon setting up operations in the Channel Islands to take advantage of the loophole and remain competitive, including the UKs biggest music retailer HMV. "We resisted that for as long as we could," a spokesman for HMV told the BBC in 2005. "But we realised that if we were to try to compete on the same level playing field then we would have to try to get the benefit and that advantage as well."

In 2007, a mail order trader called Richard Allen raised a complaint with the European Commission regarding the UK's allowance of LVCR to The Channel Islands mail order industry. Richard had been forced to close his successful online mail order business Delerium Mail Order due to the abuse of LVCR by Channel Island based traders and the huge market distortion it had created.

He wasn't prepared to give up however. By 2009, Richard had formed a campaign group called Retailers Against VAT Avoidance Schemes (RAVAS) that successfully brought together everyone suffering from the onslaught of Channel Islands VAT free mail order - not only music retailers but also traders involved in horticulture, cosmetics, health supplements, electronics and computer games. Richard's campaigning obtained large amounts of UK press coverage.

Initially the businesses who had set up operations in the Channel Islands and the UK Government claimed that the LVCR trade was not an abuse of VAT legislation. However, the European Commission agreed with Richard that the Channel Islands' LVCR trade was an abusive VAT avoidance scheme and threatened HM Revenue & Customs with legal action if they did not close it down. HMRC were forced to take action, and on November 9, 2011 announced the removal of LVCR from Channel Island mail order goods because "in recent years it has been used on an increasingly large scale to sell low value goods to UK customers VAT-free, a purpose for which it was never intended".

In March 2011 George Osborne became the first UK Chancellor to mention record shops in a National Budget when to cheers of cross party support he stated to Parliament "We are going to tackle the exploitation of low value consignment relief that has left our high-street music stores fighting a losing battle with warehouses in the Channel Islands."

Even so, the Channel Islands in a desperate attempt to hang on to their tax advantage tried to block the new LVCR legislation in the UK Courts. Richard then had to mobilise RAVAS members and raise £20,000 in two weeks to intervene in the court hearing and assist the UK Government. Everyone contributed money from the smallest record shop to large distributors and in March 2012 the defeat of the Channel Islands in the High Court established a landmark EU legal ruling that allowed LVCR to be removed from Channel Islands mail order goods. On April 1, 2012, the VAT loophole was finally abolished and the next day prices on the internet for CDs and DVDs increased by around 20%.

So why had virtually nobody outside the world of record shops been aware of the history of this loophole and why was there no publicity to celebrate its demise?

The blame lies with the humble Cornish pasty. In the same budget, George Osborne, not only became the first chancellor to mention record shops in a budget speech, but the first to mention pasties. He announced that VAT would be charged on hot takeaway food adding 20% to the cost of sausage rolls, pasties and other such savories. This was to stop supermarkets and some high street bakers undercutting chip shops and other hot food outlets who already had to charge VAT.

The Pasty Tax, as it became known, was manna from heaven for the tabloid press who jumped on the story ignoring the bigger issue of the end of the LVCR tax loophole. Politicians lined up to be filmed eating pasties. George Osborne could not remember when he last ate a pasty and David Cameron said how much he enjoyed a pasty at an outlet in Leeds Station (even though it was argued in the media that no such pasty shop existed). While the Government was accused of taxing the common man for pasties and sausage rolls, the end of the Channel Islands mail order tax abuse passed by unnoticed. The internet retailers whose VAT-free sales had been destroying UK record shops got off scot free as what became known as "pastygate" rumbled on. The closure of the loophole that had forced the closure of so many record shops passed by with hardly anybody picking up on it.

Despite this, within a year of the removal of LVCR from Channel Islands mail order goods all major music retailers based in the Islands had ceased their operations. By 2013, Play.com retail was no more, and the company sadly laid off 147 staff in Jersey. It is estimated that at its peak the use of Channel Islands LVCR cost the UK £165 million pounds a year in lost VAT on CDs and DVDs alone. During its existence the Channel Islands LVCR trade was the largest factor in the closure of more than 1,000 record shops. It is no coincidence that since its demise the record shop revival has taken off.

Independent shops should have launched their own campaign of awareness and informed the public how the internet retailers were taking advantage of this legal tax loophole. It was in their interests to point out that, traders were indirectly depriving hospitals and schools of investment. In the end one person was determined to close the abusive trade. In so doing he saved untold millions in tax, along with many independent record shops.

Over its lifetime, the use of LVCR cost the UK at least a billion pounds in lost tax and even more in terms of UK job losses, benefit payments and lost national income. For the money he has saved the country and the benefit he has given to UK business, I believe Richard Allen should be in next year's honours list.

Amazon

No organisation has changed the way the public purchases music more than Amazon has. It is hard to believe that Jeff Bezos formed the company as recently as 1994, initially specialising as an online bookseller.

Back then, when the internet was in its infancy, Bezos had the vision to realise that it would be the future of retail. Amazon expanded at an astonishing rate and turned itself from being simply an online retailer into a broad customer community. Music customers were encouraged to post their own CD reviews and Amazon profiled customer tastes to recommend further titles that they would be likely to enjoy.

Such was its rapid growth that Amazon was floated on the American stock market in October 1997, raising $54 million.

However, things did not always go to plan and in 2001 the company posted a staggering $1.4 billion loss because of problems generated by over-rapid growth. Many people predicted its demise but, essentially, Amazon was a company which had the potential to dominate cyber commerce. It had already established strong customer loyalty by offering product at an extremely low price and with a reliable delivery service.

Amazon first started selling CDs in 1995 and today, is far and away the seller of the largest number of CDs online in the UK. You can't fault the service. It is simple to order and offers multiple delivery options including next day.

There is no doubt Amazon's sales have hit independent stores hard. On the positive side, independent stores can see at a glance, via the web, what price the largest online retailer is charging, What Amazon has achieved is to raise the standards of service by independent record shops who sell via their own website. If they can't match the outstanding service Amazon offers, then they are wasting their time.

Amazon is also proactive when it comes to selling. Whenever you purchase music from Amazon they will recommend you titles purchased by other consumers who have bought the same title as you. This method of cross-selling is hugely successful, and the more titles you purchase the more titles Amazon will recommend you. However it is here that independent record shops do have an advantage. Nothing beats talking to a knowledgeable record shop employee who can not only recommend music and play it for you, but also build a relationship with you so you can hone your musical tastes.

Where Amazon has really hit the independent shops is by attracting the rarity buyers. These are the customers who would come in to the shops and search for the unusual or collectable titles. These people no longer visit as the world's biggest choice of music is available through the click of a mouse.

On the plus side for record shops, they can use the Amazon marketplace. For £25 per month, record shops are able to list and sell their product via the online giant.

Decline of the Christmas market

Another aspect of retail that has changed for the independent record shop is the loss of Christmas sales. Twenty years ago, December would be one long rush, as people purchased their Christmas presents. Now, however, the rush starts two shopping days before Christmas, when people realise they are too late to buy presents online.

The Christmas No.1 single would normally have been the biggest seller of the year for record shops. These days Christmas No.1s are not always released on a physical format, meaning record shops now make no money from this former money-spinner.

The TV programme *Top of the Pops* was a staple part of Christmas Day TV for music fans. There was much excitement generated as music fans speculated on what the Christmas No.1 would be. With the scrapping of the programme, interest in Christmas records seems to have vanished. Christmas records have become something from the past. How many Christmas No.1 records can you remember? It is likely your most memorable come from one of two decades.

The 1970s spawned such festive hits as:
John Lennon and Yoko Ono and The Plastic Ono Band – "Happy Xmas (War is Over)" (1972)
Slade – "Merry Xmas Everybody" (1973)
Wizzard – "I Wish It Could be Christmas Everyday" (1973)
Mud – "Lonely This Christmas" (1974)
Elton John – "Step into Christmas" (1974)
Chris de Burgh – "A Spaceman Came Travelling" (1975)
Greg Lake – "I Believe in Father Christmas" (1975)
Johnny Mathis – "When a Child is Born" (1976)
Boney M – "Mary's Boy Child" 1978)
Paul McCartney – "Wonderful Christmastime" (1979)

The 1980s still produced the quality, but the quantity was noticeably dropping:
Jona Lewie – "Stop the Cavalry" (1980)
Band Aid – "Do They Know It's Christmas?" (1984)
Wham – "Last Christmas" (1984)
Shakin' Stevens – "Merry Christmas Everyone" (1985)
Chris Rea – "Driving Home for Christmas" (1986)
The Pogues and Kirsty MacColl – "Fairytale of New York" (1987)
By the 1990s it was down to a trickle:
East 17 – "Stay Another Day" (1994)
Mariah Carey – "All I Want for Christmas is You" (1994)
Since then the trickle has become a drought.

The drought in new Christmas releases has not only had a negative effect on sales in record shops. According to clinical psychologist Linda Blair, too much time spent listening to old Christmas songs could even have a negative effect on the brain. I certainly feel for shop assistants who, for one month every year, are subjected to a repetitive barrage of the same old songs. Personally, I am sick of hearing these old tunes again and again, and I would be delighted if current artists could reverse the trend. No wonder that these days Christmas week sales pale in comparison to sales achieved on Record Store Day. Indeed, many shops have told me that they take more money on Record Store Day than they do during the entire week before Christmas.

Supermarkets

Supermarkets contributed in a major way to record shops vanishing on the high street. This is not a problem exclusive to the music industry. Butchers, bakers, greengrocers and many other independent businesses have all struggled to compete.

I am not sure whether or not record companies wanted to get involved with supermarkets, but in reality they had no choice in the matter. Supermarkets are experts in capitalising on products that have a high perceived value by the public. The over-priced CD was perfect for this, especially since a rack of Top 40 chart hits would take up very little space.

It is rare for a shopper to enter a supermarket to purchase just a CD. The low price of CDs can entice a consumer in, but most shoppers come out with a basket full of goods and it is on those goods that the supermarket makes their profit. By throwing their hat in with the supermarkets, the record companies allowed music to stagnate. Endless compilations, greatest hits packages, and reality TV stars produced a dull market devoid of excitement.

The supermarkets are not the sole reason why music has stagnated. It is also about the decline of musical culture. In times gone by, if there was a new Beatles or Led Zeppelin record, people would be queuing outside the record shop on the day of release. Something new from a major artist would generate a tremendous buzz. These days such excitement is created by the release of the new *Grand Theft Auto* game and the desire to purchase music is a lower priority in people's lives.

With the record companies thus forced to sell their musical souls, it was not long before the supermarkets were calling the shots. Prices were driven down. Release dates were influenced by whether a supermarket could (or would) promote the CD. The effect of this, once again, was to force record stores out of business. Before the vinyl revival, the biggest percentage of many independent record shop sales came from chart CDs. This was their core business. By undercutting prices in record shops by up to £3 or £4, the supermarkets took business away from the independent record shops and reinforced the impression that they were unnecessarily expensive places to buy music from.

Record company sales representatives being made redundant

The reduction in the numbers of sales reps on the road was a major factor in the demise of the independent record shop. Throughout the 1990s most stores received visits from around seven record company reps each week. Some would call two or three times in that week. The advantage of this attention lay in the exchange of information it generated. Reps would inform independent shops what was happening with their artists, the promotions that were in place, and the special offers that were available.

Nowadays, stores are out of the information loop. It was because of reps that shops became aware of what titles were selling well in other stores. Now the shops receive information largely by blanket email, and if they were to believe every email they receive then every release is a sure-fire success.

Many stores inform me that they receive more than 100 emails a day from record companies. To read them all would require them to employ somebody just to do that. Stores are drowning in email.

Reps also carried stock that the shops could buy, along with a collection of free promotional stock to be given away, ensuring that a company's artists were displayed in prominent positions in the store. They would also supply display material and posters. Best of all, they could offer deals on the product they sold, thereby giving the independent stores an opportunity to buy at a lower price.

Reps can make a significant difference to the sales of a record. For an artist or label, choosing your distributor is a massive decision. If you bought a car or a house you would do your research first. I am amazed that artists and labels don't seem to attach the same importance to who is responsible for ensuring their stock is out in the marketplace. If I was a band or a label I would ask the following questions of any company you are considering to be the distributor of your product.

Does it have sales reps on the road?

Do those sales reps visit all shops or just key accounts?

Do they try and secure new business or are they content to look after just their regular customers?

Do they have an active sales team happy to communicate with shops each week to talk through new releases, offers and promotions or does the company rely on emailing the shop details of new product in the hope that the shop will fill in a spreadsheet?

In the past, it had been important for record companies to look after independent record stores, as their sales provided the data used to compile the charts. The pivotal day in the decline of independent record shops was the day that Asda was invited to contribute their sales data to the chart ratings. Soon, the other supermarkets followed suit, and simply by means of their sheer buying power the balance of power was shifted decisively. Record companies no longer needed to court independent shops as the buying power of the supermarkets would virtually guarantee a release they supported to enter the charts in the Top Ten, often getting it straight to No.1.

Soon after this, downloading and streaming could be counted towards chart statistics, which further diminished the influence of the beleaguered independent shops and their relative importance to record companies. The promotional budgets that record companies had been targeting at record shops were now targeted at internet retailers and supermarkets.

The know-all behind the counter

For many years, some staff could be the record shop's own worst enemy. Many of us recall how intimidating it could be going into a record shop, taking your purchase up to the counter only to be sneered at by the know-all sales assistant behind the counter, clearly unimpressed by your taste in music.

For me nobody summed this up better than an ex-school colleague the late, great Pete Burns who, before finding fame as lead singer of Dead Or Alive, terrified the music buyers of Liverpool from behind the counter at Probe Records. Pete would wear black contact lenses and with his outlandish fashion sense and sharp wit could be an intimidating figure. He became renowned for letting customers know if he did not approve of their musical taste. One customer recalls taking an album up to Pete only to be refused service as he was wearing jeans with turn-ups. Another customer brought a record by the band Japan to the counter, only to be told by Pete to put it back and buy something decent.

The balance of power has now changed. The customer is king and the record shops that did not treasure their customers are long gone. The shops that survived did so because they looked after their customers and were prepared to go the extra mile.

Chapter 2

How Record Store Day kickstarted the vinyl revival

In 2008, only a tiny percentage of releases came out on vinyl and sales of vinyl accounted for just 0.3% of physical album sales. Fast forward to the present and almost all key releases come out on vinyl as well as the CD and digital formats. In 2017 vinyl accounted for 19% of physical album sales, making it the tenth consecutive year to witness a rise in the sales of the vinyl format.

In 2008, £2.9 million was spent on vinyl in the UK. By 2017 the sum had risen to £88.7 million, according to the Official Chart Company.

The digital generation has discovered the joy of owning vinyl and it is no coincidence that the initial rise started following the first Record Store Day (in 2008 in the USA; 2009 in the UK). Since then, sales of vinyl in independent record shops have risen from 78,400 units in 2008 to 1,280,700 in 2017. And overall sales of vinyl records have increased five-fold since 2013 – from 831,000 units to 4,319,300 units in 2017.

Much of the credit for the resurgence of vinyl must go to the inspirational idea of having a day to celebrate record shops. Record Store Day was founded in Baltimore, Maryland in 2008 by a group of record store owners: Michael Kurtz, Eric Levin, Carrie Colliton, Amy Dorfman, Don Van Cleave and Brian Poehner. It has since grown into an annual, worldwide celebration of record shops by artists, record labels and most importantly of all, music fans. For record shops the event, which takes place on the third Saturday of April is more important for trade than Christmas.

Here, in co-founder Michael Kurtz's own words, is the story of Record Store Day – how a little idea has developed into one of the most important dates in the music calendar.

"Record Store Day was originally pitched to me as an idea by Chris Brown, one of the guys who runs Bull Moose out of Portland, Maine. Bull Moose is the largest retailer of new and pre-loved music, movies and video games in Maine and Seacoast New Hampshire with 10 stores, employing over 100 people. Chris had observed how the comic book industry ran an event called Free Comic Day and suggested that we organize a similar event for independently owned record stores. I run an organization called the Department of Record Stores. DORS is now the largest of the indie coalitions in the US and Canada. Part of my job is bringing together indie retail stores for an annual event called Noise in the Basement, held in Baltimore. At the 2008 event I posed the idea for Record Store Day to folks in my group, as well as to Newbury Comics, Criminal Records, and the Coalition of Independent Music Stores. At the time, everyone was grousing about all the negative press on record stores and how, even though there had been a good deal of expansion in our world over the past few years, everything that was reported about record stores in the media was bad. Record Store Day would simply be an excuse to throw a party for ourselves and the artists we love, as well as get the real story on record stores out to the media. Chris originally pitched the idea of Record Store Day, which I took to some of the other great indie stores in the country as well as to the Coalition of Independent Music Stores and the Alliance of Music Stores (two noteworthy indie coalitions).

After getting the stores on board, I felt that the best way to see if the idea had legs was to see if the artists themselves would support us. Paul McCartney had recently released Memory Almost Full *and had celebrated its release with an intimate in-store event at Amoeba Records, in Los Angeles (with Ringo in the audience!). Shooting for the stars, I reached out to the Hear Music/Concord label (owned by TV producer, and huge music fan Norman Lear). I asked them if they would alert Paul to what we were doing with Record Store Day and see if Paul would give us a word of support. I was stunned when an email from Paul appeared in my inbox saying "There's nothing as glamorous to me as a record store. When I recently played Amoeba in LA, I realized what fantastic memories such a collection of music brings back when you see it all in one place. This is why I'm more than happy to support Record Store Day and I hope that these kinds of stores will be there for us all for many years to come. Cheers.*

Almost all the folks who run record stores grew up with The Beatles so getting a note from Paul gave us the strength to say "Yes, we are pretty cool. We can do this." From there the messages started cascading in from the likes of Chuck Berry, Mike Patton, Tom Waits, Nick Hornby and Cameron Crowe, amongst many others. I then took the message of Record Store Day to Mike Sherwood at Warner Bros and to Marc Reiter, who was based at a management firm called Q Prime to see if Metallica would get involved in their hometown of San Francisco.

One of the most exciting days of my life was getting the call from Marc saying that the band loved record stores and the idea of Record Store Day so they would help launch it at Rasputin in their hometown of San Francisco. Having Metallica participate was especially gratifying to me as I always thought Lars Ulrich got a raw deal from the media for having the audacity to speak up about not embracing peer-to-peer networks because he thought Metallica, along with other artists, should be paid for their work. What a concept.

Anyway, Metallica ended up being incredibly nice to work with and they treated their fans like royalty insisting that they be given time to meet and talk with each and every one of them circling and fanning out from the store for what seemed like miles. It was, as Lou Reed, once sang, a "perfect day". Others joined in like Steve Earle who performed at Manifest Discs in Charlotte, NC and Panic at the Disco played at Waterloo Records in Austin, TX. Pretty much all the major labels and distribution companies embraced the idea and created wonderful promotional/collectible pieces like vinyl LPs and 7-inch singles to give out freely to music fans on the day. We even had various commercial products made for us by artists like REM, Stephen Malkmus, Built To Spill, Death Cab For Cutie, and Jason Mraz. A group of about 200 or so stores in the USA jumped into the fray and before we knew it the news media was reporting our positive story pretty much everywhere from the NY Times to the BBC to CNN. This was our beginning.

2009 was our second year for Record Store Day and I don't think anyone was prepared for what took place, or how exciting it would be. The labels and distributors showed record stores a massive amount of love and created close to 100 commercial pieces made specifically for Record Store Day and independent record stores. We had Radiohead, the Flaming Lips, Wilco, the Smiths, Iggy Pop and the Stooges, Iron And Wine, Tom Waits, Bruce Springsteen, Sonic Youth, Leonard Cohen, the Killers, Bob Dylan, Slayer, Dead Weather and the Black Kids involved in one way or another.

Apple Records even gave the stores beautiful hand numbered Beatles' lithographs. Jeff Tweedy from Wilco issued a statement saying, "My introduction to a lot of great music and to the music business came from hanging around and eventually working at independent record stores. It's the life I know. Nothing beats browsing in your favourite store, listening to music, finding something new or old that you've been searching for, being ignored by the store clerks, all that. Without these stores, there's just no way Wilco would still be around. They've been there with us from the very beginning, through thick and thin. Even if I wasn't in a band, I'd still support Record Store Day.

With artist statements like Jeff's coming out with regularity and a press release from NYC Mayor Michael Bloomberg declaring Record Store Day as an officially recognised day by the city of New York, media coverage on Record Store Day began to build. By the time the day hit, Record Store Day reached the No.5 Google news item of the day, ranking #34 as the most googled term of the day. 10% of all tweets for that day were about Record Store Day, and our story went worldwide. The result was the creation of a new event that hundreds of both established and developing artists embraced, including Ani DiFranco, Wilco, Disturbed, Erykah Badu, the Eagles of Death Metal, Talib Kweli, the Silversun Pickups, Chris Cornell, Ashford & Simpson and so on. Record Store Day now brings even more people through the doors than Christmas.

The dark side of Record Store Day was having a few embittered indie stores attack the organisers of Record Store Day. This was a bit of a shocker, but as I reached out to each of the stores to work with them so that they could fully understand what we were doing, everything came together. For the most part, the American indie record store community is fully now behind Record Store Day, so all the hard work was worth it, and we accomplished what we set out to do.

The bad press, paranoia and the weirdness has gone, replaced by innovation fuelled by local community spirit. It's the essence of rock n' roll. You could see this in the indie record store that Record Store Day erected on site with Zia Records (out of Arizona) at the Coachella Music Festival in California. Over 80 bands stepped in to participate and meet fans and over 30% of everything sold was on vinyl. It was a huge success, allowing us to take our story directly to the music fans at arguably the world's coolest three-day music festival. Progress in rolling out Record Store Day internationally has gone well, with over 300 stores joining in from around the world. Our main task now is working to help international stores get commercial pieces made for Record Store Day in their respective countries so that Record Store Day can continue to grow and strengthen local record stores everywhere."

The UK record shops were first involved in 2009 but only a handful of shops took part with a limited selection of releases. Since those humble beginnings it is now the most important day in music retailing for record shops. Each store celebrates Record Store Day in its own way. As part of their individual celebrations, most shops have a day of bands playing in-store, unique offers, and product giveaways.

The record companies have embraced Record Store Day. Last year there were more than 400 exclusive releases that could only be obtained from independent record shops. The film *Last Shop Standing* featured scenes from Record Store Day of a staggering 900 people queuing outside Rough Trade East in London, and more than 400 people waiting outside Record Collector in Sheffield. People are often astonished to see this, not realising just how big the event has become.

What Record Store Day achieved was to encourage music fans back into visiting independent record shops. Once there, they discovered and, in many cases, re-discovered the pleasure visiting a record shop can bring. By releasing exclusive records, it re-ignited the interest in record collecting.

The event has attracted extra publicity by each year appointing a Record Store Day Ambassador. In recent years artists such as Metallica, Chuck D, Dave Grohl, Jack White, St Vincent, Iggy Pop and in 2018 rap duo Run The Jewel have fulfilled the role, giving media interviews and live events to help promote the day. Many artists have fond memories of making their first record and finding that the local independent record shop would be the first to stock it. By supporting Record Store Day those artists are giving something back.

In 2017 Record Store Day celebrated its 10th anniversary and each year is better than the last. Every year the event makes changes that lead to improvements both for the retailers and customers. They have done sterling work taking on the scourge of Record Store Day, the "flippers", a term used to describe the people who queue outside shops on Record Store Day, purchase the most collectable items then go home and immediately put them on eBay to make a vast profit. These people are despised by shops, labels and music fans as they deprive true vinyl fans of titles they want in the same way as ticket touts do with concert tickets. Johnny Marr referred to flippers as tossers and urged people not to buy from them. If a shop sells a collectable Record Store Day piece for £20 and a flipper turns around and sells it for £100, then the shop and the record label have made a small profit on the £20 whilst the flipper has made £80. If labels sell the record for a higher price, the artist gets more royalties, with the flipper making less profit but neither label nor shop wishes to increase the price. Record labels and shops are not in the business of making flippers a living. They are in the business of giving music fans what they want.

Record Store Day rules say that it is first come first served. In the early days of the event, shops would inform me that they would have people at the front of the queue that they had never seen in the shop before spending a four-figure sum clearing many of the collectable releases out. Since then I have always advised new shops taking part in the day for the first time to limit the queue to purchasing a maximum of five titles for one copy of each. After that they would have to return to the back of the queue if they wish to purchase more. This ensures the stock is spread out and limits the impact of flippers.

It is also the disgruntled who shout loudest. Following Record Store Day 2017, the internet was full of people complaining about flippers. Record Store Day founder Michael Kurtz commented: "There are about 600,000 pieces that were sold on Record Store Day, out of 650,000 that were shipped to stores, and of those, I think about 7,000 ended up on eBay. So that's about 1 per cent. That's good to know, that almost 99 per cent of everything goes home to a music fan."

I think that shows that things are not as bad as some media commentators would have us believe. Record Store Day organisers have done their utmost to make life difficult for flippers. They watermarked the cover photos of stock with giant anti-resale text saying "support record shops not flippers". This made the artwork unusable, thereby safeguarding it from pre-selling on the internet. Flippers had to wait until after Record Store Day to obtain the real photos up online.

Many observers lay the blame for flipping with eBay, for apparently doing nothing to stop it. Record Store Day organisers have appealed to eBay not to allow listings, but to no avail. With Record Store Day stock, flippers often post things on eBay that they don't even have. Often the stock is not even shipped yet. They are taking a gamble that on the day they can queue early and obtain the item and fulfil the order they have already taken. Flippers are the parasites of the music industry, so save your ire for them not the Record Store Day organisers.

The UK event is organised by ERA (Entertainment Retailers Association) and the work this organisation has done in shaping Record Store Day has been outstanding.

Formed in 1988, when it was first known as BARD (British Association of Record Dealers), the Entertainment Retailers Association is a UK trade organisation which acts as a forum for the physical and digital retail and wholesale sectors of the music, video and games industries.

It represents all types of retailers who sell both physical and digital music, as well as video and games sellers, and is a must-join body for independent record shops as membership has many advantages.

ERA membership benefits for record shops include:

Free sign up to Record Store Day for eligible record shops.

Payment for music data if the shop contributes to the Official Charts.

In some cases, a shop may receive more than the £100 cost of ERA subscription.

Access to chart data, free legal advice from the ERA office, plus much more.

If you are planning to open a record shop, joining ERA is essential. The ERA board is made up of 18 to 20 members covering the full spectrum of entertainment retail. Currently the board consists of representatives of 7digital, Amazon, Deezer, Game, Google, HMV, Isotope, Proper Music, Sainsburys, Sky, SoundCloud, Spotify and Tesco. Six people sit on the board to represent the independent record shops.

The organisation has a fascinating history and is modelled on a USA trade association known as NARM (National Association of Recording Merchandisers) which was formed in 1958. This trade body looked after the interests of music retailers, wholesalers and merchandisers. Each year they would hold a huge conference attended by members from all over the country.

It was re-named MusicBiz (Music Business Association) in 2013.

NARM had carried out its work for 30 years when one of its board members Russ Soloman (the founder of Tower Records in the USA) paid a visit to Steve Smith the chief of Tower in the UK. Russ asked Steve if they could meet up with the UK equivalent of NARM. Steve informed him that no such trade body existed.

Determined to do something about this, Steve Smith hosted a get-together with Russ Soloman and other NARM members with the senior executives of UK multiple retailers, wholesalers and independent record store owners. At that meeting it was agreed that retail should have a voice within the music industry and Steve Smith was elected the first Chairman of BARD.

It was not all sweetness and light at the beginning, and BARD was certainly not welcomed with open arms. There was a fair share of scepticism from the independent record stores who suspected that BARD would become a talking shop for, and controlled by, the multiple music retailers of the time such as Woolworths, Boots, WH Smith, HMV, Virgin, Andys and Our Price. However, when it became clear which issues BARD was looking to address, the independent shops realised there was a lot of common ground, and were won over. Soon BARD began to have a big impact on how the industry worked. The first major achievement was to create a joint venture with the record labels for compiling and managing the sales charts and to secure payment for its members sales data. Unbelievably, this information had previously been supplied for free. This arrangement forms the basis of today's Official Charts and has since become a regular source of income to ERA and its members.

One of the most important decisions from an environmental point of view BARD took was not to go along with the longbox packaging adopted by stores in the USA to display CDs. Millions of trees have been saved by this decision. When the CD was marketed in the USA, retailers complained that CDs did not fit into the old LP racks. Instead of informing retailers that if they wanted to stock this exciting new format they would need to purchase new racking, the record companies pandered to them by supplying CDs in long boxes which although only slightly wider than a CD were the same height as an LP. This meant record shops could use the LP browsers to rack out CDs. With millions of CDs being sold every year the sheer waste and extra cost of so much needless packaging was mind-boggling. Fortunately, BARD had the foresight to resist using the longbox packaging in the UK. It was decades before the Americans came to their senses and started packaging CDs the way we do in Europe.

Initially, the organisation was run by people who already had a full-time job in the music industry, such as Brian McLaughlin the managing director of HMV and Andy Gray owner of the Andys record shop chain. But after a while it made sense to employ somebody full time, and ex-CBS man Bob Lewis was appointed to the role of Director General. One of the first issues he addressed was the chaotic shipment of new release product. It is hard to believe now, but back then the UK delivery system did not enable all retailers to sell new releases at the same time. BARD created a level playing field and achieved cost savings by requiring all product to be shipped for release on a Monday.

Next on the agenda was to sort out the confusion created by not having a uniform standard for barcodes which made reporting chart information difficult, time consuming and costly. In addition to these administrative improvements, BARD started making voluntary contributions to support the fight against music piracy as well as negotiating with banks to reduce fees being charged to its members.

Many of today's industry events such as the BRITS and the Mercury Music prize came out of collaborations between BARD and different sectors of the industry. The Mercury Music prize was created by BARD board member David Tyrell and Jon Webster from the BPI whist BARD members participated and helped the growth of the BRIT Awards.

Bob Lewis retired from the job of Director General in 2004 having done a brilliant job of bringing together all sides of retail to work together. He had always been able to negotiate from a position of strength as more than 90% of music sales in the UK were conducted by BARD members.

Bob passed the baton of Director General on to Kim Bayley who had started her career as a commercial lawyer before joining BARD in 2002 as Director of Development.

One of her first tasks was to expand the membership to encompass all forms of retail including the nascent digital music sector. Her role also involved fighting piracy, a major problem for the industry then which was depriving artists and retailers of income. In 2002 alone almost 300 artist sites providing illegal MP3 downloads and approximately 450 auction sites were taken down.

Under her leadership and due to the changing nature of the membership the name was changed to ERA (Entertainment Retailers Association). The organisation represents those who sell music, video and games including record shops, supermarkets, online retailers and digital services so the British Association of Record Dealers was a name that no longer reflected the membership.

Kim also encouraged Paul Quirk, an independent record shop owner who sat on the board as an independent record shop representative to organise the first indie record shop conference, which was held in Birmingham. He persuaded retailers and suppliers to meet up for one day to showcase products and discuss the future of the indie retailer. It gave the record shop owners a valuable opportunity to question the policies of the suppliers at a time when many shop owners suspected that record companies no longer cared about them, and that their priorities were now selling to supermarkets and the internet companies.

Paul Quirk's message to the shops was "Be independent but don't be isolated." He emphasized that the idea of the conference was for record shops to communicate with each other and work together in unison.

Further indie record shop conferences were held in Birmingham in 2006 before relocating to London in 2007 and 2008. One thing ERA could not do was negotiate pricing with record companies. This resulted in some record shops who belonged to ERA forming a new group calling themselves The Coalition to fulfil this role and focus on independent retail. Around 25 shops signed up, the idea being that together they would be in a stronger position to negotiate deals with the record companies. The Coalition did not last long, however. Arguments on whether to allow all record shops to join or whether to restrict the membership to "cutting edge" shops created a split in the ranks.

Apart from reaffirming ERA's position as the organization best-placed to represent indie retail, one positive legacy of The Coalition's brief existence was that many of its members' shops took part in the UK's first Record Store Day. After hearing that the USA had started a day celebrating independent record shops, Spencer Hickman from Rough Trade decided to bring the event over to the UK. He was the driving force behind Record Store Day, encouraging both shops and record companies to take part and attracting some excellent media coverage of the event. With only a small selection of official releases to mark the occasion, it was up to the shops to make the day a success.

Spencer continued organising RSD, with ERA first getting involved in an administrative role and providing the services of industry PR Steve Redmond. ERA also set up the Record Store Day website with a store locator facility, which proved a significant success in putting the individual shops on the map. For the first time, potential customers could submit their postcode and immediately be pointed in the direction of their nearest independent record shop.

In 2012, it was decided that Record Store Day would stage a launch event designed to bring in extra publicity. Exclusive releases would be announced and there would be a party for retailers and the media. Spencer Hickman pulled off a coup in booking a couple of top artists – Public Image Ltd and Orbital – to play at a secret location in Shoreditch.

On the week of the event, disaster struck. The person in charge of looking after the bands and venue for the evening pulled out. Not only that, when the ERA representatives arrived at the venue, they discovered it was a shell with no facilities such as a green room.

While frantic calls were made to draft in an event organiser to sort out the mess, ERA's Kim Bailey headed to the pub across the road to see if by chance they had a room that could serve as the green room. Thankfully for the bargain price of £50 the pub agreed to let Kim rent an upstairs room, fully equipped with balcony, bar and sofas, but no staff. Although Kim and Paul Quirk had no experience in this field, they set to work on the rest of the event. They were handed a rider (catering agreement) from the bands requiring food, wine and beer. No problem, they thought. The green room was in a pub with a bar. Sadly, the pub did not stock any of the wines or beers that the band had requested. Kim and Paul set off through the streets of Shoreditch on a treasure hunt. Luckily, they found a beer and wine warehouse which could supply the required brands of booze. The warehouse even lent the duo a trolley. It was tiresome work dodging the crowds as they returned to the venue with Paul pushing the trolley while Kim held on to the stock.

They had just finished loading the drinks in to the dressing room when one of the managers approached. He informed the duo that the band would not perform unless they provided a dozen fluffy white towels. With only 30 minutes before Public Image Ltd were due to take the stage, the duo set off again. It was now 9.30pm, where on earth in London could you pick up fluffy white towels? They started popping in to hotels explaining that they had a packed venue with the legendary John Lydon waiting to perform, but the gig could not start till they had procured a dozen fluffy white towels. After some early rebukes, they found a friendly Sex Pistols fan working at the Shoreditch Premier Inn who kindly lent them the towels for the evening.

After all this palaver and against all the odds the evening turned out to be a huge success. Paul has fond memories of John Lydon and the band staying long after the event finished, happy to chat to all who wanted a word with them and Kim serving Coronas from the bar.

The following year, the Record Store Day launch party took place at Rough Trade East with Tom Odell headlining. It is now a much-anticipated day and in subsequent years many of the shops also started holding their own launch parties.

Record Store Day does attract criticism a lot of it unjust. Nothing is perfect, and each year ERA have taken steps to address any issues that have cropped up. To counteract complaints, ERA launched a communications offensive, visiting as many record shops as possible as well as holding regional meetings for shops to offer feedback on the day. In the early years the event had problems with product being sold online before the day. ERA brought in strict rules forbidding any retailers from doing this. Shops were removed from Record Store Day if they breached the rules. This eliminated the problem as no record shop in the country would risk losing the right to take part in this amazing event.

Those who criticise often have short memories. Before Record Store Day started, the only queue you were likely to see outside a record shop was for a closing down sale.

ERA have attracted sponsorship from the likes of Rega Turntables and Friels First Press Vintage Cider, Fred Perry and Sound Performance to help fund the event.

Each year for Record Store Day, Rega produce 500 RSD turntables of which thirteen are signed by artists such as Liam Gallagher, Jarvis Cocker and Tim Burgess. I am proud to say that I started the ball rolling with Rega's involvement in the day. Before the *Last Shop Standing* film was released I gave a talk at the *End of the Road* festival where I showed a trailer for the film. In the audience were a couple of the team from Rega who informed me they would be happy to sponsor the film. I was delighted they got involved, and from there it led on to them being an RSD sponsor.

Friels have proved a very popular sponsor. Anybody who sends record shops free cider is immediately loved. They even produce a Record Store Day cider and do a brilliant job of promoting the day through giveaways and competitions via social media.

Fred Perry the iconic British clothing manufacturer co-founded by our greatest ever tennis player is also a sponsor.

In 2018, Record Store Sound Performance and DIY Mag launched a nation-wide competition to offer the UK's best unsigned talent the chance to have their music pressed to vinyl. The one-off prize not only included 500 copies of the chosen record pressed to vinyl (for free!) but also a one-year distribution deal with Proper Music. I was delighted to be involved with this as part of my job was to sell the winning record into the shops. The winners were Barbudo, a trio from Havant.

ERA took on a young graduate, Megan Page, to work full time on the event and she has taken to the role with relish, working tirelessly as the link between shops, suppliers, and the media.

In 2015 they secured the support of BBC 6 Music to promote RSD. The station spends the time leading up to RSD playing tracks from forthcoming RSD releases, interviewing artists and staff in the shops taking part in the big day. The day before RSD, they broadcast the Lauren Laverne show live from a record shop. In 2016, it was Resident in Brighton, 2017 was Vinyl Tap in Huddersfield and in 2018 Spillers in Cardiff.

A great initiative has been to set up a private Record Store Facebook group for ERA members. Here, shops can communicate with each other, ask advice from other shops and even arrange to swap excess stock. What ERA have created is a record shop community. In the past record shops were in competition with each other. Now they work together in a spirit of co-operation.

A major initiative was to re-introduce a record token scheme. Can you remember when you were a child and your Gran or Auntie would be stuck for ideas on what to buy for your birthday or for Christmas? A record token was always the perfect answer. Each year thousands were sold, redeemable at any record store across the country. As well as providing a steady source of income for shops, they also enticed people into record stores who may not have otherwise considered entering. Many children's first experience of buying a record was redeeming a record token at their local shop.

The EMI-administered record token scheme was a consistent success. However, in 1995 WH Smith broke rank and decided no longer to accept universally-redeemable record tokens and, instead, introduced its own token scheme, "locking in" the customer transaction and taking advantage of its network of stores in most towns across the country. Soon, HMV followed suit. Without the support of two of the biggest retailers in the country, EMI decided to abandon the record token. At this point, independents needed to come together and start a new scheme selling tokens which could be redeemed at any independent record shop in the country. Sadly, nobody took the initiative, and this has cost them millions of pounds in lost revenue.

While many stores have begun selling record tokens which can be redeemed only at their own store, the great thing about EMI's record tokens was that if you lived in Inverness you could buy a record token for somebody living in Bude, confident that the recipient could spend it locally. During the past few years I have been in record stores dozens of times when people have come in to purchase record tokens, only to see them leave empty-handed after finding that a single-shop scheme did not suit what they needed.

ERA recognised this problem and invested considerable time and money to come up with a solution which offers the opportunity for shops to sell their own record tokens alongside a national record token scheme. For shops who do not do their own record tokens it is a godsend. If you are looking for a present, why not go out and buy a record token?

What the team from ERA have achieved is remarkable. They have made a major contribution to the vinyl revival and I have no doubt that we have more record shops trading today thanks to their efforts.

Record Store Day is always the best trading day of the year for the retailers. Despite the stress and the extra workload, it is also the most fun. Here are a few of my observations on how the day could be made even better and more importantly help to secure the future of independent record shops.

The industry ought to encourage more artists to be involved in the day itself. That does not mean just releasing product. It is fantastic to see so many groups playing in-stores on Record Store Day, but it tends to be local bands or artists yet to hit the big time. The day lacks big names playing stores. I am sure if artists were aware that record stores would like them to play then many would be delighted to support them. This is about communication. It is down to labels to reach out to their artists and let them know that shops need their support so popping in for a signing or to play a few numbers would give them such a boost. So many artists release product on the day; how about a bit more support for the shops selling their releases?

The very first Record Store Day featured both Metallica and Steve Earle making appearances in shops. I don't feel we have had any artists personally involved since then who are of that status. If you are a musician, a DJ or work in the media, offer your services to your local record shop for Record Store Day. Give something back to the people who have helped you on the road to success.

The product gets better each year. One gripe is that some of the stock doesn't arrive until the day before, or in some cases, doesn't even arrive in time for the Record Store Day itself, which is unforgivable. Staff in many shops have worked well into the night to get stock processed for the next day. This time would be better spent preparing for the day's events. Stock should be shipped earlier. It is not as if record companies don't know in advance when Record Store Day is. Every year it is the third Saturday of April. And every year some product arrives at stores after the event. This causes endless headaches for staff in the shops, who lose sales and often have to inform customers that the Record Store Day title they are asking for will be in next week.

Disaster struck in 2014 when Paul Weller released 500 copies of a 7-inch single "Brand New Toy." The minute I read this I just knew this was going to be a huge problem. With more than 200 shops taking part, it was likely most shops would receive just 2 copies. Most shops could have easily sold 25 plus. Barry Everard of Record Collector in Sheffield summed it up well:

"We opened the shop and sold the Paul Weller singles to the first two people in the queue. Not surprisingly, the first 10 people to enter the shop all wanted the single. By 11am I reckon 50 people had asked and by closing time around 75. So, what had we achieved in getting our message across that record shops are a great place to visit? I had made 2 people extremely happy but managed to cheese off another 73."

Even more galling was the fact that plenty of copies started appearing on eBay for three figure sums. This showed that it was not Paul Weller's genuine fans who snapped up the record in many cases it was touts (flippers), snapping them up to sell at a vast profit. The situation was easy to predict.

The result was Paul Weller took the decision not to take part in Record Store Day again, so everybody lost out. Having interviewed Paul for the *Last Shop Standing* film I know how passionate he feels about record shops, and to lose such a great supporter was a blow to all involved.

The Entertainment Retailers Association acted to suspend stores from the event who had sold RSD product online. The strict penalties which they introduced have since ensured that all shops stick to the rules, although there is still an issue with smaller shops not receiving a fair allocation. However, there remains a delicate balancing act to be performed between making a record sufficiently scarce to be collectable and having enough copies on hand to ensure that somebody who has queued outside a record shop for a couple of hours receives the record they came to buy. The industry learned from the Paul Weller fiasco and has since ensured that the quantities of records being pressed are small enough to make the items collectable but also sufficiently realistic to satisfy demand.

It is to everybody's credit that quantities of product supplied to shops has improved but there are still blips as the release of Abba's "Summer Night City" 7-inch picture discs for RSD 2018 proved. It was limited to 2,000 copies worldwide with around 650 of them going to UK shops. No doubt the Scandinavian countries, the USA and the UK could easily have sold 2,000 each. With 245 shops taking part in the UK the average was under three copies per shop.

Steve Meekings from X Records in Bolton commented. "Universal supplied just one copy. Over the day we had over 50 requests for the record, so I made one person happy and 49 had a negative experience. What good does that do for us? Compare that with Warner who supplied us with 35 copies of the Led Zeppelin yellow vinyl 7-inch "Rock and Roll". It rewarded most of the fans who were queuing for it. I could have sold 50 copies but at least 35 Led Zeppelin fans had a great Record Store Day. It was the perfect balance between collectable and enough stock to meet demand."

Barry Everard of Record Collector commented "As soon as we opened, we sold the two Abba singles straight away. We let the crowd know that they had gone, resulting in an audible groan with at least 10 people exiting the queue."

You did not have to be Mystic Meg to predict the Abba fiasco. There was great interest in the brand, new product coming out, rumours of a reunion and an Abba exhibition coming to London, all of which would fuel interest in the record.

It is decisions like this that give credence to the people complaining about stock appearing on eBay. As I write, it is selling for £60 while thousands of genuine Abba fans missed out.

One area Record Store Day could improve on is broadening the musical scope of the records released. In 2014 One Direction released "Midnight Memories" on picture disc vinyl. The release drew criticism from some record shops who deemed it to be too mainstream and not cool enough. But the result was that thousands of teenage girls visited a record shop for the first time. They experienced queuing outside a record shop and the thrill of obtaining a collectable item by their favourite band. For many it was their introduction to vinyl and left them with a positive view of shopping in an independent record shop. First impressions count, and you can be sure that many have carried on buying vinyl. These are the future vinyl buyers and they need to be enticed into a record shop with releases by artists that appeal to them.

It is important that shops taking part for the first time are given industry wide support. Sanctuary Records in Nailsworth opened the shop for its first day of business on RSD 2018.They made huge efforts to publicise the opening, and to let it be known that the town of Nailsworth would have a shop taking part in the great event. They had features on the radio and in the press, they hired bands to play on the day and offered goodie bags to the people in the queue.

What should have been an incredible day for the shop and the town was not as perfect as it should have been. All the record companies bar one supplied them with RSD releases for their opening. Warners, however, decided that as the shop had no trading history with them, they would not supply them. Owner Ash was left bemused. Here they were making huge efforts to promote the day and a major supplier would not allow them any stock.

On the day dozens of people asked for records by Led Zeppelin and many of the other

Warner releases only to be turned away. Many of these people had spent a long-time queuing. You can imagine what their opinion was of the town's new record shop.

Neil Harris of Bug Records in Beverley took part in RSD for the first time in 2017. As he had only opened in November 2016, two of the companies decided he had not built up enough trading history to warrant being supplied RSD stock. He reported that by 9.30am he felt he needed to attend an anger management course, as he found himself constantly having to inform customers that he was not provided with many of the key releases. Even more galling was that he was contacted on the Monday after Record Store Day being offered the key releases which had not been supplied to his shop on Record Store Day itself. Talk about rubbing salt into the wound.

According to *Save the High Street*, an organisation which champions independent shops, 48% of consumers said that the most critical time to gain their loyalty is when they make their first purchase in a shop. Many customers attending a new record shop on Record Store Day for the first time were unlikely to have been impressed.

In my view, if a shop meets the official ERA conditions required to participate in Record Store Day, then it must be allowed to stock a minimum of three copies of each title.

Another criticism levelled against Record Store Day from small independent record labels is that, because pressing plants are working flat out in the months leading up to the day itself manufacturing RSD product, there are no opportunities for smaller labels to get records pressed during this period. This issue has received plenty of negative media coverage, but it all comes down to long term planning by the labels concerned. Everybody knows when Record Store Day is and that pressing plants are going to be stretched to full capacity between January and March. The music industry is no different from any other business; forward thinking is required.

Furthermore, looked at from the other side of the fence, this is a problem that reflects the continuing success of RSD. I recently visited a new pressing plant in Portsmouth, where the owner noted with satisfaction that his order book was already full for many months ahead. Such is the continuing strength of the vinyl revival, that there are simply not enough pressing plants to cope with demand for the format.

Music fans may have noticed that on many occasions an artist releases the vinyl at a later date than the CD. This is not a clever marketing trick. More often it is a failure to plan effectively. The label will set a release date to coincide with a tour, then they discover the pressing plant can't press the vinyl in time for the release date. The CD release goes ahead, as planned, at the start of the tour. But the vinyl release is unintentionally delayed until such time as it can be pressed. It is important for all involved in the industry to understand just how long it takes to get vinyl pressed and to plan accordingly.

Then there is the accusation that Record Store Day is just a cynical opportunity for major labels to rip off music fans with over-priced product. It is important for consumers to appreciate that a small run of vinyl - maybe coloured or a picture disc, often containing a download code and/or booklet - is an expensive thing to manufacture. The artist, the writer, the sleeve designer, the label manager, the label, the distributor and the shop will all be taking a small percentage of the sale of the record. Add VAT and you get a better understanding of the true cost.

It's all very well harking back to the golden age of vinyl in the 1960s, when a record cost the equivalent of £2.99. But in those days a pint of milk cost £0.06p. And besides, big-selling albums were pressed in batches of 5,000, so manufacturing costs were far lower.

It would help if all involved sought to educate the media and the public that the event is called Record Store Day. I have had people mention to me no end of alternatives

Record Shop Day

Vinyl Day

Record Vinyl Day

Record Day

World Record Day

Record Store Day is a brand that the music industry can be immensely proud of, so all of us involved with it should take care to emphasise the correct name.

Regular customers who keep record shops going with their support throughout the year get no reward for their loyalty on Record Store Day. The "first come first served" policy is a reward for nothing more than how early you are prepared to join the queue on the day. A customer who has spent £20 in a shop every month might ask to reserve a particular Record Store Day release. And the shop owner might very much wish to oblige, not least as a reward for that customer's loyalty. But to do so would put the shop in breach of RSD rules. The regular customer must take his or her chance in the queue with everybody else on the day.

The logistics make it difficult to reward regular customers on RSD but there is an opportunity to reward them throughout the year. Although it would be difficult to have a loyalty card promotion for RSD, there is no reason why shops should not use one for offers throughout the year. The music industry should follow the example of other businesses such as supermarkets and bookmakers which provide some sort of loyalty card offering discounts, special offers and prizes. Customers who sign up for a card are then kept informed of the latest releases and offers and receive exclusive access to in-store events. Many record shops now sell coffee, giving them the chance to adopt the Waitrose model of offering a free cup to cardholders who purchase something. By giving a customer a free coffee, the customer is likely to spend more time in the shop, therefore the chances of making another purchase are increased. Shops such as Vinyl Hunter in Bury St Edmunds, Hot Salvation in Folkestone, Gatefold Record Lounge in Hitchin and Smugglers in Deal already do their own successful loyalty cards, and it is something I believe many more shops could benefit from.

I feel sometimes that the media, the shops and the public may be in danger of losing sight of what Record Store Day is primarily about. It is about making people aware of record shops and celebrating the fact that these important outposts of our shared musical culture are still bringing us pleasure. It is tempting to get hung up about the special vinyl releases when we should be concentrating on celebrating the day.

It is imperative that shops have artists performing on the day. Many shops offer free coffee or bake record-shaped cakes. Some shops continue the celebrations on through the evening, holding a pop quiz, or a vinyl listening evening where customers can bring their favourite record to be played. Many have DJ sets or more bands playing. There are endless ways for them to engage with their customers beyond simply encouraging them to buy collectable vinyl. My top tip, which has been adopted with considerable success by some stores, is to keep the celebration going throughout the whole weekend. It requires some creative thinking to entice the customers back again on the Sunday.

I always recommend to the shops I deal with to do a one-day sale where all non-Record Store Day product is 20% or whatever discount they wish to give for that day only. That way customers will stay in the shop and browse instead of just buying their collectables. I like the idea of doing a "CD is not dead" promotion where they offer a discount on the CD stock, ensuring they are appealing to buyers of all formats.

Another of my suggestions is for shops to print their own vouchers offering £5 off a £20 or more purchase in May. This ensures the customer returns. Shops who have implemented this idea tell me they receive 25% – 30% of the vouchers back.

Record Store Day is a wonderful thing despite what the doom-mongers say. It gives a boost to local economies with most shops having artists play in the shop or outside bringing free music to the masses. Independent businesses such as coffee shops, bakers, Hi-Fi dealers, fashion retailers and brewers have all linked up with record shops to make a great day even better.

The farce of Black Friday

Like Halloween, Black Friday is an American tradition that we have adopted in the UK. As with the practice of Trick or Treating, it is difficult to say whether it has enhanced our lives. But one thing is certain. It has a been a disaster for record shops thanks to the indecision of record companies over whether to embrace or ignore this new retail phenomenon. Currently they do neither.

Black Friday is the name of the day following Thanksgiving which occurs on the fourth Thursday of November in the USA. It has signaled the beginning of the Christmas shopping season in the USA since 1952. It has been reported as the busiest shopping day of the year since 2005, if not before, even overtaking the last Saturday before Christmas. The term Black Friday was originally used in a negative sense to describe the heavy traffic that clogged up the streets in American cities on the day after Thanksgiving. Its meaning changed over the years and by the 1980s it was more commonly used to denote the day when retailers began to turn a healthy profit on the year's trading and thereby go into the black (having been in the red).

We don't celebrate Thanksgiving in the UK, so how did we end up with Black Friday here? Traditionally, Black Friday was a negative term in the UK coined by the emergency services to describe the last Friday before Christmas. This was the day when their workload increased dramatically as people finished work for the holiday, went out drinking, got involved in an accident or a fight, and ended the night in hospital or the police cells.

In 2013 the phrase was adapted for retail purposes by Asda. The company was owned by American retail giant Walmart, who decided the time was right for the UK to experience the joys of this high-intensity retailing phenomenon. Other retailers both online and in bricks and mortar shops quickly followed suit, and it was not long before Black Friday also became the UK's biggest shopping day.

In the USA, nine people have died so far on Black Friday, usually the result of shootings as customers fight over bargains, although in one unfortunate case, the employee who opened the shop doors was trampled to death by over-enthusiastic bargain hunters charging in to the store. Anybody who witnessed the disgraceful scenes as UK customers fought over TVs would not be surprised if something similar were to happen here, as customer greed makes them forgo all decency.

In the USA the record companies put out expensive rarities very similar to those offered on Record Store Day. This is bonkers as Black Friday is all about discounts. Shoppers are looking for bargains not an opportunity to pay £50 for a rare vinyl album.

For UK record shops the situation is worse. Music fans read about the releases and expect their local record shop to have them. Many of these scarce items can only be obtained via a third-party music importer. Vinyl that is already extortionate is made even dearer as the importer adds their margin on top.

Come Black Friday there are queues outside the high street retailers offering their bargains. At record shops it's just another day, unless they have taken the initiative to organise their own sale. The major problem is that consumers only have so much money that they allocate for spending on leisure goods. On Black Friday they are spending their spare cash everywhere but the record shops. Before Black Friday, record shops suffer a lull in trade as consumers hold off from buying anything in order to keep their powder dry for Black Friday bargains. Following Black Friday, consumers are skint, ensuring that the lull continues for the record shops.

I always advise record shops to do their own one-day sale on Black Friday to try and claim at least a small slice of the pie. The UK music industry should re-evaluate its position. I would scrap the rare releases for Black Friday as I believe it would benefit shops more for them to be spread over the course of the year.

My suggestion instead would be for record companies to offer 200 classic titles that shops can retail for £5 on CD and £12 on vinyl. This would entice shoppers in to the stores. It would also give the opportunity for the humble CD to figure in a promotion. Record shops could then expand the promotion by reducing the price of any other stock in their racks.

Record Store Day tends to be a day of vinyl bargains only. Although Black Friday is never going to match Record Store Day, I am confident if the record companies worked together on this, there is no reason why Black Friday could not be the second biggest sales day of the year for record shops.

Chapter 3

Brave new world: the future of record shops

The world of retailing is constantly evolving. It is important that record shops avoid the pitfalls of the modern consumer landscape and maximise their opportunities for the future.

The vinyl revival has seen two new breeds of record shop open. One type is owned by young people inspired and swept along on the positive tide of media coverage about the format. The other is owned by the long-term vinyl fan who has spent his or her life in an alternative employment and is now fulfilling the dream of owning their own record shop. In both cases neither traded through the grim times that many of the well-established shops have come through.

What most of these shops have done is embedded themselves within the local music community by promoting local music, in-stores and alternative events. Many have made themselves the meeting place for the local community.

Now is the time to ensure they are in a position for when times become tougher by having their own record shop MOT. It is important to pick up on the positive things other shops are doing. Ensure if you don't have a website get one sorted, make sure you are utilising Discogs and eBay as complimentary selling opportunities. The margins make it difficult to trade profitably selling just new vinyl. It is important to consider what else they can stock.

Vinyl is in fashion

You know vinyl is fashionable when the government starts using it to advertise pensions. In 2017, they ran newspaper adverts featuring a middle aged woman flicking through the vinyl in a record shop. The tagline was "I know what travels at thirty-three and a third. But I don't know how much my pension will be."

Advertisements featuring vinyl or turntables, since 2013 include:
777.com, Alliance Trust, Auto Trader, Barclaycard, Becks, Burton, Durex
Facebook, Fiat 500, First Direct, Herbal Essence, Ikea, ITV, Mini Paceman
Nescafe, Purple Bricks, Rightmove, Robinson's Fruit Shoots, Tetley
Victoria Quarter, Vodaphone, VODKA, West Quay Shopping Centre, Whole Foods

Advertisements featuring CDs, since 2013: zero

One evening I popped into the local pub and noticed the beer mats and beer towels covered in pictures of vinyl records advertising a local ale. It was further evidence advertisers are queuing up to associate themselves with the vinyl revival in order to make their products appear to be cool. Records and all that they represent are suddenly being referenced to advertise the domestic lifestyle choices that influence your purchase of cars, shelving units and bank accounts. Record collecting has lost its image as a hobby for middle-aged men and become instead a pursuit of the most fashion-conscious consumer.

A TV series was even named after the format. Broadcast in 2016 on HBO in the USA and Sky Atlantic in the UK, Martin Scorsese's 10-part series *Vinyl* about life in the New York music industry in the 1970s, was a tale of sex, drugs and rock 'n' roll excess. It could have been called many things, but it was telling that they chose to name it after a format whose popularity was booming.

There has been a growing movement over the last few years in support of independent shops in general. Mary Portas fronted a notable TV series on the subject, and on December 7, 2013, Small Business Saturday was launched, an event featuring Jumbo Records in Leeds. The idea was to encourage people to visit their local independent shops and was deemed a huge success. Clearly people do not want the high street to die.

There has also been a shift whereby record shops who previously had been 100% second-hand have started stocking new vinyl. In many cases new product now accounts for a significant percentage of their business. They were finding it more difficult to obtain collectable product. A huge gap has developed between those wishing to buy to collect and those wishing to sell. Tens of thousands of people have taken up record collecting, making rare titles increase in value, as it is a seller's market.

Sellers are also becoming savvier as they can check the price of vinyl just by looking to sell via Discogs or eBay. They then expect the record shop to match this, which in many cases is not possible as the shops have extra costs such as rent, rates, electricity etc. to incorporate into their profit margins. Prices for buyers have become high while supply is low, resulting in spaces in the shops' racks. These have been filled by new vinyl.

There is no shortage of unsellable vinyl being offered to shops. Easy Listening is a genre that is difficult to sell. Most shops can tell a tale of somebody finding a box of vinyl in the loft containing the likes of Jim Reeves and Mantovani and expecting the shops to pay a fortune for them.

One retailer told me of how he had recently taken 3,000 of these types of albums down to the local landfill. The public can expect to receive good prices on specific genres such as punk, Britpop, reggae and classic soul while, strangely, 1980s pop is becoming more popular. Elvis is the artist that the public make the mistake of thinking is worth good money. But the market is flooded with his music and his stock has been devaluing for a long time.

Discogs

Discogs is an online platform that allows record shops and members of the public the opportunity to sell physical music. Inspired by sites such as eBay, Kevin Lewandowski had the inspired idea to start a website where music fans could list physical music they wished to sell. He launched it in November 2000 in Portland, Oregon originally listing electronic music and naming the site Discogs, a condensed version of discographies.

The site soon proved very popular and by 2004 it reported more than 250,000 releases listed.

Discogs' progress has been staggering. It is now the world's largest database of catalogued music. By 2018 it had more than 10 million releases listed by nearly six million artists. The site has been a major factor in the record shop revival as it opened a whole new market for independent record shops to sell their product. It was especially helpful for them to dispose of all the old stock that had been clogging up the racks or sitting in boxes in the storeroom. By listing the stock, it matched up the product with people somewhere in the world who had been looking for it.

Discogs earns its revenue by charging the seller a percentage in commission and through advertising on the site. The most expensive purchase on the site is $15,000 which was for a 1987 promotional copy of Prince's *The Black Album*. Should you find a copy in your collection then I reckon you can party like it's 1999.

Prince shelved *The Black Album* just a week before the intended 1987 release date, resulting in the destruction of about half a million copies that were already pressed and waiting to be shipped. Promos that had already been sent to clubs and DJs were also recalled and destroyed. A limited number of those promos made it into the hands of collectors and served as the source of bootlegs until the album was officially released in 1994.

The Discogs record for a sale pales into comparison with the highest price ever paid for a vinyl album. In an ironic twist, the most paid for a vinyl record on Discogs was for *The Black Album*, while the highest price paid anywhere, ever was for the *White Album*. Ringo Starr's copy of the 1968 Beatles record sold at Julien's Auction House for an incredible $790,000. The reason for the high price was it was numbered 0000001.

If you are in a band reading this and you wish to make your music collectable calling your next record *The Blue Album*, *The Brown Album* or *The Red Album* would seem a sensible move.

Any music fans who use Discogs should check out the new kid on the block iHaveit. Launched in 2018, iHaveit is like eBay with a music collectors function, enabling users to buy, sell, collect and get estimated prices for vinyl, CDs and cassettes. iHaveit provides a fresh new look and feel to searching, finding, buying and selling. Check it out at: www.ihaveit.io

Supermarkets join the vinyl party

Over the last few years it has become noticeable how supermarkets have cut back on the space they give to CDs. Thanks to all the hard work done by independent record shops to rescue vinyl from the scrapheap, the format has suddenly become fashionable again. It was time for the supermarkets to attach their trailer to the vinyl charabanc.

Tesco was the first supermarket to dip its toe back into the water, after abandoning the vinyl format 30 years previously. The chain had achieved success selling budget-price record players, so it was a move that made sense. Iron Maiden's first studio offering in five years, *The Book of Souls* was the album chosen for this venture. It was a triple album with a fabulous gatefold sleeve and magnificent packaging. The vinyl edition was released exclusively on September 4, 2015 in 55 Tesco Extra stores. Tesco used the album launch as an opportunity for a special promotion on Iron Maiden's own brand of beer, Trooper. Customers who bought the album or CD could purchase the beer half price at £1. Non-Iron Maiden fans had to pay £1.99. The beer is advertised as "created by Iron Maiden" which gives you the bizarre impression of Bruce Dickinson and his fellow band members mixing hops in giant steel containers. The beer was manufactured by Robinson's brewery based in Stockport.

The CD format was sold by Tesco in 850 of its UK stores and online at Tesco Direct. The triple-LP vinyl format cost £24 while the double-CD version cost £9. It was brilliant marketing by Tesco and hats off to the band's management. The story dominated music media for a while. They executed a well-thought out plan and succeeded in getting the album to No.1 in the chart. Tesco then trialed a limited selection of 20 classic vinyl titles in many of the larger stores. Retailing between £12 and £20 the product stocked included albums by artists such as the Beatles, Coldplay, Nirvana and Led Zeppelin.

In March 2016, Sainsbury's joined the vinyl party by stocking vinyl in 171 of its stores. They tied it in with a decision to stock Crossley budget-priced turntables. As with Tesco the selection of albums mostly was limited to best sellers and all-time classics and selling at a discounted price. Key artists in the promotion included Adele, David Bowie, the Eagles and Fleetwood Mac.

By June 2016, Sainsbury's claimed that they were the UK's largest vinyl retailer, responsible for 8% of all vinyl sales. It was somewhat depressing for fans of new music to know that the limited range offered by supermarkets represented such a substantial chunk of the market. Many in the retail industry questioned how a supermarket with such a limited selection could have cornered such a high percentage of the market. HMV responded with a press release openly mocking Sainsbury's claim.

"When it comes to vinyl sales HMV have over four times the market share of Sainsbury's from a range of up to 1,500 records in each of our 128 stores. Not that HMV are blowing their own trumpet, but if you are looking for some Red Hot Chili Peppers, a Hot Chip, or Black-Eyed Peas: the best place to go is your local record store. HMV stocks a huge selection of music on vinyl and CD with artists as diverse as Bread, Marmalade, Bananarama, Hot Chocolate, and the Cranberries (however, we would like to point out that we don't sell nearly as many teabags as Sainsbury's)."

A similar controversy occurred in the USA, when clothing giant Urban Outfitters announced that they were the world's number one vinyl seller, only for *Billboard* to immediately refute the claim, pointing out that Amazon sold more vinyl. Urban Outfitters could have avoided all the negative publicity by pointing out that they were the USA's number one *bricks and mortar* retailer of vinyl.

Incredibly, Father's Day 2016 turned into a high street vinyl battle between Tesco and HMV. They had both secured some fabulous product with 1,800 copies each of eight records offered for Father's Day with four available on coloured vinyl, on sale in 150 stores. The Jam's *Sound Affects* album was released on pink vinyl and sold out immediately as Jam fans - who tend to be a dedicated bunch - were alerted through social media, and there were many tales of fans driving vast distances to find a participating Tesco outlet.

Another album to be cleared from the shelves was the Clash's 1979 double album *London Calling* which Tesco had secured in pink and green vinyl. The album contained the track "Lost in the Supermarket" which was apt as many Clash fans searched Tesco in vain for the limited pressing.

Other limited editions were *Searching for the Young Soul Rebels* by Dexys Midnight

Runners in green vinyl and a gold coloured pressing of Status Quo's *12 Gold Bars*.

Four other titles were included in the promotion, all perfectly chosen to appeal to dads who were returning in droves to purchasing vinyl. *Changesonebowie* by David Bowie, *Purple Rain* by Prince, *Parklife* by Blur and *The Ultimate Collection* by Paul Simon.

Nobody was expecting supermarket staff to have the specialist knowledge of people who work in record shops. Even so, there were some comical responses from staff when customers enquired if the supermarket stocked vinyl records. One customer was asked to clarify: "Are vinyl records like giant CDs?" Another was asked "Are they the black things that go round and round?"

Urban Outfitters vinyl departments continue to do brisk business which can only be a good thing for the format. The more vinyl that is produced, the cheaper it will become. Supermarkets have followed suit with a chart-based vinyl range. The benefits for the non-chart vinyl fan will surely outweigh the disadvantages. With the promise of shelf space in supermarkets, major labels will almost certainly deem it worth their while to press more vinyl.

The downside to this is that, just as they did with the chart CDs, the supermarkets have helped create a dull, stagnating vinyl album chart. The UK Official Chart's best-selling vinyl albums of 2017 makes depressing reading for fans of new music. Fleetwood Mac, the Beatles, Amy Winehouse, Pink Floyd, Radiohead, David Bowie, Bob Marley, Stone Roses, Queen and Nirvana dominated the chart, taking up 14 spots in the Top 20. With supermarket favourite Ed Sheeran at No.1 the chart certainly does not reflect the records being sold in independent record shops. The supermarkets policy of stocking limited titles in bulk quantity is having a huge impact on the chart. I find it embarrassing that the industry is prioritising the promotion of albums on vinyl released decades ago rather than embracing new music.

In 2017 the vinyl supermarket story took a bizarre twist when Sainsbury's announced plans for their own record label. It should not be a surprise as they have sold more than 300,000 vinyl records since 2016. With more than 160 branches stocking vinyl, the chain claims it is responsible for selling one in every 20 albums bought in the UK. Whimsically called Own Records, the Sainsbury's label is curated by well-respected journalist, author and Saint Etienne band member Bob Stanley.

The first two releases were compilations of 1960s and 1970s music. *Hi Fidelity* features a rather eclectic mix of artists including Tangerine Dream, Gallagher & Lyle and Elton John. The other release titled *Coming From Los Angeles (A Taste of the West Coast)* is as good a vinyl collection as you will find for those wishing to explore the sound of the American West Coast. Fleetwood Mac, Love, the Byrds and Little Feat are among the artists featured. Both are 20-track, double-vinyl albums with eye-catching sleeves. You also get Nectar points on your purchase, something you will never get in an independent record shop.

The problem with purchasing your vinyl in a supermarket or an Urban Outfitters is that it is a bland shopping experience. You get none of the feel of a music community that you automatically find in an independent record shop. There is nobody who can advise you on a record in the same way that dedicated record shop staff do. This is best summed up by the pictures on the internet that showed a supermarket putting a security tag through the sleeve of the vinyl records they were stocking, leaving a hole in the cover. In an instant, they had turned a piece of art into a damaged product.

The CD is not dead yet

When it was invented in the 1980s the CD was viewed as the future of music. It looked space aged, a gleaming silver disc that the industry told us had a superior sound and no matter how much wear and tear it suffered, would always play perfectly. We were encouraged to change our vinyl collections over to this exciting format, and the industry was happy to sell us our record collections all over again.

The problem with the CD is that it has not improved in more than 30 years. We are on iPhone 8, Windows 10, but still on CD1. The industry has still not produced a plastic CD case that is unlikely to smash or crack if dropped on the floor. The alternative they came up with was the digipack made of card. Unlike the plastic case it did not smash, though offered less protection to the plastic tray inside which held the CD in place. If crushed, the teeth of the plastic tray would break so when you opened your CD lots of little pieces of plastic would drop out. CDs are wrapped in that irritating plastic that is difficult to tear off. You end up using your teeth or getting a knife. We can send a spacecraft to the edge of the universe but have still not invented a satisfactory CD case. It is as if the format has been sentenced to a long lingering death and nobody is prepared to save it

Compare it with vinyl, where you often receive a free download or CD of the album with your purchase, meaning that you get multiple formats for the price of one. The LP often comes with a booklet and is now manufactured on higher quality, 180-gram vinyl, giving a better sound than in days gone by. The LP has evolved. Yet the CD is stuck in the past.

People treasure vinyl and take great care not to damage it, yet people don't value the CD in the same way. My job involves driving all over the UK to visit record shops. On these trips, I take the opportunity to listen to many of our forthcoming releases that I will be selling to the record shops. When I have finished listening to a CD, I throw it on the seat of the car or in to the glove compartment. When I have finished listening to vinyl, I don't hurl it across the room like a frisbee. The record is carefully replaced in the inner sleeve, before being inserted in the album cover.

Despite the lack of development, the CD is far from dead, with talk of a complete digital dominance being misplaced. Many observers predicted that the CD would go the way of the audio cassette, but I am pleased to say that CDs show no sign of becoming a format consigned to our memories. Indeed, with more than 41 million CDs sold to UK audiences in 2017, the figures show clearly that the format is proving resilient in an era of rapid change. So why do we often talk the CD down?

Research conducted for ERA's 2017 Yearbook noted that the subscription streaming market now accounts for 48% of market spend. Physical and digital methods of consuming music are not mutually exclusive. In fact, they're often consumed hand-in-hand, as part of the diverse, innovative and ever shifting way in which we access the work of our favourite artists.

I firmly believe that CDs will continue to be a resilient fixture in our musical landscape for a good few years to come. Time and time again music lovers vote with their hard-earned cash and choose to invest in physical formats.

Nobody can deny that the CD is undergoing a long and steady decline but talk of "the death of the CD" is premature. It is important to recognise that all formats are integral in ensuring that music prospers. The CD should not be a format we ignore, they are an integral part of the British music industry success story that ought to be celebrated.

We have a Record Store Day in celebration of vinyl, and a Cassette Day to celebrate the cassette, and yet we have no celebration of the physical format that sells more than all the others put together: the CD.

It is fair to say that Cassette Day has not exactly captured the imagination of record shops and the public. The event, which began in 2013, takes place in October and has received a lukewarm reception. A minority of record shops have persevered with the format, but only 16 shops took part in Cassette Day in 2017.

The volume of sales speaks for itself. The cassette format accounts for significantly less than 1% of physical sales of music. According to the Official Chart Company, the best-selling cassette in 2017 was the Original Motion Picture Soundtrack *Guardians of the Galaxy Vol.2: Awesome Mix Vol.2*, which sold 3,120 copies (compared to 70,000 plus copies on vinyl). This was way ahead of the year's second-best seller on cassette, Kasabian's *For Crying Out Loud* with 1,026 sales. About 20,000 cassettes were sold in the UK *in total* in 2017, a similar figure to 2006.

The format hit rock bottom in 2012 when a grand total of just 3,823 cassettes were purchased in the UK. If artists use cassettes at all, it is often as a promotional tool which they produce in limited runs to sell at gigs and via their own website, cutting record shops out of the picture.

Chapter 4

Last chain standing: the story of HMV

How HMV came back from the brink and learned to love vinyl

It is easy to underestimate the role of HMV in facilitating the vinyl revival. If the chain had not taken decisive action to reverse its earlier (catastrophic) decision to remove the format from their shops, then vinyl sales would be considerably below current rates. Not only did they put vinyl back on the shelves, they embraced the format with gusto, giving the format a timely and much-needed boost.

I had the pleasure of working at HMV Liverpool for eight years during the mid-1980s. They were some of the best years of my life. To work in an environment with fellow music enthusiasts, selling to music fans while listening to new music was my idea of heaven. My previous job had been manufacturing the flavour for cheese and onion crisps, so it is easy to understand why I enjoyed working at HMV so much. These were the glory days of record retailing, when people queued outside the store on a Monday morning to purchase the new releases. It was also the period when CDs were retailing for up to £15 each.

Thirty years on, high street rents and rates have rocketed while many CDs sell for less than £10, so the profit margin on what was once HMV's core product has been slashed dramatically. At its peak, the chain had 320 stores spread all over the globe with the majority being in the UK. HMV is the Last Chain Standing. Past competitors such as Zavvi, Our Price, Tower, MVC, Music Zone and Andys have all closed, leaving just HMV and the independent record shops to fly the flag for those wishing to buy physical music product on the high street. In 2013, HMV went into administration and if they had not been rescued by Hilco, 40% of our record retailers would have been lost in one go.

To understand both where it all went wrong for HMV and their remarkable comeback, you need to know the history. The inaugural HMV store in London was opened in London on July 20, 1921 at 363 Oxford Street, by the composer Sir Edward Elgar. They sold sheet music, recordings and HMV-brand gramophones, which were available for a mere £5. At that point, HMV was part of the Gramophone Company. In 1931, a merger with the Columbia Gramophone Group formed EMI, which stood for Electric and Musical Industries. The decision to use Nipper the dog as the HMV logo was an early stroke of marketing genius. The dog, which has become synonymous with the brand, was a stray fox terrier found on the streets of Bristol in 1884 by Mark Barraud. He was named Nipper due to his tendency to nip the backs of visitors' legs. After Mark's death, his brother Francis Barraud, the Liverpool artist, took care of the dog. The picture titled *His Master's Voice* was painted in 1899 and showed the dog listening to a cylinder phonograph. William Barry Owen of The Gramophone Company bought the picture for £50, which proved to be a very shrewd move. In 1901, the Gramophone Company registered the *His Master's Voice* Nipper painting as a trademark in the UK. It was used in advertising by the Gramophone Company and became one of the world's most recognisable trademarks.

For the next four decades selling recording equipment was the core business. This all changed during the 1960s, thanks to the huge popularity of artists such as The Beatles and Elvis Presley. The stores stopped retailing record players and recording equipment to concentrate on selling singles and LPs.

I am grateful to a former work colleague and respected music journalist, Cliff White who wrote a piece for me (reprinted below), describing his time working at HMV during the Swinging Sixties. A wonderful man, Cliff, sadly, passed away in January 2018. As you will see his memories of HMV in a bygone era are fascinating.

"I am happy to offer a few off-the-cuff memories of my time working at the original HMV record store - 363 Oxford Street, London - from mid-1964 to some brain-swiped day in early 1968. Once employed there I was ever-ready to recommend my music preferences to customers but selling the hottest wax was the name of the game: across the spectrum service with a smile.

Among those I served were Vera Lynn, Del Shannon, The Who (in full Union Jack regalia - them, not me), Jimi Hendrix and Kim Fowley who pranced around the department shouting, "Freak Out!" Jimi came in to buy blues and soul records and I insisted he include Screamin' Jay Hawkins' "The Whammy" amongst his purchases - which may account for his subsequent career.

During my tenure with HMV it was owned by EMI who began experimenting with a self-service department and started acquiring other record shops to convert into suburban and regional HMV outlets. More of which later. When I was first employed it was still the sole flagship, managed by the rotund figure of Mr Robert (Bob) Boast, who had reputedly joined the store before the Second World War. All staff were issued with uniform jackets or blouses and obliged to address each other as Mr., Miss or Mrs.

Song publishers Ardmore & Beechwood occupied the top floor of the building. This was a bonus as they'd occasionally offload boxes of American 45s they'd been sent for review. It was important to get wind of this bonanza in advance to be first at the trough for the freebies. There were usually obscure soul gems among the discarded discs.

Adjacent to them, was a small recording studio where engineer Jim Foy taped Cliff Richard, the Beatles and others recording messages of gush for their fan clubs. I believe other artists recorded demos in this little-known hidey-hole. History tells that after the Beatles had been rejected by Decca it was Jim Foy who recommended Brian Epstein to Ardmore & Beechwood who then sent him on to George Martin at EMI - so the mop tops' success was all Jim's fault, folks.

Cosmopolitan Corner, specialising in what is now termed "world music", was tucked away on the mezzanine. Ground floor was the classical department. "Pop" music (including folk, jazz, blues, soul, easy listening, etc.) was consigned to the basement.

It was a lively basement, descended upon each lunchtime and end of working day by hordes of young persons asking to be played the latest hits in the open sound booths around the walls. We also had a couple of enclosed listening rooms for the more "serious" customers, who tended to drop in during the afternoon lull. Bribing me with a lunch, The Who's manager Kit Lambert used one of the listening rooms to promote an acetate of "I

Can't Explain" to likely takers. Apparently, he didn't have an office at the time.

The stockroom extended under Oxford Street, where in quiet moments one could lift a hatch in the floor to watch thousands of cockroaches scuttling from the sudden light, presumably back down to the Central Line that rumbled below.

Pop sales staff were corralled in a large enclosure in the middle of the basement, surrounded by a ring of browser boxes full of empty record sleeves - the 45s had hand-written cardboard inserts. The discs themselves were filed on our side of the fence, where we also had record playing turntables for all the listening booths. It was then the store's policy to stock at least one copy of every UK record release still in catalogue. As the record companies didn't delete their products, particularly LPs, as rapidly as they might cast them aside today, we were the custodians of an impressive library of vinyl, some items dating back to, ooh, when I was a lad.

Being under the EMI umbrella, HMV staff were urged to "bump up" sales figures of EMI releases. In a shocking exposé I can now reveal that EMI releases were automatically ranked higher than they should have been on the in-store sales chart, which was then a key contributor to the national pop chart. As EMI had acquired the Motown franchise from Oriole and launched its Stateside label this didn't conflict too much with my sensitivities.

Every so often we'd get wealthy owners of continental discotheques swanning in, flashing wads of cash and requesting "the latest two hundred hip 45s" (or words to that effect). Oh joy! As a responsible salesman it was my bound duty to include all the most recent Brit beat group hits but that still left plenty of room to fill up the box with blues kings, James Brown, Guy Stevens' Sue releases, other soul favourites and whatever else I fancied. In my imagination, somewhere in France or Spain or Italy or Germany there is now a demented record collector who was sparked off by something I snuck into a care package to their local disco.

At the other extreme, another colleague was a big fan of Cilla Black. He contrived to get an invitation to meet Cilla backstage at a London theatre, masquerading as a PR person from EMI's Manchester Square headquarters, looking after three visiting delegates from EMI Sweden, aka the HMV store. As one of those "delegates" I put on my best Swedish accent to chat to Cilla in her dressing room before nipping along the corridor to say hello to the stars of the show, the Everly Brothers.

I don't think I bothered to try to be Scandinavian with Don & Phil. Have occasionally thought about confronting Miss Black again and saying "Surprise! Surprise!"

I'm bound to also mention in passing a memorable colleague who shall remain nameless. A tall, grey-faced, ravaged-looking individual (with whom I shared a flat for a time; he wasn't as scary as he appeared to be), he'd had an unconventional upbringing and was a clinically diagnosed schizophrenic. This did not affect his salesmanship except in moments of extreme stress, when the hordes were swarming. He'd then lie on the floor in the middle of our corral and howl like a rabid dog. Always guaranteed to grab the customers' attention. A real crowd pleaser.

In January 66 I left HMV for five months to tour Germany as lead "singer" (I use the term loosely) with my cousin's beat combo, and then to loon about with Screamin› Jay on his second UK tour. That's an entirely different ramble. In my second stint with the store, now managed by former assistant manager Ken Whitmarsh, there were grand plans afoot. Incidentally, Ken, who had employed me in the first place and remained a friend until his premature death, was principally a jazz man - a knowledgeable buff - but that didn't blinker his retailing acumen. However it did mean that HMV always had as strong a stock *of jazz albums as our specialist competitors Asman's, Collet's, Dobell's and Ray's.*

Circa 1966 HMV opened its first self-service department (where the discs were now in the sleeves in the browser bins) and bought a shop in the Edgware Road to be run on the same principal. Our in-house prototype, by the main entrance on the ground floor, was of immediate benefit to a trader who had a record stall just off Cambridge Circus at the junction of Charing Cross Road and Shaftesbury Avenue. He'd come in, select an armful of albums of his choice, and then sprint off with them along Oxford Street. Our security guard, an elderly ex-war sergeant with a gammy leg, was thwarted every time. I believe the arrangements were eventually tightened up.

Being part of the team revamping purchased shops could be interesting. We'd go in and log all the existing stock for removal; builders would follow us to convert the premises into an HMV; we'd go back in to restock the new store. I clearly remember one shop in North London that had been harbouring a stockroom full of unsold LPs and 45s, piled high in dusty boxes. I picked the sellotape off the first box I came to: Jeez, 25 mint copies of Gene Vincent's "Be-Bop-A-Lula". Unfortunately, I was only a poorly paid salesman otherwise I'd have bought the entire contents of the room. Never did know what happened to all that old stock, although I suspect a couple of copies of Mr Vincent's single inadvertently fell into my knapsack.

Towards the end of my days at HMV I had been promoted to the dizzy rank of Assistant Manager of the Pop department and was earmarked to manage one of the growing number of branch stores. At the same time, I had been initiated into the mysteries of marijuana by a summer-break temping university student and to LSD by a young temptress in Bayswater. No contest: I tuned in, turned on and dropped out." Cliff White (1945-2018)

HMV went through rapid expansion in the late 1960s and 1970s. Although the chain faced stiff competition from Richard Branson's Virgin Records shops, which were set up in 1971, and the iconic Our Price, which appeared on the scene in 1972, they became the country's leading music retailer.

The 1980s were a huge decade for HMV, as they were in the perfect position to capitalise on the new exciting format of CD. They could use the power of MTV to promote music via the rapidly expanding video market. Sales of 12-inch singles were showing dramatic rises as many music fans would buy multiple copies of the same song on various versions. Cassette singles were also big sellers.

In 1988, they acquired the 18-shop Midlands chain Revolver, which increased HMV UK's stores to 126. HMV believed in promoting from within, so the key positions in the company were filled by people who had worked their way through the ranks. The environment was incredibly competitive with store competing against store, area against area and, at head office, department against department.

A particular emphasis was placed on league tables. When I worked at HMV in Liverpool, each Monday we would discuss our position in the regional table. It was like a football league. We always wanted to finish above Manchester and were always confident we could beat the likes of Bolton, Blackburn, Preston and Blackpool. If you were near the bottom of the league you knew that the area manager would virtually camp in your store so that he could monitor everything you did to see how he could improve things. Stores that finished top of the league were rewarded with prizes such as holidays. These were the golden days for HMV. The 1980s was the decade of "loadsamoney". People seemed to have money to burn and the increasing value of property was the main conversation at UK dinner parties.

HMV thrived during this period, with the CD being a badge of honour. As the CD buyer for HMV Liverpool at the time, I was instructed to buy at least one of every CD released by the record companies. It is now hard to believe that from 1985 until 1992, the cassette was the biggest-selling music format in the UK. Its advantages over vinyl were that it was a small, portable way of listening to music. The CD offered the same advantages in a vastly superior format, which boasted greater resilience and higher sound quality than cassettes as well as the option to skip back and forth between tracks.

With the arrival of CDs, the vinyl format was abandoned by record companies as music consumers were encouraged to replace their LP collections. HMV positioned itself at the heart of the CD revolution. A new flagship store at 150 Oxford Street, which had more than 50,000 square feet dedicated to customers' listening pleasure, was opened by Bob Geldof.

The tragic famine in Africa that prompted such an admirable response from the international music industry through Band Aid and Live Aid, energised interest in music, across the board. I had numerous customers at HMV who bought 10 or more copies of the Band Aid single "Do They Know it's Christmas?" to give away as Christmas gifts to family and friends. HMV and all record shops gave their share of the sales of the record to the appeal. As is often the case, it was the music industry that led the way when it came to helping in a time of need.

The good times continued throughout the 1990s with the great Blur v Oasis battle and the Spice Girls helping fuel demand for the physical format. HMV was quick to recognise the potential of the DVD, just as they had done a decade earlier with CDs, and dedicated a much greater percentage of the store to promoting the new format than any of its rivals did.

A fundamental change occurred during this period when HMV began purchasing the majority of its stock via its head office. Central buying as it was called made economic sense as it gave the company stronger bargaining power with the record companies, and improved consistency and sales in most areas. Previously, individual shop managers had a lot of flexibility to stock titles they wanted, resulting in HMV promoting a lot of local music. Head Office certainly considered local variations when they scaled product out to the stores, but stocking local fanzines and small local releases were no longer a priority.

HMV had profited from selling talking books, and took a major decision to buy the book chain Waterstones, merging them with Dillons, another bookseller they already owned. Later, Ottakar's bookshops were also added to their portfolio. The timing turned out to be poor and, in hindsight, there was no practical benefit to the merger with Waterstones. It coincided with a slump in book sales as Amazon steamed into that market and drove prices down. There was not enough space in HMV or Waterstones to introduce proper cross-merchandising, which might have been a good strategic move for the long-term.

In the early 2000s HMV took the decision to remove vinyl from all but their largest stores. This opened the door for the independent record shops to be the gatekeepers of the format. In a strange twist of fate, by abandoning the format it created a vacuum that the indies were happy to fulfil. It was from the momentum created by this that the seeds of the vinyl revival were sown. Suddenly independent record shops had a virtual monopoly on the format. The decision was taken, not because the chain did not like the format, but for a purely economic reason. The ratio of sales to stock was very poor compared to CD. For example, 5 feet of LP racking held around 160-200 titles of vinyl whereas CD held 400-500.

Vinyl had become a low priority for record companies due to the massive sales being achieved by CD and DVD. During this period the industry and the media were all telling us how superior the CD was. Many releases were not released on vinyl, so if you were a fan the only way you could purchase a lot of music was on CD. With the extra cost of manufacturing, storage and a higher return of faulty product, it is easy to understand why the record companies lost enthusiasm for vinyl and why HMV took the decision to decommission it in all but their larger shops.

In 2002, the HMV group was floated on the London Stock Exchange. It was valued at around a billion pounds. Senior staff received shares which turned out not to be a great investment. It was a critical point in the history of HMV. The timing was unfortunate insofar as the flotation occurred just before it became evident how much iTunes and Amazon would impact on the music retailing business. The requirement to report quarterly to the city on what became, within months, a downward trend, meant there was a media story about CD decline which was constantly fed.

This coincided with a change in the broader cultural context. Traditionally, the business pages in newspapers tended to be dry, boring and stuck to the facts. But by this point, the business pages were becoming as sensationalist as the rest of the papers, and there was more of a narrative spin put on the facts. Lazy journalism and a desire to reiterate that physical music was dead started to dominate reporting. Young, rich, city types were not early converts to the vinyl revival, quite the reverse and there was a uniformity of opinion in the business pages that digital music was the future.

A major problem created by the floatation was that HMV constantly made short-term decisions to improve the figures in an effort to satisfy shareholders and supply the press with good news. In retrospect, a proper long-term plan with external input, commitment to investment in streaming (the HMV jukebox was an early subscription model very similar to Spotify which they gave up on) and investment in HMV.com which was competing with Amazon for a while, would have made more sense.

HMV had benefited from the demise of other music chains. When the independently-owned Fopp chain was forced to close in 2007, HMV bought the name and six of its best performing stores from the receivers: Glasgow, Edinburgh, Cambridge, Nottingham, Manchester and Covent Garden.

By 2008 music retailing was in big trouble. Independent record shops were closing at an average rate of one every three days and things were to get worse. In January Woolworths closed. The high street retailer employed more than 30,000 people and though music was only a part of its business, it was a massive blow to the music industry. However, many former Woolworths music purchasers took their custom to HMV. On Christmas Eve the Zavvi chain of music shops entered administration, ensuring its staff had a woeful Christmas. HMV took this opportunity to purchase 20 of their best performing stores.

Being the last chain standing did have some advantages. But HMV was also beginning to feel the pinch. There were many reasons beyond HMV's control for the decline in sales, but the key mistake they made was not to plan for the next decade but to keep concentrating on being the number one entertainment retailer on the high street. HMV had been a major player in the video market and were in the perfect position when the DVD took off to replace the videos. By the late 1990s DVDs accounted for more than 50% of HMV's business.

There was not much HMV could do about the many illegal downloading sites that sprang up, but as people were now obtaining music free of charge, the feeling among the public was that CDs were overpriced. The media picked up on this, reminding the public that CDs could be manufactured for 50p but were being sold for £12. Nobody in the music industry was countering this argument. The content of a CD had to be written, recorded, produced and then marketed and distributed. All these things cost money and they were still fantastic value for the pleasure they gave.

The internet created both challenges and opportunities for music retailers. At first HMV embraced it, as the first major music retailer to set up a website. However, instead of aggressively promoting the website in their stores and on their carrier bags, it was left to limp along unsupported. HMV were slow out of the blocks when music started being sold online. Amazon and Play and several other online traders recognised the potential of this new concept in selling music. The HMV website was always playing catch up and was never able to attract enough customers away from other online retailers. The fact that Apple launched iTunes in 2001, but it wasn't until 2010 that HMV Digital started up is a measure of just how slow they were. Like a lot of other companies in the music industry, the powers-that-be at HMV were convinced that digital downloading was just a passing fad.

The policy of promoting from within was a mistake in an industry that can change so quickly. With the emergence of Amazon and digital music, HMV needed fresh people who understood these new competitors and could enable HMV to compete with them. There was a general feeling within the company that selling physical music in bricks and mortar stores on high streets was the cornerstone of the business and that is what they should concentrate on. The result was that Amazon had a free run at establishing itself as the website from which to purchase CDs. It was internet and digital that exposed the flaw in HMV's policy of internal promotion. There were no young, dynamic personnel within the company with the vision to see that in the future, digital and internet sales were going to be a big part of music retailing. HMV had the opportunity to be one of the biggest players on the internet, but they did not grasp the nettle and others took advantage.

Events such as the London bombings of 2007 and the dramatic rise in parking charges in city centres contributed to a sea change in consumer attitudes. People were less inclined to come into town with all the associated cost and hassle of getting there when, with the simple click of a mouse, they could purchase music without leaving the comfort of their armchair. Things were looking so grim that even Nipper the dog was retired to the old dog's home. Gromit, the dog from Nick Parks's *Wallace and Gromit* replaced Nipper during a promotional period. The public wondered whether they had seen the last of Nipper, but the faithful old dog later returned to carry on representing the chain.

The stock market crash of 2008 was the last thing the beleaguered chain needed.

When times are tough, non-essential items such as CDs are among the first things that consumers cut back on. HMV began to lose its identity as it desperately tried to encourage customers to visit the shops. It had been known to the public as a great record shop - probably the best music chain in the world - but it now decided it no longer wanted to be the best music retailer, it wanted to be a one-stop shop for all things entertainment. The chain stopped stocking vinyl records, just as vinyl sales started to pick up again. Stocks of music genres such as metal, jazz, folk, blues, country, world music as well as classic rock back catalogue were greatly reduced to make way for computer games, books, headphones and clothes. They gave over more sales space to computer software and hardware, DVDs, Blu-ray discs, MP3 players and tablet computers.

This all seemed a great idea to the people in head office, but the message did not get through to the public, who still thought of HMV as a music store. Soon the chain was forced to cut back. If you are selling mobile phones and clothes, you don't need specialist music knowledge. They started losing many long-term staff who had become disillusioned with the direction HMV was taking. These staff members had joined the company because they loved music not fashion or technology. HMV had always had a policy of employing music fans to work there. Product knowledge was deemed fundamentally important. As the chain had expanded there were not enough people with that expertise for the number of stores they opened.

Opening new shops was the quickest return on investment but created major overheads and impacted on the quality as they were appointing increasingly inexperienced staff to management positions while stretching the resources of regional and divisional management too far.

It is fair to say that the exceptional customer service HMV offered did contribute to standards rising through the whole of music retail. One of the reasons for the decline of indies was the standard of service in many shops. HMV identified merchandising and service as priorities back in the 1980s and really went for it (sometimes to an extreme). The revival of independent record shops has seen a growth not just in vinyl but in standards of presentation and communication.

Many music fans abandoned the chain and turned to independent record shops or the internet to purchase the genres HMV had chosen no longer to stock. Other retailers sold clothes and computer games far more cheaply. Independent record shops were the place to go if you wanted advice on records, and especially to buy vinyl - the format HMV had virtually given up on.

In 2006 Simon Fox was appointed CEO of HMV. He launched a radical three-year plan to turn around the company's fortunes. The aim was to engage with the customer more. In a blaze of publicity, HMV launched the "Get Closer" social network. The idea was that fans would discover content through the site and buy more music. Thus It allowed users to import music and film files and create their own library. They were then linked to other users with similar tastes. Once again the message did not seem to get through to staff or the public. Surprisingly, they did not take the opportunity to advertise the scheme on their carrier bags and promote it at every opportunity and the idea failed to catch on. The site was popular with the people that were using it but there were not enough of them. Reluctantly, HMV closed the site in 2009.

At this point, the cash reserves HMV had at the beginning of the decade were no longer there. It was more important than ever to prioritise where they were going to spend their money. They had invested heavily in "purehmv", a loyalty card scheme where members paid £3 to join. More than 2 million people had signed up and these members collected points every time they shopped either online or in the shops. Points could be exchanged for money-can't-buy rewards such as tickets to gigs, film screenings, VIP experiences and signed items. They could also be exchanged for digital tracks. These experiences included opportunities to meet bands backstage or at sound checks before gigs. The most famous event was probably an exclusive preview screening of the Take That DVD *The Circus Live* at the Hammersmith Apollo. The band was in attendance and the event was free to purehmv members.

HMV borrowed extensively to purchase MAMA's live venue business at a cost of £46 million. It was a long-term investment as MAMA ran thirteen music venues including the Hammersmith Apollo, the Forum, the Jazz Cafe and the Borderline. The idea was sound, as HMV had become one of the UK's largest ticket sellers. It also started a joint venture with Curzon Artificial Eye to bring cinemas to the high street. The first trial store was in Wimbledon, south west London. The cinema was located above the store in a former stock room that had been converted into three separate screens and a bar. It had its own entrance so it could be accessed outside store hours. In the short term, it had swallowed up more money and was beginning to make the banks jittery.

The company had lots of great ideas and in order to implement them, investment was more important than ever. Christmas 2010 was the crunch moment. Already under extreme pressure from their banks to reduce borrowing, HMV needed good Christmas sales to relieve the pressure and ease their cash flow situation. Unfortunately, it was a disaster for all high-street retailers. Appalling weather conditions kept many shoppers at home. Shopping Centres such as Brent Cross were closed completely.

HMV's profits were down by £6 million on the six-week run up to Christmas 2010. HMV would normally do 45% of their annual sales during this period, which would usually generate 65% of HMV's profits. January 2011 got off to a bad start as VAT was increased to 20%, which had a negative effect on trade. The media vultures were circling, speculating who would be the first high street retailer to close. It was clear they had HMV down as the next victim, drawing unfair parallels with Woolworths.

Soon, four profit warnings were issued. These are statements issued by a company advising the stock market that profits will be lower than expected. This triggered more negative publicity from the press, who were already giving them a hard time. Every bit of bad news was seized on by the media, who would start articles with the phrase "Troubled music retailer HMV". Any good news was virtually ignored. The company had still managed to post a £30 million profit despite its troubles. But the negative publicity was sufficient to make people uneasy about using the stores.

In May 2011, HMV sold Waterstones to Russian billionaire Alexander Mamut to reduce debt. The following month they agreed new credit facilities with the Lloyds Banking Group and Royal Bank of Scotland. With a £240 million loan, it was going to take a monumental effort to turn the chain around. Other assets soon followed as in 2012 they sold the Hammersmith Apollo to AEG Live, the concert promoter, and Eventim, the ticket agency. Later in the year they sold the remainder of the MAMA group to Lloyds Development Capital.

HMV was still much loved by the music industry, which supported the changes. The chain's long-term vision made sense, but it needed the support of the British public more than ever. Unfortunately, it was too late. HMV had too many stores, and they were now in a position where, due to the high overheads of prime high street locations and staff wages, they were no longer competing with the online retailers on price, could not offer the personal service of independent record shops and were missing out on the beginning of the vinyl revival as they were excluded from Record Store Day. HMV no longer had anything much to offer music fans.

In January 2013 HMV announced that it was going into administration. It would continue to trade whilst they tried to find a purchaser for the business. HMV's shares were suspended from trading while financial firm Deloitte was appointed to administrate the chain's 239 stores. The chain was bought out of receivership by Hilco who have turned out to be true knights in shining armour. They restructured the company by keeping 141 of the 239 stores as well as the nine Fopp shops, saving more than 2,500 jobs. Rents were renegotiated with landlords and trading terms improved with suppliers. At the time of going into receivership HMV accounted for more than 20% of physical music sales, which is why the music industry did all it could to get the chain up and running again. Helped along by the industry itself, some amazing offers appeared in the shops to encourage people back in. Hilco recognised that it had been a mistake to pull away from vinyl and embraced it with gusto. Soon the shops had new racking installed and were bulging with vinyl bargains.

HMV had lobbied the Entertainment Retail Association to be part of Record Store Day. The Entertainment Retail Association balloted their members on whether the chain should be allowed to take part. This was akin to asking foxes if they wanted to bring back hunting. Most Entertainment Retail Association members are record shops. With many releases on Record Store Day only being pressed in quantities of 500–2,000 copies, why would any record shop vote for a major chain to come in and take half the cake away? The decision of the ERA ballot was a resounding "No."

HMV therefore founded their own version of Record Store Day, which has been highly successful. They offered big discounts on vinyl they already stocked. The limited-edition vinyl exclusives were available in all stores and online on a first-come-first-served basis. These were the exclusive titles:

Sex Pistols: *Never Mind the Bollocks* (1000 copies on pink vinyl)
Manic Street Preachers: *Everything Must Go* (1000 copies on blue vinyl)
Various Artists: *Let's Bop – Sun Records Collection* (1000 copies on black vinyl)
Teenage Fanclub: *Bandwagonesque* (500 numbered copies on pink vinyl)
The Clash: *The Clash* (1000 copies on green vinyl)
Velvet Underground: *Loaded* (1000 copies on white vinyl)
Deep Purple: *In Rock* (1000 copies on marbled vinyl)
Alex Turner: *Submarine OST* (500 copies on 10-inch black vinyl)
Ben Salisbury & Geoff Barrow: *Ex Machina OST* (500 copies on frosted vinyl)
John Martyn: *Solid Air* (500 copies on green vinyl).

Hilco have done a fantastic job of turning HMV around, and in January 2015, the company overtook Amazon to become the largest retailer of physical music in the UK.

I feel that HMV should be more loved than it is. The pleasure it has given us music fans for more than 90 years is such that it should be held in the same regard as HP sauce, Heinz baked beans, Marks & Spencer or the Mini Cooper. We should cherish the brand and recognise the joy it has brought to millions of music fans.

Chapter 5

The making of Last Shop Standing, and other record shop movies

Last Shop Standing (2012; 50 minutes)
Last Shop Standing (2013 RSD deluxe-DVD; 124 minutes)

My book *Last Shop Standing: Whatever Happened to Record Shops?* was published in 2009, and to publicise it I did several filmed segments for the BBC One current affairs show *Inside Out*. In 2012 I was contacted by two film companies, both interested in turning the book into a film.

I met producer Rob Taylor and director Pip Piper of Birmingham-based film company Blue Hippo Media in a local pub and was immediately impressed with their enthusiasm and passion for taking on the project. Having read a story earlier that week about an author who received $1 million to turn his book into a film, I was feeling optimistic about the financial benefits of such a project. Pip and Rob kindly bought me a ploughman's lunch and a pint of bitter shandy as they gently brought me down to earth. They convinced me that it would be no problem to raise funds for the film, but after six weeks the *Last Shop Standing* bank account balance stood at zero.

We decided to go down the crowdfunding route. We chose Indiegogo as our platform to launch the appeal. The target was to raise £7,500 in a 3-month period. And a further £10,000 for post-production. A donation of £25 would be rewarded with an advance copy of the film signed by Pip the director, and a name on the credits. A donation of £200 secured two tickets for the film premier. For £500 we would enable a screening of the film at a venue of the donor's choice with either the director, producer or myself on hand to talk about the making of the film – the donor to keep any money made on the door.

Pip had decided that the film would tell the story of the independent record shops through the voices of the record shop owners themselves. I picked out 23 shops that we could visit that all had interesting tales and charismatic owners.

The initial plan was to film an interview with one of the shop owners and post it on the Indiegogo website to kickstart our crowdfunding appeal. I knew straight away the shop we would visit. Kane Jones owned Kanes Records in Stroud. In all my years of visiting record shops a visit to Kane was always great fun as he had a vast array of funny anecdotes about his time in the music industry. I looked forward to getting these tales on film as I knew the British public would enjoy them. I called Kane up. He told me he had the band ahab playing in the store soon. Perfect! We could also film the band.

It turned out to be a disaster. Kane telling anecdotes down the pub or in a shop was not the same as telling them to a film camera. He could not get the stories right, or when he did they were just not funny. After studying the footage, Pip decided that he could not use any of the interview. Despite this setback, he cobbled together a trailer and set it to the music of the James Clarke 5 who had kindly offered us the use of their music free of charge.

The finished clip looked impressive. We posted it on Indiegogo and donations started trickling in. After three days, we noted that Andy McCluskey of OMD had donated £200. Securing his endorsement and reading his comment, about how he remembered the times he had spent in Probe Records in Liverpool, was a tremendous early boost.

The big day arrived for us to do our first day's proper filming. With myself, Pip, Dave the cameraman, Billy the sound recordist and a pile of equipment all crammed into a Vauxhall Estate, we set off to the West Country with the car's suspension nearly touching the road. The first shop we visited was Acorn Records in Yeovil to interview Chris Lowe the owner and his long-time assistant Mavis Slater. At the age of 83, Mavis was a local legend. Her son, Mutter Slater, the singer with the band Stackridge, had been the first artist to play the first Glastonbury Festival.

From there we drove to Dorset to visit Piers and Steph Gardner at Bridport Music. The husband-and-wife duo gave us some thought-provoking material on chart hyping before one of the shop's regular customers, Billy Bragg joined us to speak of the importance of record shops. That night the film crew stayed at my house in Wiltshire. Our entire tour of the UK was involved staying at a combination of houses of friends and families and Travelodge.

The next day it was off to London where we had arranged to meet the broadcaster, author and musician Sid Griffin, of Long Ryders and Coal Porters fame, at Sister Ray Records in Berwick Street. Sid has an endless supply of anecdotes about his life in music. He told me great tales about growing up in the USA, of buying his first record and the thrill of when you first visit record shops as part of a band to see if they are displaying your record. When the interview was concluded, Sid commented that he looked forward to seeing the film, but expected to be on the cutting room floor as it was where he normally ended up. I assured him he would be in the film.

Unfortunately, Sid was correct. He did end up on the cutting room floor. The film was telling the story of the UK record shop and Pip decided Sid's tales of American record shops did not have any relevance with the story we were trying to tell. All was not lost though, as Sid's anecdotes ended up being included among the 74-minutes of extra footage on the extended, deluxe-DVD version of the film.

While at Sister Ray we interviewed the owner Phil Barton. Nobody was more forthright than Phil. He had seen the industry from both sides. He started off by being a sales assistant at the fondly remembered Selectadisc Records in Nottingham before moving on to become a sales rep working for various record companies. "Our job was to hype the chart," he memorably said.

At Rough Trade East we interviewed Nigel House and vinyl champion Spencer Hickman who at the time was organising Record Store Day in the UK and gave us a bullish account of the way forward for independent record shops.

The following day we went to Brighton, a city which had three quality record shops to visit. At Resident Music, co-owner Derry was upbeat about the future of record shops and confidently predicted that Resident would still be going long after the supermarkets had given up on selling music. He may yet be proved right.

Just a short walk from Resident was Borderline owned by the charismatic Dave Minns a man famous for wearing bright and sunny shirts. This day however Dave's mood was not as sunny as his shirt as he was recovering from a heavy night and was unusually lethargic. The shop had some fantastic collectable pieces of vinyl, so I asked Dave to point some out to the camera. As he pointed to a Robert Johnson picture disc on a shelf behind him he knocked it off the shelf. Trying to replace it, he knocked it off again to much hilarity. This clip ended up in the opening sequence.

We met Norman Cook aka Fatboy Slim at a local coffee shop and then paid a visit to Rounder Records where he used to work, before he became a member of the Housemartins and a world famous DJ. His role at Rounder used to be to look after the 30 or so DJs that frequented the shop each week to purchase the latest imports from the USA. Many 12-inch singles were often released in the USA months before the UK. Shops such as Rounder would import these records ahead of the official UK release date. Norman has many happy memories of working at the shop even if at times it sounded like a chapter from the Nick Hornby novel *High Fidelity*.

Sadly, since our filming trip to Brighton, both Borderline and Rounder have closed down.

In Bristol we met Lawrence Montgomery at Rise Records who spoke about the early days of using social media. Lawrence and Rise have since joined forces with Rough Trade. We journeyed over the Severn Bridge to visit Ashli Todd at Spillers Records in Cardiff who kindly stayed behind long after the shop had closed to do her interview.

As we travelled around the country, money kept trickling in via the Indiegogo site. As we visited each shop, they would start promoting the project via their own social media and gradually the momentum built up. By now around 200 people had donated and they became a highly effective mini-PR team on our behalf.

We started receiving donations from Austria and Germany. These were from fans of Clara Luzia, a Vienna-born musician, whose song "How the Mighty Fall" would be used in the film. I had contacted her to seek permission for this and she had responded by posting about the film to her following on social media.

The film benefited from the kindness and support of many musicians. Bands including Half Man Half Biscuit, the Pretty Things and Wagon Train all donated their music free of charge. Just as importantly, they spread the word on social media, resulting in another surge of donations.

It was time to head north and our first stop was Birmingham, a city that had lost many record shops in recent years, and home to the Blue Hippo team. Our location was one of the UK's most famous record shops The Diskery, a shop that had not changed much in the 30 years I had been visiting it. Here we interviewed Jimmy Shannon the long-serving manager who turned out to be one of the stars of the film. Jimmy could have had a career as a comedian with his constant stream of quips and jokes. He had gone to the trouble to dig out some interesting vinyl records for us to listen to - or not, in the case of the 1980 record "The Wit and Wisdom of Ronald Reagan" an album that is 30 minutes of silence. This idea was followed-up in 2015 by the makers of "The Wit and Wisdom of Nigel Farage", a 7-inch single on the ALCOPOP label. Unlike the Reagan release, one side did contain music that incorporated some of his speeches. In a neat twist some of the profits were donated to The Migrants Rights Network. It can only be a matter of time before somebody releases "The Wit and Wisdom of Donald Trump".

The highlight of the encounter with Jimmy was his presentation of a record by the American jazz singer Slim Gaillard titled "Chicken Rhythm." The record features what appears to be the sounds of chickens clucking, but the sound that Gaillard is making sounds more like the word "fucking". Jimmy noted that he has a regular customer who was a butcher who would love the record, as he is into chickens and all that.

In Liverpool we interviewed Geoff Davis of Probe Records and met up with Paul Quirk, at that time chairman of the Entertainment Retail Association (ERA), who gave us an industry point of view on how record retailing had changed since the days when he used to run a small chain of record shops in the north west called Quirks.

We interviewed Diane Caine and her son Tony at The Musical Box in West Derby. Their banter had everybody chuckling, especially when Tony informed his Mum that when she died he was going to get her stuffed and stand her in the corner. Diane captivated us with tales of selling the first single by Elvis as well as serving The Beatles when they were customers of the shop. Another documentary could be made on this shop on its own.

We interviewed Johnny Marr at one of his favourite record shops, Kingbee Records in Manchester. In Manchester city centre we interviewed DJ Jo Good in her favourite record shop, the Northern Soul specialist Beatin' Rhythm Records.

Clint Boon of Inspiral Carpets spoke to us in the XFM studio where he was recording his radio show. "I'm not denouncing the digital age," Clint said. "It's brilliant, and as a musician I always say embrace that technology. But there are some things you can't replace. There are some experiences that, if you've never been to a record shop and bought a record on vinyl and gone home and played it on your record player, and your dad's not shouting upstairs saying – 'Turn it down! Turn it down!' You've not lived. You might think you have, but it's all been a digital illusion."

We travelled to Chesterfield to meet Keith Hudson, owner of the oldest family-owned record shop in the world, Hudson's Music Store, established in 1906. Keith, 78, was determined to keep the tradition going and pass the business on to his daughters. He had been working there since he was a teenager and regaled us with tales about his incredible life in music, including many experiences I had never come across in any other shop.

Back in the early 1950s, Keith would post the orders for records to London and the stock would arrive by overnight steam train on Saturday mornings. Keith would pick up the stock from the station at 4.30am – by taxi, since the shop didn't have a van and he didn't own a car – so he could have the stock on the shelf by opening time.

In those days, every record had to be checked before going on display, as shops suffered a high percentage of breakages – 78s were very brittle and needed to be packed carefully. The record companies delivered their product in tea chests packed with straw; the straw came in handy for the local horses but was useless at protecting records.

One Christmas, the delivery was so big it hardly fitted in the taxi. The driver was reluctant to set off with so much weight on board, but Keith promised him a big tip. Just as well. Each time they went over a bump one of the taxi's wheel hubs flew off.

When he started working in the business, more than 60 years ago, one of Keith's jobs was that of string cutter. Back in those days they did not have carrier bags, so when they sold a 78rpm record, the assistant would thread a piece of string through the middle of the record and tie the two pieces of string together to create a handle that the customer could carry the record with.

Keith's favourite comic request from a customer is the occasion he was asked if he had Marsha Cup. "Where did you hear Marsha?" he asked the customer, presuming she was a soul singer he hadn't heard of.

"Marsha Cup is the name of the song," said the customer. "The one that goes 'I'm in love, I'm Marsha Cup."

"I think you'll find the lyrics are 'I'm in love, I'm all shook up' and the song is by Elvis Presley," Keith said.

Barry Everard at Record Collector in Sheffield made many trenchant points about how difficult it had become to stay in business. He pointed out so many shops had closed that, even though Record Collector was about 100 miles from the coast, "the next decent record shop that you'll find heading east of here will be in Amsterdam, which is a sobering thought."

We interviewed Richard Hawley at Record Collector. As we were packing away the equipment we noticed Richard at the till with a batch of vinyl in one hand and a wad of notes in the other. He had come to do an interview and ended up discovering some new vinyl to listen to.

Later that evening we met up again in a Sheffield pub called The Greystones which doubles as a music venue. After a few drinks, the manager Mike suggested that the pub put on a fundraising evening to raise money for the film. Thanks to Mike and Kit Bailey (daughter of Roy Bailey and wife of folk musician Martin Simpson), an unbelievable group of local musicians performed for us to raise money for a film about record shops – because they cared about them. The gig has since become part of Sheffield folklore, and anyone who saw Richard Hawley, Martin Simpson, Sam Sweeney from Bellowhead, Hannah James, Roy Bailey, Fay Hield and Andy Cutting all perform that night will not forget it in a hurry.

True to their word they donated every penny from the evening to our film. The financial benefit was very welcome. So too was the boost to our moral to know that these musicians were prepared to do this as a thank you to the record shops that have supported them. Buoyed by the goodwill, and with the bank balance improving thanks to a donation from Martin Mills at Beggars Banquet plus a timely cash injection from Proper Music, it was off to Scotland for our next round of interviews.

Mike Dillon of Apollo Music in Paisley was scathing in his condemnation of the major record companies. "It was OK when we were hyping the charts for them but as soon as we outlived our use they dropped us like a bag of stones," he said.

At Monorail Records in Glasgow, we met up with one of the owners, Dep, who stressed how important supporting local music was. One of the reasons the shop thrived was due to the support it gave and received from the local community. He also stressed the importance to the shop of Record Store Day saying it was "the equivalent of ten Christmases rolled into one."

After our Scottish trip, we did one more day of filming on Record Store Day itself with one crew at Rough Trade in London where there was a queue of 900 outside, while Pip went back up north where he found a queue of 400 waiting outside

Record Collector in Sheffield.

We had nearly run out of money and Pip felt we had enough footage to make the film when, out of the blue, we got a message that Paul Weller had heard about the project and wanted to lend his support. We met him in the record shop that he frequents, Honest Jon's in London. Paul was nostalgic as he recalled the happy days of his youth in Woking where he and his mates would cram into the listening booth to listen to the latest releases. Paul is a massive vinyl fan and said he always makes a record visualising it in vinyl terms. He will pick the order of the tracks based on track 6 being the last track of Side One, then the listener would turn the record over, so it was important to have a strong track to start the second side.

As we had the crew in London, we called in on vinyl shop Intoxica which was managed by ex-Echobelly and Curve bass player Debbie Smith. With her unique look and charismatic personality Debbie became one of the stars of the film.

Just when we thought the filming had finished we received a call from Keith Hudson at Hudson's Music Store, who informed us that after 106 years of trading the shop was going to close. It was devastating news. We filmed his last day and the footage that Pip shot was so powerful. The images of Keith carrying the last bits out of the shop in bin bags and saving what he could of the racking had an incredible impact. At many of the screenings the scene reduced people to tears.

Now it was time for Pip to do his editing and turn the footage into a film. I could not wait to see it. A few weeks later I was leaving for a trip to North Korea with my son Ben. As I left the house the postman came up the drive and delivered a package. Inside was a disc of the film. I had no time to view it before the flight, but I assumed I would be able to do so in North Korea. This turned out to be more difficult than I thought.

On arrival in North Korea our tour group were allocated three minders who between them were meant to stay with us during every waking hour. We hit it off with one of these minders, Mr. Lee, an ex-army captain who was happy to chat with us each evening about his life growing up in the country.

I asked him if there was anywhere we could view my film and after several days of pestering him he took us to a library to watch the film. The place was so quiet you could hear a pin drop. And "view" was all we could do, as to begin with our guide would not allow us to turn the sound on. When we did manage to get the sound on, Mike Dillon of Apollo Music in Paisley was on screen, expressing in the strongest terms possible his disenchantment with the UK record companies' lack of support for independent record shops. Something about his broad Scottish accent and bullish manner seemed to strike a chord with our North Korean minder.

"This man is like me," he said, gesturing at the screen. "He is a military man. Is he a captain or a general in your army?"

"No. He owns a record shop," I said.

"But am I right in saying he used to be a military man?"

"No. He used to be a DJ," I explained, attempting to stifle my laughter.

"Is DJ a rank in your military?"

"No. He plays records."

"Why does he speak like that?"

"Because he is Scottish."

"So Scottish men are military men?"

And so it went on.

When I eventually had the chance to view the film properly back in England I was impressed by how well Pip and Rob had managed to tell the story of record shops and capture the spirit of the many great characters who were determined to keep bringing exciting music to the public. To make such a film on a budget of less than £30,000 was a remarkable feat. We laughed when we read that *Pirates of the Caribbean* had cost £268 million pounds. How many films could Pip have made for that amount?

We held the premier of *Last Shop Standing* at The Ritzy in Brixton on September 5, 2012. The venue was packed with people who had donated to the crowdfunding campaign, along with musicians and shop owners who had contributed to the film. It received a rapturous response. The most memorable moment of the night came during the Q&A when Richard Churchyard the owner of Raves From The Grave record shop in Frome announced that he had entered the cinema thinking he was likely to close down his business, but after watching the film he had been inspired to start thinking of the future instead.

It received rave reviews. Q magazine gave it five stars and featured it in their best videos of the year, and it was generally acclaimed as one of the best films about record shops (of which there have been a few).

The film was shown across the UK at independent cinemas, released on DVD and chosen to be the official film of Record Store Day 2013. Pip produced a deluxe version with 75 minutes of extras including full length interviews with the musicians who contributed, along with the record shop owners telling more anecdotes.

In the run up to Record Store Day, 87 shops in places as far flung as Singapore, South Korea and New Zealand organised screenings of the film. Blue Hippo sold the rights to screen the film to Sky Arts who first screened it the day before Record Store Day and have since screened it more than 30 times.

The most satisfying thing about having made the film is that so many people email me or talk to me at screenings and book readings to say that the film persuaded them to change their habits and buy music from an independent record shop. Even more humbling, is the number of new owners who have told me that reading the book or watching the film was the catalyst for them to open their own record shop. lastshopstanding.com

Other record shop films that contributed to the vinyl revival

I Need That Record! (2008; 77 minutes)

Brendan Toller's thought-provoking *I Need That Record!* was the first film to highlight the perilous state of record shops. The film examines why more than 3,000 independent record stores closed across the United States between 1998 and 2008. Brendan interviews many record shop owners just before they closed down, and the result is a sobering and illuminating spectacle. The film won 17 awards.

I Need That Record! is a eulogy for the hip indie record stores that have disappeared in the United States, a change which Brendan calls a "cultural crime". In a documentary, which inspired me personally, Brendan rails against supermarkets, deregulated radio behemoths and unrestrained corporate capitalism. He points the finger of blame for the demise of record shops at greedy record labels, media consolidation, homogenised radio playlists, big-box stores, e-commerce, and the digital revolution.

The movie features an impressive cast list including Thurston Moore of Sonic Youth, Lenny Kaye of the Patti Smith Group, Chris Frantz of Talking Heads, Patterson Hood of Drive-By Truckers, political activist Noam Chomsky and many indie record store owners across the USA.

The film pulls no punches, making it clear that unless we support independent record shops they will quickly become a thing of the past.

Brendan was way ahead of his time.

Record Store Day (2011; 27 minutes)

Jason Wilder Evans' film Record Store Day covers the history of how the vinyl record has been manufactured over the decades and the equipment it has been played on. Some great vintage footage is intercut with the story of Record Store Day as told by USA record shop owners and musicians such as Duff McKagan, formerly of Guns N' Roses and Peter Buck of R.E.M.

Duff comes up with the film's best line: "Every day should be Record Store Day, as I'm a music fan 365 days a year."

Sound it out (2011; 75 minutes)

Sound it out is a delightful fly-on-the-wall documentary film directed by Jeanie Finlay which provides much laughter and a feel-good dividend.

Sound It Out Records is tucked just off the high street in Stockton-on-Tees, one of Britain's most deprived towns. The shop is situated next door to the job centre and opposite a pub. It is an oasis of culture in a desert of charity shops and pound stores. Many other shops in the area have passed away to the great high street in the sky. Struggling to keep afloat in the face of recession and changes in technology, Sound It Out Records is the last record shop standing in Teesside - an old-fashioned enclave in an old-fashioned town.

Tom Butchart, the shop's owner in this distinctly male environment, is our guide through the film. "I sell hard music, it's a hard area," he says. A shop-counter philosopher, whose clients hang on his every word, he seems to know each of the 70,000 records in his shop. "When I look at the records on the walls, I can hear them all in my head," Tom says. "It's memories, all of them, every single one."

Shot over a period of 18 months, the film gives an insight into today's vinyl addict as well as offering a window into life in modern day Teesside. The camera follows an eclectic stream of customers out of the shop and accompanies them as they go home to listen to their new purchases, or play them as part of a DJ set.

"I met Tom at school and decided to make the film when I discovered that his shop was the very last vinyl record shop in Teesside," Jeanie says. "My mum was very ill, and I was spending a lot of time at home. The shop became a haven for me, and when I looked around I realised it was also a haven for many other people. Making a film offered me an opportunity to explore a musical community, as well as what 'home' means and the emotions and memories wrapped up in vinyl discs."

Tom is the star of the film. No matter how messy the shop, he knows where every single CD or record is. Woe betide any member of staff who tidies the racks without informing him of any stock they have moved.

The DJs, the lone female customer, the junkies, the blaggers with carrier bags of stolen goods and the *Makina* fans (*Makina* is a subgenre of hardcore techno, popular in Spain and Stockton) make this a fascinating film that anybody who has visited or worked in a record shop can empathise with.

Some of the most enjoyable scenes feature Status Quo superfan Shane Healy. Shane is a B&Q employee who boasts that he has seen the Quo 354 times and has bought everything the band has ever released including European, American and Japanese versions of the same album, many with the same track listings. Despite all this he insists he is "not obsessive". This argument falls flat, however, when he reveals that after he dies he wants his Status Quo record collection to be melted down and turned into a vinyl coffin in which he is to be buried.

I am glad to report that the film gave the shop a huge boost and customers now travel from all over the world to visit Sound It Out. As soon as you finish this book, you should go and buy the DVD or watch it online at sounditoutdoc.com - unless you have already seen it.

Sound it out was the official film of Record Store Day in 2011.

Vinylmania: When Life Runs at 33 Revolutions per Minute (2012; 75 minutes)

Vinylmania is a documentary about the love of records, an epic tale, filled with fascinating characters. The director Paolo Campana loves vinyl and the film is full of passion and enthusiasm as he takes us on a world tour to meet collectors, DJs, musicians and artists. He visits 11 cities on a global road trip, to find out what role vinyl records play in the 21st century.

Like many independent film makers, myself included, Paolo turned to the crowdfunding site Kickstarter to raise the money to make the film. A total of 395 vinyl fans donated $37,173. The film was screened at 15 international film festivals and is available as a beautifully designed two-disc DVD set.

The film was well received and brought a lot of positive publicity for record shops by reminding music buyers why they loved them.

Vinylmania was the official film of Record Store Day in 2012.

The Record Store Day Film (2013;15 minutes)

Produced by Greatcoat Films this little film captures just how big Record Store Day has become. It features musicians who have championed record shops such as Paul Weller, Tom O'Dell, Ghostpoet, Frank Turner and Smoke Fairies.

Filmed in London, Manchester and Leeds it shows the impressive turnout of music fans on the big day. Many fans are interviewed while queuing to get in to shops. My favourite quote: "Record Store Day is Christmas for nerds".

High Fidelity (2000; 113 minutes)

An honourable mention must go to *High Fidelity*, the most famous record shop film ever, which told the story of the oddball staff and customers who inhabited the fictional record shop Championship Vinyl. This entertaining film starring Jack Black and John Cusack did much to publicise and romanticise a certain hipster image of record shops. But in all my time travelling around the country to visit new record shops, no owner has told me that he or she was inspired to open a shop after watching *High Fidelity*.

Nick Hornby wrote the book in 1995 and set it in London (although, disappointingly, the shop in the film was based in Chicago). What he did was brilliantly capture the musical snobbery that was prevalent during that period. I used to visit many record shops who employed staff with a similar approach to the men behind the counter at Championship Vinyl. They felt their taste was all that mattered, and if you did not purchase something they approved of you could expect a sarcastic comment or sneering look.

In the years when record shops were in steep decline, it was precisely that type of shop that disappeared from the high street. These days record shops treasure their customers or they quickly find themselves out of business.

Chapter 6

Turntable tales and the jukebox of jokes

Since writing the book Strange Requests and Comic Tales from Record Shops, *published in 2013, I seem to have become a magnet for people wishing to share their funny, sometimes bizarre record retailing experiences. Here are some more of my favourite tales.*

After 18 years of trading in Portobello Road, Intoxica, the vinyl specialist in Kentish Town, North London was hit with a 90% rent hike. Regretfully, the owner Nick Brown was forced to close the shop and now trades online instead.

On Nick's last day in the shop, Mark Lamarr, presenter of *Never Mind the Buzzcocks*, came in and asked if he could have the Intoxica sign hanging above the door. Nick said that he was welcome to take it, provided it was removed before midnight, when the property reverted to the landlord. That evening, after the shop had closed, Mark returned in a hired pick-up truck with comedian and fellow music fanatic Bill Bailey to do the deed.

The next day, Nick took his morning stroll to buy his paper and, to his horror, saw the headline on the front page: "Man killed in North London by falling sign." His stomach churned. Had Mark Lamarr met his end? Or, more likely, the bungling pair had dropped the sign on the head of some hapless passerby. He picked up the paper and could not hide his relief when he read that the unlucky gentleman had been killed by a William Hill sign. A minute or so later, Nick composed himself, and reflected that a man had sadly lost his life.

Blissfully unaware of this unfortunate coincidence, Mark and Bill had delivered the sign to Mark's house without mishap. Mark has now restored the sign to its original, pristine glory and it is proudly displayed in his basement, where Nick has since been over to view it.

Many shops have tales of telephone sales people not understanding requests. But Nick Brown from Intoxica recalls a telesales pitch that surely takes the biscuit. A young woman from the distributors Pinnacle called to persuade him to stock some of their priority releases.

Telesales woman: "We have a brand new album from Nico Peelsessions called *You Will Sell Loads of This One*."

Nick: "Can I confirm the artist is Nico Peelsessions?"

Telesales woman: "Yes."

Nick: "And the album is called *You Will Sell Loads of This One*?"

Telesales woman: "Yes."

Nick: "I think the artist is Nico, the title is *Peel Sessions*, and your boss has typed out a bit of advice."

Telesales woman: "You could be right."

Since writing *Last Shop Standing: Whatever Happened to Record Shops?* I have been invited to give many readings, talks and Q&A sessions at record and book shops around the country. The shop may charge a small fee for people to attend, and in return they lay on a glass of wine and other refreshments. These talks provide a great opportunity to engage with true music fans about our shared love of vinyl and record shops – and to sell some books. Usually they are highly enjoyable. But things do not always run smoothly. On one occasion I ended up in hospital thanks to an injury sustained at a book reading.

I was giving a talk at Solo Music in Barnstaple in North Devon. Solo's staff were in a generous mood and the event was free (either that, or they had no confidence in me pulling a crowd). I arrived about 30 minutes before the start of the talk. Usually, I would find a back room and read through my notes. But Solo was quite a small shop and they did not have a back room available. However, I was welcome to sit in the toilet, if I wished. I thanked the owner, Maggie, for this kind offer, but decided to stay out front and mingle with the people who had come to the event. Maggie had laid on a lavish spread with a choice of wines, soft drinks, nuts, crisps and various snacks. I poured myself a glass of wine and stood by the counter.

A man sidled up to me and whispered, "This is a bit of alright."

"What do you mean?" I replied.

"Free food and drink."

"Are you here for the talk?" I enquired.

"No, I just noticed the sign in the window saying complimentary food and wine. This is my third glass. Who is this geezer Graham Jones?"

When I identified myself, he mumbled something about his wife having his tea on the table and scarpered, leaving me thinking "there is somebody who won't be buying my book."

I tried talking to a gentleman in his fifties who had a glazed look on his face and was constantly looking over my shoulder at what was going on behind me. I guessed I was boring him and decided to move on. Just then one of the staff came over.

"He won't be buying your book," she said

"Why is that?"

"He is the shop stalker," she replied. "He only attended because he thought the girl that he fancies would be working. Luckily, she heard a rumour he was coming, so asked for the evening off." Another wine guzzler who wouldn't be buying my book, then.

I was then approached by a middle-aged couple. Two things immediately struck me about them. The first was how in love with each other they clearly were. I found it touching that people of that age could still be romantic and hold hands. The second thing was that he certainly thought he was a cool dude as he had his shades on. One of my pet hates is people who wear sunglasses when it is either dull or in the evening. The music industry is full of these types wearing sunglasses when it's not sunny thinking they are being cool. The lady asked me if I was doing the talk and I informed her I was. She told me that although she was not a great music fan her husband was a fanatic who spent all day playing his favourite records. Throughout the conversation the gentleman never contributed. We were then interrupted by Maggie who asked if I was OK to start the talk. I bade the cool dude and his wife farewell and told them that I hoped they would enjoy reading *Last Shop Standing*.

"Oh, we won't be buying your book unless you put it out in braille as my husband is blind and I have no interest in it," she told me.

A gentleman tapped me on the shoulder and introduced himself as Steven Seagal. He was clearly not the famous actor, being only 5ft 4in and rather rotund. But he was clearly an enthusiastic music fan and engaged me in a conversation about his favourite purchases. I explained that I was about to start the talk. He responded by producing a bunch of receipts from his wallet, which turned out to be for every purchase he had made at Solo since he had started shopping there a few years back. He then started telling me the story behind every receipt. After five minutes, just as I turned to make my escape he shouted "Graham check this one out." It was for *Last Shop Standing* £9.99. Another satisfied customer who would not be buying the book tonight.

I started the talk, and everything seemed to be going well… until I was interrupted by the sound of snoring. Surely, I am not boring someone so much that I have sent him to sleep, I mused. It turned out that a gentleman in the audience suffered from narcolepsy, a sleeping disorder which can cause the sufferer to drop off in an instant. Whenever the audience laughed the gentleman woke up and joined in the laughter before a few minutes later dropping off and starting to snore again.

By now, I was looking forward to finishing and going home. Although the talk was in the evening, the shop had stayed open, and halfway through my talk, just as I was finishing a story, a customer came up to me and said, «Excuse me mate, can you move? I want to look through the jazz CDs and you are in the way." Everybody laughed, and I observed that this was exactly the kind of dedicated customer all record shops need to attract. As I moved out of his way, I cracked my elbow on the CD racking. It was very painful, but I carried on as if nothing had happened. The jazz customer then proceeded to drop all his money on the floor, so the talk stopped again while I helped him pick up his coins.

I eventually finished this most eventful of talks and started the long drive home in considerable pain. My elbow had swollen up so badly that I took a detour to the casualty department of the local hospital. Luckily it was not broken, and the swelling was just excess fluid.

A few weeks later, I gave a talk at Raves From The Grave record shop in Warminster in Wiltshire. Afterwards a young man came up to me with great enthusiasm asking if I could sign a copy of my book to Rory. I signed it, in front of him, "To Rory, best wishes Graham Jones."

"That's no good," he said. "You've spelt my name wrong. It's R-A-U-R-I. Please can I have another book?"

It would have been nice if he had told me that before I signed it. I gave him another book with Rauri spelt correctly. If you know anybody called Rory send me their address and I will send them a signed copy – half price.

Have You Got?
Genuine requests from customers in record shops
"Go and Get Stuffed" by Billy Ocean? ("When the Going Gets Tough")
Kathy del Mar? (Café del Mar)
Pablo Martini? (Paolo Nutini)
Fun Lovin' Cannibals? (Fun Lovin' Criminals)
Internal? (Eternal)

A singer called Simon Garfunkel? (Simon & Garfunkel)

"Albert Ross" by Fleetwood Mac? ("Albatross")

"I Can't Stand Gravy" by k.d.lang? ("Constant Craving")

That song they play on the radio? I have no idea who sings it. I think his surname is Ferry. His first name might be Bryan. (Take your pick)

That song they sing at New Year, "Old Mount Zion"? ("Auld Lang Syne")

The blues guy T.J. Hooker? (John Lee Hooker)

Have you got any music that will help rid my house of evil spirits?

Tanya Zafta? (Ten Years After)

The Immaculate Conception by Madonna? (*The Immaculate Collection*)

Spangle Barry? (Spandau Ballet)

Anklepert Humpelstink? (Engelbert Humperdink)

Storm C? (Stormzy)

Any Floyd albums? There's nothing in the F section. (Pink Floyd)

One of the regular customers at Save Records (since closed down) in Bury Market, Greater Manchester, told the owner Maxine that he was going away for a week to the Lake District. He asked her to keep his order of LPs to one side until he returned, as he needed his holiday spending money. A few days later he came in and said he would like to buy his LPs, after all.

"I thought you were on holiday," Maxine said.

"I am," he replied.

It had been a rainy morning in the Lake District and, walking through town he had noticed a Mystery Tour coach trip. Thinking that would be a perfect way to spend the day, he bought a ticket. After travelling for a couple of hours, he noticed that the "mystery" route looked familiar. As the bus arrived at its destination he realised that the Mystery Tour was to the world famous Bury Market, right next to his home town and home to Save Records. Since he was there anyway, he decided he would spend his holiday money in the shop he visited every week.

Chapter 7

How to open a record shop

With more than 40 new record shops opening in 2017, these are exciting times. I expect the revival to continue in the short term as there are still plenty of towns which could sustain an independent record shop.

However, it may not be as easy as you think and there are important questions to be asked. Will I be able to compete in the marketplace? Will I have a better range, better product knowledge, better pricing and better service than my competitors?

Without confidence in your ability to deliver these and other factors the chances of survival are not good. You will need to put a lot of hard work into the financial and administration details, a process that can be far removed from the fun and excitement of running your own store.

Location
As Kirsty and Phil from the TV programme *Location, Location, Location* stress, this is by far the most important consideration. Are your intended premises right in the centre of town and a natural stop off for regular shoppers, or are they on the outskirts making it more reliant on passing trade? Is the proposed shop on main bus routes and is there adequate parking nearby? Do your research before taking any practical steps to set up a shop.

Competition
If there is another music retailer across the road it is going to be difficult to compete. It is important to take a long, hard look at any sort of competition, be it specialist or mainstream, and assess the implications. Today's greatest competition is likely to be in the form of supermarkets or online sellers.

Local Demographics
Is your location in a university or college town with a high population of teenagers and young adults, or is it more family orientated? Is it a commuter town with a station off loading office workers in the evening. Even if your intended location is somewhere you're familiar with try to be as scientific as possible in your research to get an accurate idea of your likely success. What sort of disposable income do the most likely record buyers in the area have?

Formats
What kind of releases will your store stock and what formats will sit most comfortably within it. Selling home entertainment products has become increasingly complex in recent years as more formats jostle for shelf-space. CDs remain a key player for most stores and depending on your catchment area, it is worth considering stocking both CD and vinyl formats.

Of the new record shops I have visited since 2016 around 50% of them sell coffee.

The vinyl café has been a welcome addition to our towns.

And don't forget audio accessories, electronic gadgets and T-shirts. The latter can be racked comfortably alongside companion audio products and sell particularly well in the summer on the back of chart hits or a local tour.

Premises

Once you have outlined a detailed business plan and cash-flow projection you should have a fairly good idea of the sort of premises you can afford. A high street which is accessible to both regular shoppers and passing consumer traffic is ideal, but this will have to be balanced against the available capital and the higher rent demanded for such a location. A list of vacant premises can usually be obtained from the Local Authority and it is worth considering the benefits of leasing as opposed to buying. Before you sign any lease document, ensure you have legal advice. It will put your mind at ease.

If you want to play music in-store you will have to obtain a PPL and a PRS licence. If you are an ERA member you receive discounted rates for these.

Operations

In-store operations will be dictated by whether you decide to display product live (the whole package) or dead (just the empty cases), and this will also determine the layout and appearance of your store. Opting for dead displays generally means adopting the master bag system, where the product itself is filed behind the counter. Although this works well with the CD format, most vinyl fans prefer the album to be sealed.

Investing in a good Epos (Electronic Point of Sale) digital system will save you endless hours of work in the long run. It is a computerised system, used in retail outlets, that facilitates the most efficient way of letting people pay for goods or services. The software to run these programs can vary greatly in cost and it's best to shop around for one that suits your needs and stock. Epos allows a retailer to record precise information by either scanning a barcode or keying in a number printed on the packaging, which is then matched to a central product database. An electronic till is thereby transformed into an accurate stock control system. Epos not only identifies the sale but also the item sold and amends stock records accordingly.

Security tagging remains an important issue for those retailers displaying live and EAS (Electronic Article Surveillance) works neatly with Epos by matching the product bar code with an electronic security tag. The EAS electronic tag attached to a product's packaging sets off an alarm if a customer tries to leave without paying.

Stock

It's a good idea to contact wholesalers and manufacturers (see listings) before you open the shop to enquire about their terms and services. Reps will explain how to open an account, when to order, minimum levels of orders and discounts, what percentage returns to expect (if any) and delivery details. Regarding what items to stock I have a saying that I pass on to all new shops: If in doubt leave it out.

Distributors' telesales departments are equipped with information about forthcoming promotions and the latest releases, while calls from reps will also provide

POS (Point of Sale) support, details of promotions and new products. Minimum order requirements and sale or return conditions vary between distributors so it is important to gather this information well in advance. Many retailers also sell online through their own websites or third-party sites like Amazon, Discogs, etc. This all deserves serious consideration.

Social Media

I am amazed that some record shops don't have a website and many do not use Twitter. The use of social media has revolutionised how record shops engage with their customers. In the past, larger shops would spend a fortune with the local paper, advertising new releases. Many of these adverts would be paid for, in part, by the record companies in return for featuring their priority product. Some advertised via local radio and others produced leaflets to be distributed amongst the local community.

Those days are gone. Instagram, Tumblr, Twitter and Facebook are now the norm for informing customers of new releases, offers and in-store performances. It is imperative if you are planning to open a record shop, that you have somebody in your team with social media skills.

New releases can be photographed then posted on the sites and videos of the bands shared. This has all helped to fuel the vinyl revival among a young demographic, contradicting the idea that the vinyl revival is a result of males over 40 replacing their CD collections with vinyl.

It is crucial to have a website both for selling product and promoting the shop's brand. Independent record shops are all different. The product they sell is influenced by the owner's personality. It is important for shops to get their customers to buy into the character and personality of the shop. This can be done by writing a blog and sending out a monthly email newsletter. Many shops do this and many are an excellent read. It is a reliable way of connecting with their consumer base. It is perfect for informing their customers what exciting new records are to be released, what special offers they have and if they have any performances coming up in the shop. Blogs and newsletters are perfect for building up the excitement of Record Store Day and forthcoming releases. And they keep customers interested in the shop. Use your blog to offer views on the industry and to put across your personality. Keep stressing why it is so important that customers should shop at independent stores.

If you are planning to sell vinyl, taking part in Record Store Day is essential. ERA (Entertainment Retailers Association) have strict rules on participation. Shops are required to have accounts with at least three of the following distributers: Ace, Cadiz, Cargo, Kudos, Little Amber Fish, Orchard, Pias, Plastic Head, Proper, Republic of Music, RSK, Shellshock, Sony Music, Universal, Warners. New shops should open accounts with all these distributers to ensure they are offered all the RSD releases.

A store must register to participate no later than the end of January for that year's event. A store may only participate if it is defined as an Independent Retail Store engaged in the sale of music products. An Independent Retail Store is defined as "any independent shop selling music, which is open to the public for at least 48 weeks of the year for at least 25 hours per week". For clarification, mail order-only stores or stores which only operate for limited days during the year are not eligible.

Participating stores must adhere to the spirit of RSD, which is designed to encourage music buyers to visit record shops both on the day and after the event. By signing up to RSD, shops agree to use reasonable endeavours to be active and positive on social media and to generate awareness and interest in the event.

Participating stores may not open prior to 8am on RSD and may not take pre-orders or reservations for customers not able to come into the shop to make their purchase. No store may hold back product to sell at a later date, either in shop or online. All RSD product has to be sold on a first-come, first-served basis.

Participating stores or their staff members may not sell any RSD products online or by mail-order for a period of seven days after the event. Any retailer found to be selling online before the seven-day period will not be eligible to participate in future RSD activities.

Finally, anybody planning to open a record shop is very welcome to drop me a line at graham@lastshopstanding.co.uk. I'm always happy to offer encouragement and advice if it helps to set up somebody with the best job in the world.

Downloading and Streaming
Some media commentators would have us believe that soon the only way you will be able to obtain recorded music is by downloading or streaming. If you are buying music digitally, it is more profitable for the record company. They do not need to pay for manufacturing, storage, distribution and coping with faulty product. Nor do they have to employ sales reps.

On numerous occasions I have been in a record shop and heard a customer say that they had downloaded tracks of an artist and now they want to purchase the album. In that respect it is remarkably similar to the days when I would buy albums after recording tracks from Radio 1's chart show. Figures show sales of downloads decreasing as consumers prefer to stream digital music.

Chapter 8

A warning from history

Will the vinyl revival continue?

The independent record shops started the vinyl revival but so many parts of the music industry are chipping away at their market that I fear tough times are ahead.

We now have more than 2,000 retail outlets selling vinyl. This statistic makes me fear for the future as I watch record companies failing to learn the lessons of the past.

In 2013, independent record shops accounted for 44.4% of all vinyl sales. Just 4 years later, in 2017, it had dropped to 26.1%, as others have gate-crashed the vinyl revival. It is imperative to learn the lessons of history. The music DVD was once a staple of independent record shop sales. The record companies then started doing deals with supermarkets, which resulted in some major titles being cheaper for a *record shop* to buy (let alone a customer) from a supermarket than direct from the company. Independent record shops, not surprisingly, abandoned the format in droves.

The same mistake was made with Top 40 CDs, which the supermarkets used as a loss-leader to attract customers. This resulted in the absurd practice of many record shops making a Friday evening visit to their local supermarket to buy chart CDs cheaper than they could get them supplied direct from the record companies. The chart CD was once a key part of independent record shop sales. But this grossly disadvantageous pricing policy, resulted in many of the shops moving away from the CD to concentrate on selling vinyl.

In 2014, no vinyl was stocked in UK supermarkets. In 2017 a whopping 344,000 units were sold in supermarkets. The vinyl album chart is dominated by rock and pop re-issues from decades back, which is stifling new talent from entering the chart and receiving the exposure a chart position creates. The best-selling album of 2017 was Ed Sheeran's ÷ (*Divide*). But, according to the Official Chart Company, only 4.6% of that album's sales were in independent record shops.

Instead of giving independent record shops exclusive releases, as they used to do, the major record companies have started offering "bricks and mortar exclusives". This means it is "exclusive" to independent shops, HMV and the supermarkets – a half-hearted approach which isn't very "exclusive" at all. It is no way as helpful as having a special release that you can only purchase from an independent record shop. That's what will get people in through the door.

Another threat to independent record shops is the rise of the Vinyl Record Subscription Clubs. These are not a new phenomenon. The Britannia Music Club, which started in 1969, would advertise extensively in the UK press. It worked by offering you four albums for a £1 each. Then if you signed up, you would be contracted to purchase a further six albums that year, at full price.

The new breed of vinyl clubs doesn't offer those dubious incentives to get you to sign up, but they do offer exclusive product. This sector is flourishing with vinyl clubs such as Wax & Stamp, That Special Record, Trax & Wax, Flying Vinyl, VNL, Prescribed Vinyl and Stylus (who provide an album with a bottle of wine) being the most well-known. In each case, the customer pays a monthly subscription and the company sends them an album of their choice. Leaders in the field are the USA-based Vinyl Me Please. Each month the customer is sent a vinyl version of a classic album that won't be available anywhere else. Usually it will be coloured vinyl with an art print and, for some strange reason, a cocktail recipe. They often tag on extras such as lyric sheets, patches or stickers. Their tagline is "The best damn record club" and it is hard to argue. Their website is always an interesting read and, ironically, often has articles on record shops. To purchase from the club's website you must be a member.

I find the concept of an organisation sending me an album and telling me I will like it a bit strange. I find it comparable to when I make a purchase on Amazon and they recommend something else, based on my choice, that is seldom anything I would wish to purchase. The joy for me is discovering new music for myself and the independent record shop is the place to do that.

The point, however, is that there are tens of thousands of vinyl sales every month that are not going through independent record shops.

Artists selling direct to the public
Whether it is via an artist's own website or at an artist's gigs, vast quantities of physical product are now sold direct to the public, thereby cutting out the record store. It is easy to understand the artist's perspective. Why give part of the profit to the distributor and the record shop when the act can keep it for themselves? This is short-term thinking though, as both the distributor and the record shop bring the artist to the attention of a wider audience.

An especially damaging practice is for artists to sell a new release on tour or via their own website, *in advance of the release date*. Music fans hear about these exclusive/advance releases and expect their local record shop to be stocking them, only to be informed the product is only available via the artist's website. It is only fair that artists can sell via their own websites, but they should give record shops the opportunity to sell at the same time. Artists should take in to account the work independent record shops do in promoting new bands. Why deprive them of a fair portion of the pie for some short-term gain?

Steve Meekings of X-Records in Bolton recently hosted an in-store performance by Ginger Wildheart. Steve, a big fan, describes Ginger as a true professional who put on a brilliant performance to a packed crowd. After the event, Ginger took time to speak to fans and sign whatever they wanted. And yet Steve found that he was hardly selling any of the vinyl he had bought in for the event. Ginger's album *Ghost in the Tanglewood*, had been part-funded by a Pledge crowdfunding campaign. Fans who donated, were rewarded with a deluxe, limited-edition version of the vinyl. The result was that a lot of fans brought their deluxe copies down for Ginger to sign, while Steve's display of the normal black-vinyl version was neglected. For all Steve's efforts in providing a brilliant free show for the music fans of Bolton, along with the stress of organising the event, his reward was a handful of sales.

"Artists crowdfund projects, via Pledge or similar ideas, and offer a range of product bundles at various prices," explains Andy Oaten of David's Music in Letchworth. "These include the vinyl LP itself with added merchandise, signed items, gig passes, hand-written lyric sheets, etc. As most of these artists have a very loyal fan-base and a strong presence on social media they get a large uptake and easily raise the money to pay for the recording of new material. Which is fine, but surely isn't what the music business is all about. The downside for record shops is that these artists' fanbases are often our sort of customers, but when the album gets a commercial release there is barely any point in us stocking it, because most of them already own it."

D2C (Direct to Consumer) – Record company website exclusives

Over the past few years the major record companies have started to offer exclusive vinyl albums that can only be purchased through their websites. Trade account customers – ie record shops - are not allowed to buy them to sell on to their customers. This practice is grossly unfair to the retailer and is having a detrimental effect on both the sales and the reputation of the record shops. I fear that the situation will worsen unless steps are taken to include independent record shops in all releases.

It is beyond frustrating for a record shop when a customer asks for an item that is only available from the record company direct. Even worse, the shop must direct the consumer to a company website that is effectively destroying their business. Not only does D2C hit record shop profits, it is a disastrous source of negative PR for them. Customers are leaving their shops disappointed and puzzled.

Mark Wills of Hundred Records in Romsey highlighted two releases that have had a profoundly negative effect on his trade and relations with his customers. The Lorde album *Melodrama* was offered to Hundred Records as a normal black vinyl album or as a limited-edition, deluxe version in translucent blue vinyl with a double-gatefold jacket, a double-sided record sleeve and a lyric booklet with six double-sided photo inserts.

Mark spread the word via social media and plenty of his customers ordered copies of the deluxe version. None ordered the plain black version. He therefore decided to order 10 copies of the deluxe version. A couple of weeks before release, he was informed that the deluxe version was now going to be D2C only. Mark suspects that they had taken so many orders for it via their own website that they had decided they could sell all the stock themselves. He then had to refund all the customers who had ordered the deluxe version and explain that they could only obtain it via the record company's own website. So, Mark had advertised it for the record company, obtained sales for them and what was his reward? All his customers ordered it off the website and now the company has their contact details so they can market direct to them with other records. Where are those customers going to look first when buying their next album? As for Mark, if anybody would like to purchase the normal black version (the only version he was allowed to order himself) do get in touch, as his stock is still sitting unsold in the shop.

A similar scenario occurred with the Jam's 6-CD box-set *Fire and Skill*. Each CD featured a historic concert by the band and the box-set was available for all music retailers to order. But when it came to the vinyl, each concert came out as a single album that was only available D2C. Mark was inundated with requests for these releases. Through gritted teeth, he had to direct his customers to the record company's D2C site, losing dozens of sales. What other industry does this? Can you imagine going in to Tesco, asking for a product, and being directed to Asda's website?

This also creates a moral dilemma for shops, as Gary Smith of Rapture in Witney pointed out. When U2's *The Joshua Tree* box set came out, Gary was selling it for £82.

Having made considerable financial commitment to stocking and supporting what he thought was an exciting release, he was disappointed to discover that there was an even better version of the box set available online. This put him in an awkward position. One of his best customers, a big U2 fan, came to the counter to purchase the box set he was stocking. What should he do? Advise the customer that there was a better version online, or recoup some of the money he had invested in the (inferior) box set? I don't think the record companies have given any consideration to the invidious position that independent record shops are placed in, thanks to their dubious marketing strategies.

What can be done?

Record Companies: Bricks and mortar store offers are not a great idea. "Only available through independent record shops and all supermarkets" does not sound very exclusive. Give more indie record shop exclusives not bricks and mortar exclusives. If HMV, the supermarkets, Amazon, etc have an exclusive version of an album, then give independent record shops an exclusive version that is equally attractive. If Amazon have a red-vinyl version, give the indies a different colour.

Artists: When releasing an album via a crowdfunding site, press up twice as many (it is far cheaper.) Give your distributor 50% of the stock to be available through an independent record shop. Simplify what your extras are. Lyric sheets and signed copies are perfect. Think long-term, not short-term gain.

I recently bumped into Pete Wylie, the singer with Liverpool band Wah! I had been a fan long before he released his first big hit "The Story of the Blues". We chatted about the past and then he started enthusing about his forthcoming new album *Pete Sounds!* I asked to hear it and told him that Proper, the company I work for, would be interested in distributing it. Pete was delighted and sent me a copy. It was magnificent, up there with the most splendid stuff he has ever recorded.

However, he had raised the money to record the album via a crowdfunding campaign on PledgeMusic. When my colleagues and I discovered that the 1,240 fans who had contributed would be receiving a copy of the album direct from Pete, we passed on the project.

Although Pete had raised a lot of money, I am convinced he would have made a lot more by having his record distributed by Proper. We would have sold the record to independent record shops, HMV and online retailers and enabled it to get in to the album chart. In a situation like this we all lose; fewer sales for Pete, no sales for us and fewer people being aware of the album.

Music Fans: Think where you buy your music from. Vinyl is thriving because of independent record shops. They are the champions of new music and are preventing the scene from stagnating. It is they who nurture and grow the local music scene.

Warning

I started this book with a description of the little-known tax loophole Low Value Consignment Relief (LVCR) which created unfair trading conditions that decimated the independent record shops. Now we are back to the beginning, and D2C (Direct to Consumer) has become the new LVCR.

Record companies are treading the same path of chipping away at record shops as they did in the past. Unless they stop making the mistakes they did with music DVDs and CDs, and re-think the D2C model, another record shop decline is surely on the cards. "Some record companies would like to see the back of us," one record shop owner said to me. Surely not. Or would they?

Travelling around the country a decade ago I would often hear the phrase "I remember when our town had a record shop." I have no wish to hear those words again in the future.

Graham Jones
graham@lastshopstanding.co.uk
© 2018

THE SHOPS THAT MADE IT HAPPEN
The Vinyl Guide to UK Record Shops

Working as a sales rep, travelling around the UK for more than three decades, I have lost count of the amount of guide books I have been bought for Christmas. Good Food Guide, Good Hotel, Best B&B that sort of thing. It occurred to me I could write several guide books myself: Worst Traffic Warden Guide (I would start with Hull); Guide to the worst places to drive around in the UK (a big entry for Milton Keynes); and I can always recommend good-value places to stay and eat throughout the country.

But with all the guides bought for me, I would never read them from cover to cover. I would just dip into them and read about the area I was staying or eating in.

With this book I hope I have produced a practical guide that you will want to read from start to finish. Many of the shops featured on my travels explain the reasons for the vinyl revival. They have supplied me with many interesting anecdotes and outlandish tales that will give you a taste of life in the somewhat crazy world of record retailing.

The guide is organised in alphabetical order by region or county, and includes address, contact and social media details, and a description of stock. For London shops I have included the nearest tube or rail station.

Bedfordshire, Berkshire & Buckinghamshire

This used to be a woeful area for vinyl fans, but in recent years there has been a resurgence in trading. Except for The Record Shop in Amersham, all the stores featured in this chapter have been open for three years or less. Windsor, Slough, Luton and High Wycombe all offer opportunities for those interested in opening a record shop.

Beyond The Download

Unit 10B, Holme Grange Craft Village, Wokingham, Berkshire RG40 3AW
01189 962965
beyondthedownload.uk; sales@beyondthedownload.uk; @beyondthedownload
Monday-Saturday 10am-5pm
Sunday 11am-4pm
Established 2016
Stock: Vinyl, Pre-owned, Accessories, T-shirts, Turntables

Ian Biles started his wonderfully named business in 2012, selling vinyl online. He now owns a record shop in what is essentially a posh shed situated in a craft village.

When he opened, it was the smallest record shop in the UK. Things changed in 2017 when he moved to a larger premises opposite. It is not too much bigger, but it is now the fifth smallest record shop in the UK.

It is the only record shop that has a hand pump, a wishing well, a flagpole and a chocolate café all within 25 square meters of the shop. Pride of place though goes to the working 65 Rock-ola jukebox sitting proudly inside the shop. It is worth a visit just to see this magnificent specimen.

Ian had worked in sales for more than 40 years before he opened his own record shop. You soon pick up on his background, and his charming sales patter and passion for music brings in plenty of extra sales.

The Craft Village is described as "Wokingham's best kept secret". It is crammed with independent shops selling product you won't find on the high street. It is well worth spending a few hours here and, if possible, timing your visit for one of Ian's regular gigs by local bands in the Chocolate Café. On Sunday afternoons in the summer, the bands play on the green outside the shop.

Black Circle Records
2 Roebuck Mews, 2a Hockliffe Street, Leighton Buzzard, Bedfordshire LU7 1HJ
01525 839917
blackcirclerecords.co.uk; david@blackcircle records.co.uk; @blackcirclerecordsuk
Monday-Friday 9.30am-5.30pm Saturday 9am-6pm Sunday 11am-4pm
Established 2004
Stock: Vinyl, CD, Pre-owned, Accessories, Turntables

David Rosky spent his career working at record chains of the past including Our Price, Titles, MVC, Virgin Shop and Sanity. With unfortunate timing he was made redundant by Sanity not long after he had married Lynne, and the couple had purchased a house.

Disillusioned with his experiences at the retail chains, he decided to take a gamble and launch his own business from his bedroom, selling cult and horror videos. Online selling was in its infancy, so the business started well. The only downside was storage. He did not have the finances to rent warehouse space, so the videos were stored in the spare room. Gradually he started using more rooms in the house and it was not long before the house no longer looked like a home but an offshoot of the Blockbuster Video chain.

To solve the problem, the couple decided on a complete change of lifestyle and bought a video rental shop in the seaside town of Ilfracombe in Devon. In those days video rental was a licence to print money. Dave would buy the videos for £13 then rent them out at £5 per time. If he rented a video out three times he was in profit. With his background in music retail it was sensible for him to convert part of the store for selling music.

The advent of the DVD kept things ticking over for the shop. The rental market peaked in 2005, then suffered a rapid decline. DVD rental shops closed, faced with many of the same problems record shops were experiencing. Supermarkets had embraced the format and were happy to use it as a loss leader to entice people into their stores. Mail order operations based in the Channel Islands were selling them to the UK market VAT free. People had started downloading movies both legally and illegally. Dave phased out DVD rental replacing the format with vinyl.

In August 2016 Lynne was offered a teaching post in the area she grew up in, so the couple took the drastic action of relocating the record shop 215 miles to Leighton Buzzard. They found a property in an historic mews which was being renovated which the landlord informed them would be ready to trade from in September. Work dragged on with it being December before they could eventually move in. Even then it was not finished, but the couple desperately wanted to catch some Christmas trade. Dave named the new shop after Pearl Jam's only Top 10 UK hit "Spin the Black Circle". The song features on the band's 1994 album *Vitalogy*.

The shop has blossomed. It has a distinctive red design with some low prices. There is a 50p-each or 3-for-a-£1 vinyl section which has a superior selection of clearance vinyl than you will find in many other record shops I have visited. When I was there, Aswad, Rose Royce and Rita Marley were amongst the bargain offerings. And it was cheaper to buy three records than it was to park my car. Not many record shops offer that.

Slide Records *The shop where you can take a class in mixing and scratching*
9, The Arcade, Bedford, MK40 1NS
01234 261603
sliderecordshop.com; info@sliderecordshop.com; @sliderecordshop
Monday-Saturday 10am-6pm
Established 2017
Stock: Vinyl, CD, Pre-owned, Books, Cassettes

If there is a more well-travelled vinyl purchaser than Slide Records shop owner Warren Alsop, then I am not aware of him or her. Warren describes himself as a "vinyl addict and DJ". He previously worked in banking where his job enabled him to buy vinyl wherever he visited. He would travel with a portable turntable in his luggage. Amsterdam, Antwerp, Beirut, Brussels, Edinburgh, Ghent, Havana, Istanbul, Liverpool, London, Los Angeles, Manchester, Melbourne, New York, Osaka, Paris, Philadelphia, Rio de Janeiro, San Francisco, Sydney, Tokyo and Utrecht are just some of the places he has been crate-digging. He could also win an award for the most impressive beard in record retailing, which makes him easy to spot when you enter his store.

The shop is in a beautiful arcade, opened in 1905, which is full of independent shops. Slide Records fits in perfectly. Warren has made the most of the natural light, with the shop sporting a minimalist design, utilising wood and chipboard, creating a clean and well-ordered look.

Warren and his wife Nerys had careers at opposite ends of the spectrum with Warren being in banking and his wife an aid worker. Then came a time in Warren's life where he felt it was now or never to fulfil his dream of opening his own vinyl shop. Warren's wife came from the Bedford area, so Warren packed in the banking and the couple moved to an area lacking a record shop and where there were some family connections.

Warren also hosts DJ masterclasses in mixing and scratching. He likes to get budding DJs started on the decks young, so you can take a class at any age from 8 upwards. The shop has a little seating area with leather sofa, chair and a coffee table festooned with music related books. The area is situated next to the listening decks and as Warren always has the kettle on, this is the perfect place to spend some time.

The Record Shop
37, Hill Avenue, Amersham, Buckinghamshire HP6 5BX
01494 433311
therecordshopltd.co.uk; therecordshop@btconnect.co.uk; @The RecordShoplt
Monday-Saturday 9am-6pm
Established 2005
Stock: Vinyl, CD, Musical Instruments, Record Players

Not the most original name, but this is an all-round record shop stocking a bit of everything. Owner Graeme Campbell started in the industry in 1976 when he was formerly a manager at Record House, which had three shops in the area. When the owner decided to sell up, Graeme bought one of the shops. It was a measure of his self-belief that he did so at a time when an independent record shop in the UK was closing on average every three days.

In 2017 the shop masqueraded as Record Collector in Sheffield for the Sky TV programme *Urban Myths*. This was a dramatic reconstruction of the story of a taxi driver who rescued the hip-hop band Public Enemy from missing a performance in Sheffield after doing a personal appearance in Record Collector (for the full story see Record Collector in the Yorkshire section).

To save money the production company decided they could recreate Sheffield in Amersham. A factor was that Record Collector in Sheffield is on a very busy main road and the production involved parking six large vehicles outside. Fortunately, The Record Shop in Amersham was able to accommodate their requirements. The shop received a fee as they had to close the business for a couple of days, although the cast and crew did purchase some goods and even borrowed a few guitars from the shop to belt out an acoustic session after filming had concluded. The main character was played by Phil Glenister famous for his roles in *Life on Mars* and *Ashes to Ashes*. It is well worth checking out.

Bristol & Avon

No other city has suffered as much record shop closing carnage as Bristol. It used to take me two days to visit the record shops of the area which sold new product. Park Street was the hub where I would sell to five different independent record shops: Imperial Music, Onyx, Rayners and Replay (who had two other branches in the city). They all closed within a few years of each other. Add to that Disc-n-Tape, Music Stop, Revolver and Kays (which had 4 shops), all of which have bitten the dust.

In recent years, some new entrepreneurs have opened shops and the scene is on the up again. The publicity Bristol received when Rough Trade opened a branch there in December 2017 was welcome. In 2016 Friendly Records in Bedminster and Longwell Records in Keynsham both opened, starting the revival. With Specialist Subject Records re-locating to Bristol from Exeter, record retailing in the city is now buzzing.

Bristol would rate as one of the best three cities in the UK, along with Manchester and Brighton if you are looking to buy pre-owned vinyl. Amongst the pre-owned stockists, are Prime Cuts, PK Music Exchange, Plastic Wax, Playback Records and Clifton Arcade Music, which are all well worth checking out.

Friendly Records *The record shop which lives up to its name*
8 North Street, Bedminster, Bristol BS3 1HT
07701 027824
friendlyrecords.co.uk; tom@friendlyrecords.co.uk; @recordsfriendly
Monday-Saturday: 12-6pm
Established 2016
Stock: Vinyl, CD, Pre-owned, Books, Hi Fi Equipment, In-stores, T-shirts

Friendly Records is Bristol's only record shop located south of the river, just a 15-minute walk from the city centre. Sandwiched between two bars on the vibrant North Street, the shop fills a void left by Replay, which closed its doors over a decade ago.

Having spent countless hours in Bristol's record shops during his youth, where "grumpy" seemed the default setting for many of those who worked there, Friendly Records owner Tom Friend was determined to ensure that he would offer a vastly different experience. And he does. It must be one of the cheeriest and happiest record shops I have ever visited. The walls are adorned with some of the popular T-shirts they sell, all featuring the shop's logo (designed by Pete Fowler, the man behind the Super Furry Animals records sleeves) of a happy face inside a vinyl record. The face looks remarkably like Tom's.

The Bristol Post ran a feature on the 50 Coolest Bristolians alive. Stephan Merchant, George Ezra and J K Rowling were all prominent. So was none other than Tom Friend, a sign of not only the importance of music to the city, but of the shop's success in creating an inclusive experience for likeminded individuals. It is a place where not only are records bought, but stories shared.

Tom's early claim to fame included a cheeky attempt to play at Glastonbury when he was only 15 years old. In an impressive display of youthful bravado, he and his bandmates, who called themselves A Moveable Feast, set off from Bristol for Worthy Farm in Pilton the home of Glastonbury Festival owner Michael Eavis. The idea was to give the Eavis family an impromptu gig in the hope they would be added to that year's festival line up. They turned up at the farm and knocked on the door. It was opened by Michael's wife, a friendly woman called Jean. She invited the boys in for a cup of tea and tracked down Michael to come and meet them. He turned down the offer of a live performance there and then, but he was happy to listen to the demo tape they had brought down.

Tom remembers the event with fondness and was impressed by the hospitality shown to them by the Eavis family especially as he now regards the music they were playing as appalling. "If I had my way, I would not have let music as bad as that out of the rehearsal studio, never mind playing Glastonbury," Tom says now. Sadly, Michael Eavis agreed with Tom's latterday assessment and politely turned down the opportunity to put A Moveable Feast on the Pyramid Stage.

A Moveable Feast had a short-lived career the highlight of which was playing The Thekla, the legendary Bristol music venue housed on board a ship in the harbour. The local paper reviewed the gig, comparing Tom (the lead singer) to a poor-quality Shaun Ryder (of Happy Mondays). Tom took it as a compliment at the time, although with hindsight the review no longer seems quite as positive as it once did.

Since his early teens Tom had bought records. As his musical horizons expanded so did his collection. Hundreds become thousands. His love of music would eventually lead to a career in the music industry, where as an A&R man he worked for the likes of Island Records and 679 Recordings and with artists ranging from The Streets to The Polyphonic Spree. But still the collection grew. Acknowledging an addiction is hard but Tom's wife only had to point to the sagging shelves that filled their house as clear evidence of his problem. So Friendly Records was born, a place for a collection that grew too large, but also an exciting business opportunity that is now paying dividends.

One thing that surprised Tom when he opened the shop was the amount of people who came in and told him that they don't play the vinyl records that they buy, but display them like works of art. While most music fans would find this strange, you only have to check the internet to find evidence of this trend. Accor ding to an ICM poll, 48% of people who buy a vinyl record don't play it within a month of purchasing it, while 7% don't even own a record player. The poll also found that half of people who buy a vinyl record listen to it online first.

Don't leave the shop without purchasing a Friendly Records T-shirt, guaranteed to make even the most miserable person smile.

http://www.bbc.co.uk/news/entertainment-arts-36027867

Longwell Records

36 Temple Street, Keynsham, Bristol BS31 1EH
01173 826104
longwellrecords@gmail.com; @LongwellRecords
Established 2016
Stock: Vinyl, CD, Pre-owned

Longwell Records owner Iain Aitchison recalls living on a council estate in Southmead in the 1980s as a tough gig. Listening to records eased the pain of the Thatcher era and his musical tastes were shaped by artists such as the Style Council, Billy Bragg and various ska and reggae bands connected with the Red Wedge politico-pop movement. Having worked as a drug counsellor for many years caring for people high on heroin, he now finds encounters with the occasional troublesome customer a piece of cake.

During the 1990s Iain frequented the many local charity shops in his area building up his vinyl collection. This was the period when most people were dumping their vinyl collections and replacing them with CDs, and many of the vinyl albums that he found selling for 50p or less would one day be worth considerably more.

He opened Longwell Records in Keynsham, a town with its own music festival and some distance away from the plethora of music shops in Bristol. The shop has its own logo based on a cartoon of the family dog Jaffa. A huge picture of Jaffa dominates the window and he also appears on the shop's bags and T-shirts. Iain is grateful for the support of his most famous regular customer and big vinyl fan, actor Stephen Merchant, who has promoted the shop through his extensive social media activity.

"I love the fact that on Record Store Day I can make someone's vinyl dreams come true, like a great big record fairy," Iain says. "Since I opened the shop I have been genuinely shocked by how many fantastic stories I have heard from customers, regular and new. I have lost count of the amount of times I have been informed that a customer saw the Beatles in Bristol or at Weston-super-Mare, their eyes glazing over with fond memories of seeing the Fab Four in the west country back then. One customer attended Eddie Cochran's last concert, a few hours before he was killed in a car accident on the A4 at Chippenham. The crash scene was attended by a young policeman [David Harman] who later became the leader of the band Dave Dee, Dozy, Beaky, Mick & Titch.

"Many customers also tell me of witnessing Hendrix playing Bath Pavilion; others about being one of the 36,000 who watched the Rolling Stones in the pouring rain at Ashton Gate in Bristol in 1982. My favourite story was from the old punk guy who informed me he had Sid Vicious's release papers from when he was nicked in New York. He told me he used to visit Sid's mum up in Croydon and she let him have them. He had lost them many moons ago, the sad look on his face a testament to his regret, though the memories will always be there."

Rough Trade (see main feature in London section)
3, New Bridewell, Nelson Street, Bristol BS1 2QD
01179 297511
Monday-Saturday: 9am-7pm
Sunday: 11am-6pm
Stock: Vinyl, CD, DVD, Books, Clothing, Coffee, Food, In-stores, Licensed

Try and time your visit to coincide with one of the many in-store performances (check out website for details). Allow plenty of time to look through the racks and enjoy some food and drink in the café.

Specialist Subject Records *Shop that shares its space with a punk-rock yoga class*
First Floor Exchange, 72 Market Street, Bristol BS2 0EJ
07828 943754
specialistsubjectrecords.co.uk; info@specialistsubjectrecords.co.uk;
@specialistsub
Monday-Sunday 12-6pm (late night when gigs are on)
Established 2016
Stock: Vinyl, Pre-owned, Books, Cassettes, Tickets, T-shirts, Zines

The Old Market area is a part of Bristol that is on the up. Located just off one of the busiest roundabouts in the city, the Exchange, it is a three-story, multipurpose building that is a creative hub for the music community. It houses a 250-capacity venue that has been graced by artists such as Rag'n'Bone Man, George Ezra and the Sleaford Mods. It is home to a recording studio and for those requiring sustenance there's also a vegetarian café which has become extremely popular. The building also works as a rehearsal space and has even played host to punk-rock aerobics and yoga classes. I am not sure myself if I could relax and stretch to the sounds of Sex Pistols even if it was "Holidays in the Sun".

The latest addition to the building is punk/indie/hardcore record label and shop Specialist Subject Records, owned by Kay Stanley and Andrew Horne.

Andrew has been self-releasing music since he was 15. The name was coined for a fictional release as part of his university coursework, but he resurrected it in 2009 when he decided to start the label. Since then the label has gone from strength to strength and has now amassed more than 60 releases.

Andrew and Kay previously ran the label and an online shop in Exeter before taking the decision to relocate to Bristol in 2017. The vibrant Bristol music scene seemed a more suitable home for both the label and the shop. The shop is up two flights of stairs and situated close to the building's toilets. For selected gigs they'll keep the shop open late. It is amazing how many people have walked up the stairs to use the toilet, discovered the shop and are now regular customers. Don't expect to find regular back catalogue in the shop. The racks are full of contemporary punk, indie and hardcore releases. If that is your music taste, then it is a must visit. You can find more about the label's own releases through their yearly CD samplers, quarterly physical newsletter and (almost) weekly email newsletter.

The label also runs a "Season Ticket" subscription. For a one-off amount, recipients get the most limited colour vinyl pressing of every Specialist Subject Records release for a year, digital downloads emailed to them before official release dates and a year-long 10% discount on everything in the shop and on their website. Every person who signs up receives a goodie box, and if you can't visit the shop in Bristol to collect, they offer worldwide postage.

The DIY ethos of Kay and Andrew's label is a 2018 replica of the punk spirit of 1976, with Specialist Subject Records being everything that independent retailing should be.

The Centre For Better Grooves
33 Gloucester Road, Bristol BS7 8AA
07736 638568
centreforbettergrooves@gmail.com; @cfbgbristol
Monday-Friday 11am-6pm Saturday 10am-6pm
Established 2014
Stock: Vinyl, Pre-owned

Gordon Montgomery started working as a Saturday assistant at HMV in 1973. He quickly impressed and went on to manage the shop. For the next eight years he managed branches all over the country for both HMV and later Virgin Records. Coventry, Liverpool, Manchester, Glasgow & Tottenham Court Road London were some of the locations he ended up at. Gordon was the founder of the Fopp chain of record shops.

Fopp started on a stall in De Courcy's Arcade in the west end of Glasgow. He departed Virgin, for whom he had set up their first Megastore in Scotland, taking £3,000 in severance pay, and arranged a £3,000 overdraft to begin building a business. By the turn of the new millennium, the business was racking up sales of £30 million plus.

Sadly, the Fopp chain closed in 2007 at a time of very difficult conditions for independent record shops. The name still trades today, now owned by HMV. For his latest venture Gordon has returned to his roots. After the challenge of running major record stores he is now selling the vinyl he loves in a relaxed environment. Focusing on quality pieces and recordings, laid out to suit the traditional record browser, there are more than 5,000 mostly used titles on offer covering all genres, including classical.

Gordon is one of the most knowledgeable record shop owners you could ever meet and is always happy to offer his words of wisdom on prospective purchases. The smell of freshly-brewed coffee adds to the ambience. Take your time looking through the racks and check the unusual sections such as "Going to the disco?" and "Weird Shit".

Around half of the used records are from the USA, and this is especially true of Gordon's excellent and extensive Jazz, Soul and Funk selections.

Wanted Records
Unit 1, St Nicholas Market, Bristol BS1 1HQ
01179 290524
wantedrecords.co.uk; info@wantedrecords.co.uk
Monday-Saturday 9.30am-5pm
Established 2009
Stock: Vinyl, Pre-owned

The shop with the name that tells you what it requires, is housed in a prefab in the famous St Nicholas market. Although specialising in Pre-owned, the shop has recently started selling new vinyl stocks, including a great range of African, reggae and world music. It also has an extensive range of styli. The shop is fascinating to look, at both inside and out, with a chimney on its roof and the outside decorated with giant labels of 7" reggae singles. Inside it is equally a feast for the eyes as owner and renowned local DJ John Stapleton has acquired some bizarre memorabilia, including an antique trombone, a children's record player and an illuminated Technics Music Academy sign.

Cambridgeshire

When Head Records moved out of Cambridge in 2013, the city was left without a single independent record shop selling new vinyl. This was a city that once had Andys Records, Parrot, Streetwise, Garon, The Beat Goes On and Jays, to name just a few. I found it hard to believe that a student city of Cambridge's size, which hosts both a famous folk festival and a lively gig scene, was a wasteland when it came to buying new vinyl. Often people would ask me if they were going to open a record shop where should it be? Cambridge would be my suggestion. Luckily three budding entrepreneurs agreed with me and now, for vinyl lovers, the city has gone from famine to feast. Blackbarn, Lost In Vinyl and Relevant Record Café are outstanding record shops, all different from each other.

Black Barn Records *He won £148 million and set up his dream record shop*
15 Burleigh St, Cambridge, CB1 1DG
01223 464888
blackbarnrecords.co.uk; bbrcambridge@gmail.com; @RecordsBarn
Monday-Tuesday, Thursday-Saturday 10am-6pm
Wednesday 10am-8pm Sunday 10am-4pm
Established 2015
Stock: Vinyl, CD, Pre-owned, Memorabilia, Toys, Posters

For the wow factor, nothing can beat the first impression when you enter Black Barn Records. This is more than a record shop, it is a tourist attraction.

In what other record shop in the world can you purchase a signed Elvis single as well as a Lady Gaga dress? Even more startling is the shop's warehouse. This houses 1.5 million records which are filtered into the shop at a rate of around 1000 per week. This is a shop with a high turnover of vinyl.

Owner and passionate music fan Adrian Bayford has done an amazing job of creating his dream record shop. Back in 2012, he won £148 million on the Euromillions lottery. At the time, Adrian ran a small music shop the Suffolk Music Centre in the small town of Haverhill, but due to financial restrictions could not stock it with everything he would like. After his win he spent a couple of years enjoying himself before deciding that he missed the retail life and would like nothing better than to create his perfect record shop. The win enabled him to open in a high street location in Cambridge. He has created a dream shop the like of which many music fans, myself included, would try to replicate if we had won the lottery.

The shop is a great supporter of local talent. It has a separate section for recordings by local bands as well as stocking clothing and prints by local designers and artists.

Although the Cambridge Rock Festival had become a regular feature of the local music scene, in 2017 it looked as if its days could be coming to an end as it struggled to finance that year's event. Adrian stepped in to keep it going. He helped to fund it with sponsorship from Black Barn Records and offered to host it in his grounds. The festival is now on the up. In 2018 artists of the calibre of Focus and Atomic Rooster played the event and it has been short-listed for the award for best medium-sized UK festival.

Black Barn is a truly wonderful record shop with a pre-owned section second to none. It is a must visit for any vinyl fan visiting the county.

Lost In Vinyl
14 Magdalene Street, Cambridge, CB3 0AF
01223 464882
lostinvinyl.org; lostinvinylsales@gmail.com; @LostInVinyl
Monday-Friday 10am-5.30pm
Saturday 9.30am-6pm
Sunday 11am-5pm
Established 2013
Stock: New and Pre-owned Vinyl

After thirty years of working for the major music chains HMV, Woolworths and Virgin, as well as a spell as commercial manager in West End theatre, Rob Campkin decided it was time to start working for himself. He had the vision to see that the vinyl format he loved was the future for music retail. He started selling online in 2013 before taking a chance on opening a bricks and mortar store in 2014. The shop is neat and tidy and concentrates mainly on promoting new music, though does have a good selection of pre-owned vinyl too.

In 2018 Rob moved five doors down to a shop that enabled him to stock twice as much vinyl. He's still not quite sure why or how he has opened a record shop, but he's quite pleased he has.

Marrs Plectrum *The owner forced to stand outside when his record shop gets busy*
387, Fulbridge Road, Peterborough, Cambridgeshire PE1 6SF
07884 357021
marrsplectrum.co.uk; matt@marrsplectrum.co.uk; @MarrsPlectrumRecords
Monday-Friday 10am-4pm
Established 2014
Stock: Vinyl, Pre-owned

The downtrodden man of the house, forced to sit at the bottom of the garden by his wife and children, has long been a staple of sitcoms…usually taking refuge in a barrel of home-brew. The *Shed of the Year* series on Channel 4 has been shining a light on this scenario for a few years now. With the spiraling of property prices and rents, it makes total sense to maximise what you have. The result for Matt Houghton was to open a record shop in his garden shed.

When he first opened Marrs Plectrum, Matt thought the size and location would hold him back. He called me for advice, and I convinced him that being the smallest record shop in the UK at that time would be the shop's greatest strength.

Indeed, I suggested he use "The UK's smallest record shop" as his tag. Both of us are delighted that the slogan has worked. Marrs Plectrum shop has received some amazing publicity. Local TV, radio, *NME*, *Vinyl Factory* and *Fact Magazine* are just some of the people who have knocked on Matt's door. The shop has become a tourist attraction. People love the notion of someone living their passion out in a shed at the bottom of the garden. And they all want to take a photo. Unfortunately, at 79 square feet, Matt's shop is now the second smallest.

I asked Matt what the disadvantages were in owning such a tiny shop. "Well, the only passing trade is birds and squirrels," he said. "And I'm assuming they're all downloading as they've never spent a penny here. Storage space is the biggest issue. The lines of domestic bliss can be crossed when you try to store 50 Led Zep records in the airing cupboard. I don't understand the issue – the heating wasn't on."

One day Matt took a phone call from a customer asking if he had to book an appointment to come. Matt told him he did not, and informed him of the opening hours. A couple of hours later Matt's wife came in to the shop and asked him what on earth was going on in the front garden. Matt went to have a look and there was a band unloading a drum kit, amps and guitar cases onto the lawn. The man who'd phoned thought the shop was a recording studio and was hoping to lay down some demos. I like to think he was the drummer.

I asked Matt what was the best thing about working at Marrs Plectrum. "I love standing outside the shop," he said. "If I am doing that, it means we are busy and I am making room to accommodate everyone. Also, the commute to work is ace."

The Music Box

94, Norfolk Street, Wisbech, Cambridgeshire PE13 2LW
077794 45034
vertigodma@hotmail.co.uk
Monday-Tuesday 9.30am-4.30pm
Thursday-Saturday 9.30am-4.30pm
Established 2002
Stock: Vinyl, CD, Pre-owned, DVD

This beautifully blue-painted store is owned by Dave Allen whose hobby is finding obscure records for his customers. It is worth asking if you can't find what you are looking for as Dave owns a lot more stock than he can fit in the shop, and keeps the rest in storage. Wisbech is not one of the wealthier parts of the UK, so Dave keeps his prices as low as possible. There are plenty of bargains, if you are prepared to travel in on the notorious fen roads.

Relevant Record Café

260 Mill Road, Cambridge CB1 3NF
01223 244 684
relevantrecordcafe.co.uk; andy@relevantrecordcafe.co.uk; @Relevant_Cambs
Monday-Wednesday 8am-6pm Thursday-Saturday 8am-10pm
Sunday 11am-4pm
Established 2014
Stock; Vinyl, Pre-owned, Coffee, Food, In-stores, Licensed

"You're never going to run into an old friend on Amazon, or grab a spontaneous coffee browsing on Spotify." Andy Powell – Relevant Record Café

With a desire to set up their own business together, combined with a passion for music and great coffee, husband and wife partnership Andy and Angie Powell set out to create a space for both in Cambridge's bustling Mill Road. It is a shop of great contrasts; the coffee shop is bright, clean and has a cheery atmosphere, but venture down to the vinyl emporium in the basement and you're in for a big surprise. Described as both "an Aladdin's Cave of records" and "the vinyl dungeon", it's creatively designed with sofas, sideboard and retro wallpaper; it's as if you have stepped into a living room from the 1970s, but with thousands of great records.

Relevant is a great supporter of local music, and you can find performances in the café most Thursday, Friday and Saturday evenings, when the café transforms into an atmospheric cocktail and pizza bar. Music quizzes, comedy evenings, board game nights and open deck events are also regular crowd-pullers. Relevant also hosts numerous DJ nights including the Relevant Disco, which has obtained cult status in the city.

A keen sense of humour is evident from the staff, whether it's their tote bag slogans, cinema-styled light box messages or puntastic A-board.

Displayed outside the shop the board has a different humorous message each day to entice the public in to the shop. Amongst my favourites they have displayed are:

"Words Cannot Expresso How Much You Mean to Me"

"Cake is Nature's Way of Making up for Monday"

One day they even cooked up a Liam Gallagher soup, advertising it with the slogan "You Got a Roll with It".

It is a popular hang-out for local musicians and music lovers, and it's this social aspect that is key to the revival of independent record shops. Regular customers often spend hours hanging out at the weekly Record Club each Friday evening, sharing their newest favourite music with each other over a drink while sampling some of the week's new releases.

The vinyl demographic has certainly become a lot younger since the great vinyl resurgence, as Assistant Manager Tom observes "We have had a few of our younger customers return records (or 'vinyls as some call them') complaining that they're pressed at the wrong speed, until we point out that turntables are generally equipped with TWO speed settings!"

I asked Andy how Record Store Day had impacted on his business.

"The whole phenomenon of Record Store Day and limited-edition, indies-only pressings have created this whole competitive element to record collecting which, for all its faults, could be partially responsible for independent record shops like ours becoming sustainable businesses for the first time in years.

Obviously, it's very fashionable right now, but we're optimistic for the future; there's so much history behind vinyl as a format and record collecting in general. Some people crave original copies of their favourite albums, so they have that little slice of authenticity and a piece of history they can own for themselves, while others want brand new, pristine 180g reissues that they can blast through their top-end hi-fi. Either way, we're happy to cater to both, and hopefully introduce a few people to music that they may not have been aware of along the way too."

The Vinyl Revival Store *aka The Only Record Shop in the Village*
3 Church St, Buckden, Cambridgeshire PE10 5TE
07971 792461
vinylrevivaluk.com; ian@vinylrevivaluk.com; @ShedloadsofSheds
Established 2015
Stock: Vinyl, Pre-owned, Turntables

Based near St Neots and housed in a barn you will find one of the smallest record shops in the UK at just 138 square foot. Opening hours are limited, but if you call owner Ian Gosling up he will open anytime just for you. That is what you call customer service.

This is a special place to visit on Record Store Day. Ian's daughter spins 45s on an old Dansette with many customers combining vinyl shopping with a visit to the local pub before returning. Ian has some nice memories of last year's event, such as the first-time customer who enquired "Do you do this every weekend?" On RSD it can often pay to visit an off-the-beaten-track record shop as is typified here.

About 10:30am a customer called his mates who'd gone to a different shop. "How's it going? It's great here. I have got everything on my list." After he hung up, he laughed and said "They're still in the queue."

Channel Islands

Seedee Jons

47 Halkett Place, Saint Helier, Jersey JE2 4WG 01534 769405
seedeejons@mail.com; @seedeejons
Established 1993
Stock: Vinyl, CD, DVD, Art, Games, T-shirts

John Holley set up See Dee Jons after having worked as manager in another record shop for 12 years. After five years, he moved into bigger premises in St Helier, where sales were healthy due to the popular local rave scene.

He has more recently moved into a fantastic location with a reasonable rent in the town centre, where business has been helped by the departure of both HMV and Blockbuster from the island.

The shop's most memorable customer was the slightly drunk Meaty Big Balls Lady who asked "Do you have the DVD *Meaty Big Balls*?" After detailed and patient questioning from an initially bemused John, the lady walked out of the shop with a DVD of *Mrs. Brown's Boys*. Another happy customer.

Vinyl Vaughan

40 Fountain Street, St Peter Port, Guernsey GY1 1DA. 07781 124828
vaughan.davies@cwgsy.net; vinylvaughan.com
Established 2017
Stock: Vinyl, CD, Pre-owned, Coffee, In-stores, Memorabilia, Tickets

Vinyl Vaughan has evolved from a Christmas pop-up charity shop to fully fledged record store. After a 40-year career in the travel industry, the owner, Vaughan Davies has embarked on a musical journey inspired by the vinyl revival. "In 2015, I suffered a severe stroke and was looking at ways to recuperate and above all be my own boss again," Vaughn says.

Vinyl Vaughan has become a typical indie store boasting an incredible atmosphere complete with a revolving door of local and casual buyers all talking vinyl and swapping tales of their favorite bands and gigs. Vaughan is keen to support local charities Headway, GMND as well as supporting The Vale Earth Fair and is grateful to the Guernsey public for their generous donations.

Cheshire

Four of the five shops in this county have been trading for under two years. The county still has room for more, Crewe, Wilmslow and Knutsford have all sustained record shops who sold new vinyl in the past and are worth considering if thinking of opening a record shop.

A&A Music   * The record shop with its own music school*
12, High Street, Congleton, Cheshire CW12 1BL
01260 280778
aamusicmail@aol.com; @A&AMusic
Monday-Saturday 9.15am-7.15pm. Established 1977
Stock: Vinyl, CD, Pre-owned, Books, Musical Instruments

Owned by the popular local musician Dave Wedgbury A&A Music will even teach you to play an instrument as they run their own music school. Originally the shop was a traditional record shop, but through the darker days of record retailing Dave branched out to stocking musical instruments to help keep going.

The Electric Church
Birtwhistle Buildings, Over Square, Winsford, Cheshire CW7 2JP
07928 897413
electricchurchrecords@hotmail.com
Monday-Saturday 10am-8pm Sunday 10am-4pm
Established 2017. Stock: Vinyl, Pre-owned, Cake, Coffee, In-stores

Named after a Jimi Hendrix documentary, The Electric Church is a brilliant vinyl café. Don't make the mistake of driving in to Winsford town centre to find it. The shop is located out of town just off a main roundabout. The good news is you can park outside.
   The shop is owned by Jim Coppack who runs the record side of the business with his mum Toni looking after the café. Jim is lead singer with up and coming band 1968. If he is not in the shop it is likely to be due to touring or recording commitments.
   Jim loves his customers, but he has a couple who are extra special. Both are in their eighties. They come in every Wednesday for a coffee and to purchase a vinyl record with their pension money.

Cornwall

Back in the 1980s most towns in Cornwall had a record shop selling new vinyl. If you are a vinyl fan coming here on holiday it is now slim pickings and you are best off staying on the beach. It is hard to believe towns like Bude and St Ives have made no contribution to the vinyl revival, none of them in the area hosting a shop which participates in Record Store Day. However, Hurley Books in Mevagissey and Museum Vinyl in St Austell are welcome additions to shops participating in RSD.

Hurley Music & Books *The only record shop incorporating a Tourist Information centre*
3, Jetty Street, Mevagissey, Cornwall PL26 6UH
01726 842200
enquiries@hurleybooks.co.uk
Monday-Saturday 10am-4pm
Longer hours and open Sunday in the summer months
Established 2016
Stock; Vinyl, Pre-owned, CD, books

Serving a population of just more than 2,000, no record shop has a smaller catchment area than Hurley Music & Books. To survive in this village, owner Steve Hurley must wear three hats: that of record shop seller, book seller and manager of the Tourist Information centre.

One of the advantages of this is that he gets lots of crossover trade. It is incredibly satisfying when somebody calls in for advice on local attractions and walks out after Steve has sold them a record or book. It is even better when they walk out with both.

Originally a bookshop, Steve started introducing second-hand vinyl. It is displayed in flat pack boxes that he has painted and looks far more appealing than it sounds. Sales of the format have been so successful that he is a regular visitor at the DIY store buying more flat packs.

Like creeping ivy, the vinyl is gradually taking over the shop, much to the chagrin of his wife, who just wanted a traditional book shop, but to the delight of his children, who are vinyl nuts.

One surprising thing when looking through the racks was the amount of vinyl copies of *The Mevagissey Male Voice Choir* Steve had in stock, selling for £3 each. Much to my surprise, Steve informed me it is not a great seller. If a male voice choir is not your thing, the Wurzels recorded a song called "Mevagissey" which appears on their album *The Wurzels Collection*. Sadly, Steve seemed to have sold out.

This is a lovely shop and should be your first port of call when visiting the village. Not just because it is the Tourist Information office, but because it is the perfect place to pick up your holiday reading and listening.

Top tip - Turn right when you leave the shop, walk to the end of the street and be dazzled as it opens on to a beautiful vista, encompassing the harbour and surrounding hills.

Jam *Lauren Laverne, this shop would love you to call in*
323 High Street, Falmouth, Cornwall TR11 2AD
01326 211722
jamrecords.co.uk; mandy@jamrecords.co.uk; @Jam_Records
Monday-Saturday 10am-5pm
Established 2003
Stock: Vinyl, CD, Books, Coffee, Food, Art, Photography

Owner Mandy Camp describes her shop as shabby and quite groovy and stuffed with comfy sofas. Formica shelving and battered old standard lamps gives it a lived-in feel. It is half-record shop, half-café based in the town's old quarter in a street full of independent shops. Jam brings an esoteric collection of music, film and art to locals and visitors alike, serving exceptional coffee and I can highly recommend the muffins.

One of the shop's customers described it as "a culture shop, sort of like the Culture Show but without Lauren Laverne popping up every five minutes." Not that Mandy has any objections to Lauren popping in, and indeed, if she did, she would be welcome to share a coffee with an equally committed music fan. Mandy has created an atmospheric meeting place in which just about anybody would love to spend half an hour or more.

Museum Vinyl
Unit 10, St Austell Market House, Market Hill, St Austell, PL25 5QB
07792 834509
museumvinyl@hotmail.co.uk; @museumvinyl
Monday-Wednesday 9.30am-5.30pm
Friday/Saturday 9.30am-5.30pm
Thursday/Sunday Closed
Established 2016
Stock; Vinyl, CD, Pre-owned, T-shirts

Located in a historic and architecturally-impressive building, you will find Kevin Hawkins' delightful shop, Museum Vinyl. A market has been on the site since 1791, but was inadequate for a growing town until, in 1842, an Act of Parliament was given Royal Assent by Queen Victoria to permit the building of a Market House. Both William Gladstone and Winston Churchill have made speeches there.

It seems you must be called Kevin to own a record shop in St Austell as the fondly-remembered Saffron Records traded in the town for 30 years, owned by Kevin Matta.

Music Nostalgia *An inspirational story: from homelessness to record shop owner*
Unit 56-58, Pannier Market, Back Quay, Truro, Cornwall TR1 2LL
01872 274998
musicnostalgia.co.uk
peteburywillis@hotmail.com; @MusicNostalgia1
Monday-Saturday 9am-5pm
Established 1999
Stock: Vinyl, CD, Pre-owned, Merchandise

The story of Pete Willis and his wife Hannah who went from being homeless to running the largest record store in Cornwall is heart-warming and inspirational. After leaving school, Pete started working at WH Smith before being persuaded by a local trader to take over the running of his gift and bookshop. Finances were tough for the young couple and when the owner of the shop returned from a few years abroad to run the shop himself, Pete was left without a job. He and Hannah had purchased their house when interest rates were 6%. During the next few years the rate rose to 15%. When the couple could not make the repayments, they had to move out.

Over the next few years Pete and Hannah rented at nine different addresses before moving in with Pete's mum. This arrangement ended when his mum remarried and moved up to Lancashire. Now homeless, Pete took the decision to start selling his beloved record collection at a local car boot sale to raise some much-needed cash. Before he set up, he would always tour the rest of the stalls, and being knowledgeable about music, he was able to snap up a few bargains that he knew he would be able to sell at a higher price himself.

The council found the couple some temporary accommodation. Pete retrained at the Riverside Business Centre and, with the use of an old computer, began selling records on eBay. In 2006 he took to selling records at a local flea market. He jumped at the chance to expand into the larger, and permanent, setting of the Truro Pannier Market, when a friend working in the stall next to him offered to lend him the money for the deposit.

It was a gesture Pete and Hannah will never forget, and they have not looked back since. With the help of Nicky and the shop's other amazing staff, Music Nostalgia has built up an impressive range of stock. As the name implies they specialise in music of the past, but it is the kind of shop that stocks a bit of everything, including selected new releases. Pete and Hannah can be proud of what they have achieved, and it shows what you can do if you have the determination to succeed.

Retro Sounds

Unit 7, Morfa Hall, Cliff Road, Newquay, Cornwall TR7 1SD
07964 043364
retrosoundsrecords@yahoo.co.uk; @RetroSoundsrecordsNQY
Monday-Saturday 10am-4pm
Established 2014
Stock: Vinyl, Pre-owned, Hi-Fi Equipment, Memorabilia

Steve Goodwin-Day had been a DJ for more than 30 years when he bought what was then a second-hand record shop. The exterior is painted sky blue which fits in well with the surfing vibe of the town. Steve has stamped his own mark on the shop filling it with some wonderful memorabilia. As you walk in the selection of original reel-to-reel tape recorders on the shelf catches your eye. These incredible machines were invented in the 1920s, initially using steel tape to record music. Steve has a fine selection and hardly a week goes by without a customer trying to buy one. He has no intention of selling any of them as they are just for show.

The shop has a large retro red sofa for you to sit on and take in the atmosphere. It also has a selection of pre-owned, music-related books which you are welcome to flick through. Another eye-catching feature is that the vinyl is separated by sleeveless old records with the genre painted on the records in white. My favourite feature in the shop is normally used at road junctions telling cars to stop or proceed. It flashes red, amber and green. He calls it his Steve Winwood light (you are a true music fan if you can work out the reference).

In his youth Steve was a supporter of the American civil rights movement, and a framed album cover of Malcolm X hanging on the wall testifies to this. The piece he is most proud of displaying is the 1960s photograph of his dad's group standing next to their trusty van with the band's name Margo & the Marvettes emblazoned on the back. Having the name on the back of the van was responsible for giving them their break. On November 22, 1963, the day of John F Kennedy's assassination, the band was in London when a gentleman approached them. He had seen the name on the back of the van and informed them that a band he had booked for an event that evening had cancelled. He asked if they would stand in. The band agreed to do the gig, despite such short notice. It was a real success and one man in the audience was so impressed he offered them a residency in the Gresham Ballroom in Holloway. This in turn led them to being signed by Parlophone, a label which had also signed an up-and-coming Liverpool group called the Beatles. Margo & the Marvettes went on to release four singles and play with Roy Orbison and Johnny Cash. They never quite hit the big time, although their last single, „When Love Slips Away" is regarded as a cult classic by many Northern Soul fans.

Steve inherited his dad's love of music and since taking over the shop has developed it, with new vinyl selling well. He is also a great communicator and is happy to chat to customers for as long as they like, about music. He is always happy to recommend music. The shop is especially strong on Afrobeat and world music vinyl.

Top tip: Newquay can be expensive to park. The Asda car park opposite allows 90 minutes of free parking for customers.

Room 33

2 Market House Arcade, 17 Forge Street, Bodmin, Cornwall PL31 2JA
01208 264754
room33records.com; room33records@gmail.com
Established 2014
Stock: Vinyl, CD, Pre-owned, Posters, T-shirts

Although stocking all genres, Richard Burke's shop Room 33 specialises in rock and metal. A large window enables you to view many of the wares from the street outside. However, it would be a mistake not to enter, as the shop has lots of interesting items tucked away in the nooks and crannies.

Cumbria

For music fans looking to buy new vinyl while on their holidays in the UK, it may be wise not to take a trip out to the Lake District. Cumbria is great for lakes, Beatrix Potter and beautiful scenery but not for the number of record shops. Windermere sustained a record shop for many years called Action Replay, but that is now gone. If you are looking for a new direction and a high quality of life, then opening a record shop here could be ideal. If planning to visit the Laurel & Hardy museum in Ulverston check out The Music Room, 28 Queen Street, LA14 4NB. Although stocking mainly CDs, it does have a small vinyl section.

Replay

Unit 28, Westmoreland Shopping Centre, Kendal, Cumbria LA9 4LR
01539 634050
netdiscltd@yahoo.com
Monday-Saturday 9am-5.30pm
Sunday 11am-4pm
Established 2011
Stock: Vinyl, CD, DVD

Replay was started by Phil Ames, a man who entered the music retail sector in 1959 and once owned a chain of record shops with the appalling name of 4Play. Over the years he downsized until he owned just the one shop. Lizzie May had been a customer since she was a child and when she left school she started work there. When Phil announced he was retiring Lizzie grasped the opportunity to buy the shop herself.

Over the years Replay has had some strange requests. Here are a few of the shop favourites.

Customer – "Have you got that Constellation CD of 1997 hits?"
Shop - "Yes, it is the one with all the stars on it."
Customer, enquiring about a *Tom and Jerry* three-hour double-DVD - "There won't be any on here that I already seen, will there?"
Customer - "Have you got the DVD *Professor Nutter*?"
Shop – "Would you mean *The Nutty Professor*?"
Customer – "I would like the *Best of Eurosmith* please."
Shop – "Would that be Aerosmith?"
Customer - "I got a CD from you about a year ago. I would like it for the car. Have you got it on cassette? I can't think what it was called or who sang it."
Customer - "Have you got the new CD by America?"
Shop - "Yes."
Customer - "Brilliant, you have never let me down yet. I always come here if WH Smiths don't have it."

Vinyl Café *The only record shop I know where wedding photos are displayed*
4 Abbey St, Carlisle, Cumbria CA3 8TX
01228 522845
vinylcafecarlisle@gmail.com; @vinylcafecarlisle
Monday-Saturday 10am-5.30pm
Sunday 11am-6pm
Established 2016
Stock: Vinyl, Pre-owned, Coffee, Food, In-stores

Based in the historic quarter of Carlisle, Vinyl Café is run by the record shop owner with the best name in the business: James Brown. As a youngster James grew accustomed to people responding to the announcement of his name with their own "hilarious" version of "Living In America" or "Sex Machine". After a lifetime of collecting vinyl he took the plunge and changed his career from landscape gardener to the owner of Vinyl Café.

The shop is a feast for the eyes filled with art, antique record players, a ghetto blaster, a banjo, lampshades and tables that include 7-inch singles built inside 7-inch single coasters. Everything is for sale, apart from the lovely photographs of James and his wife Lynn taken on their wedding day, proudly displayed on the wall. The shop has two impressive busts of Beethoven. When customers ask about them, James points out that Jimi Hendrix was a huge fan of the composer.

The most famous member of staff Is Deborah. Although deaf, blind and mute she is responsible for a lot of sales. Deborah is the shop mannequin who is displayed standing in a listening booth. She is a notable talking point and likely to be the first thing you notice when you enter. She is dressed in a wardrobe tailored to the season, so in summer she wears a wristband, straw hat and wellies to celebrate summer festivals, yet in the winter she will be in a thick coat, gloves and a stylish hat.

The shop has an unusual method of displaying the vinyl. Nothing is divided into genres, so you will find Beethoven in the same section as The Beatles. James believes that this encourages browsing.

The menu in the café is full of record-themed food and drink. My favourites included
Miles Davis Tea - Kind of Brew
You Sexy Thing Hot Chocolate
Flat Jack White Coffee
Nick Drake Coffee – Bryter Latte

Although James loves his customers he can become exasperated by some of their requests. Recent ones include:
"Where is the plug on a wind-up gramophone?"
"Are the records for sale?"
"How do I skip to the next track on vinyl?"

Top tip – Time your visit for when Vinyl Café host one of their popular listening evenings, when people can hear the whole of a classic album while relaxing with some food and drink.

Derbyshire & East Midlands

The vinyl revival seems to have bypassed the East Midlands. While Leicester had a winning team in the Premier League, they are battling to escape the relegation zone in the Vinyl Revival league. The area once had three of the UK's best independent record shops: Selectadisc in Nottingham, Ainleys in Leicester and Reveal in Derby. The gap has been partially filled by Rough Trade and Forever Records providing welcome additions to the Nottingham music scene.

It is hard to believe that neither Derby nor Lincoln are home to a record shop that takes part in Record Store Day. Following the closure of CE Hudson's, a permanent fixture in Chesterfield for 105 years, newly-opened Tallbird Records' fresh, vibrant approach is proving popular with the locals.

When visiting Nottingham, jazz fans are well catered for by Music Inn, 42 West End Arcade, Nottingham NG1 6JZ. Tel 01159 470754. David Rose is an expert and the shop has been trading for nearly a century.

Forever Records *Motto: We love music because music is Forever*
2a, Cobden Chambers, Pelham Street, Nottingham, NG1 2ED
01159 476237
forever-records.com; foreverrecordsuk@gmail.com; @records_forever
Tuesday-Thursday 10:00am-5.30pm
Friday 10.00am-6.00pm
Saturday 10.00am-5.30pm
Sunday 12.00-3.30 pm
Established 2016
Stock: Vinyl

Joey Bell has been working in music retail for 20 years, most of it at Selectadisc and The Music Exchange, both of which, sadly, are now closed. The loss of the Music Exchange was a particular blow to the community since the shop was run as a social enterprise by Framework, a local charity for the homeless managed by Joey. When government cuts forced The Music Exchange to close, Joey decided to open his own store. He wasted no time in making his mark, and Forever Records was nominated in the Music Week Awards for Independent Record Shop of the Year in 2017.

The shop is located near the Bodega Social music venue, where most of the city's up-and-coming bands perform.

Herrick Watson Ltd
8 High Street, Skegness, Lincolnshire PE25,3NW
01754 763481
herrickwatson.co.uk; hwatsonltd@btconnect.com; @herrickwatsonlmtd
Monday-Saturday 9am-5.30pm
Sunday 11am-4pm
Established: The Dawn of Time (owners not sure of exact year)
Stock: Vinyl, CD, DVD

Sunny Skeggy wouldn't be the same without this family-run independent record shop. Going by the name of the current owners' grandfather, Herrick Watson Ltd has been firmly planted for more than 80 years at the west end of the area known as "Chip Pan Alley" (due to the sheer volume of fish & chip shops located there).

Taking to music trading in the 1960s, twins Rob and Jan have more experience than most when it comes to being the public face of the music industry. Trading for six decades, during an ever-changing music landscape in a town better known for its ice cream, chips and beach, rather than its music heritage, has not always been easy. Longevity is not Watson's only selling point. A genuine enthusiasm for music, through all the highs and lows of fashion, has never faltered.

Skegness offers a unique opportunity for a shop like Herrick Watson. The flow of tourists and changing faces suggests that close customer relationships should be few and far between. But the shop's regulars come from far afield, often just to visit the shop. The owners often hear comments like "We always come straight to your shop from the station" or "You don't get great shops like this anymore."

Diversity and adaptability are the key attributes of the shop. Rob's vast experience has given him an instinctive understanding of what the public are likely to want and to buy.

Nevermind
10, Church Street, Boston, Lincolnshire PE21 6NW
01205 369419
nevermindboston.co.uk; nevermindthemusicstore@gmail.com
Monday-Thursday 10am-5pm
Friday 10am-5:30pm
Saturday 9.30am–5.30pm
Established 2001
Stock: Vinyl, CD, DVD, Clothing, Merchandise, Skateboards

Fanatical Sunderland football fan Gareth Skinner has established his shop Nevermind as a meeting place for music fans on the cobbled streets of Boston. He is happy to chat to all his customers over a cup of tea about anything music or football related. The shop stocks all types of music but specialises in punk, metal and rock.

Gareth started working in a record shop earlier than most people. His dad owned Discount Records in Durham and from the age of 6 he would spend a lot of Saturdays and school holidays accompanying his dad to work. When Gareth was aged 10, his dad closed the Durham shop and opened The New Record Inn on Sunderland's high street. It was next door to a Sunderland landmark, the fondly remembered Old 29 pub. It was demolished many years back but was a haven for live music in the city. The shop did a roaring trade in ex-jukebox singles. These were 7-inch singles with the middle punched out and, as jukeboxes had to keep up to date with the latest releases, the companies that ran the operations would flog the old stock off cheap to record shops. The shop would do a roaring trade at 25p each, or 5 for a £1. It was also a major vendor of pre-owned comics which his dad would buy in huge quantities from the USA. Gareth has fond memories of taking his break in the basement, sitting on a huge pile of comics whilst reading some of them. He would sit opposite an iconic poster on the wall of Frank Zappa sitting on the toilet, known as the "Zappa Krappa" poster. Zappa once joked that he was probably more famous for that poster than anything else he did. Young Gareth thought the sight of a man sitting on the toilet was very amusing.

Soon Gareth was given his first opportunity to make money as his dad put him in charge of the badge board. These were the days of punk rock, and button badges were incredibly popular. Selling them at 20p a badge, he experienced his first taste of business. Like all good family concerns, Gareth kept his money in the family by using his wages to buy Marvel comics. Working in a record shop means you will often be recognized on the street and Gareth recalls, with no fondness whatsoever, people commenting "There goes the little ginger badge boy from the record shop" as he walked around Sunderland. His dad decided to expand, and they moved to a new location and re-named the shop Chartz (probably not the best name ever for a record shop). His father had also taken over the premises next door, which he used to sell alternative clothes. Gareth's dad sure had a thing for basic names; he called it The Alternative Clothes Shop. Gareth now combined his time helping in both shops, and even modelled the Oi T-shirts and bondage trousers the shop did so well with.

When Gareth was 18 his dad announced that he had sold the shop, as in his view the music industry was finished, and he was off to Spain where he had bought a pub. It was a shock for Gareth who suddenly had to stand on his own two feet. For a while he worked in another clothes shop, then spent some time selling audio books before obtaining a job with Impulse Promotions. They were one of several companies, such as Full Force and Platinum, who were employed by the record companies to get their singles higher up the chart.

Gareth gave me a fascinating insight into how these chart promotions companies worked and his job role. Every Monday he would visit the Woolworths stores of the North East where he would leave quantities of stock. Record companies would pay Impulse to take this stock – which was then given to the shops free of charge. In those days, the shops would display the Top 40 singles next to the counter. Positioned in a prominent position next to the Top 40 was a "recommended" board of new releases. These releases were recommended not because Woolworths thought they were fantastic records, or because they came from exciting new bands. The criterion was simple: give us the records for free and we will recommend them to our customers.

The records that received such favourable exposure in all the chain's stores were almost certain to be in the Top 40 the next week. A place in the Top 40 would ensure plenty of radio and media exposure and would qualify the artist to appear on *Top of the Pops*, a major influence on the singles chart.

From Tuesday to Thursday, Gareth would sell stock to independent shops and the HMV stores of the North East. This would involve him visiting the shops with a car packed full of stock. Fridays were spent visiting the independent radio stations of the area. Here he would try to meet the head of music to leave free stock and talk through the releases Impulse were promoting. Interestingly, he would never visit BBC stations.

On a Saturday, he would work as part of the Weekend Team. Record companies would receive a mid-week chart position, so if one of their records was just outside the Top 40, the team would be employed to visit as many shops as possible and leave them free stock of the record and explain to the shop that any help with promotion of the record would be appreciated. For Gareth, Saturdays were a mad rush to get around the shops in time to make sure he never missed a Sunderland home game. Impulse would often give out gifts to record shops to make them aware of certain records. To promote a single by an act called the California Raisins, Gareth was instructed to give boxes of raisins to his customers. The campaign was a flop as it did not achieve its aim of *raisin'* the song up the chart. The California Raisins were a fictional rhythm and blues animated musical group of cartoon raisins featuring the American drummer Buddy Miles on lead vocals. Amazingly, they released four albums and their biggest hit was the aptly titled "I Heard It Through the Grapevine". Personally, whenever I hear that song I think of the person who came into a record shop and asked, "Have you got that record by Marvin Gaye where he hurdled through the grapevine?"

An even stranger promotion involved the Fat Les record "Vindaloo". This song, written by Alex James of Blur, session bass player Guy Pratt and comedian Keith Allen, was released as a single to tie in with the FIFA 1998 World Cup, and peaked at No.2 in the UK chart. Gareth would pick up his parcels of stock at the local Securicor depot. One day he had a few extra boxes and when he opened them, they were full of Sainsbury's pre-cooked chicken vindaloos. The idea was for him to give away the chicken vindaloos to the shops to remind them of the record. The first thing that he thought of was these meals were normally kept in the chiller and the boxes he had been sent were anything but cold. There was only one thing for it, he needed to test the batch. That evening his family dined on vindaloo and as none of them suffered any negative consequences he thought it was safe to drop them off to his customers. The only problem was that it took him a week to get around them all and by the end he was seriously worried that he was giving his customers pre-packed food poisoning. Luckily there seemed to be no ill effects amongst them. A few did mention that they got a bit of Delhi belly. I wonder if they thought of the Fat Les record while they sat on the toilet, or was it par for the course with Vindaloo?

Things seemed to be going well for Gareth at Impulse, so much so that after much discussion with his wife they decided to splash out £800 on some bedroom furniture. Back in 1997 it was a big investment for the couple. After much sweat and frustration, they finally got it all assembled. Just as they were admiring their handiwork, the phone rang. It was Gareth's boss with the untimely news that Impulse had been sold and the promotions team would all be made redundant. It was unfortunate timing. If he had received the call a few hours earlier he could have taken the furniture back and saved himself a lot of stress and money.

What Gareth really wanted was to run his own record shop. An opportunity arose when he heard that Volume, which had a few record shops in the North East were looking to dispose of an outlet they had in Washington shopping centre, creatively named The Washington Music Store. Gareth's bid was accepted. However, to raise the money, he had to re-mortgage his house, sell his car and trade in his prize possession, a vintage jukebox. He even considered selling his new bedroom furniture.

It was an exciting time running his own business, though not easy. He loved his little shop but one thing he did not like was the shop next door which constantly roasted chickens, so that his shop always smelt like a KFC outlet. After a couple of years of trading there, the Washington Centre informed Gareth that his rent was to rise by 40% prompting him to relocate to Boston. He decided to rename the shop Nevermind after the classic Nirvana album, a title which, in keeping with his positive mindset, also happens to be Gareth's favourite catchprase.

He found a shop with a flat above and although it was a bit cramped for his three children it was within the budget, so he and his wife purchased it. After a few days of getting the shop ready they announced to the local media that the big opening of Boston's new record shop on the following Saturday. Unfortunately, on the Friday evening, his eldest daughter Natalie fell through the floor of the upstairs flat, causing a collapse of part of the shop's ceiling. They postponed the opening until the Monday and called in a builder in to make urgent repairs. If you are visiting Nevermind, you can still see the part of the ceiling that they call 'Natalie's patch' where she had the accident.

The most memorable day in the shop's history occurred on the December 7, 2013.

Gareth heard the news that an extremely high tidal surge was expected in the town at 7 o'clock that evening, and those living near the River Haven were advised to seek alternative accommodation and secure their homes. As he lived just 50 feet from the river it was, to quote the mod band Secret Affair "time for action".

With the help of his family, Gareth started the monumental job of removing his stock from the shop downstairs to the upstairs flat. He could hear the commotion in the street below as the sound of police sirens and people knocking on doors could be heard. As predicted, at around 7pm, he heard the water gushing down the street and discovered water pouring into his basement through the air vents. In what seemed no time at all the basement was full, and he was splashing around in ankle-deep water. His wife and children left the building, got into the car and reversed down the street through the fast-rising water. Film of his family fleeing the flood was shown on TV and YouTube and was used in an advertisement shown in local cinemas warning of flooding in the area.

With the flat upstairs full of stock, Gareth started piling stuff up on the stairs. Soon there was a loud knocking on his glass door. It was a policeman shouting that he must leave immediately as his life was in danger. Gareth was surprised how quickly the water had risen, it had now passed his knees. He shouted back that he would leave in five more minutes. He just had a bit more stock to move. The noise of the water made it difficult for the policeman to hear him and he continued knocking and ordering him to get out "NOW".

So enthusiastic was the policeman's knocking that he smashed the window of Gareth's door. It really was time to go and Gareth performed the rather pointless task of locking the front door, which by now had no glass in it. Around 10.30pm the water had subsided, and he returned to survey the damage. The shop was a disaster area with debris floating about. The next morning the fire brigade pumped out the basement and with the help of family and friends, they went about the task of cleaning up. The timing could not have been worse. With Christmas just three weeks away, the shop had never had so much stock in. All his CDs between B and D were ruined so the Beatles, Bowie and Dylan were all missing. Also completely lost were artists from P to S including Pink Floyd, Queen, the Rolling Stones and the Sex Pistols.

His insurance company sent around an assessor. Gareth's experience was not like the adverts where a smiling insurance man sorts everything out in minutes. Having lost

8,000 CDs and DVDs and more than 1,000 vinyl records, Gareth did not agree with the valuation, and it was clear he would not be getting any money until after Christmas. Gareth had a serious cash flow problem: he had lost half his stock and had nothing in the bank. He phoned the record companies to ask if they would give him a bit longer to pay his December bills and if they would give him some extra credit so that he could re-stock the shop. Some were sympathetic while others refused.

He went to B&Q and spent the last of his money on six heaters, while the one good thing the insurance company did was rent out some humidifiers to help dry out the air in the shop. With his financial position perilous, Gareth put an appeal out on social media announcing that the shop would re-open on the Saturday with a flood sale, and asking those people of Boston who were planning to buy music for Christmas to check out his shop first. This only applied to people who wanted to purchase albums by acts whose names started with A, or E through to R or T through to Z.

The people of Boston did him proud and a queue formed outside before the grand re-opening. One of the first people in the shop approached the vinyl rack and pulled out the whole section of over twenty LP's and brought them to him at the counter. As Gareth surveyed the artists, Abba, Anthrax, Alien Sex Fiend, AC/DC, etc., he knew that it was unlikely the man could have such a broad taste and asked him why he wanted to buy all the vinyl in the shop beginning with A. "I just want to help you out for Christmas," the man replied. Gareth was incredibly moved by this kind gesture but explained that he would much rather the customer buy something he was going to listen to. The man put the A section back and instead picked out twenty LPs that he did like. This was typical of the spirit shown by his regular customers and by many people of the town who were visiting the shop for the first time. They all wanted to help a local independent business.

As feared, the insurance company paid out nowhere near the amount Gareth had valued the stock at, and it has been a long process and a financial struggle to get the stock back to its 2013 level. He reckons he is 90% there. There is one album that he always keeps in stock and whenever he looks at it in the racks it reminds him of the pre-2013 days when things were a bit easier. It is Bob Dylan's *Before the Flood*.

Music in The Green

Rutland Square, Buxton Road, Bakewell, Derbyshire DE45 1BZ
07929 282950
musicinthegreen@gmail.com; @musicinthegreen
Monday 11am-5pm
Tuesday/Wednesday Closed
Thursday-Sunday 10am-5pm
Established 2015
Stock: Vinyl, CD, Pre-owned

Steven Free has the perfect background for running a record shop. For more than 30 years he was a psychiatric nurse and therapist. The job was incredibly stressful, and he would unwind at the end of the day by listening to music. Steve is an enthusiastic attendee of gigs and festivals. His favourite genre of music being folk, he would travel all over the UK to attend many small folk festivals. He noticed a gap in the market as some of these festivals did not have anybody selling the artists' CDs.

He bought some folk CDs from a distributer and hired a stall at the Wath-upon-Dearne folk festival. Where is Wath-upon-Dearne? It is a small village near Rotherham. On arrival, he would approach the artists and ask if they would like him to sell their CDs for them. The festival was a success and soon Steve was spending most weekends trading at small folk festivals. Steve really enjoyed selling and talking to fellow music fans, so decided to rent a stall on Bakewell market. He now had a lifestyle he was enjoying, combining selling music and still doing therapy work part-time.

The UK has some great record stalls in markets, but the downside is the weather. It can be fun in the summer, but selling records in a gale force wind, torrential rain or heavy snow is not so much fun. Steve decided it was time to find a permanent home and found a lovely property just outside the town centre on the town green.

If you walk from the town centre on a winter afternoon towards the beautifully-lit shop, it looks as if you are heading towards a cottage from a Hans Christian Anderson fairy tale. The theme does not change when you enter. The shop is painted green and decorated with branches, giving it the feel of a record shop within a forest. Most unusual of all, Steve has fifteen carvings and statues of green men hidden all over the shop. If you have young children, this is the record shop for you. They can be amused finding the green men while you look through the vinyl and CDs.

Music In The Green has the most comprehensive collection of folk vinyl that I have come across in England. Steve is a charismatic chap who appears perfectly at home in this environment. Not for Steve a record shop of silence. He will engage you to find out your taste in music and is happy to make recommendations. Steve is proud that few people leave the shop empty handed. He recalls the day a man came in looking for a Depeche Mode album that was out of stock. Steve persuaded him to buy a Led Zeppelin album instead.

One day an elderly woman came in and asked if the shop had any Pink Floyd. Steve took her over to the section and started talking her through the different albums.

When he had finished, he asked her which one would she like. "Oh none," she replied. "I just thought you would be interested to know that my daughter once babysat for Dave Gilmour from the band." With that nugget of information, she left.

If there is one song that causes more arguments in record shops than the 1980 Bob Marley song "Three Little Birds", then I am unaware of it. The song was taken from the album *Exodus* and reached No.17 in the UK chart. The problem is, many of the public think the title is something else. The lyrics that Bob Marley sings are:

"Don't worry about a thing as every little thing is gonna be alright."

So many record shops have told me about people coming in and asking for the Bob Marley song "Every Little Thing is Gonna be Alright", thinking this line from the chorus is the title. In this case a woman came in asking for Bob Marley's "Don't Worry". Steve explained that the song was called "Three Little Birds". The woman became quite upset, giving Steve the impression that she thought he was clueless. Before Steve had the chance to play the song to prove his point, she stormed off. She came back the next day to apologise, having discovered Steve was right. Steve's reply: "Don't worry."

The shop's least knowledgeable customer was the gentleman with whom Steve got into a conversation about the merits of Nick Drake. The man expressed the view that he enjoyed Nick's dad a lot more, Charlie Drake. Not much you can add to that.

Off The Beaten Tracks

36 Aswell Street, Louth, Lincolnshire LN11 9HP
01507 607677
offthebeatentracks.org; offbeatstock@yahoo.co.uk; @offbeatentks
Tuesday-Saturday 10am-5.30pm
Established 2004
Stock: Vinyl, CD, Pre-owned, Books, DVD

A well-named shop. The town seems further away than it is. Traveling slowly along country roads often behind tractors it can seem like an eternity to reach. But those who persevere will be rewarded by visiting this gem. Located in an old whitewashed cottage, this is a charming shop run by friendly Mancunian Mark Merryfield. If you are a Neil Young fan, you will enjoy a chat with Mark who describes himself as "an obsessive."

Replay Records

62-64 Freeman St, Grimsby, Lincolnshire DN32 7AG
01472 351125
replayrecords.co.uk; replay-records@btconnect.com
Tuesday-Saturday 9.30am-5.30pm
Established 1999
Stock: Vinyl, CD, Pre-owned, DVD, Badges, Tickets

Now in its fourth location in the town, Scott Wardle's shop is a sanctuary in an area that is otherwise a desert for vinyl fans. If you are a fan of button badges, it is well worth the trip. Scott has a collection larger than any other shop I am aware of.

Scott is one of the great record shop survivors. Ten years ago, his wife, his family and his accountant all advised him to close the business down as he was not making any money. Instead of Replay becoming another of the hundreds of other record shops who closed during that grim period Scott decided he would work in the shop of a day and in the evening as a taxi driver. Although exhausting, his efforts paid off. Thanks to the vinyl revival and Record Store Day the shop came through that period and is now doing better than ever, so much so that Scott no longer has to ferry the good people of Grimsby around in his taxi.

One problem with the vinyl revival is that some people get the impression that all vinyl is worth a fortune, as Scott relates:

"A guy walks into the shop with what looks like a bin bag, or as it turned out several bin bags carefully covering his prized LP. He stood at the counter peeling the layers off whilst telling me I will be amazed at what is going to appear and how lucky I will be to see this item! After removing literally several bin liners, carrier bags and finally a cardboard mailer he stands there proudly holding the *Flash Gordon* soundtrack LP by Queen.

"He could clearly see I was unimpressed as he said, "Do you not recognise a £500 LP when you see one?"

"I confirmed I would indeed recognise a £500 LP when I see one, but unless what he was holding was either fully-signed or was a white-label test pressing with different tracks/mixes from the original, then what he had was an LP worth £5. He was flabbergasted and a little annoyed.

"I directed him to the Queen section where there were four other copies of the LP sat there priced at £5 each. He told me I had made a mistake, the LP is very rare and quickly snapped up the four copies and paid for them. After carefully wrapping them in the black bin liners, he couldn't get out the shop quick enough! For seven months he visited the store, and bought every copy of *Flash Gordon* I had on each visit. I even put the price up to £6.99 and he still bought them. During this period, he bought 27 copies in total.

"Each time he came into the shop and found more copies of the LP, he would punch the air to express his excitement. There would be gasps of 'Oh yes!', giddy smiles and always many black bin liners to protect his purchases! On his last visit I asked why he still thought the LP was a mega-rarity. Only when I pointed out to him that he had at least 28 copies of a supposed rarity did the light bulb appear above his head. Never saw him again."

Rob's Records

18, Hurt's Yard, Nottingham NG1 6HL
@robsrecordsnottingham
Monday-Saturday 11am-5.30pm
Established 1992
Stock: Pre-owned

Setting foot in Rob's Records is a problem as you do your best not to stand on the boxes that cover most of the floor. It is less a crate-digger's paradise, more a box lifter's utopia. I found myself constantly moving boxes to find out what is underneath.

Rob only sells pre-owned product and is a charismatic Northern Soul DJ who had previously worked in other record shops in the city.

Top-tip: do not visit on a rainy day. On a sunny day, Rob takes boxes of records and piles them in the alleyway, giving you at least a tiny space to move around in. If it is raining those boxes are brought in ensuring you have virtually no space. Rob's Records is a true one off.

Rockaboom

18, Malcolm Arcade, Leicester, LE1 5FT
01162 538293
carl.rockaboom@gmail.com; @rockaboomshop
Monday-Saturday 10am-5.30pm
Established 1989
Stock: Vinyl, CD, Pre-owned

This longstanding record shop has been based in various locations throughout the city. It has always been a family business which was started by the owner Carl Petty with his dad Ian. The shop has an excellent range of reggae and keeps prices low. The shop has a loyal following in the city.

Spun Out

57 Gold St, Northampton, East Midlands NN1 1RA
01604 230064
Spunout.net, sales@spunout.net
Monday-Saturday 9am-5pm
Sunday 10am-4pm
Established 2000
Stock: Vinyl, Pre-owned, Merchandise, T-shirts

Chris Kent's Spun Out is hard to miss with its bright orange frontage. It is part-record shop, part-clothes shop with an impressive selection of body jewellery. It stocks a wide range of merchandise as well as bags and accessories. The shop offers a loyalty card for regular customers.

Tallbird Records

10, Soresby Street, Chesterfield, Derbyshire S40 1JN
01246 234548
tallbirdrecords.co.uk; tallbirdrecords@gmail.com; @TallbirdRecords
Monday-Saturday 9.30am-4.30pm
Established 2013
Stock: Vinyl, CD, Pre-owned, Art, Books, In-stores, Merchandise, Turntables

"Who doesn't want to own and work in a record shop?
It is the best job in the world." **Maria Harris -Tallbird Records**

Maria Harris walked into Richard's Records in Canterbury and asked them if they needed any part-time staff. The answer from Richard Rodgers, the shop owner, was "Yes" and so she took the first step towards realizing her dream of owning a record shop. Maria stopped off at a few other legendary record retail establishments along the way, including another part-time job at Beggars Banquet in Kingston-Upon-Thames, manager of a branch of Alto in Carnaby Street, and a head office product manager role at Virgin Megastores.

Maria opened Tallbird Records in Chesterfield in 2013, a couple of years after the closure of HMV and the much loved CE Hudsons (Keith Hudson appeared in the *Last Shop Standing* documentary film and was the proprietor of the oldest, family-run record shop in the world, having traded for 105 years). Not content to live in a town without a record shop and looking for a new challenge after more than 10 years as a stay-at-home mum, Maria decided the time was right to open a new shop to take advantage of the resurgent interest in vinyl.

CE Hudsons had been forced to close because of spiraling rents and rates, but Maria was fortunate to secure an affordable, small retail premises just around the corner from the old Hudsons site. Chesterfield is famous for its Church of St Mary's and All Saints with its crooked spire, so she toyed with the idea of calling the shop Spire Records, but that seemed a bit too obvious. As Maria has spent her entire life being told how tall she is (more than six foot in her heels) she thought it would be fun to call the shop Tallbird. Maria's graphic-designer dad designed the much admired Tallbird logo which now appears on T-shirts, mugs, slip mats and even the own brand record cleaner (years of working for a corporate brand like Virgin has obviously rubbed off!)

The first record sold when the shop opened its doors on October 4, 2013 was a pre-owned copy of *The Man Who Sold the World* by David Bowie, which, as a Bowie fan, Maria took as a good omen. The shop has gone from strength to strength ever since. The new vinyl and CD section has expanded, and the shop stocks a wide selection of new music and reissues across most genres. There's also plenty of great, reasonably priced pre-owned vinyl and CDs, which are topped up weekly with dozens of new titles to keep the racks interesting and fresh, plus four bins of bargain vinyl at £2.99 each or two for £5. Maria has managed to cram in as much stock as the little shop can hold without looking cluttered and untidy. Everything is well laid out and titles are easy to find. Pre-owned vinyl is all given a clear, colour-coded grade and there is a loyalty card scheme for regular vinyl customers.

The shop has built up a great reputation for its good product range and excellent customer service and has had visits from vinyl junkies from around the world including Japan, Australia and the USA. The shop has also had a few celebrity visits. There was one occasion when it felt like the shop had been transported back in time to a 1980s episode of *Top of The Pops*, with visits from Marco Pirroni of Adam & The Ants, Tom Bailey of the Thompson Twins and Captain Sensible of the Damned, all popping in on the same day. Marco is a regular and came in with his girlfriend who was promoting the Damned gig that evening, hence the visit from Captain Sensible. Tom Bailey was up visiting his dad who lives in the town. Tom is from Chesterfield as are most of the original Thompson Twins. So, if you are a vinyl fan passing by Chesterfield, call in and you might meet a 1980s star. If not, you will find Maria the extremely likeable "tall bird" behind the counter and star of the shop.

The Attic
74, Market Street, Ashby De La Zouch, Leicestershire LE65 1AN
01530 588381
theatticashby.com; ben.duncombe4gmail.com; @TheAtticAshby
Monday-Saturday 9am-4.30pm
Established 2010
Stock: Vinyl, Pre-owned CD, Comics, DVD, In-stores, Turntables

Ben Duncombe spent his early career working in catering and has gone from working with bread, jam, cream, sugarcubes and salt and pepper to catering for music fans who wish to purchase artists of the same name. Ben had always been an enthusiastic collector and recognised early on that car boot sales were the perfect place to pick up vinyl bargains. He started only buying records that he liked, but the temptation to buy stock to sell on proved irresistible since many sellers did not recognise the value of the records they were selling.

Soon, Ben had accumulated so much stock that he decided to hire a stall for one day a week in the market in Ashby De La Zouch. When an upstairs room above the market overlooking the high street became available, he snapped it up and founded The Attic. As the name implies, the shop is situated at the top of the building with access via a long staircase. To take your mind off the climb, Ben has decorated the walls with some fabulous movie memorabilia. It would be easy to walk past the doorway to the stairs on the street, but to ensure everybody sees it, Ben has installed a beautiful, well-lit jukebox in the entrance. The stairs have proved too much for one of his regulars a 90-year-old Johnny Mathis fan. She buys anything Ben can obtain for her. She calls Ben to tell him when she is planning to visit and, on her arrival, will ring the bell and Ben will come down to show her what he has to offer.

Ben does a great job of marketing the business. If planning a trip, try and visit during his twice yearly "1000 records for a £1" promotion. These happen just before Record Store Day in April and the following Black Friday in November. These events create big interest due to the quality of product Ben includes. All the albums included in the promotion had previously been on sale for £8 or more. The last event included a copy of the Beatles album *Sgt. Pepper's Lonely Hearts Club Band*. On the day of the promotion, a large queue waits for the shop to open. When the doors open there is a mad rush to the racks where Ben and his team have mixed the 1000 albums priced at £1 in with all the other records in the shop to create a lively treasure hunt.

Another popular promotion involves a tie-in with the local cinema. Ben bulk purchases 50 tickets for a current blockbuster. Then for each purchase in his shop, the customers receive a raffle ticket that entitles them to go into the draw to win two tickets for the film screening at the end of the month. The draw itself brings many customers back into the shop, keen to see if they are one of the lucky winners.

The Attic is not just a record shop. Ben has a huge selection of comics on sale and one of the largest collections of 7-inch singles that I have ever come across.

Vinyl Lounge

4 Regent Street, Mansfield, Nottinghamshire NG18 1SS
01623 427291
vinyllounge.mansfield@gmail.com; @vinylloungeuk
Monday-Saturday 9.30am-4.30pm
Established 2016
Stock: Vinyl, CD, Pre-owned, Art, Coffee, Food

Richard Vickerstaff had spent his life working with beer, He had run a country pub, a nightclub and ended up being the Operations Director for Whitbread. At the age of 50 he re-evaluated his life and decided to swap his love of beer for a love of vinyl. He took the plunge, returning to the town where he was born and opened a vinyl café in Mansfield.

With its distinctive red sign, the shop stands out and is easy to find. On the day I was there, the local butcher over the road from the shop was shouting bargains through a head microphone such as "All you can eat meat", "Get your pies here" and "A bag of chicken pieces for £5". I thought he needed better catchphrases. But if you are looking for the Vinyl Lounge just follow the sound of the noisy butcher and you will find it.

To step inside and hear vinyl playing instead of a butcher's noise pollution was very welcome. Richard has done a fantastic job in creating a relaxing atmosphere. The walls are covered in a combination of vinyl and spray paintings of rock stars by talented local artist Splat. Next to the window sits a nest of stools perfect for watching the people outside. Richard informs me that on a Saturday the shop attracts many couples, one of whom will spend their time looking through the vinyl selection while the other sits in the window reading a book or newspaper and enjoying a coffee.

In my travels throughout the country I often find certain bands do well in areas you would not expect them to, The Vinyl Lounge is the best example of that I know. If you have any vinyl sitting around by 1970s pop star Alvin Stardust or 1980s new wave band B–Movie get in touch with Richard as he struggles to keep up with demand for these local heroes. The town of Mansfield is crazy for the music of Liverpool band Cast. The shop's all-time best seller is the Cast album *All Change*. Richard will order it in batches of ten. It is interesting that his other top selling artists are of a similar ilk: Oasis, Blur, Arctic Monkeys, Stone Roses. Richard is a fan of Cast, so if anybody reading this knows John Power the band's frontman, let him know to include Mansfield on his next UK tour. Even better, pop into the Vinyl Lounge and do an acoustic PA. You will be warmly welcomed.

Devon

What they lack in quantity, the record shops of Devon make up for in quality. Drift in Totnes, Phoenix Sounds in Newton Abbot and Rooster in Exeter are amongst the finest. It is difficult to believe that the UK's ocean city Plymouth has no record shop that takes part in Record Store Day: It is a great location for somebody looking to open a record shop or a vinyl café. Barnstaple which once had three independent record shops, would be high on my list of suggestions. Bideford, Tiverton and Torquay are also worth considering.

Book Stop

3 Market Street, Tavistock, Devon PL19 0DA
018226 17244
bookstoptavistock.co.uk; @BookStop1
Monday-Saturday 9am-5.30pm
Established
Stock: Vinyl, CD, Books

Book Stop is the epitome of all that is good about an independent shop. Housed in a quirky, three-story, historic building, with books on the first two floors, it is worth the trek up to the third floor to check out the vinyl and CDs. Watch your head though if you are tall. The shop has a low ceiling.

Cavern Record Store

9a Bolton Street, Brixham, Devon TQ5 9BZ
01803 414101
thecavernbrixham@gmail.com
Tuesday-Saturday 10am-4pm
Established 2012
Stock: Vinyl, Pre-owned, CD, DVD, Memorabilia

Without the bright yellow canopy and "open" sign plonked on the pavement, it would be easy to miss Roger Stafford's shop Cavern Record Store. It is certainly the narrowest record shop I have visited in the UK. It carries an excellent selection of 1950s and 1960s records. Roger has lived in the area all his life and has plenty of anecdotes about the local music scene.

Drift
103 High Street, Totnes, Devon TQ9 5SN
01803 866868
driftrecords.com
info@thedriftrecordshop.com; @driftrecordshop
Stock: Vinyl, CD, Pre-owned, Tickets, In-stores
Monday-Saturday 10am-5pm Selected Sundays 12-5pm.
Established 1995
Stock: Vinyl, CD

Totnes seems to feature in every list ever compiled regarding the best places to live in the UK. The town centre is a quirky mixture of shops selling new age merchandise, vegetarian cafes and no end of galleries, situated on a steep hill. The unique-looking Drift record shop sits well in the laid-back atmosphere that prevails.

"We take what we do really seriously, but there is always an underlying element that amuses us about how deeply inappropriate it is to run a record shop in the middle of a small farming town," co-owner Rupert Morrison explains.

Stocking new music from everywhere on CD and vinyl, Drift is deliberately undefinable in its approach to buying. The shop will stock anything from contemporary classic and avant-garde, through to hip hop, electronica, rock, metal, stoner and "sludge". Drift is family owned, run by Rupert with parents Jenny and Graeme taking care of the front of house and finance department respectively. The original shop was a lot smaller renting VHS tapes then DVDs before gradually introducing more CDs and vinyl. A rebrand in 2009 incorporated a move to the stylish current location.

"I think people have latched onto what we're doing as we try not to take ourselves too seriously," Rupert says. "It is a tough balance to get right, you know? We're passionate guys and we think we're pretty good at curating music, but in the grand scheme of things, against all the stuff going on right now, are record shops all that important, especially in small towns? But then – and bear with me here – that's the most important thing, right? Drift and other stores like us change lives... deal with that!" (laughing) The shop has a reputation for supporting new music. It is just as likely to be championing left-field minimal tech house as home-recorded roots music from the Appalachian Mountains. The staff genuinely enjoy listening to something new and then putting it in the shop for their customers to get turned onto as well.

Working like a Whirling Dervish, Rupert wasted no time in getting the online shop established. Soon after opening, Drift was organising regular in-store performances that consistently attracted a crowd of both locals and tourists. Subsequent years brought new innovations, from a highly-recommended quarterly newspaper called *Deluxe* which can be found in many independent British record shops, to their 2016 initiative launching a town festival called *Sea Change*. Rupert is one of the most switched-on independent music retailers I know. I asked him what had changed at Drift in recent years as they had gone from being one of the smallest record shops in the UK to being a relatively large store. His in-depth answer was full of both passion and frustration:

"We opened up the new shop on April Fool's Day 2011. This was deliberate. I mean, it's kind of ridiculous to move from a small and successful safe space to a large building with double the rent, double the rates and huge windows to fill. I think that is why people have responded so well to what we're doing. We're ambitious and felt that we couldn't display the music in a way we'd want to view it. So, we risked it all. Do it right or don't do it at all. Record shops are no longer essential. I hate to say it, but it's just the case. There was a time in the not so recent past (as well documented in your Last Shop Standing film) where shops were the conduit from band to bedroom and had their hands around how physical music was distributed. Two things have happened: music is no longer just a physical thing and shops no longer hold the monopoly."

"I regularly go to other shops and buy records as I love the experience of doing so. If a shop is good, I'll likely spend loads as I love getting totally off-my-head excited about how the music is presented to me. I went to Spillers in Cardiff a while back and Ashli the owner bothered to give me five minutes to run through the 'Welsh wall', which is a wall of new releases by Welsh bands which she thought I might enjoy. I made away with an absolute gem and that made a huge impression on me. The internet will often beat you on price, availability, ease of transaction but it will never be able to replicate what it is like to walk into a record shop and feel that you are part of something."

"We keep the shop clean, we fill it with plants and records and we try and write a little something about them all", Rupert continued. "The shop is polished hourly. It's a bit like being invited into the living room of an uptight record obsessive and being given full permission to snoop about. It works for us, but I strongly believe that the specifics won't matter. Some people love the way we rack stuff; some people walk out furious because they can't find what they are looking for. There are no rules anymore, just free range to get people enthused, well, try to anyway.

It has got harder and harder though. Distribution is a balancing act, likewise, depth of stock is impossible compared to online shops and patience no longer is an option. The culture to buy music cheaply is supported online in such sophisticated mechanisms, that Amazon is considered by many consumers to be the benchmark for prices. Fair prices? Worse still, the high street shops like HMV are starting to try and price match. Quite literally, no one wins in that market. Bands, labels, distributors are broke, small shops go bust, bigger shops look to be going bust and the online shops make pennies. Legal or not, streaming and downloading is so convenient that it has irreparably changed the landscape. The old models are redundant, and many stores are too scared or naive to change. So why keep doing it? Because it matters. It makes a massive difference to people's lives and if you can get it, it's a pretty great job.

"But all of this does need a little bit of caution you know. The rise and rise of the record shop scene has ironically – and this is my opinion – watered down what shops did. Shops died, the whole sector nearly collapsed, but it didn't. Somehow spiritually and intrinsically linked to vinyl, the culture lived on and grew and grew... but it has become insipid. There are just too many cookie cutter stores who are saying the same stuff, they are not curators or experts. I think the bit that gets me, do they even care? On a buying level alone, pick what you want for your narrative, if you hear something and hate it, don't buy it, likewise, follow your ears, back something wild and weird you know?! Have courage, have an identity. This is all about cycles and waves, this can't go on and shops are going to need to be accountable sooner or later for their worth... they deserve nothing on a plate. I hope that the legacy of Record Shops for the next decade is taking the concept of 'the record shop' and just getting rid of it entirely. We sell the same stuff, but we should only be identifiable across the sector by our friendships and passion. No rules, just passionate people doing good work. I don't have the answers, but I am ready for a change."

Martian

Unit 13, Exmouth Indoor Market, Exmouth, Devon, EX18 1AB
01395 225981
marcus.martian@yahoo.co.uk; @martiancentral
Monday-Saturday 10am-5.30pm
Established 1989
Stock: Vinyl, CD, Pre-owned, DVD, Merchandise, Lego, Musical Instruments,
T-shirts

Martian used to have shops in Exeter and Weston-super-Mare, but now just the one survives based inside Exmouth Market. The great majority of stock is pre-owned, but they take part in RSD. Check out the guitars made from petrol cans.

Phoenix Sounds

Queen Street, Newton Abbot, TQ12 2AQ
01626 334942
phoenixsound.co.uk; phoenixsound1@gmail.com; @phoenixsoundsuk
Monday-Friday 9am-5.30pm
Saturday 9am-5pm
Sunday 11am-3pm
Established 2003
Stock: Vinyl, CD, DVD, In-stores, Merchandise

Will Webster found his way into the music industry via the unusual route of Jobcentre Bristol which landed him a post in Virgin Records as a singles buyer. It was once the most important job in a record shop. Order the correct quantities and the store would make good money, order too many non-selling titles, and the shop's profits would be tied up in dead stock. The role has been redundant for many years, because so few single releases come out as a physical format.

Will quickly impressed the management in Bristol and was given the chance to manage his own store in Torquay. The chance to have his own shop by the sea appealed to Will, and he packed his swimming trunks, bucket and spade. By the time he had moved to the coast, the smaller Virgin record stores had been bought by music retailer Our Price. Will was asked to take over the running of the Newton Abbot branch, which was known as the "managers' graveyard". This was the store you were moved to when Our Price wanted to get rid of you, and Will was no exception.

Disillusioned at working for Our Price, Will turned his back on music retailing and took up teaching. He remained a teacher for 10 years and found it challenging and rewarding. However, once in your blood, music never goes away, and Will accepted an offer to go into partnership at local independent record shop Phoenix Sounds. Unfortunately, he returned to the music retailing business at a time of major downturn. His disillusioned business partner offered him the chance to buy out his share in the store, and suddenly Will had his own business. Despite the pessimism of his former partner, he was determined to make it work. Swimming against the tide, Will invested heavily in new racking, increased the stock level and moved Phoenix Sounds to a new site, which was more than twice the size of the original. It seemed to have worked, helped by the fact that Will had no competition after the local Our Price closed.

Phoenix Sounds is a wonderful record shop and Will is one of the unsung heroes of record retailing. He never wins awards, never gets media coverage but is delighted just to be making the music fans of Newton Abbot happy. In return, they appreciate having one of the largest record shops in the South West in their town.

Rooster *The shop which had a genuine fire sale*
98 Fore Street, Exeter, Devon EX4 3HY
01392 272009
roosterrecords.co.uk; jaimiefennell@gmail.com; @RoosterRecords
Monday-Saturday 10am-5.30pm
Established 1995
Stock: Vinyl, Pre-owned

Jamie Fennell sacrificed more than most to follow his dream of opening a record shop. He gave up a career as a lawyer, having been in a practice for ten years, and along with his partner Sheryl opened Rooster. The duo has not looked back since. He gave his old pin-stripe work suit to his brother-in-law, who runs a gardening shop in Bath, to put on his scarecrow. His first shop was in Taunton, but when the lease ran out he had acquired so much stock that he needed a much larger shop and re-located to Exeter in November 2006.

Jamie displays the shop's vast array of collectable product on the wall. It makes an impressive sight. Collectable vinyl continues to rise in value. Whether this upward trend is set to continue remains to be seen, but for now Jamie would rather invest his money in these dusty, round, groove-ridden artefacts than in anything else.

The shop has an excellent selection of pre-owned vinyl and CDs, and Jamie often visits people's homes to purchase record collections. On one occasion, he went to see a collection and came across a whole pile of CD cases with Rooster Records stickers on them. However, they were all empty. He remembered the titles having been stolen from the shop about a year earlier and here he was in the perpetrator's house. Instead of confronting him (well, he was twice his size) he discreetly placed them in his bag while his host was making him a cup of tea. Back in the shop he matched them up with the caseless CDs, which he had kept, and returned them to the racks. The would-be thief was none the wiser.

One day Jamie was playing a CD by the Byrds in the shop when who should walk in but Gene Parsons from the band. Jamie was going to see Gene Parsons in concert that evening, so he was getting in the mood for the gig, but he had absolutely no idea that Gene was planning to visit the shop. Gene shook his head in disbelief and then shook Jamie's hand to introduce himself, congratulating him on his fine taste in music.

The upsurge of interest in vinyl has astonished Jamie who makes the point that, five years ago, he would consign many of the pre-owned albums he bought off the public to his £1 bin. Nowadays, many of the same pre-owned albums are promoted to the main racks and sell for decent money. Although he is paying more to the public to purchase their records, his overall margin is now better. Despite Jamie's comment about putting fewer records in the £1 bin nowadays, I think his selection of vinyl for £1 is among the best I have seen. Do not leave the shop without checking these bargains out. They are all kept in boxes under the racks.

Another positive thing he has noticed in recent years is the greatly increased number of female customers of all ages buying vinyl of all genres. If you go back 20 years many record shops could be intimidating places for women, with staff who made you feel it was a private male-dominated club. The good news is that those record shops have long since closed down. Rooster is typical of the modern record shop, where all music collectors receive a warm welcome regardless of age or gender.

Disaster struck Rooster in June 2017 when a light fitting caught fire. Staff evacuated the premises as the shop filled with smoke and the fire took hold. Having lost a lot of stock, Jamie organized a fire sale and was soon trading again as usual.

One of Jamie's customers suggested that working at Rooster was an expanded hobby, not a job. Jamie tended to agree.

Dorset

The county is an excellent place to visit for vinyl enthusiasts and you would struggle to get around all the shops in a day. Poole has three shops selling second-hand vinyl and it would make sense for one of them to grasp the nettle and commit to selling new vinyl and taking part in RSD. Dorchester would be the ideal town to open a record shop selling new vinyl.

Bridport Music *Have you got any Jose Mourihno records?*
33a South Street, Bridport, Dorset DT6 3NY
01308 425707
bridportmusic.co.uk; info@bridportmusic.co.uk; @BridportMusic
Monday-Saturday 9am-5pm
Established 1976
Stock: Vinyl, CD, Books, In-stores, Merchandise, Musical Instruments

I experienced the madness of dealing with the British public the last time I was in Piers and Steph Garner's shop Bridport Music. An elderly woman approached the counter and asked "Do you have any Gene Krupa?"

Piers: "Yes, "I have this compilation and it is only £9."

Elderly woman: "Oh, £9."

Piers: "It has all his best tracks on."

Elderly woman: "It is for a friend of mine who is not very well, and I thought it might cheer him up. The only problem is he is so unwell that he may not pull through. I think it is best if I wait a couple of weeks and if he survives I will come back and get it."

Piers and I looked at each other, unsure if we should laugh. Surely, an ill friend is worth £9 of anybody's money. She never came back, so I guess he didn't make it.

This incident started Piers off and he was soon regaling me with some more crazy happenings from the shop including the tale of the customer they nicknamed The Crow Woman after the following conversation:

Customer: "Have you got any classical music for crows to dance to?"

Piers: "I am sorry madam, we do not have any classical music for crows to dance to."

Customer: "Ok, can you tell me what other type of music you stock suitable for crows to dance to?"

The shop also had a visit from the world's least knowledgeable blues fan:

Customer: "I am after a CD by a blues guitarist and I think his first name is Jose."

Piers: "Jose Gonzalez?"

Customer: "Not him."

Piers: "Jose Feliciano, the guitarist famous for his version of The Doors 'Light my Fire'?"

Customer: "Not him either."

Suddenly the man's face lit up as he had a lightbulb moment.

Customer: "Got it, I think his name is Jose Mourihno."

Piers pointed out that he used to manage the Blues as opposed to playing them.

It turned out, after some brilliant detective work by Piers, that it was none other than

Joe Bonamassa that the customer was after.

Not long after, the world's least knowledgeable metal fan visited the shop.
Customer: "Do you have any metal albums in by Maidenhead?"
Piers was not sure if this was a new supergroup featuring members of Motorhead and Iron Maiden or if some new metal band had been named after a Berkshire town. It turned out he was after Motorhead.

Not long after they had a visit from world's least knowledgeable disco fan.
Customer: "Do you have a CD of disco classics?"
Piers showed him the disco compilation section. Each time he picked one up he would study the track listings before placing it back in the racks.
Piers: "Is there a disco track you are looking for? "
Customer: "'Rhinestone Cowboy' by Glen Campbell."

Piers became involved in music when his brother-in-law Andy Bell phoned him to say he had taken out a lease on a new shop. Andy already had his own general store but wanted a record shop and asked Piers if he would be interested in running it. At the time, Piers was studying law at Sheffield, but had become disillusioned and was desperately seeking an alternative career path. He packed his bags, headed to Bridport and in 1979 The Record Centre opened. Piers married Steph in 1980, and since then this dynamic duo have run the store. It is a credit to them not only to have stayed married for nearly 40 years but to be running a business together at the same time.

The first thing you notice as you enter the store, is the bongos, guitars and ukuleles hanging from the ceiling. Piers and Steph work on a raised platform at the far end of the store, looking down on their kingdom below. Like most shop owners faced with a CD industry in slow decline, they realised that survival depended on diversification. After visiting a stand at a music industry conference, they decided to stock musical instruments. It proved a wise move, and one which I am surprised more stores have not followed. In recent years, I have noticed more space being given to instruments not only in Bridport Music but also in other successful shops I visit. Piers has even been known to bring his ukulele out and give the customers a tune, always a good tactic at closing time when looking to clear the shop.

Unusually, the shop stocks a range of nose flutes. Following a comical interview with daughter Hannah by Mark Radcliffe on BBC Radio 6 Music about the instrument, which included some funny attempts at playing it by the renowned DJ, the shop has received great interest from the public. As the name suggests you play the flute by blowing through the nose instead of the mouth. It normally has four holes which can partly be covered by fingers to make the sounds. Piers has a couple of tips for would-be purchasers. Always blow your nose first, and don't lend it to somebody else to have a go.

Bridport Music used to be known until 2009 as Bridport Record Centre. The name change reflects the new, broader philosophy. "If it's music-related then we will have a go at stocking it," Piers says. Piers and Steph feel that if they were to concentrate on just one of the many strands that they do then they would inevitably fail, but by combining them they are successful. They have listened to what customers have asked for and try to stock it, especially if there is nowhere else in town to buy it.

They love living and working in Bridport. The town is full of independent shops, and given the difficulties faced by independent shops elsewhere, visitors seem amazed to discover that business is thriving. "I wish we had a shop like yours where we live," is a comment they constantly hear. In 2016, they celebrated the 40th anniversary of the shop opening. The trouble is that no one can remember the exact date when they started. If you are in the area, pop in and offer your congratulations. If you have a wicked sense of humour, you may prefer to ask them for an iTunes voucher. It is the only time you will find the smile leaving Piers' face.

Replayed Records
4 Daisy May's Arcade, Kings Rd East, Swanage, Dorset BH19 1ES
01929 421717
replayedrecords.com; music@replayedrecords.com; @ReplayedRecords
Monday 11am-4pm Tuesday/Saturday 10am-4pm Thursday/Friday 10am-5pm
Wednesday/Sunday Closed
Established 2012
Stock: Vinyl, Pre-owned

"Running a record shop is far better than working." **Nick Wells – Replayed Records**

Opening a record shop was a completely unplanned, spontaneous decision made by Nick and Dawn Wells. They had sold up a long-established car repair and skip hire business in Buckinghamshire and moved down to Swanage at the end of 2010. While downsizing after their children had left the nest, one of Nick's tasks was to reduce his huge vinyl collection so he started selling online. This turned out to be a big mistake. As soon as he went online, Nick kept finding vinyl that he found irresistible and soon he had amassed more than ever before.

The couple were walking through Swanage in February 2012 when they passed an empty shop and Nick said "It would make an ideal record shop". Within an hour they were checking the availability to rent. They opened their shop on March 1. The change has been positive in every way. They love their relaxed lifestyle on the coast and what could be better than selling records and chatting to fellow vinyl enthusiasts all day?

Revolution Vinyl Café   *The record shop with a beautiful view of the harbour*
8 Trinity Road, Weymouth, DT4 8TJ,
01305 788664
revolutionvinylcafe.com; team@revolutionvinylcafe.com; @revovinyl
Monday Closed
Tuesday/Wednesday 10am-5pm
Thursday-Saturday 10am-6pm
Sunday 11am-5pm
Established 2016
Stock: Vinyl, Pre-owned, Cake, Coffee, Turntables, Vintage Clothing

Chris O'Connell and Sarah Whiteside own this delightful harbourside café with a good selection of vinyl. In the 1990s the South West became renowned for its mad and exciting free dance party scene, and Sarah cut her teeth in the industry as part of the Chemical Element Drum and Bass promotion company who put on free dance events across the local area. This was a steep learning curve into the intricacies of running an independent music-based business and the responsibilities involved in creating a safe and vibrant space for people to party in. Sarah was involved in all aspects of it. She made ceiling drops and banners out of parachute fabric to decorate the dated venues to make them look the part. She babysat endless party-goers who had overdone it or lost contact with their friends. Running the door was like running an overgrown creche some nights. Eventually the events were proving too popular. With people travelling all over the South West to attend, things got out of hand and with the hassle they were getting from the police, it all became too much. Sarah has many happy memories of those days; when the night flowed and the music peaked, there was no better feeling.

Family life took over in the coming years and she utilized her skills in new ways, developing a charitable live music event, The Big Grove Summer Festival, that ran for more than seven years, raising money for local schools and voluntary sector organisations. What started out as a chairmanship role on the PTA, morphed into an annual music festival that won awards and recognition for its positive impact on the local community. The day job, meanwhile, was running a dressmaking and design company, commissioned to make bridal wear and historical costuming. She also developed a range of retro clothing from her own designs.

Chris was based in London when they met, working as a driver, but it did not take long for him to fall in love with life by the sea. He relocated, and the duo began working together on Sarah's business, Frank Designs. The duo spent the summer hitting the road with a pop-up boutique, attending tattoo conventions, vintage weekenders and music festivals, mixing work with pleasure and pushing the business in new directions. Adding a mobile coffee bar and vinyl booth to the set-up added to the vibe and made them stand out.

A trip to see Massive Attack got them talking on the journey home about the dream of building up enough of a reputation to put the concept into premises one day, with music at the heart of it all. The combination of vinyl, coffee and retro clothing convinced the duo there was a future. By the time, they arrived home, the seeds of the Revolution Vinyl Café had been sown.

One thing to look out for on your visit is the 1950s radiogram that they had restored so they can play vintage vinyl in the shop. It's a talking point for customers, most of whom recall their parents or grandparents having one in their front room.

I asked Sarah what life is like in the Revolution Vinyl Café and is she pleased they took the bold decision to open. Her answer summed up the satisfaction people get from dealing with fellow musically-minded people.

"It's been all about the music and the people here at Revolution. We never tire of choosing new music to stock in store and are constantly pushing our own boundaries and introducing our customers to new sounds. We have been welcomed into the town with open arms and have had so many awesome and interesting people through the door and the laid-back vibe in here puts everyone in a positive frame of mind. It's become a place to hang out and catch up with friends, in many ways, with the family-run ethos, it's an extension of our lives at home and we wouldn't have it any other way."

If you are planning a visit, try and go on a Sunday to catch one of the Sunday Acoustic Sessions. Sample the coffee and the highly rated lemon sponge (check out the reviews on the Facebook page), look through the vinyl and watch a local band. What a perfect way to spend a relaxing afternoon.

Square Records

14, High Street, Wimborne, Dorset BH21 1HU
012028 83203
rob@square_records
Monday-Saturday 9am-5pm
Established 1975
Stock: Vinyl, CD, Photographic Art

Located close to the beautiful Wimborne minster, Square Records was founded by electrical goods retailer Roger Holman. He decided to utilize some space in the shop by selling vinyl. Sales were soon booming so he opened a record shop in the high street. His son Paul has run the shop for the last three decades with help from his sister Julie and the punk expert of Dorset, Rob Hoare.

Paul has an interesting history being a member of 1990s cult band the Lemon Trees. The band featured a young Guy Chambers who went on to great success as Robbie Williams' songwriting partner. In fact, "Lazy Days", one of Robbie's Top 10 hits, was an old Lemon Trees number that Paul sang.

The loyal, wonderful and sometimes bonkers customers remain the lifeblood of the shop's business. One man came in asking if they had anything by a brilliant American duo he had seen on TV called Daryl Hall and John O'Groats.

They still have a lady who phones every Saturday who knows nothing about pop music and relies on the staff to finish her crossword. She does not even say "Hello", she just starts with "Four letters, song by Queen, We Will **** You". The staff wonder what she would do if they were not there.

In 2018, there was much upset in the town when the shop announced it was closing. I am delighted to report that the team behind the excellent Gullivers bookshop have bought the business and service is continuing as normal.

The Vault *Turning a slaughterhouse into a record shop*
1 Castle Street, Christchurch, Dorset BH23 1DP
01202 482134
thevaultchristchurch.co.uk; rotationmedia@aol.com; @thevaultxchurch
Monday-Friday 9am-5pm
Saturday 9am-5.30pm
Sunday 10.30am-4.30pm
Established 2011
Stock: Vinyl, CD, Pre-owned

Like most kids who were introduced to music in the early 1970s, Alan Rowett lived on a radio diet of Radio 1 and Radio Luxembourg, plus the weekly TV show *Top of the Pops*. The radio was on all the time during his early years, and it was not until he was nine that he was given a record player and his mother's collection of middle-of-the-road singles from the 1960s. Funds were tight. A small amount of pocket money did not stretch far in his home town of Christchurch. Although it had a large high street, it only had a branch of Woolworths and a second-hand shop called Exchange and Mart which sold records. Buying new singles was beyond his budget, so the second-hand store was his regular weekly call to spend those few pence. However, he soon found out that Tuesday afternoons was a good time to visit Woolworths. The new chart was announced every Tuesday at lunchtime on Radio 1, and the local branch used to discount all the records that had dropped out of the Top 40 that week into their bargain bin. Alan was first there after school and got the goodies that were only a third of their usual price, a business head already at a such a young age.

He was asked at school by his careers teacher, "What do you want to do when you leave?" He replied "Work in a record shop. It would be a fantastic dream job". The reply was along the lines of "That's nice, but aim a little higher, my boy". Also, around this time he read an article by Radio 1 DJ John Peel. It had a picture of him surrounded by records on his desk and the floor. In the article, he said one of the best things about being a DJ is that you get all your records free. "Fantastic," Alan thought. "That's what I am going to do." The idea of working behind a record store counter disappeared.

Throughout the remainder of the 1970s his Saturdays were spent walking round the many music shops in the nearby town of Bournemouth. These record-buying jaunts continued until the early 1980s, when Bournemouth gained its first ILR (Independent Local Radio) station Two Counties Radio. Alan soon got himself involved, obtaining a Saturday job doing everything that no one else wanted to do. His payment was that he could help himself to the massive chuck-out box of records that none of the presenters wanted. He would arrive home on Saturday evening with a bag full of free records, sometimes 40-50 singles a week. His dream had come true, a tap of free vinyl and an introduction to all genres of music. Radio became his full-time career at which point record shops disappeared from his radar.

During the next 30 years he worked not only in ILR but moved up to London and joined the BBC, working as a producer across programmes on Radio 1, Radio 2 and The World Service, during which time he received free promotional copies of every record, weeks before they came out. He even produced John Peel for a few years, and once over lunch told John about the article he had read in the 1970s, which was the reason he had ended up there with him.

But, in the back of his mind, he still had that other dream. What would it be like to run his own record shop?

Alan left the BBC in 2006 and formed his own production company, producing several weekly shows for stations across the world, including a weekly chart show for BBC World Service, inheriting the legendary *Top of The Pops* brand he had grown up with. His family had moved to a village in North Dorset called Stalbridge, and in the courtyard at the back was an old coach house from the 19th century. During the 20th century it had become a slaughterhouse and cold store for the butcher's shop which once occupied the front of the house.

Inspired, so he kindly told me, by reading my book *Last Shop Standing,* Alan decided to convert the old slaughterhouse into a record shop, and in March 2012 The Vault opened for business. After 30 years of playing new records on the radio, he now had the task of trying to sell those same items to a declining record-buying public. It was not the easiest thing to do in a tiny village like Stalbridge, which had no through traffic and a population of 3500, and Alan found himself on a steep learning curve. Someone told him at the start "Don't just stock what you like, no one else will like it." That was true.

Slowly a few people did come through the door, as much out of amazement as anything else. Why open a record shop in a village like this? was a popular question, one that Alan would regularly ask himself.

One memorable customer stood in the middle of the shop and said in a very strong Dorset accent: "I remember killing the chickens, sheep and pigs in here, right here." And, pointing at the floor, "The blood used to run down there and out the door." Although it was great fun, the shop in Stalbridge never made any money. It just about broke even, although some months not even that.

In 2014 the opportunity arose to move to a more viable, high street location in his hometown of Christchurch, just 100 yards away from the site where that Woolworths store used to be in the 1970s. Fighting off competition from a wine shop, an estate agent and a gift store, Alan convinced the landlord that the town was more urgently in need of a record shop, and The Vault suddenly had a new home.

With Alan's wife Chrissy giving up her job to help run it, the new shop was decorated, stocked and opened within three weeks. The new Vault felt like a proper shop, and best of all, people came in. The shop is a partnership and shared joy for Alan and Chrissy. Open every day of the week, it has quickly established itself in the town, and built up a good number of regular customers. Every corner has been filled with stock and the shop boasts the largest range of new vinyl in the county, alongside a wide range of high quality, pre owned records.

The shop has become a favourite stopping place for the dog walkers of the area. Indeed, several dog owners make regular stops at the store while out on a "long walk". It is here where the walk ends for the dog. The staff look after the animal while the owner looks through the shelves.

The Vault has taken on the supermarkets and major online retailers and when it comes to the popular chart titles, they either match or beat them on price.

It has been a period of rapid expansion for The Vault. In 2016 they opened a brand-new store further along the coast at Old Christchurch Road, Bournemouth, Dorset BH1 1LR (Tel: 01202 559 511). Having seen the record shops in which he spent the happiest times of his youth closing down over the years, Alan was especially proud to be reversing the trend not only in Christchurch but also in Bournemouth.

The Vault shops have the atmosphere of a classic record shop, run by two people who love music and enjoy meeting and talking with anyone who pops into the store. They are open 7 days a week, and you will always be very welcome. If you arrive on a day when Chrissy or Alan are off, then you will be welcomed by record store veteran Simon, who has been in the business since the early 1970s. Just don't ask him about classic rock music, you will never leave.

Essex

Essex has gone through a transition, with long-established stores such as Adrians and Fives reducing their outlets to just a single shop. Slipped Discs is also down to one shop but now incorporates an excellent café. Colchester is in need of an independent record shop selling new vinyl.

Adrians

36-28 High Street, Wickford, Essex SS12 9AZ
01268 73 3318
adriansrecords.co.uk; sales@adrians.co.uk; @AdriansRecords
Monday-Saturday 9am-5.30pm
Sunday 10am-4.30pm
Established 1969
Stock: Vinyl, CD, Pre-owned, Memorabilia, In-stores

Anyone who bought the NME throughout the 1970s and 1980s will be aware of Adrian Rondeau's shops in Wickford. For twenty years, they had an eye-catching advert highlighting the latest releases.

"If you can't get it at Adrians, you can't get it anywhere" is the shop's motto.

At one-point Adrian had four shops, but after years of decline he now has just the one, plus a thriving online business. Things did not look great at the beginning of the decade when Adrian became seriously ill and was away from the business for a lot of the time. I am delighted to report that, following numerous operations, he is back to his usual effervescent self. He has also had a huge stroke of luck – although I am sure Adrian will see it as brilliant long-term planning. Back in the 1980s, Adrian had bought, along with his partner, Richard, an old Victorian house that had belonged to a brewery. The huge cellars that came with the house were full of old slate shelving on which ale barrels used to be stored, and which were perfect for stacking up boxes of limited-edition vinyl that he was buying by the van load. Sometimes he would buy up remaining stock from small record labels and importers.

When CDs took over, vinyl sales slumped dramatically. This period coincided with Adrian being in and out of hospital, so the stock in the cellars was rarely visited.

When he was declared fit again, and with no more operations on the horizon, he and Richard fulfilled a lifelong ambition by moving into a rambling house in the countryside. Of course, the existing house had to be sold and the cellar emptied. It took nine months to sell the house and almost as long to empty the cellars. To his amazement, in those long-neglected cellars he discovered box after box of wonderful finds: Beatles picture discs; Oasis white labels; and boxes of rare vinyl from artists such as the Smiths, Abba, the Cure and David Bowie. Adrian started feeding the vinyl into the shop. The result? Once again record collectors have been looking up where Wickford is on the map and business is better than in 2009, as vinyl fans make a beeline to the shop, where long serving manager Mike Dalby will be happy to show them the many collectable items for sale.

Fives Records

103 Broadway, Leigh-on-Sea, Essex SS9 1PG
01702 711629
fivesrecords@gmail.com; fives-records.co.uk; @fives_records
Monday-Saturday 9am-5.30pm
Sunday 9am-4pm
Established 1977
Stock: Vinyl, CD, Accessories, In-stores

Founder Peter Driscoll was a fully qualified heating engineer who designed and fitted systems for schools and offices but was looking to do something different. Peter loved music and deep down had always wanted his own record shop. When he noticed that Leigh-on-Sea did not have a record shop, he decided it was time for a career change.

Fives Records is a true family business. The store has been staffed by Peter's daughters Sandra, Julie, Cheryl and Tracy, as well as his grandchildren Danielle, Kyle and Sarah. Behind the scenes keeping the website and social media ticking along and fixing all the computers when they decide to be awkward, is Sandra's partner Tony.

Peter allegedly went into semi-retirement in 2006 when the Fives Records shop in Rayleigh closed, but he still cannot keep away and, now aged 78, still gets up around 5.30am and walks more than a mile to the shop to clean, and pack the online orders that have come in overnight. Peter still works Wednesdays and Sundays when it is Sandra's days off. When at home he is constantly listing stock, some going back 40 years, for sale online. Sandra is now the joint owner and manager and has a regular spot on the BBC Radio Essex show Vintage Vinyl, hosted by Mark Punter every Sunday (12-2pm) where vinyl records from as far back as the 1950s are played. New and upcoming vinyl releases are also discussed, and Mark runs various little competitions for the listening audience.

Over the years they have had many bands play in-store. The shop received its first complaint from the local council, as reported in the local papers, when the band The Ends played and decided during their set to venture outside onto the high street to entertain passers-by. People stopped to watch and listen as well as dance for about 20 minutes. These events always go down well, as did this one, except for one person complaining. Fives Records was rather pleased with all the publicity generated by the incident, following which, they tell me, all bands playing the shop are welcome to venture onto the pavement.

Intense Records

33-34 Viaduct Road, Chelmsford, Essex CM1 1TS
0124534 7372
intenserecords.com; info@intenserecords.co.uk; @intenserecords
Monday-Saturday 10am-6pm
Established 1999
Stock: Vinyl, CDs, DJ Equipment, Tickets, T-shirts, Turntables

This shop is easy to visit by public transport, being located under the viaduct of Chelmsford railway station, which in turn is next to the bus station. It is an atmospheric location as the shop roof is constructed of corrugated iron within two arches. The trains pass directly overhead so the constant rumbles mix in with the music.

Jonathan Smith was always going to open a record shop. When studying at Chelmsford College, he wrote a business plan on how to open one. A few years later, studying Business Management at Birmingham University, he wrote a thesis on "Why people buy vinyl off the internet". Both projects turned out to have been instrumental in shaping his career.

While at university, Jonathan started organising student nights that gave him the opportunity to test out his blossoming DJ skills. He moved into a house with four fellow DJs and there was great competition among them to be the first to get their hands on the latest vinyl releases.

Jonathan had a brainwave. He decided to open accounts with record companies, informing them he was a mail order company. The problem was that record companies would only ship orders if they reached their minimum order level, which was normally around £50-£75. Jonathan therefore began ordering extra copies and selling them to his housemates and fellow students. Soon he had a genuine mail order operation as he was also supplying his mates back in Chelmsford.

As part of his course in Business Management, Jonathan was required to set up a pretend business. But he was already doing it for real. Having based all his coursework on his experience of setting up the mail-order business, he duly graduated with flying colours.

Jonathan bought the domain name www.intenserecords.co.uk and proceeded to build a website where customers could search and listen to all the tracks before ordering, and the records would be posted from his office, which was his bedroom. During the next break from university he returned to Chelmsford, where he discovered a new record shop had opened. It was not stocking much drum & bass, which was his forte, so he struck up a deal with the owner to supply the shop with all the latest drum & bass vinyl. Jonathan would collect any profits due when he returned during term breaks. This arrangement continued successfully until he graduated from university and needed a job.

He persuaded the record shop owner to go into partnership with him, Jonathan would sell drum & bass while the owner concentrated on other genres of music. The shop was divided into two, with both having their own counters and walls to display their records. Unfortunately, they both had a set of decks resulting in "counter wars" as they both vied to play their own records. It soon became clear that Jonathan was attracting a greater share of the customers and that he had outgrown the shared premises. He thus resolved to find his own site where he could play drum & bass to his heart's content.

Jonathan opened his own shop in December 2003. On a memorable first day he played Santa, wrapping 50 packages of 12-inch singles in Christmas paper and giving them away to his first 50 customers. He held a launch party that was a huge triumph, with more than 500 people attending. It was so successful that after the "launch" party he had a "landed" party a couple of weeks later.

The Essex Chronicle came down to interview him for a feature. It was arranged for early morning. Jonathan had been playing a club the previous evening, so the combination of excess drink and minimal sleep resulted in the paper printing a picture of a rather bleary and dishevelled record shop owner to accompany the piece. The next day when walking to work, he noticed the less-than-flattering picture on a lamp post. Soon he was to see dozens more as, unbeknown to him, his mates had printed off 50 posters and fly-posted them all over Chelmsford.

For Jonathan, the best thing about owning Intense Records is that it was where he met his wife Jen. She had been a customer of the shop for more than three years, but always came in with a guy called Pete. Jonathan assumed that they were partners. One day Jen came in on her own and Jonathan enquired if she was still with Pete. Jen explained that Pete was just a mate she went shopping with for vinyl. The rest, as they say, is history.

From 2002 things got tough as record retailing went into a steep decline. Jonathan did everything in his power to keep the business on an even keel. He was organising dance parties, running a website, working in the shop and even set up a separate company running coaches to house parties, although they were never hired to transport the local Women's Institute for a day trip to Clacton.

Jonathan also became a DJ on various pirate radio stations producing a two hour show each week featuring his own Top 10 dance chart. He would produce adverts for his shop on the radio and noticed that whatever background music he used on his adverts would immediately become the shop's best seller over the following weeks.

With business still slow, he decided to rent out half the shop to another business. Luckily, he found the perfect tenant. Jen, his wife, had started a merchandise printing company called Get Customised, and she moved her operation into the shop. In 2013 the shop's fortunes revived. It was no coincidence that it was the first year that Intense Records took part in Record Store Day. As the shop was new to the party, Jonathan only dipped into the many releases available. He was apprehensive that the music fans of Chelmsford would not come to a drum & bass shop to buy rock and pop releases. The shop had its best sales day ever. Many people commented that they had never come in before because they thought it was only drum & bass. It was a turning point in the history of the shop. With the new-found customer base that they had gained, they changed direction and started selling all genres of music.

By 2017, Jen's business had outgrown the shop and she moved out to her own offices.

Most people reading this have probably owned one of her products. In 2015 she was commissioned to print the official Record Store Day plastic carrier bags and other memorabilia supplied to participating shops. If you bought a record on RSD it is almost certain that you carried it home in one of these bags and many UK record shops have continued to use her services.

Jen's departure allowed the record shop to expand and Jonathan has since allocated one arch of the shop to dance music while the other arch sells a range of genres. The best time to visit Intense is the first Saturday of the month. That is when Jonathan organises the Chelmsford Record Fair in The Ale House, a few doors down from the shop. Live bands and DJ's play on the day and Jonathan organises his own burger and coffee stalls.

Intense is an ideal name for the shop as it describes how Jonathan's life has been for nearly 30 years. Jonathan and Jen are great examples of how independent record shops have had to diversify to survive. In this dynamic duo's case they have diversified to thrive.

Music Mania   * Does anybody know Madness?*
18 High Street, Clacton-on-Sea, Essex CO15 1NR
01255 222844
malcolmstone68@yahoo.co.uk
Monday-Thursday 9am-5.30pm Friday/Saturday 9am-6pm
Established 2002
Stock: Vinyl, CD, Pre-owned, DVD, Merchandise, T-shirts

Unlike other seaside towns, such as Margate and Broadstairs, Clacton still has a way to go before it becomes fashionable. Walking down to Music Mania, I pass the brilliantly-named Codgers of Clacton selling comfy beds, next door to Easy Mobility, selling mobility scooters, shops which rather sum up the atmosphere of the town. It reminds me of seaside resorts such as Skegness and Great Yarmouth that look as if they might benefit from investment and which I would describe as cheap and cheerful. Sitting comfortably in this environment is Malcolm Stone's shop Music Mania.

Malcolm is definitely cheerful and his vinyl is undeniably cheap. Indeed, his prices are among the lowest I have ever come across in UK record shops. Vinyl fans in the town are spoilt, and several dealers from London are happy to travel through the notorious Colchester ring road to make regular visits to the shop.

Malcolm has always been an enthusiastic record collector so much so that between 1983 and 1990 he bought every single to enter the Top 40. If you are a fan of the band Madness, then this is the shop for you. Malcolm owns the largest Madness collection in the world (as far as he knows). He claims not to be obsessive, but nevertheless owns more than 100 variations of the *One Step Beyond* album on cassette, CD and vinyl from all over the globe. Other Madness product he owns includes:

A Madness fruit machine in full working order of which there were only 50 made.

All manner of different shaped picture discs.

Acetates signed by Suggs.

Discs awarded to members of the band.

"One Step Beyond" 7-inch on clear vinyl which Malcolm believes to be the only one in existence.

A vast collection of memorabilia, posters and badges.

An extensive knowledge of the band.

The shop's favourite customer is known as the Alphabet Woman. Every week she comes in and shouts out a letter. It is then Malcolm's job to recommend a record by an artist whose name begins with that letter. So far, she has never complained about any of Malcolm's choices. He did think he would struggle when she asked for Z, but she seemed happy enough with a record by the Romanian pan flute player Gheorghe Zamfir. Even Malcolm had to concede defeat with X as the Alphabet Woman is not really a fan of indie, rap or punk so The xx, Xzibit and X-Ray Spex were out. Recently she is becoming more specific, so instead of asking for an artist beginning with J, she will ask for one beginning JU.

Before he retires from record retailing, Malcolm's great hope is that one day a member of Madness will walk into the shop and purchase something from him. If you know any of the band members, please pass this message on. Malcolm promises to wear his baggy trousers for the visit.

Slipped Discs
57- 59 High Street, Billericay, Essex CM12 9AX
01277 631422
slipped-discs.co.uk; s.discs@btconnect.com
Monday-Saturday 10am-6pm Sunday 11am-4pm
Established 2008
Stock: Vinyl, CD, Pre-owned, Coffee, Food, Licensed

Slipped Discs is one of the most aromatic record shops you will ever come across due to the smell of fresh coffee wafting out of the Brown Sugar Café located at the back. As the name implies, owner Carl Newsum is a big Rolling Stones fan (as opposed to injuries of the vertebrae).

The shop has a great location right in the middle of the high street and is extremely popular with locals. On arrival you are greeted by a vast selection of CDs and vinyl along with some comfy chairs to relax in. As you venture further in, you notice that the back of the shop is a cafe and there is hardly a spare seat as people relax over a coffee or something from the extensive menu.

The walls are adorned with some magnificent pop art, many items created by local artist Nick Dillon (check out the Noel Gallagher collage). Pride of place is taken by a Ronnie Wood print that Carl obtained from Ronnie's brother. While the shop plays music at normal volume, it is much quieter in the cafe. Customers are encouraged to select music they would like to listen to while they sip their lattes. The shop attracts mothers and toddlers and Carl does a roaring trade in children's CDs.

Carl has invested £50,000 in turning what was previously a bookshop into the record store he has always wanted. It was a brave move to invest so much at a time when many shops were closing, but others have since followed his model. The old record shop model was not working. Slipped Discs would not be here today if Carl had not had the vision to diversify.

Carl is a genuine Essex boy and, in his youth, spent his spare time travelling into London to buy records. By the time he left school he had acquired a vast collection. He wanted to work in music but ended up working as a greengrocer, which certainly gave him a grounding in how to sell.

At the age of 22 he took the plunge and rented a tiny shop in an alley off Billericay High Street. He had saved and borrowed a total of £5,000 but made the mistake of buying premium racking, which set him back £3,500. He spent the rest on stock, but £1,500 did not go far. Everybody could see what great racking he had, because hardly any of it was obscured by stock. Carl felt he had no option but to add his whole record collection to the stock.

After a year, the shop moved from the alley onto what Carl describes as "the dog-end of the street". It was the very last shop on the street, but the new location at least had some passing trade. Then, in 1997, Carl heard on the grapevine that a musical instrument shop in Chelmsford was looking to rent out a floor. He contacted the landlord and they agreed a deal where Carl would have the ground floor to sell recorded music, and the instruments would be sold upstairs.

Carl was excited by this opportunity to expand and quickly agreed terms. Unfortunately, due to a breakdown in communication, when he arrived with a truck full of stock to move in, the ground floor was still racked out with musical instruments. There was

Top photo is of The Record Shop in Amersham which was turned in to Record Collector Sheffield for the Sky TV programme Urban Myths.

The original Record Collector in Sheffield. I visited this shop on my first day as a sales rep 32 years ago and am still selling to owner Barry Everard

King of self-publicity Iain Aitchison wearing his Longwell Records hat-shirt and jacket. If you enlarge this photo you will see nine references to the shop.

Pure Vinyl, a reggae and soul specialist in Brixton. The charismatic owner is local DJ Claudia Wilson who is so passionate about playing you music that I would be surprised if you left the shop without a purchase.

The queue outside Drift in Totnes on Record Store Day.

81 Renshaw Street in Liverpool. A must visit for Beatles fans.

Jam Records in Falmouth with Bob, the shop's resident dog.

Maria Harris, owner of Tallbird Records in Chesterfield. The humorous name of the shop refers to what she was called in less PC times.

Owner Laurie Dale with long-time assistant Richie Westmacott of Dales in Tenby.
Photo Gareth Davies Photography Tenby.

X Records in Bolton who have the most artistic shutter that I have ever seen.

Jacaranda Records in Liverpool, home to an original 1948 Voice-O-Graph machine, which allows customers to cut their own two-minute record.

The perfect destination for lovers of good food and vinyl records.
The wonderful Pie & Vinyl in Southsea.

Phonica Records is one of the many great record shops in Soho. Check out the sofa that looks out on to Poland Street giving you the chance to people watch whilst listening to music.

The Record Deck. A record shop that floats any vinyl lovers boat. You will find it touring UK canals when not moored on the River Lea in Hackney.

chaos as members of staff struggled to move the instruments upstairs while Carl was loading his stock in through the front door. He decided it would be easier to help them, before bringing any more stock in. As he moved a display cabinet of saxophones, part of the chimney collapsed, and bricks tumbled down around him. When the dust had settled, he surveyed his new premises. All the CDs and racking were covered in dust and bricks were strewn over the floor. It was not the best start, and trading was delayed while builders repaired the chimney breast.

Carl based himself at the new location in Chelmsford while his assistant Paul Moody, who still works with him today, took over the running of the original Billericay shop. Among the first of the regular customers were Liam Howlett and Keith Flint from The Prodigy, one of the UK's most successful dance music groups. Carl describes Keith (whose scary look was known to send young kids scurrying behind the sofa) as one of the nicest people he has ever met. He would often hang about the shop for hours talking about music.

Carl took the biggest gamble of his life in 2010, when he and his wife Karen moved into their current premises in the middle of the High Street. Formerly a bookshop, it is three times the size of their previous shop. Karen runs the café and the couple have done a brilliant job of creating the perfect meeting place for music fans. All the cakes are homemade (by Karen) and I can vouch for the almond slice. If other record shop owners are considering adding a coffee shop, pay Slipped Discs a visit to see how it should be done.

South Record Shop

22 Queens Rd, Southend-On-Sea SS1 1LU
01702 826166
southrecordshop.com; shop@southrecordshop.com; @southrecordshop
Monday-Saturday 10am-7pm Sunday 11am-4pm
Established 2013
Stock: Vinyl, CD, Pre-owned, In-stores

Canvey-born Richard Onslow could not believe that a town such as Southend did not have an independent record shop. After working with the biggest names in music, such as the White Stripes and Katy Perry, during stints as a PR for major record labels EMI and XL Records, he decided to rectify the situation.

With an impressive array of collectable vinyl, the shop has a welcoming atmosphere and if you ask nicely Richard may even make you a cup of liquorice tea. He has established the shop as a musical hub and a meeting place for music fans in the town. One feature you can't help but notice is the safe located to the left of the counter. It offers no worthwhile purpose other than to display leaflets on. It was built into the shop so when Richard acquired the premises the safe came with it. Unfortunately, there are no keys for it and you could only access it with dynamite. Still, it looks impressive and is a big talking point.

Richard always makes a big effort for Record Store Day and in 2015 he secured the services of locally-based comedian and broadcaster Phill Jupitus to DJ in the shop. Phill has been a great supporter of record shops and had spent a previous Record Store Day working behind the counter at Spillers in Cardiff.

Vinyl Van
Various markets in the Essex, Hertfordshire area and music festivals
07939 956065
vinyl-van.com; sales@vinyl-van.com
Established 2018
Stock: Vinyl, Pre-owned, T-Shirts

Vinyl Van is the UK's only mobile record shop.

Jon Morris was unhappy about the lack of record stores in his local towns, so he built a mobile record store to provide vinyl fans with product. It took a while to source the right vehicle, but he eventually found a 1996 Citroen Relay that was formerly used as a mobile RAF recruitment office. Jon's mobile shop can pitch up anywhere to sell records and play tunes thanks to the batteries and solar panels he has fitted. Don't leave the van without purchasing one of his music-related doormats.

If you would like Vinyl Van to attend at your event, get in touch with Jon.

Gloucestershire & Worcestershire

Anybody considering opening a record shop should investigate Gloucester. Not only is it the largest city in the UK not to have a team in the English football league but it is also the largest city in the UK without a record shop that participates in Record Store Day. It has a population of just over 128,000, yet nearby Cinderford in the Forest of Dean with a population of just 8,000 manages to sustain two record shops. However, for those in need of a vinyl fix in Gloucester, Darren Wilks at Vinyl Vital Signs in the Eastgate market, stocks new and pre-owned vinyl - but is only open on Saturdays.

Worcestershire is famous for the Lea & Perrins sauce it produces, but not for record shops selling new vinyl. Worcester, Kidderminster and Bromsgrove are worth exploring for those thinking of opening a record shop.

Badlands

11 St George's Place, Cheltenham, Gloucestershire GL50 3LA
01242 246242
badlands.co.uk,shop@badlands.co.uk; @BadlandsUK
Monday-Saturday: 9.00am-5:30pm
Established 1985
Stock: Vinyl, CD, Tickets, In-stores

Cheltenham is a town famous for its spa and horse racing festival. But for Bruce Springsteen fans Cheltenham means one thing: Badlands Records. Not only is Badlands a great record shop but it is the world's number one specialist in Springsteen. As well as his music, they also sell a vast range of merchandise, concert tickets and even organise holidays around the world to see The Boss perform.

The shop was started by two Manchester-born brothers, Phil and Steven Jump who have lived in the area since they were toddlers when their parents moved to the Cotswolds. After leaving school, Phil worked in insurance while Steven started a painting and decorating business. Phil left his job after the company refused to give him time off to travel to Leicester to see The Jam. He started working with Steven in the painting and decorating business, but profits were increasingly being spent on expanding Steven's record collection. One day while at the top of a ladder above a butcher's shop in Cheltenham high street, Phil shouted down to Steven that he had had enough of painting and wanted to pack it in. They stopped there and then, and never went back to the butcher's to collect their brushes and half-used tins of paint, which may be still up there on the roof.

The following Saturday, on a cold October day in 1985, they set off with a pile of records to Evesham market where they hired a stall for £3.50. They took £38 on the first day of trading. The brothers had different tastes in music but the one artist they both loved was Bruce Springsteen. They chose the name Badlands after the opening track from the album *Darkness on the Edge of Town*. A song about a man down on his luck, angry with the world and looking for a better life, it resonated with both of them.

The turning point for Badlands was when one of the biggest collectors of Springsteen memorabilia contacted them to say he was moving abroad and wanted to dispose of his collection. The asking price was £3,000 and much as they wanted to buy the lot, the brothers did not have that much spare cash. They contacted another avid fan and between them they raised the money. The purchasers decided the best way of splitting the collection was to put all the records on the floor and take turns at picking what they wanted.

Choosing the name Badlands turned out to be an inspirational move. Soon Springsteen collectors throughout the world were sending them their wish lists. By accident Badlands was becoming a Springsteen specialist. Soon an opportunity came to move to bigger premises (well 10-foot by 10-foot) in an outlet above BHS in the Regent Arcade. Thanks to a government initiative, their rent was covered by a grant. The only stipulation was that they had to attend college one day a week to study business skills.

They took customer service to new levels. If somebody asked for a title they did not have they would say it would be in later that afternoon. When the customer had left one of them would rush out of the shop and call in to one of the other record shops in town to purchase the item. They would then sell it to the customer on his return but make no money on the deal. For them it was more important that the customer came back and the constant running between the shops kept the boys fit.

Not long after opening, Badlands had another stroke of good fortune. Sony, one of the UK's biggest record companies, had a dispute with Our Price who at that time had a large branch in Cheltenham. The result was that they stopped offering product to the Our Price shops temporarily. Sony phoned Badlands to ask if they would like a credit account and offered most favourable terms. Phil and Steven took up the offer and filled the shop with Sony product, enjoying the fact that Our Price had no Sony new releases or back catalogue in their Cheltenham shop. They then phoned the other record companies to inform them how well they were doing with their new credit account from Sony and all then offered them credit terms.

In 1989, Badlands founded The Ties That Bind, an unofficial Bruce Springsteen fan club which has proved a great success. They produce a quarterly magazine and give the club's 2,000-plus members' discounts on mail order and shop purchases.

The shop is so successful at selling tickets that they are the only alternative outlet that the Harvey Goldsmith organisation allows to be official Bruce Springsteen ticket sellers. It is thanks to the Springsteen connection that Badlands continues to thrive. According to Sony the shop is responsible for 10% of all Springsteen sales in the UK. Badlands regularly has artists playing the shop. They are still waiting for Springsteen to turn up and do an acoustic set, but they count passionate performances from Frank Turner and Billy Bragg among their favourite events so far.

The shop was voted Independent Record Shop of the year in 2010. Jump Travel Ltd is the Badlands Travel Company, set up to create well-designed holiday packages for the greatest shows around the world. Initially concentrating on tours by Springsteen, Bob Dylan and the Rolling Stones along with a host of other legendary acts, their packages combine excellent seats for the show with top class hotels near the concert venue itself or within the city center of the holiday destination.

Having been avid concertgoers themselves (both brothers have seen Springsteen more than 100 times), Phil and Steven know what makes a well-designed package.

They will often arrange social gatherings or pre-show parties where you can meet up with like-minded fans from around the world. They recommend bookings at some of their favourite restaurants for a pre-show get together and where possible arrange excursions or guided tours of the area. The Memphis packages include visits not just to the concerts but also to Gracelands, Sun Studios and The National Civil Rights Museum.

Phil informs me that they have had people who have met on their trips and got married. One couple had their wedding on a trip. Many of these couples now have children. They were impressed with one customer's dedication to Springsteen, when the fan left the trip to go back for the birth of his child before returning to finish his holiday.

The shop suffered a desperate blow in September 2013 when Steven unexpectedly passed away at the age of 56. He brought joy into the lives of thousands of music fans throughout the world, and his memory lives on in this great record store.

Carnival Records
83, Church Street, Great Malvern, Worcestershire WR14 2AE
016844 38120
carnivalrecords@icloud.com; @carnivalrecords
Monday-Sunday11am-5pm
Established 2011
Stock: Vinyl, Pre-loved, CD, Coffee, T-shirts, Vintage Hi-fi

Carnival Records, owned by Rachel and Chris Heard, is a delightful, quirky record shop in the scenic Malvern Hills. In 2014 it was voted one of the best 10 indie record shops in the world in a poll in *The Guardian*. Rachel and Chris also run their own record label, Three Black Feathers, releasing top quality folk albums by artists including Dick Gaughan and Lal Waterson. The label was praised by Kate Rusby on BBC Radio 2's Radcliffe and Maconie show, when she rhapsodised about her all-time favourite LP, *Penguin Eggs* by Nic Jones, which was reissued in a special "audiophile" 200g heavyweight vinyl edition by Three Black Feathers in 2009.

Now that Rise in Worcester has closed, the county does not have any record shop officially taking part in Record Store Day. Carnival Records celebrate RSD each year with a half-price vinyl sale and a live mini-festival featuring many bands. Although you won't be able to purchase any of the official RSD releases, I guarantee you will enjoy the carnival atmosphere.

Ceritech Audio

Drake House,1 Pavilion Business Park, Cinderford, Gloucestershire GL14 2YD
01600 716362
ceritech-audio.co.uk; sales@ceritech-audio.co.uk; @CeritechAudio
Tuesday-Saturday 9.30am-5.30pm
Stock: Vinyl, Audio Equipment

Cinderford is a small town on the eastern fringe of the Forest of Dean and despite having a population of less than 9,000, it has the highest percentage of record shops per head in the UK.

To enter Ceritech Audio, you must press the buzzer and be let into the showroom. Owners Simon and Sam Jackson run one of the UK's most renowned hi-fi dealerships with systems costing up to £25,000. Over the last few years the interest in record players has been phenomenal and they felt it was a logical progression to start stocking high quality new vinyl. The shop has listening rooms where you can experience the quality of the sound. With its proximity to the famous Rockfield recording studios the shop attracts many musicians and can count the Manic Street Preachers as regular customers.

Forest Vinyl

Unit 7, Hollyhill Park, Hollyhill Road, Cinderford, Gloucestershire GL14 2YB
07751 404393.
forestvinyl.co.uk; info@forestvinyl.co.uk; @ForestVinyl
Tuesday-Friday 11am-5pm
Established 2015
Stock: Vinyl, Pre-owned, Cassettes, Memorabilia

This shop is a rock vinyl store and although most stock is Pre-owned there is a good selection of new product too. Steve Helsdown was an area manager for a bingo company before a heart attack made him re-evaluate his priorities. Having been a vinyl collector for more than 40 years, he decided to start trading on eBay to bring some cash in. Steve's dream had always been to have his own record shop and with the vinyl revival in full flow and with support from his wife he decided the time was right. He had been a regular customer at Ceritech Audio (see previous entry), where he was able to start out by renting the upstairs of the premises. Nobody was happier than Steve's wife who, after years of having vinyl records in every room, now has her house back.

In 2017 Steve moved out of Ceritech and now runs Forest Vinyl in a separate store.

The shop offers a fine assortment of rarities. It also has a stunning collection of music-based clocks, including one shaped like an electric guitar. The shop is also home to some antique gramophone players. Pride of place goes to a Wilson-Peck model from the 1930s. To control the sound, you open some wooden flaps, and to change the tone you shut the lid, quite a contrast to the modern equipment.

It is also one of the few record shops I know which sell cassettes, 8-tracks and mini-discs. Check out Steve's memorabilia. He has some collectable items, and many are signed. Forest vinyl makes fresh coffee for its customers (no instant here) and is happy to offer you a cup of tea if you prefer.

Sanctuary Music

Acorn House, 42 Nailsworth Mill Estate, Nailsworth, GL6 0BS
01453 704481
sanctuary-music.co.uk; ash@sanctuary-music.co.uk; @SanctuaryMusic2
Monday-Saturday 9am-5pm
Established 2018
Stock: Vinyl, Pre-owned, Books, T-shirts, Turntables

The attractive Cotswold town of Nailsworth, sited in an Area of Outstanding National Beauty, is full of fascinating independently owned shops but is probably best known for its football team Forest Green Rovers. Due to the efforts of the club chairman the Club, as well as being completely vegan, is the most environmentally friendly club in the league. The football pitch is organic with solar panels fitted on the stands and is mowed by a robot!

It is in this town where you will find a fabulous new record shop that opened its doors on Record Store Day 2018. Ash Hunt had a Medico-Legal Reporting company which his record shop partner and friend, Adrian Couborough, worked at. Unfortunately, Ash had to take a long time out of the business due to a serious health problem and it gave him a chance to contemplate his future.

His twelfth birthday which was on 28 October 1977 coincided with the release of the Sex Pistols releasing *Never Mind the Bollocks*. Ash has never forgotten the excitement of purchasing that album from Sanctuary Record Shop in Lincoln. In honour of the shop, in which he would spend so much of his youth, he has named his shop Sanctuary Music.

Although in the centre of town this beautifully designed shop is located in an unusual place. It is in a courtyard with a huge mill being renovated on one side and Morrison's supermarket on the other.

As you step in the door the first thing that will catch your eye is a wonderful genuine 1976 American Rockola jukebox. Customers are encouraged to put a record on and it has the bonus of being free. If you ask nicely and they are not too busy they will even open it up, so you can see how it works!

Sound Records Stroud
24, Gloucester Street, Stroud, Gloucestershire GL5 1QG
07941 46359
Soundvinylrecords@gmail.com
Wednesday-Friday 11am-6pm
Saturday 10am-6pm
Established 2018
Stock: Vinyl, Pre-owned

Sound Records Stroud is a partnership between local DJs and record dealers Sean Roe and Tom Berry, whose dream of opening a record store became a reality after they snapped up an empty lot in Stroud. After weeks of crate digging and assembling Ikea furniture, the shop opened.

Sean and Tom have got a few decks set up in the shop, so there is always something groovy playing when you walk in. Being DJs, they open later than most record shops. "Because the shop is so small we have to be a little fussy about the stock we carry," Paul says. "So if you want Paul Young's *No Parlez* you'll need to ask elsewhere."

Trading Post
26 Kendrick Street, Stroud, Gloucestershire GL5 1AQ
01453 759116
simon@tradingpost.freeserve.co.uk; @TradingPostRecs
Monday-Friday 9.30am-5.30pm
Established
Stock: Vinyl, CD, Pre-owned

Stroud, once described by the *Evening Standard* as "Notting Hill with wellies", is the kind of town I could live in. Acknowledged as one of the founders of the organic food market, it is home to an artistic community with many studios, including one owned by Damien Hirst. It is full of independent shops, including many great cafés and on Saturdays it boasts an award-winning farmer's market full of local produce. It is no surprise that no record store chains such as Our Price or HMV ever opened in the town.

More in keeping with Stroud's spirit of independence is the Trading Post owned by Simon Vincent. Simon was born and grew up in Stroud before moving to Staffordshire. One of his early musical memories was his mum taking him to see Hawkwind. Not only did the band include Lemmy, who went on to form Motorhead, but also featured the model Stacia, who danced on stage topless and covered in luminescent paint, a sight that Simon has never forgotten.

Simon began writing songs from an early age. He rates "Angels" as the best song he ever wrote – together with Adam Gamble as one half of the duo Stumpy The Pigeon Slayer – although it never quite achieved the success of the Robbie Williams song of the same name. After leaving school, Simon spent 15 successful years in banking. At the age of 33 years, 4 months (33-and-a-third) he had made enough money to start working for himself. In 1982 he found himself hanging out at Trading Post, his local record shop, where he became friendly with the owners Jo and Phil Walters. Jo was a former Chrysalis records employee who had opened the shop in the punk era. It was the only shop for miles around that promoted punk, and fans from as far afield as Cheltenham and Gloucester would congregate there on Saturday afternoons.

Business slowed down drastically over the years, partly due to a redevelopment of the town centre that left the shop (in Nelson Street) cut off from the main shopping area. Simon sensed an opportunity and asked Jo if they were interested in selling the shop. Jo told Simon that she "could not think of a better father for her baby". Simon was relieved to realise she was referring to the shop and a deal was done.

Simon soon found out that enthusiasm was not enough to make the business profitable. He looked at many avenues to increase income and soon came up with an idea that other record shops might well consider in future. He advertised for people to leave their unwanted records with him. After taking the person's address and phone number he would sticker the collection, with each customer's records having their own code. He sold them and split the proceeds 50/50. The owners of the records could come in whenever convenient to collect cash for what had been sold. Word quickly spread about the scheme and Simon's half-empty shelves were soon overflowing with stock. For Simon, it has helped his cash flow and he describes the scheme as "fair trade", which is apt as Stroud is a fair-trade town. His scheme also attracted publicity in the local press.

One day a man brought in a box of records, asking if Simon would sell them for him. Later that day another man came in and mentioned to Simon that a collection of his records had been stolen from a boot sale the previous Sunday. Simon realised they were the records that had been brought in a few days earlier, and immediately took them down to the police station to announce the solving of the case. As he had taken the thief's details it was an easy task for the police to trace him. Simon returned the records to their rightful owner who expressed his gratitude by making a donation to a local charity. It was good news all round and the publicity brought more people in to sell the fair-trade way. Simon was later interviewed on the BBC One programme *Inside Out* about his scheme.

Among the famous faces that have visited the shop is actor Keith Allen, a regular customer, who buys new recordings by his daughter Lily. Another regular is Mike d'Abo, the singer in Manfred Mann, who introduced himself by holding one of his own CDs - with a picture of his much younger self - next to his face and saying "Recognise anybody?" One of the UK's most successful singers, Sade, lives near Stroud. She has yet to grace the shop with a visit. "She walked past one day on her way to the Chinese takeaway opposite," Simon notes, wryly.

In 2009 Simon moved Trading Post to a more central location in the town, since when business has more than doubled. If you are in the Gloucestershire area for Record Store Day, then a visit to Trading Post is a must. Each year Simon brings in celebrities to do DJ sets in the shop, including Neil Arthur (Blancmange), Carl Harrison (Sisters Of Mercy), Patrick Baladi (*The Office*, *Stella*) and Keith Allen. The bar they set up for the day is run by the Australian singer-songwriter Emily Barker.

Best-selling author Rachel Joyce lives in the town and shops at the Trading Post. Her 2017 novel *The Music Shop*, which is set in a record shop, has been a great international success and was adapted for BBC Radio 4's *Book at Bedtime*. Many people come to the Trading Post thinking it was the inspiration for the book. Simon tells them it is not, but it does not do trade any harm to let people think otherwise.

The shop has become an important part of the community. The people of Stroud support their local independent businesses and I am sure they will continue to support the Trading Post.

"It is an experience putting a record on and hearing the needle hit the groove and I don't think that can ever really be matched with other formats," Simon says. "People have tried to get rid of vinyl, but it keeps coming back."

Hampshire

When Record Store Day started, Hampshire did not have a single record shop selling new vinyl. Luckily, plenty of visionary vinyl fans have since had the foresight to open shops there, with seven new shops since 2016. Every music fan should make a pilgrimage to the wonderfully quirky Pie & Vinyl in Southsea. Romsey is lucky to have such a great new record shop as Hundred Records, a new musical oasis in the town. And, thankfully, someone has finally had the vision to open a record shop in Southampton: Vinilo which incorporates a vegan coffee bar.

A Slice Of Vinyl
134 High Street, Gosport, Hampshire PO12 1EA
keironvinyl@hotmail.com; @sliceofvinyl
Tuesday-Saturday 9.30am-5pm
Saturday 9am-5.30pm
Established 2018
Stock: Vinyl, Pre-owned, Memorabilia, Musical instruments

When Keiron Howes was a toddler, his Mum would place him in front of the TV where they would watch *Top of the Pops* together, while Keiron bashed away on a "drum kit" of pots and pans.

Growing up, Kieron always wanted to own a record shop and started out selling vinyl on Gosport market. After a few successful years, he opened A Slice Of Vinyl, the perfect name for a record shop café selling vinyl and cakes. The shop has a wonderful logo of a vinyl "cake" with a slice cut out.

Kieron trialled the idea at a pop-up shop in Gosport, but his skill-set was more Chuck Berry than Mary Berry and the baking was a disaster. He reverted to selling just records until a local café owner offered him a permanent base. Now you can go for a bite at Katie's Vinyl Bar and Café, then pop upstairs to purchase your vinyl.

The saying you can never judge a book by its cover will resonate with all record shop owners, as this tale from Keiron shows.

"This guy, who was a massive punk in the full get up, looking very scary, came up to me carrying a couple of albums. We started talking music and it turned out he was in the Vibrators and had been an original member of the Lurkers. We had an enjoyable chat with him telling me tales of the past and what the bands are up to now. After the conversation this massive punk handed me albums by Aretha Franklin and Roberta Flack. This taught me that anyone can fall in love with any sort of music no matter what background. It didn't put my nose out of joint - it realigned it, helping me understand that people don't just like the music you expect them to. It encouraged me to broaden the range of genres I stock and to make my stock as varied as possible."

Elephant Records *The shop with a name you are unlikely to forget*
8 Kings Walk, Winchester, Hampshire SO23 8AF
07871 188474
elephantrecordshop@gmail.com; @elephantrecshop
Monday-Saturday 10am-6pm Sunday 11am-4pm
Established 2016
Stock: Vinyl, CD, Pre-owned

Alex Brown worked at the Winchester Discovery Centre for 15 years. He jumped at the offer of voluntary redundancy, using the money to help him open his own record shop. Elephant Records has been a voyage of discovery which started off with Alex selling his own vast vinyl collection and is now known for the selection of cutting-edge new releases it stocks. It is not an easy shop to find, but it is well worth the effort to do so.

Harbour Records *"What did you get for Christmas?" "A record shop"* *
29, High Street, Emsworth, Hampshire PO10 7AG
harbour-records.co.uk; harbourrecordsemsworth@gmail.com
Monday-Saturday 10am-4.30pm
Established 2017
Stock: Vinyl, CD, Pre-owned

Emsworth is a beautiful town with a great sailing tradition. It is not somewhere you would expect to find a record shop. But I am happy to report that I did. Colin Thomas was asked by his friend (and then owner of Harbour Records) to look after the shop for three months while he went to visit family in Australia. Colin enjoyed himself so much that when the owner returned, Colin enquired if he was interested in selling it. Having been informed that he was, that evening Colin went down the pub with his mates Ken Brown and Rob Moore. All three of them already being involved in music through promoting gigs in the Portsmouth area.

  Colin: "Fancy buying a record shop lads?"

  Ken: "Why not?"

  Rob: "Good idea."

  The boys decided it would make a perfect Christmas present for themselves, as all three harboured (forgive the pun) the dream of opening their own record shop. The rest of the evening was spent talking about how they were going to transform a sleepy old second-hand record shop into a vibrant, exciting place with new vinyl too.

  A deal was done and the week before Christmas they opened their doors. I'm pleased to report they have done a great job.

Heathen Chemistry

130 West Street, Fareham, Hampshire PO16 OEL
01329 600303
heathenchemistryrecords.com; info@heathenchemistryrecords.com;
@heathenchemistryrecords
Monday/Friday 10am-5pm Tuesday/Thursday 12noon-8pm
Saturday 9am-5pm Sunday 12noon-4pm Wednesday closed
Established 2017
Stock: Vinyl, Pre-owned 7-inch, Art, T-shirts

Heathen Chemistry is named after the fifth album by Oasis. Released in 2002, it is owner Simon Dampier's favourite record by the Mancunian band. If you too are a fan, then this is the shop for you. Simon has amassed some very collectable Oasis records and memorabilia, including exclusive prints, all of which are for sale. A good reason to visit is that he has some of the cheapest pre-owned singles I have come across. While the collectable singles sell at reasonable/normal prices, his "15p-each or 10-for-£1" singles section is understandably popular.

The shop is situated in an area in which independent shops have been encouraged to open. West Street is very long and at one end you have the usual high street shops, while the other is the independent sector. The area has attracted a lot of publicity, though the local paper reporting that an independent funeral director has recently opened is unlikely to bring much crossover trade for Simon.

The layout of Heathen Vinyl is long and narrow, with pre-owned vinyl on one side and new product on the other. Simon sits at an illuminated counter which he has turned into a work of art. Decorated with vinyl, it is an impressive sight, especially in the evening.

Hundred Records

47, The Hundred, Romsey, Hampshire SO51 8GE
01794518655
mark@hundredrecords.com; hundredrecords.com; @HundredRecs
Monday-Friday 10am-5pm
Saturday 9am-5pm
Established: 2014
Stock: Vinyl, CDs, Books, In-stores, Merchandise

Mark Wills opened Hundred Records after taking voluntary redundancy (or as his wife Anna puts it, "being paid to go away"). The investment (or "gamble" as Anna calls it) has enabled him to squeeze a living out of doing something that he loves. No one gets rich from running an independent record shop and holidays are more likely to be in Southend than the South Pacific.

Hundred Records is part of the new wave of independent record shops which have opened as an anti-digital reaction that has contributed to the vinyl revival. The shop is based in a historic street called The Hundred, so named because it contains 100 buildings. Although quite small, the shop looks spacious and the decor is impressive. Most of the fixtures are wooden, and Mark displays much of the vinyl in wine crates.

Mark has always been a vinyl collector. Growing up in Southampton, he bought his first record at Henry's Records and remembers the independent shops the city used to have such as Weasels, Underground and Subways. His working life as a sales manager for Lloyds Bank required him to drive around the country, and whenever time allowed he would pop into local record shops. His job was thus the opposite of mine. I would drive around the country selling records, he would drive around buying them.

Mark remembers with absolute clarity the first thing a customer bought from his shop. After months of planning and promotion, Hundred Records opened at 9am on November 15, 2014. Mark had been expecting a queue, but by 9.20am not a single person had walked through the door. Visions of bankruptcy were looming when, much to his relief, Mark's first customer bought a set of headphones and a Peter Gabriel CD. A steady stream of people followed many of whom said how delighted they were that Romsey now had its own record shop.

Mark describes Hundred Records as a "curated shop". Realising that he can't stock everything, he tries to ensure he knows everything he does stock, and tries to play as much new product as possible. Mark is a staunch supporter of local music and stocks all releases from local artists and musicians on a non-profit basis. It is a fabulous gesture, but as Mark puts it: "I want the local record shop to be a hub for musicians and I want people to talk about Hundred Records".

Another great initiative is the shop's Record of the Month. The criteria for qualifying is that Mark must like it. He will contact the distributor to see if they can offer any promotional stock, give extra discount or get the artist to visit the shop. Often, he will have a pre-release evening where customers can listen to the album over some refreshments and pre-order it. This is an idea other shops would do well to consider. When he had *Preternatural* by West Country art-rock band the Moulettes as his album of the month, he sold 135 copies.

"Running a record shop is the most fun you can have with your trousers on," Mark says, and working in the shop has certainly provided many laughs. On Record Store Day, Mark drafted his wife, Anna, in to help man the barricades. A teenager asked if they had the Front Bottoms in stock. Anna and the teenager blushed in bright tandem, as other customers burst out laughing, betraying their ignorance of this genuine, but unfortunately-named band.

The shop's most unusual customer is a man who always buys the best-known record by the most recently deceased music star. He is a medium who want to help the departed performer to reach "the next plane of existence". Listening to their hits helps him talk to these dead people. During 2016 alone, he came in for records by David Bowie, Prince, Merle Haggard, Glenn Frey, and Cilla Black. He came in to the shop soon after Lemmy died, and Mark had some Motorhead CDs lined up to offer him. But for some reason he did not ask. Either he wasn't a fan of speed metal or had decided that Lemmy did not need any help to pass over to the other side.

Hundred Records also claims to have the country's best-dressed customer. The gentleman concerned is never seen without either his top hat or his bowler. He always wears a yellow waistcoat and green cravat and carries a silver topped cane. His musical taste is described as "progressive" and he buys everything released on the KSCOPE label - Steven Wilson, Porcupine Tree and Anathema being among their top acts.

One ill-tempered customer asked for "Nights in Black Satin" by the Moody Blues. Mark told him that the song was called "Nights in White Satin", but the customer was so adamant that he convinced Mark to spend the next 10 minutes looking it up.

Even more ill-tempered was a woman who burst in to the shop, marched up to the counter and shouted at Mark for allowing her partner to spend too much money in the shop. She ordered him to stop selling her husband records and then promptly walked out. To this day Mark has no idea who the woman's husband is.

The shop puts on as many in-store events as possible. Any musician reading this who plans to be near Southampton should get in touch with Mark. He has hosted performances by Martin Simpson and many others. The most memorable event involved Larkin Poe, the American roots band fronted by the Lovell sisters. The band had not grasped how small the shop is and turned up on a hot summer's day with all their equipment, including a full drum kit. The shop can normally accommodate around 70 people for an event but by the time everything was set up the capacity had been reduced to about 40. It was an amazing gig, with people packed in like sardines. When the band finished, instead of signing their new CD from behind the counter, Mark set up a table on the pavement with some drinks, so that everyone could cool down.

Sales have grown steadily. The support from the independent distribution sector has been plentiful, from the majors, less so. Mark has been puzzled to find that major distributors don't seem to care about new businesses and small independent record shops. The companies he does most business with are Proper, Pias, Cargo and Discovery all of whom give him good credit terms and promotional support. The attitude of Sony, Warner Music and Universal is the complete opposite. According to Mark, "If you phone an independent distributor the first question is 'How can we help you?'. If you are speaking to a major it is more likely to be 'Why don't you just go away?' You don't feel like a customer you feel like you are being milked."

The industry needs to embrace shops like Hundred Records and it would benefit the major labels to get out of their offices and pay shops like this a visit. Being relatively new to music retailing, Mark is brimming with opinions and passion and sees things through fresh eyes. To see him in action enthusing to customers about the latest exciting record he has heard is a joy. So many of his customers end up leaving the shop with something they did not come in to buy, which is what can be so great about a good record shop.

The Record Shop IOW

Units 6-7, Central Market, Newport, Isle of Wight PO38 8JF
07709 708744
therecordshopiow.com; info@therecordshopiow.com; @therecordshopiow
Monday-Thursday 10am-4pm
Friday 10am-6pm
Saturday 10am-5pm
Established 2018
Stock: Vinyl, Merchandise, Turntables

I am delighted to report that enthusiastic couple Clive and Effie Moss have opened The Record Shop IOW, a dedicated vinyl shop in the heart of the Isle of Wight. The shop is close to where the historic music festival is held. The couple have had a fabulous response from both locals and tourists alike who enjoy digging through their genuine crates.

Pie & Vinyl *The record shop that produced Nick Cave pies*
61 Castle Rd, Southsea, Hampshire PO5 3AY
02392 753914
pieandvinyl.co.uk; steve@pieandvinyl.co.uk; @PieandVinyl
Monday-Wednesday 10am-7pm Thursday-Saturday 11am-9pm
Sunday 11am-5pm
Established 2012
Stock: Vinyl, Art, T-shirts, Pies

Steve Courtnell was thoroughly bored, sitting at his desk in a dead-end job at Estée Lauder, when he had his eureka moment. He vowed to open his own record shop and, from that moment on, began planning his great escape from the corporate world.

Having been a keen music fan from a young age with an obsessive personality, Steve feels that he is still on an eternal journey to find a piece of music or a song that makes him feel the way he did when he first heard a Neil Young record or watched Nirvana on MTV or listened to the Beatles in his dad's car. His father was very keen on music, and played in a band called Clint Cortell and the Confidentials. Having initially been inspired by his parents' record collection, Steve then began to like exactly what his parents didn't like.

Pie & Vinyl is situated on Castle Road, where Sir Arthur Conan Doyle first wrote *A Study In Scarlet*, and the Sherlock Holmes legend began. Steve can remember trawling the pre-owned record shops around Portsmouth in his youth. He remembers the way the shops smelled and the minimal eye contact from unhelpful staff who treated the records they were selling as if you weren't supposed to touch them. When opening Pie & Vinyl, he resolved to do the opposite.

Steve spent his spare cash on vinyl and became hooked on the superior sound. He speculated that other people would feel the same way and decided to sell only the modern format of vinyl and to do his utmost to be as approachable and honest about any genre of music and to learn from his customers.

Record shops were dying, so he needed a new approach. Like others, he decided to combine selling records with a café/catering experience. But instead of the usual muffins or pastries, he wanted to provide his customers with a different kind of taste sensation; something old-fashioned, something English, something with lots of tradition and soul… a food as satisfying as vinyl records. It came to him in a flash: pie and mash with gravy and liquor. He remembered at a music festival eating some fantastic pies made by a company called Pieminister, and approached them to be his supplier. He canvassed the idea in the industry and among his friends. The Pie & Vinyl story had begun.

With a selection of 40 different pies to go with the high-quality music, Pie & Vinyl has won the support of people not only in Southsea and nearby Portsmouth but also in the surrounding areas and even nationally. There are regular in-store performances and in November 2013 Steve expanded the shop and started his own record label to encourage local and new talent. He also opened another shop a few doors down called Pie & Hi-Fi which sells and repairs turntables. Pie & Vinyl also sells its own merchandise including T-shirts bearing the gramophone label. For serious collectors, there is The Pie & Vinyl Record Adventure, an arrangement whereby for a £100 subscription each quarter you receive a record chosen by the team, along with mystery gifts, discount vouchers and priority access to gigs.

Pie & Vinyl is planning to open another store in 2018. The team DJs at many festivals and events across the country and have curated a poster exhibition and gallery.

When Nick Cave released his album *Skeleton Tree* in 2016 it was accompanied by a documentary film *One More Time with Feeling*. The evening before the record was available in the shops, the film was screened in 86 cinemas across the UK. Pie & Vinyl did a joint event with their local cinema and after the screening patrons could buy the record and also purchase Nick Cave-themed pies which they had produced especially for the event.

Here was the menu:

Push the Pie Away - British beef steak with Stilton Cheese (after the album *Push the Sky Away*)
Abattoir Blues - butternut squash, mushroom & spinach in a coconut Thai Curry sauce (vg) (after the album of the same name)
Stagger Me - British free-range chicken with leeks and staggeringly good ale (after Nick's version of the old American song 'Stagger Lee')
Nick Cave and the Sesame Seeds – goat's cheese, sweet potato, spinach, red onion, roasted garlic and sesame seeds

It was a fantastic event and it just shows what a shop can do if they think about their promotion and marketing.

Steve says "Can you remember when you first hit the return button on your keyboard, and downloaded your first song? Me neither, but I bet you will always remember the first record you bought in Pie & Vinyl."

You will probably remember the first pie too.

Vinilo Records *The vegan record shop*
55 Queensway, Southampton, Hampshire SO14 3BL
02381 847674
vinilo.co.uk; ken.robshaw@me.com; @vinilorecstore
Monday-Saturday 10am-5pm Sunday 11am-3pm
Established 2017
Stock: Vinyl, Pre-owned, Vegan coffee and cakes, In-stores

For the last couple of years whenever I have been asked "Where would you open a record shop?" I have always suggested Southampton – a city full of students, with a premiership football team and a vibrant live music scene, but for many years no independent record shop.

Thankfully, Ken and Virginia Robshaw have taken the bull by the horns. Ken worked at the last independent record shop based in the city, Essential Music, which had branches in Southampton, Brighton and Greenwich before closing 20 years ago. Ken spent the next few years touring in bands which didn't quite make the big time.

Once you have experienced music retailing it is always in your blood and the lure proved too much for Ken. He and Virginia envisioned a shop with a difference. Beautifully designed by Virginia, with everything made of wood and decked out with lots of greenery, the store serves fresh vegan coffee and cakes (all plant-based) and has two listening stations where customers are welcome to hear the pre-owned records before buying them.

Ventnor Exchange

11 Church Street, Ventnor, Isle of Wight, Hampshire PO38 1SW
01983 716767
ventnorexchange.co.uk; store@ventnorexchange.co.uk; @VentnorExchange
Friday and Sunday 5pm-11pm Saturday 10am-11pm
Established 2014
Stock: Vinyl, Pre-owned, Books, Coffee, Food, In-stores, Licenced

Ventnor Exchange is a creative hub that combines a theatre, a Belgian beer bar and a record shop all located under one roof in the Victorian seaside town of Ventnor. It is instrumental in organising the Ventnor Fringe Festival. The records are displayed on tables in the centre of the room surrounded by a bar and lush seating to help you chill out. Check out the extensive range of Belgian beers.

Be aware of the unusual opening hours before you visit

Vinyl Matters

Bakery Lane, Petersfield, Hampshire GU32 3DY
07720 244849
vinylmatters.net; vinylmatters@outlook.com
Monday-Saturday 10am-5pm
Established 2016
Stock: Vinyl, Pre-owned, CD, In-stores

Steve McGuiness went from adversity to living the dream when he opened Vinyl Matters in the beautiful market town of Petersfield. Having been made redundant from his job at a law firm, Steve had no income, when his wife Bridget helpfully suggested that he start selling off some of his massive vinyl collection online. Steve decided to open a record shop instead.

A town full of independent businesses, Petersfield proved be an ideal location for a record shop. Vinyl Matters can be found down a small lane beside the Waitrose car park. The shop is a crate-diggers paradise with vinyl crammed into every nook and cranny. What is impressive, given the dimensions of the shop, is that Steve regularly hosts in-store performances. The shop can only accommodate around a dozen people, so the bands often end up playing in the alley outside the shop.

Steve has a "pay what you want" selection of records, which are laid out on tables with an honesty box, where customers are requested to place whatever payment they think the records they have chosen are worth.

Hertfordshire

This county has plenty of record shops. Lovers of coffee and vinyl should try the vinyl-coffee "triangle" where you can visit three record shops who all do fantastic coffee (I have tried them all). David's, Stylus and Gatefold Record Lounge are within 5 miles of each other. All are different in their own way but well worth taking your time when you visit.

David's

12 Eastcheap, Letchworth, Hertfordshire SG6 3DE
01462 475900
davids-music.co.uk; andy@davids-music.co.uk; @DavidsMusicLGC
Monday-Friday 9am-7pm Saturday 9am-6pm
Sunday 10am-5pm
Established 1963
Stock: Vinyl, CD, Pre-owned, Coffee, Food, In-stores

David's is an institution, tucked away in the most unassuming of provincial towns. Some sources claim there are more trees than people in Letchworth, but that doesn't stop people making their pilgrimages from far and wide to check the shop out. Opened originally as a bookshop, it has now established itself as one of the UK's leading independent record stores. In the early days the shop advertised for used books but soon found people offering them more pre-owned records to purchase than the shop could sell. One day, in a moment of inspiration, they decided to hire a local warehouse and organise an auction to sell their surplus stock. These auctions became legendary, with dealers travelling from all over Europe to attend.

In 1975 David's moved into larger premises in a building that was previously the NatWest bank. By 1984 the business had stagnated, and David's decided to inject some fresh blood into the staff. They appointed a young man named Andy Oaten to run the record shop, and he is still there today. Upon his appointment Andy quickly realised that the store desperately needed a revamp. His shrewdest move was to convert the bank's vault. This original feature had walls 12 feet thick, but it was being used to store hundreds of pre-owned copies of the National Geographic which were piled high on wooden tables and being sold for 10p. Andy dumped the magazines in the skip, adorned the vault with posters and moved all the second-hand vinyl in. Back then smoking was still allowed, and on a sunny day it was a surreal sight to see crowds of people, sweating profusely, flicking through the vinyl while enveloped in a haze of heat and smoke.

The shop was bought by David Wallace in 2009 and he added an in-store coffee shop that serves fabulous cakes and has been a huge success. My tip would be to attend one of the regular free events they hold. Manager Andy works tirelessly to bring high-calibre artists such as Ash, Divine Comedy and the Thrills in to the shop. He is always on the lookout for artists who have played London and for whom the next gig is in Cambridge. The shop is a perfect halfway house.

The team who work there are all great characters and always up for chatting about music. Andy goes weak at the knees if you mention the Smiths or Morrissey but don't think he's just an 1980s indie-loving dandy. He knows most things about most kinds of music, including classical and jazz. He is assisted by Ashlie Green, a woman who describes herself as "Andy's right-hand man".

David's has many loyal customers. Among them is a certain Mr. Vinyl, whose name always raises a wry smile, as he does not own a record player and only buys CDs. It was a great disappointment the day the shop took an order for a CD from him and discovered his name is spelt "Vinell".

Another customer who did have an interest in vinyl came in to sell his heirloom, leading to this memorable exchange:

Customer – "I have this Beatles LP that I want to sell and wonder if it is worth much."
Shop – "Which album is it?"
Customer – "I don't know the title, but it is the one where they are wearing all the Sergeant Pepper outfits on the front".

If you have never visited the shop, check out the website as they are constantly putting on free in-store gigs. Arrive early and browse through the books and the vinyl, then enjoy a coffee and cake before settling down to enjoy the entertainment. What a wonderful way to spend a few hours.

Empire Records

Heritage Close, High St, St Albans, Hertfordshire AL3 4EB
01727 86 0890
empirestalbans.com; sales@empirestalbans.com; @EmpireStAlbans
Monday-Friday 11am-5.30pm
Saturday 10am-5.30pm
Sunday 12-4pm
Established 2013
Stock: Vinyl, CD, Pre-owned, In-stores, Record Players, T-shirts

Empire Records founder Derek Watson originally owned the Chaos City comic shop based in St Albans town centre. When the city's HMV closed, he was convinced St Albans would still appreciate a record shop, especially one that stocked a good range of vinyl. When the shop next door to his comic shop became vacant he snapped it up and opened it as a record shop, named after one of his favourite films, *Empire Records*. Released in 1995 and starring Rene Zellweger and Viv Tyler, this was the story of a giant chain called Music Town trying to take over the local independent record store, a tale many long-standing record shops in the UK can relate to.

It has been a tough few years for the shop as, tragically and unexpectedly, Derek passed away in 2015, just two years after opening his dream store. Derek's partner Marina DeSclavis has taken over the store and, helped by ex-HMV manager Dave Burgess, has steered the shop through some difficult times. It looks impressive, with its wooden surrounds to highlight the vinyl and its green and pink retro chairs where you are encouraged to sit, chill out and listen to some good music. The shop aims to have an in-store a week and has hosted some very successful events involving artists of the calibre of Stephen Wilson and Frank Carter.

The LP Café *The record shop that will have you in stitches*
173 The Parade, Watford, Hertfordshire WD17 1NJ
07749 979880
Monday-Saturday 9am-6pm Sunday 11am-5pm
info@thelpcafe.com; thelpcafe.com; @TheLPCafe
Established 2013
Stock: Vinyl, Pre-owned, Coffee, Food, In-stores, T-shirts

The LP Café is a much-needed cultural meeting place in Watford, offering quality food and coffee (the coffee is so good I bought a bag to take home). Key titles are displayed on an old-fashioned peg wall, which helps them stand out, while the shop is decorated with flags of the world. Jazz fans should head down on a Wednesday, when the genre gets its own day to be played. The Café holds comedy evenings and has something completely original: its own sewing clubs. So, one way or another, they will have you in stitches.

As well as owner Paul Terris, two other members of staff are vinyl DJs – Leila Fireponey and Leo Morestyles – the three comprising Watford's finest vinyl-only DJ group. Catch the trio spinning funk and soul tunes most Saturdays at Bar Bodega, located just down the road from the shop. Every Sunday from 4pm-6pm Team LP Café also broadcasts an online radio show live from local internet station I'm In Radio; and the shop was recently used as the meeting place for a young couple on the Channel 4 TV programme *The Undateables*.

Gatefold Record Lounge
61 Hermitage Road, Hitchin, Hertfordshire SG5 1DB
01462 433300
jak@gatefoldmusic.com; gatefoldmusic.com; @GatefoldMusic
Tuesday-Thursday 9am-5.30pm Friday-Saturday 9am-8pm Sunday 10am-4pm
Established 2016
Stock: Vinyl, Pre-owned, Coffee, Food, In-stores

Gatefold Record Lounge offers carefully curated vinyl, specialising in hip-hop, electronic and rock, as well as spanning a breadth of genres such as funk, soul jazz, reggae and world music styles. The shop also offers direct-trade specialty drinks, from hand-roasted coffee to superb beer from craft breweries across the country. Husband and wife team Jack and Nicola Utley originally dreamt up the idea of Gatefold after moving to Hitchin in 2015. Tired of the rat race, they chose to create their dream hang-out and to share it with a vibrant town like Hitchin. This is a beautifully designed shop with a happy vibe.

Nicola and Jack constantly play interesting vinyl, trying to engage their customers with new music. This is a lovely place to relax and pick up a record or two. Most record shop cafes I visit tend to take more money on food and drink than they do on vinyl. Jack tells me that Gatefold are 90% vinyl and 10% coffee. This is probably a good thing for as I leave the shop and walk back through the town, the number of outlets I pass serving coffee is in the high double figures. I pass a rather packed Starbucks. This homogenised chain is brilliant at what it does, and you can find them everywhere in the world, but there is only one Gatefold Record Lounge. I would be surprised if anybody told me they had a more pleasurable experience or a nicer cup of coffee at Starbucks than in Gatefold.

Stylus *The record shop where you won't be disturbed by the phone*
35a High Street, Baldock, Hertfordshire SG7 6BG
07854 908425
jason@styluslounge.co.uk
Monday-Saturday 9am-5pm Sunday 10am-4pm
Established 2017
Stock: Vinyl, Pre-owned, Cake, Coffee, Gifts, Licensed, In-stores

Stylus Record Shop Coffee Lounge is a relaxed and stylish place in which to chill out while listening to records. Owned by husband and wife team Jason and Susan Kitchener, with business partner Abigail Skinner, they offer a "phone-free zone" to help people enjoy the music while being able to have an uninterrupted conversation. Visit on a Sunday morning for a spot of the highly praised brunch which you can combine with vinyl buying.

Kent

No county has witnessed a greater transformation in the fortunes of record shops than Kent. Only eight years ago, Kent had just one shop taking part in Record Store Day: Gatefield Sounds in Whitstable. By 2018 the number was in double figures. Londoners have chosen to move out of the capital to relocate to coastal towns where house prices are cheaper, and quality of life is higher. This has coincided with the government making substantial investment in towns such as Ramsgate and Folkestone. A decade ago Kent was the last county I would recommend a vinyl fan to visit. Now you will be doing well if you can visit the wide variety of shops in a weekend.

B Side The C Side *This shop still has an original listening booth you can try*
176 High Street, Herne Bay, Kent CT6 5AJ
01227 360400
bsidethecside.co.uk; chriseastman@outlook.com; @BsidetheCside1
Monday-Saturday 10am-5pm
Established 1995
Stock: Vinyl, Pre-owned

Is there a better named seaside-based record shop than this? Partners Oz and Chris have refurbished the shop they bought in 2013 from a crammed crate-diggers' space into a modern but retro-themed record shop, aiming to recapture the atmosphere of how record shops used to be when they were growing up in the 1960s. Pride of place goes to an original listening booth, a set of Belisha (road crossing) beacons and a beautiful settee (called the Vinyl Resting Place) where partners of vinyl junkies can sit and read magazines while relaxing with a coffee. Comics are also provided for children to read while their parents peruse the racks. One woman remained seated on the Vinyl Resting Place for six long hours while her partner looked through the racks. Despite downing endless cups of coffee, she did not visit the toilet once. Never has Herne Bay witnessed such amazing bladder control!

This is a shop of great character and other features include an Abbey Road-themed entrance and a Pink Floyd "wall" for well-known artists to sign. Oz and Chris have also brought back the connection between music and local community, as every first Saturday of the month they have live music in the shop, while the monthly vinyl club enables like-minded vinyl junkies to socialise as they listen to vinyl.

The shop also offers a record cleaning service for £1 an album and advertises this in the window. One day a man came in and asked what the service involved. Having been taken by Oz through the process of cleaning a record, he seemed very enthusiastic and asked a few questions before saying "Great, I'll take the job - when can I start?"

The Compact Disc
57 London Road, Sevenoaks, Kent TN13 1AU
01732 740889,
bluesandjazz.co.uk
Monday-Saturday 9.30am-5.30pm
Established 1985
Stock: Vinyl, CD, Pre-owned

The shop has a very good reputation for seeking out hard to find product and is especially knowledgeable on classical, blues and jazz. If you have not visited for a while it is worth a return visit. They have taken over what was the chocolate shop next door to expand the vinyl range.

Cruisin Records
132 High Street, Welling, Kent DA16 1TJ
02083 045853
roastbeefrob313@gmail.com;
Monday, Wednesday, Friday, Saturday 9.30am-5.30pm
Tuesday, Thursday 10am-6pm
Established 1978
Stock: Vinyl, CD, Pre-owned, DVD
Established 1978

John Setford, ably assisted by Ralph White, is the great survivor of Welling music retailers, having seen off at least five competitors. Previously a builder, John started off by selling records down the local market and has never looked back.

Elsewhere Records (formerly Monkey Boy Records)
21-22 The Centre, Margate, Thanet, Kent CT9 1RL
monkeyboyrecords.co.uk; alex@monkeyboyrecords.co.uk; @monkeyboyrcrds
Monday 12-6pm
Wednesday-Saturday 12-6pm
Sunday 12-4pm
Established 2017
Stock: Vinyl, Pre-owned

Alex Barron started out with an online store in 2012 selling mainly modern American pop-punk and emo records. He started doing pop-up stalls at gigs around Kent as well as a regular stall selling at a burrito bar in Canterbury called Club Burrito. He finally realised his dream of opening a record shop, Monkey Boy Records, on Record Store Day 2017.

His shop was too small for the amount of vinyl he wanted to stock, so in the summer of 2018 he moved to a much larger premises, incorporating a music venue, in Margate and renamed his shop Elsewhere Records.

Gatefield Sounds
70, High Street, Whitstable, Kent CT5 1BB
01227 263337
gatefieldsounds.co.uk; rhomadi16@yahoo.co.uk; @Gatefieldsounds
Monday-Saturday 9am-5pm
Established 1972
Stock: Vinyl, CD, Pre-owned, DVD, In-stores.

Mike and Jan Winch opened the first of their Kent-based chain of record stores in Faversham in 1972. They didn't expand too quickly; in fact, they seemed to operate on seven-year plans as their second store (Whitstable) opened in 1979 while the third (Herne Bay) came on stream in 1986. These were the golden days of retailing and they couldn't quite wait another seven years to open their fourth (Deal) branch in 1992. Sadly, due to changing market conditions, only the Whitstable shop still trades. Mike and Jan retired in 2015, selling the shop to nephew - and former Saturday boy - John and his wife Erin, who have increased the range of vinyl by 500%. They hold regular in-store events and have turned the upstairs into a gallery where they display music-related art and photography. The shop has noticed a dramatic increase in customers visiting from London, as Whitstable has become an ideal day out from the capital. The town is famous for its Oyster Festival held in July when, never one to miss a sales opportunity, you can rely on John to have plenty of records by the Oyster Band in stock.

Hot Salvation Records
32 Rendezvous Street, Folkestone, Kent CT20 1EZ
01303 487657
hotsalvation.com; hotsalvationstore@gmail.com; @hotsalvation
Monday-Saturday 10am-5pm Sunday 11am-4pm Established 2014
Stock: Vinyl, Pre-owned, Books, Coffee, Food, In-stores, Jewellery, Stationery, Turntables

Folkestone has enjoyed a tremendous revival in recent years thanks to huge investment in the old quarter of town. A ground-breaking regeneration project, funded largely by the Roger De Haan Charitable Trust, has seen the development of a creative quarter populated by artists, independent retailers and creative businesses including several cafés, restaurants and record shops. Contributing to the area are ex-teacher George Clift and his partner Natalie Barker who both had a background in record shops. George worked at Richard's Records in Canterbury while Natalie had her own shop in Sheffield, Selfworth Records. The couple got together in 2010 after both stores had closed. Both harboured the dream of opening their own shop and the vinyl revival enabled that dream to become reality. George resigned from teaching in April 2014, spending the next six months sourcing premises and stocking it up. In 2016 Natalie resigned from her job and now the shop is their joint source of income. With two young children to support it is by no means easy, but they are both doing what they love.

The interior is bright and minimal with a shiny black floor and space to sit and enjoy a coffee or look through the vinyl in the well-curated chipboard racks.

The shop concentrates on selling new music as opposed to music from the past. It has a great selection of African and world music vinyl. As well as its coffee, Hot Salvation has its own record label, releasing LPs by UK acts Cowtown, Sans Pareil, Mass Lines, That Fucking Tank, Kind Eyes, and Spanish noise-rock duo Za. The shop is also involved in curating an annual experimental music festival called Profound Sound. It produces a monthly radio show for Ramsgate Music Hall and a monthly vinyl night at a local bar.

House Of Martin
60 High Street, Broadstairs, Kent CT10 1JT
01843 860949
houseofmartin.co.uk; shop@houseofmartin.co.uk; @HouseOfMartinUK
Wednesday-Saturday 10am-5pm
Stock: Vinyl, Clothing, Coffee, Figurines
Established 2017

With a name like Dean Martin it was almost certain that Dean would end up working in the music industry. His path to owning a record shop took him via club promotion, retail work and band management. He had been working in HMV before he took the plunge to open his own shop, a mixture of fashion clothing leaning slightly to the mod era and Dean's taste in vinyl, which includes a lot of 1960s releases and is also strong on Britpop. Check out the band artwork on the walls of the shop which include postcards created by former Specials bassist and artist Horace Panter, and images from Shed 7 and the Rifles.

Oasis fans should check out the exclusive comic figurines of Noel and Liam stocked in the shop. Dean is the perfect record shop owner as he could chat for ages about his music loves, and it is no surprise that he won HMV's award for customer service. When he opened the shop, HMV were reluctant to lose such a key member of staff, so they came to an arrangement whereby after working in his own shop till 5.30pm Dean would then go over to HMV and work the late shift. This dedication and work ethic should ensure the success of House of Martin.

Smugglers *Gary Lineker inspires record shop owner's love of music*
9 King Street, Deal, Kent CT14 CHX
smugglersrecords.com; will@smugglersrecords.com; @smugglersrecords
013043 62368
Wednesday-Saturday 10am-5pm
Sunday 10am-3pm
Established 2015
Stock: Vinyl, CD, Pre-owned, Coffee, In-stores, Licensed

Will Greenham has spent his career helping local musicians, either by booking them to play venues, releasing their records on his Smugglers Records label or giving them a place to sell their recordings via his shop. It helps that he is a musician himself, playing guitar in local favourites Cocos Lovers. Will comes from a musical family and initially showed great reluctance to play an instrument, preferring to spend his time playing football. It was only when his mum told him that his football hero Gary Lineker loved playing the recorder that he agreed to take up the instrument. Despite internet searches

Will has since found no record whatsoever of the England legend playing the instrument but is grateful to Gary - and his mum - for getting him started on the road to becoming a musician. On leaving school he went into nursing and combined it with playing in the band and promoting gigs.

Deal was becoming a magnet for musicians who were disillusioned with London house prices and looking for a higher quality of life. As one might expect in a small town, it didn't take long for them to find each other. They met, they drank, they sung, and they played; and so, Smugglers Records grew, like many wonderful things, out of a series of chance encounters, its core members drawn together by a love of music and good nights out. From the humble beginnings of small club nights to busking-led adventures across Europe, the ethos of Smugglers Records existed before the label did. Built on a love of music and community, adventure and memories, for those involved with it Smugglers Records is more than just a label - it's a way of life.

In 2009 Cocos Lovers self-funded and pressed their first album, *Johannes*. They put a Smugglers Records logo on it and the label was born. Eleven releases later, they have gained a great reputation for quality records and achieved some success. One of the label's artists, Will Varley, who was responsible for sanding down the wooden floor in the shop as well as playing in-store numerous times, now sells out major venues. With Smugglers Records putting on regular music nights in Deal, Kent and London, the idea of hosting a three-day festival in woodland near Deal was born. The Smugglers Festival is now in its tenth year, with performances being spread between two forests. The theatre in the woods stage, due to its incredible acoustics, has become the place where musicians want to play. All artists perform acoustically and when music is not filling the air, you can hear a pin drop. If you are becoming tired of big commercial festivals, with their exclusive VIP areas for people who are not really VIPs and big brand sponsorship, do yourself a favour and check out a festival run by musicians for music fans. As you watch an artist playing in a forest under the stars with a craft beer in your hand, you will wonder why you have not done this before.

The festival has so many highlights for Will but there is one incident he would prefer to forget. Each year they build a sauna for people to relax in. They never struggle for wood. They employ two local music fans to look after it. One year after the festival had finished, the sauna burnt down. Luckily everybody had gone home by then and in an ironic twist, the music fans who were looking after the sauna turned out to be firemen. After the success of the festival, opening a record shop was the next step. By now Will had left nursing to concentrate on his various musical projects. He has done a fantastic job of designing the shop to look like a smugglers' cave. With its old wooden floors and lots of the product being displayed on old barrels, if it wasn't for the racks of vinyl you might think you had walked into a scene from *Pirates of the Caribbean*. Will has created a meeting place for the local music community and realising that most musicians like a drink, decided to devote a corner of the shop to stocking craft beers. This has been a very successful venture and they stock over 40 different beers.

The shop offers a membership scheme which I think is the best deal in Deal. From as little as £15 per month, Smugglers members receive a free CD or half price on any vinyl, free coffee in the shop and invites to in-store gigs.

The Record Shop *The shop with a floor made of vinyl records*
Kiosk 4-5, Park Mall, Ashford, Kent TN24 8RY
01233 660360
therecordstoreashford.co.uk; therecordstoreashford@gmail.com
Monday-Saturday 9.30am-5.30pm
Established 2016
Stock: Vinyl, Pre-owned, CD, Memorabilia

Vincent Monticelli combines his telecommunications job with helping his daughter Tahlula, run The Record Shop. Housed in a U-shaped kiosk outside Wilkinson's it is easy to locate. It is the quirkiest shape of any record shop I have visited. Check out the amazing floor, which is made from vinyl records. It is worth visiting for that alone. If you struggle to find the shop, just ask for the tank. Since 1919, a World War 1, Mark IV tank, Number 245, sits under a specially constructed covered area in St George's Square, not far from the shop.

Transmission
105 Northdown Road, Margate, Kent CT9 2QY 075251 66386
transmissionrecords.co.uk; orders@transmissionrecords.co.uk;
@Transmissionrecordshop
Friday-Saturday 12-4pm Established 2015 Stock: Vinyl, Pre-owned, Cassettes, Art, Toys, Skateboards

"Record Store Day has captured the imagination of the public and the shop owners proving that customers are still willing to spend money if they can get an experience that's not available online"
Spencer Hickman - Transmission

The seaside towns of Kent have suddenly become the hip places to visit - and nowhere epitomises their transformation better than Transmission. The renovation of Margate from run-down seaside town to the place to visit on the Kent coast has been remarkable. The 2011 opening of Turner Contemporary, the art gallery which specialises in the work of one of Margate's greatest ever artists, JMW Turner, was a cultural coup. The town's connection with other modern artists and designers such as Tracey Emin and Wayne Hemingway also helped bring it positive publicity and visitors in search of culture. The regeneration of the Old Town has resulted in the opening of many independent shops. Chic eateries, galleries, and vintage clothes shops rub shoulders with traditional seaside delights such as candy floss stands, fish and chip shops, and seafood stalls.

In the hub of this hip area, you will find Transmission Records, which specialises in horror soundtracks but also stocking Post-Punk, Metal, 1960s & 1970s, Jazz, Anime, Blues and Indie vinyl. The shop was founded by Spencer Hickman and Kimberley Holladay. It is worth a visit just to view the most incredible shop floor of any record shop in the UK, painted by the owners themselves in the style of the Black Lodge from *Twin Peaks*. There isn't a dancing dwarf on the shop floor that talks backwards, but there are two small dogs Earl and Flynn that resemble something from *Gremlins*!

Spencer is the label manager for both Mondo Records and Death Waltz Recording Co. He was formerly manager of Rough Trade and co-ordinator of Record Store Day.

Through his Record Store Day work, he has made a major contribution to the vinyl revival. Kimberley is an artist with a background of computer visual effects in film and hand-drawn graphics including the *Forbidden World* soundtrack sleeve art. The idea behind Transmission was to offer an expertly-curated selection of new and used records concentrating on Soundtracks and Japanese pressings. The store is a haven for any fans of soundtracks and anything connected with cult horror. The shop even has an extensive selection of Japanese pressings supplied direct from Tokyo.

In 2018, they became the only record shop I am aware of with its own bourbon bar.

Except the unexpected when you pay them a visit.

Vinyl Head

2-3 The Broadway, Addington Street, Ramsgate, Kent CT11 9JN
07901 334653
Humbi35@yahoo.co.uk; @vinylheadkent
Sunday-Thursday 9am-5pm
Established 2014
Stock: Vinyl, Pre-owned, Cake, Coffee, In-stores, Memorabilia

Vinyl Head is mainly a second-hand record shop that stocks a small amount of new vinyl and which takes part in Record Store Day. The shop has decks on which to play used records, as well as sofas on which to chill out. The café is highly-rated with 83% of reviews on Trip Advisor being excellent.

Vinyl Store Jr

20 Castle Street, Canterbury, Kent CT1 2QJ
01227 456907
vinylstorejr.co.uk; contact@vinylstorejr.co.uk; @Vinylstore-Jr
Tuesday-Saturday 9.30am-5.30pm   Sunday 11am-4pm   Closed Monday
Established 2016
Stock: Vinyl

Vinyl Store Jr has a distinct focus on the new and exciting, with new releases, limited editions and willfully obscure psychedelia from places as far flung as Russia, Scandinavia and South America - the kind of things you are not likely to find in HMV. Owner Nick Pygott had wanted to run a record shop all his life, but was diverted by other work opportunities such as selling wine, working for charity and running a castle - as well as less arduous pursuits such as sitting in beer gardens and going to festivals. During his time selling wine, his customers included David Gray, Morcheeba, Turin Brakes, and Engelbert Humperdinck.

Nick stocks only vinyl and reasons that it is not so much a purist decision as a pragmatic one. Vinyl is a "growth sector", as they say in business. He couldn't afford to duplicate stock by selling everything in more than one format, so he is sticking with vinyl "because it sounds better, it looks better, and it feels better. And it's just cooler."

Vintage & Vinyl
57, The Old High Street, Folkestone, Kent T20 1RN
01303 246715
vintageandvinyl.co.uk; alison.wressell@yahoo.co.uk; @VintageandVinyl
Monday-Wednesday 10.30am-5pm
Friday-Saturday 10.30am-5pm
Stock: Vinyl, Pre-owned, Ceramics, Turntables, Wine and all manner of oddities

"What goes better with music than a glass of wine?" **Alison Wressell - Vintage & Vinyl**

Situated in the wonderful creative quarter of Folkestone, you will find this unique record shop. To locate it simply walk down the hill of the old high street and look out for the beautifully painted violet arched windows highlighting many of the unusual lines the shop sells. The shop is owned by Alison Wressell and her partner Kev. As a teenager Alison worked at Virgin in Durham, later spending 10 years of her life living in a wine-making area of France. With that background it is understandable that the shop specialises in both vinyl and wine.

It is a true independent shop using local wine-growers and supporting Kent-based companies. This is a great combination, as one of the great joys of life is relaxing over a favourite vinyl record whilst drinking a quality wine. The shop is not just about award-winning wine - they also sell cider, gin, beer, vodka and local liqueurs. The way that they display their vinyl is unique too: by year of release. The idea is that if somebody is looking for an album recorded in 1968 it is likely they will enjoy other music from that period. It is amazing how often somebody buys something that they were not looking for in the first place. Less of a surprise is the sight of so many people leaving the shop carrying a vinyl record in one hand and a bottle of wine in the other.

Lancashire

There are not many new openings of record shops in Lancashire and locations such as Blackburn, Blackpool, Fleetwood and Lancaster could do with a good independent record shop selling new vinyl.

Action Records

46, Church Street, Preston, Lancashire PR1 3DH
01772 884772
actionrecords.co.uk; mail@actionrecords.co.uk; @ActionRecords
Monday-Saturday 9am-5.30pm
Stock: Vinyl, CD, Pre-owned, In-stores, Tickets
Established 1979

So many long-established record shops opened during the punk and post-punk periods. One of these was Action Records, owned by Gordon Gibson, who originally started selling pre-owned vinyl in a Blackpool market. At first it was tough going and he wondered if he had made the right decision. One day he only took £2 in takings whilst his bus fare home was £2.40. Luckily for music fans he stuck with it, appreciating how much he enjoyed chatting to people and persuading them to buy things that they had not intended to purchase originally.

Action expanded and moved to Preston in 1981. It is a testament to Gordon that 38 years on, it is still as popular as ever. Anybody speaking with him will quickly realise that he is not a Lancashire lad and although it is nearly four decades since he left his native Stranraer, he has lost none of his Scottish brogue. He ended up in Lancashire following an appeal on Bob Harris' radio show back in 1971. He had hitchhiked down to the Lincoln festival to see The Byrds, James Taylor and Tim Hardin amongst others. On the journey down he was picked up by fellow travellers Alan and Sheila Cookson. The three had a fabulous weekend and vowed to stay in touch. Easier said than done, back in 1971, with no email or Facebook. Soon they had lost touch, so Alan and Sheila put out an appeal on Bob's show for Gordon to give them a call. Luckily Gordon was tuned in and heard Bob read out their phone number. Can you imagine Radio 1 giving out somebody's phone number these days? Gordon duly moved down to Preston to live near his friends and has stayed there ever since.

Between 1982 and 2009 Action had its own record label releasing records by artists such as the Boo Radleys and three albums by the Fall. It all started when Gordon releasing a single by his brother's band the Genocides. That started a pattern where he was happy to release recordings by customers and friends, providing he thought the material was decent. Cornershop drummer Dave Chambers once worked at the store. Another early employee was Nick Brown who went on to open Intoxica Records in London.

The resurgence of vinyl has given the business a great boost and one thing Gordon has noticed is the younger people who come in and only buy vinyl. His CD sales amongst the under-20s is negligible. Back in 1995, though, Gordon appeared on TV saying that vinyl would vanish unless somebody started manufacturing needles for record players. He could not get them anywhere and predicted a grim view for vinyl unless this problem was rectified. Lucky for everybody, it has been.

Action is always keen to have bands play in the shop. One gig has reached legendary status with the music fans of Preston. A young Devon band yet to taste fame called Muse rocked the shop and it seems like half the music fans of Preston have told Gordon they were there, but he recalls the band only playing to around 30 people. This was not the case when Bastille recently played the shop. This time more than 100 music fans from Preston can say they were there, as the shop was packed. Other successful events have included signings with ex-Mansun singer Paul Draper and, a week later, guitar hero Steven Wilson, the queue for whom was like Record Store Day, with fans travelling from as far afield as Glasgow, Edinburgh, Newcastle and Sheffield to meet the man.

Gordon intends to be selling vinyl to the people of Preston until the day he retires. Nearly 40 years after opening, he is still passionate about music. He is the sort of person the music industry should be honouring. In 2015, an excellent short documentary *Chasing by Nuns* was produced, telling the story of the shop. It can be viewed on YouTube.

Astonishing Sounds
3 Hall Street, Burnley, Lancashire BB11 1QJ
012824 55339
astonishingsounds.co.uk; shop.astonishing.sounds@googlemail.com
Monday-Saturday 10.30am-5.30pm
Established 1986
Stock: Vinyl, Pre-owned, CD, Badges, Posters, T-shirts

If you like old-school record shops, then Burnley is the place to go. Neil Kinder has been selling music since the age of 16, when he started at Record Fairs. After six years, he moved to an indoor market and one year later opened Astonishing Sounds. Neil offers a similar service to Waitrose, who give a free cup of coffee to anybody who spends £5, as he constantly has the kettle on and is happy to give his customers a cup of tea free of charge.

One day a man entered with an unusual request. He enquired if the shop had any drugs. Neil explained that this was not that sort of shop. The gentleman did not take kindly to this and repeated that he wanted drugs and all good record shops would keep drugs in stock. At this point, Neil realised the heavily-accented man was asking for the Troggs, the West Country band led by Reg Presley whose hits included "Wild Thing" and "Love Is All Around". Along with Neil's own thick Lancashire accent, the request had been lost in translation.

If you want to see what both Neil and the shop look like, Jellybelly films posted a documentary on YouTube. Neil has been called "the Brian Potter of record retail" after the *Phoenix Nights* character, and anybody who has spoken with Neil can understand the comparison. The shop has a fantastic Northern Soul section. My only advice to visitors is don't get Neil started on his views on DJ Tim Westwood.

Electron Records *The owner went off for a pint while the Beatles were playing*
2, Hall Street, Burnley, Lancashire BB11 1QJ
01282 428118
electronrecords@hotmail.co.uk
Monday-Saturday 10.30am-5.30pm
Established 1946
Stock: Vinyl, CD, Pre-owned

Les Baxter took over Electron Records from his father in the early 1980s having previously run its sister store in nearby Nelson. With its eye-catching green front and white steps situated on a hill, Electron is a true, old-fashioned record shop that does not look like it has changed in decades. The original listening booth and collection of cassettes harks back to the past, but the shop has a modern outlook when it comes to vinyl, devoting much more space to the format in recent years. If you have seen the film *Northern Soul* you may recognise Electron, as many of the record shop scenes were filmed there.

The Beatles called in to Electron in late 1962, when John Lennon bought a Dinah Washington EP. The band returned to the area in May 1963 to play a gig at The Imp in Nelson where they had been booked a while before for the tiny sum of £20. 5,000 tickets were printed for a venue that officially held 2,000 (where was health & safety back then?). Les was one of the lucky attendees, but he could not hear the band above the screaming. So, he retired to the bar for a pint, instead of watching what was to become the most famous band in history.

Malcolm's Musicland
Chapel Street, Chorley, Lancashire PR7 1BW
0125 726 4362
malcolm@malcolmsmusicland.co.uk
Monday-Saturday 9am-5.30pm
Established 1972
Stock: Vinyl, CD

This longstanding Chorley institution stocks mainly CDs but does take part in Record Store Day.

Quicksilver Music *The owner who only stocks product from before he was born*
24, Market Street, Southport, Lancashire PR8 1HJ
0170 454 2939
quicksilvermusic.co.uk; dave.thornley@yahoo.com
Monday, Tuesday, Thursday-Saturday 9am-5pm
Established 2009
Stock: Vinyl, Pre-owned, Musical Instruments

Owner Dave Thornley has an unusual policy: he stocks as much product as he can that was released before 1975 – the year of his birth. He started the business after being made redundant, and his opening stock was his own vast collection. The shop is named after his all-time favourite band, the psychedelic San Francisco-based Quicksilver Messenger Service, best known for the album *Happy Trails* released in 1969. The shop is easy to find as it is opposite Southport market.

Townsends
30 Queen Street, Great Harwood, Lancashire BB67 QQ
0125 488 0145
townsend-music.com; townsend-records.co.uk; @TownsendRecords
Monday-Saturday 9am-6pm
Established 1978
Stock: Vinyl, CDs, Tickets, Merchandise

Also, at: 18 Moor Lane, Clitheroe, BB7 1BE

Townsends is a record retailer that seems to have slipped under the radar. Owner Steve Bamber's entrepreneurial spark was ignited during his early working life selling luxury cars. He discovered Jerry's Records, an old-fashioned, enigmatic music shop in Great Harwood which opened only three days a week.

Steve could see that the shop had tremendous potential. His brother already owned a musical instrument shop locally and Steve reckoned that the two businesses could complement and promote each other and bought Jerry's Records.

As the glory days of record retailing were ending, Steve realised that if the business was going to thrive he had to do more than just sell from his bricks and mortar stores. With the support of Bruce McKenzie, who joined from HMV Bolton, two projects he initiated bore fruit. The first was to establish Townsend's own label, offering many exclusive-to-Townsend's releases. Artists they are associated with include Mike Harding, Ian McNabb, Puressence, David Sylvian, Thunder and Black.

The next phase of the expansion was to start their own marketing "Direct to Consumer" (D2C). The idea was to work with bands to offer the consumer exclusive product. It might be a CD signed by the band or a signed lyric sheet, or exclusive postcards. It had to be something which the consumer could not buy anywhere else.

The next step was to offer artists to have their online stores managed by Townsends. They offered the opportunity to sell both the physical and digital sales as well as tickets for the tour. One brilliant innovation was to offer artists a print on demand T-Shirt service. For the artist, gone were the days of printing 500 T-shirts and having to store them: Townsends could print as many as was required. They also managed the artists' Facebook stores. It was no surprise that the likes of Noel Gallagher, The Pixies, The Prodigy, Marilyn Manson and The Charlatans signed up for the service.

In 2015, they opened a brand-new state-of-the-art fulfilment centre on a new industrial estate in Burnley. The building was designed by the Townsend team. It is an impressive operation and Steve can be proud of what he has achieved. Even he couldn't have thought, when he bought Jerry's Records, that 35 years later it would have turned into a multi-million-pound business.

London

The capital has enjoyed a tremendous resurgence in record shops in recent years. Previously it had been decimated by closures. The big chains such as Tower, Virgin and Our Price all closing. The area once known as the Golden Mile of record shops around Soho lost more than 20 record shops since the 1980s. It is heartening to report that the area is thriving again. Within close proximity to each other you can visit Sister Ray, If Records, Sound of the Universe, and Phonica. Between them they can satisfy all your vinyl needs.

Areas once unfashionable such as Dalston, Hackney, Clerkenwell, Hoxton, Peckham, Deptford, and Norwood all now have shops selling vinyl.

North London is not covered as well as it should be and there is still potential for more record shops to open there. Don't miss the opportunity to visit Brixton. A wonderful few hours can be spent visiting Lion Vibes, Supertone Records, Pure Vinyl and Container Records which are all within a few minutes walk of each other. Take a break for some fantastic food either at Brixton market or the Container Village. No trip to London for vinyl fans would be complete without a visit to one of the Rough Trade shops. If looking for accommodation, then treat yourself to a stay at the Ace Hotel in Shoreditch which has a branch of Sister Ray in the lobby.

All Ages *The UK's premier punk rock shop*
27, Pratt Street, Camden, London NW10 OBG
0207 267 0303
allagesrecords.com; shop@allagesrecords.com
Monday-Sunday 11.30am-6.30pm
Established 2003
Stock: Vinyl, CD, Pre-owned, Books, Cassettes, T-shirts
Nearest station - Camden Town

Google "punk record shop in London" and All Ages will be the name that hits the top of your screen. It has a reputation that spreads far beyond the borders of the UK, attracting punk fans from all over the world. The last time I was in there the place was buzzing with music fans from Brazil and Germany. They have become a broader church, however, with Hardcore, Oi, Ska, Garage, and Psychobilly fans all well catered for.

The shop is owned by Leeds lad Nick Collins whose journey into work each day entails taking a longboard (a sort of safer version of the skateboard) from his home in Luton to the train station, where he takes the train to Camden then longboards down to the shop.

His earliest punk memory was hearing Poly Styrene of X-Ray Spex belting out "Identity". This experience left a lasting impression on eight-year-old Nick, surely one of the UK's youngest punk fans at that time, and inspired him to start buying records.

Nick spent his pocket money on building up his punk collection and recalls his local record shop refusing to sell him a record by the Dead Kennedys because he was too young. His great hope when he left school was that he could get a job in one of the two local record shops he frequented, Jumbo and Crash Records. No job was ever forthcoming, and Nick has a theory that because he spent so much money with them they were reluctant to employ him because they would be losing one of their best customers.

Nick would supplement his dole money by running his own disco. You would not find the sounds of Chic or Donna Summer blasting out from the speakers at Nick's disco, which specialised in hardcore and hip-hop. Bands such as Public Enemy, Ministry, Ice Cube, Nirvana, Cyprus Hill, Rancid, and Helmet were the order of the day.

His evenings proved extremely popular and he received an offer to become an events manager in the Corporation nightclub in Sheffield. He left Leeds to take up the job, but also took a part-time job at Jacks Records, a shop that has since closed, but is fondly remembered by the music fans of Sheffield.

His role in the nightclub was to book the bands and present his own hardcore/hip-hop disco. He was also required to devise unique events to attract people into the club. One idea he came up with was an under-14 disco.

After advertising the event in the local media Nick received a call from the local council who thought this was a great opportunity to offer sex education to the youngsters and inquired if they could send a team down to the evening. This was the time when the country was gripped by the Aids epidemic and the Council were keen to educate the youngsters on safe sex. Nick had no objection and on the evening of the disco they turned up with a plastic penis and boxes of condoms.

They set themselves up in the corner of the disco and demonstrated the art of putting a condom on a plastic penis to a bunch of teenagers who were more interested in dancing and snogging. Soon the team from the council left but before they did they dished out the remaining condoms like confetti. One bunch of lads vanished off to the toilet with a batch of condoms where they discovered that they would make brilliant water bombs. A mass condom water fight broke out.

Nick did not attend the event and remained blissfully unaware of the chaos it had caused until his boss asked to see him the next day. She started talking about the team from the council turning up with a plastic penis and enough condoms to keep the youth of Sheffield safe for the next month. Nick started laughing, but his boss did not join in. Instead, she gave him the sack, leaving Nick to conclude that he was one of the few people ever to have been dismissed because of a plastic penis.

A friend in London asked Nick if he wanted to DJ in London one night a week. Nick was happy with the work travelled down and slept on his friend's sofa in Luton.

His friend regularly hired out videos from a local independent video shop to watch in his flat. Nick accompanied his friend to the shop, one day, and they got chatting to the owner who asked Nick if he would like to buy the business.

Nick suggested he take a few hundred videos down to Camden market at the weekend and they would split the proceeds 50/50. The owner was happy to give it a try. Nick was a huge fan of classic horror and selected as many of those genres as possible.

The stall was a huge success. People could not get enough of the videos he stocked. After he had exhausted the shops supply of videos, Nick did a bit of detective work to track down the wholesaler who had been supplying the shop. His timing was perfect. The film industry was promoting the new concept of the DVD and many videos were being deleted so the market was flooded with unsold videos which Nick was picking up for rock bottom prices.

Nick soon had a business that was thriving. He called it Up the Video Junction, named after one of Nick's favourite films. Released in 1968, *Up the Junction* had an impressive British cast including Dennis Waterman, Suzy Kendall, Maureen Lipman and Susan

George, and a soundtrack by Manfred Mann.

After four years of trading on an outside stall he was offered a permanent unit. Despite being surrounded by food stalls, the business thrived even though video stores were closing in their hundreds. It was not long before he became the "last independent film shop in London". He commemorated this by hanging up a sign outside the unit asking people to support it.

When the unit next door became vacant, Nick snapped it up and decided to start selling punk records. After trading for several years, he took the plunge and rented a property just off Camden High Street and started his dream record shop. He named the shop after one of his favourite records "All Ages" by the Bristol hardcore band Five Knuckle.

All Ages has become *the* place for fans to meet and find out what is happening in the world of punk. Vintage posters adorn the walls, though one wall is taken up with a huge message board. If you are a drummer in London, it's worth a visit. I counted six requests for a drummer whilst I was there. Nick stocks lots of fanzines, has a superb range of badges and T-shirts and the biggest collection of punk music of any UK record shop.

Nick's greatest worry is the regeneration work going on in the borough of Camden. The area is going through a period of modernisation with old buildings being knocked down to be replaced by the sort of building you can see in any town.

Many people will recall how Carnaby Street and the King's Road were once cool. There is nothing cool about them now. Camden is still cool, but Nick worries it won't be for much longer. With the future of his film shop uncertain, Nick is not confident about the future so if you have never visited All Ages, now is the time to check out London's only punk record shop.

Audio Gold *Donate your old hi fi and raise money for charity*
308-310 Park Road, Crouch End, N8 8LA
0208 341 9007
audiogold.co.uk; info@audiogold.co.uk; @Audio-Gold
Monday-Saturday 10am-6pm
Sunday 11am-5pm
Established 1992
Stock: Vinyl, Pre-owned, HI- Fi Equipment, Turntables
Nearest station - Highgate

If you are thinking about buying hi-fi equipment and are based in the London area, Audio Gold is the shop to check out first. Owned by Ben Shallcross, the shop stocks an incredible selection of new and pre-owned record players ranging from wind up gramophones to recent models. Ben is happy to advise and will recommend what system is best for you based on the budget you have. The shop is packed with product, so much so that record display cases are hanging from the ceiling, to free up space on the shop floor.

Ben started off as a motor engineer and was keen to move into something more music connected. So he got a job in the shop repairing hi-fi equipment. Ben assured me the skills are similar.

In 2002, he took over the business, but it was not until 2013 that they started selling vinyl which came about by accident. Ben had been called to a house to bid for a pre-owned hi-fi. The owner told Ben she had a vast collection of vinyl to dispose of and would he be interested in purchasing that too. Having picked up on the vinyl revival, Ben decided to give it a go. Most of the vinyl sold quickly, and from then on selling vinyl has been an integral part of Ben's business.

It is amazing how many people purchase a record player in the shop, then also buy a selection of records from the racks. The shop is in quite a wealthy area. One gentleman came in and told Ben that he had heard that vinyl was cool, so he wanted to purchase a top of the range hi-fi and would Ben pick out 100 records for him that would impress his friends. Ben was delighted to oblige and is always happy to recommend the best records along with the best hi-fi system, if requested.

Ben's passion is to convert people to listening to music on the best quality equipment they can afford. He finds it frustrating to see so many places stocking budget record players which do nothing to enhance the listening experience. Ben can put a deck together that will create a high-quality sound for as little as £200. He also has a green ethos and feels passionate about repairing and recycling equipment in our world of throwaway consumer durables.

The shop has a couple of lovely touches. If people donate them hi-fi stock, then the money raised from the sale is given to charity. Each month a different charity benefits from this kind gesture. Ben buys job lots of pre-owned vinyl, and any titles he feels are not worthy of a place in his curated racks, he puts in boxes outside and encourages people to take, free of charge.

If you are making a visit to Flashback in Crouch End, then you must not miss out this shop. It is a mere 10-minute walk away.

Banquet Records "Banquet is the best record shop in the universe." Frank Turner
52 Eden Street, Kingston upon Thames, London KT1 1EE
0208 459 5871
banquetrecords.com; shop@banquetrecords.com; @banquetRSDfeed
Monday-Wednesday 10am-6pm
Thursday-Friday 10am-7pm
Saturday 10am-6pm
Sunday 12-5pm
Established 2002
Stock: Vinyl, CD, In-stores, Tickets

The borough of Kingston upon Thames is the birthplace of musicians John Martyn, Steven Wilson, Dave Swarbrick, Rat Scabies (drummer with the Damned), Peter Cox (from Go West) and Richard Butler (singer with the Psychedelic Furs). These days the town's musical connections extend to being home to one of the UK's most innovative record shops, Banquet Records, which rose from the ashes of the Beggars Banquet record shop chain, formed by Martin Mills and Nick Austin in 1977. In that year zero for punk rock, Martin and Nick quickly decided to start releasing records themselves, the first being "Shadow" by Uxbridge band the Lurkers - a song now regarded as a punk classic. I always thought the band should have been called the Petes, since the line-up included Pete Stride, Pete Haynes and Pete Edwards. Maybe the name did not sound punk enough. Or maybe it was due to the fourth member of the band being called

Nigel. The label went from strength to strength, achieving worldwide success with artists including Gary Numan, the Cult and the Charlatans, and eventually the shops were closed, the last one standing being the Kingston branch.

Former employees Jon Tolley and Mike Smith bought the Kingston business, which at the time was in a sorry state. With the help of Jane Unwin, they have transformed it into one of the most creative record shops in the country. The numerous in-stores they put on have featured such top acts as Laura Marling, Frank Turner, Babyshambles, the Maccabees, the Cribs and the Foals.

In 2016, the shop showed its solidarity with the NHS by offering all junior doctors a free album of their choice (up to the value of £20). It also dishes out free veggie burgers to people who queue outside the shop the evening before Record Store Day, and sponsors the local football team, Kingstonian FC. The shop has its own five-a-side team. They don't make any claims to greatness but would be happy to have a game against any other record shop.

Jon works as a local Liberal Democrat councilor, and in 2015 polled more votes than all other parties put together. It was music that started him on the journey into local politics. Already disillusioned with the council's attitude to closing venues, it was the cancellation at short notice of the Kingston Carnival in 2014 that proved the final straw. It was galling for Banquet as they had booked the bands, and Jon could get no clear answers on why the successful carnival had been pulled when other years had gone so well. His experience of promoting records through social media was, he found, easily transferable to local politics.

One inspirational decision Banquet took was to stop using carrier bags. Please check out the video on YouTube under the title No More Plastic Bags. This is a huge undertaking, but I hope it inspires other independent shops to do the same. Let's not stop there. If you are reading this, and work in a retail company, share the video with your fellow employees and make a difference.

Banquet have involved themselves in as many ways as possible with the locals and customers who travel from far and wide to visit this unique shop. They are a community record shop and in 2017 were voted Best UK Independent Record Shop in the *Music Week* awards. Banquet is a record shop with a conscience.

Book & Record Bar *The record shop with its own radio station*
20 Norwood High Street, West Norwood, London SE27 9NR
0208 670 9568
bookandrecordbar.co.uk; michaeljpjohnson@gmail.com; @BooknRecordBar
Tuesday-Saturday 10.30am-6pm Sunday 10.30am-5pm
Established 2013
Stock: Vinyl, Pre-owned, Art, Coffee, Food, In-stores, Licenced
Nearest station - West Norwood

Only a minute walk from West Norwood station and on the site of an old pub is where you will find this quirky emporium. From the outside, it looks like the Queen Vic (the fictional pub in *EastEnders*) so it is a bit of a surprise when you step inside to be greeted with a huge selection of vinyl and books with the walls decorated by art from local artists.

The pub had an incredible history and was named The Gipsy Queen after a remarkable woman from the 18th century, whose skills at thievery and fortune-telling became part of local folklore. Margaret Finch was well into her nineties before she could no longer travel and settled down at last in the gypsy community based in Norwood. She was a formidable sight, with a long nose and curved spine, and could usually be found sitting on the ground, chin resting on her knees, smoking a pipe, with her faithful dog by her side. She earned money by telling fortunes in the local hostelries where huge crowds would gather to hear what the future held for them.

Her body became so contorted that when she died in 1740, she had to be crammed into a specially-constructed square coffin. It was claimed that she was 108 when she died. Her funeral was paid for by the local publicans, whose coffers she had greatly swelled, and the first recorded pub was named in her honour in 1870.

I am no fortune teller, but I am convinced the future is bright for this historical venue thanks to the hard work of current owner Michael Johnson. The Gipsy Queen closed as a pub in 2007 and lay derelict over the next few years. Squatters had moved in and the interior was badly burned by fire. It was a huge job to turn this shell into Michael's vision of an atmospheric shop, café and venue.

Michael was a semi-legendary local record collector and house DJ. His collection of more than 8,000 vinyl records helped stock the shop when he opened. He is a music expert who helped to compile the *Rare Records Price Guide*, and music fans visiting will enjoy chatting with him. If you are a fan of ambient, electronic or psych music this is the shop for you as these genres are Michael's great passion and he has lots of listening recommendations.

Michael has spent all his life involved in music. In the 1990s he was DJ at many house and rave parties all over London. One regular event he deejayed at was held in a closed down pub. It had no neighbours and the promoter would cover all the windows with blackout curtains to prevent unwanted attention. The regular events were extremely successful until Michael received a phone call from the promoter informing him that that evening's gig would have to be called off. The previous day the pub had received a demolishing order and was now in the process of being knocked down. With that evening's event completely sold out, this was a catastrophe.

To the promoter's credit the show still went ahead in a hastily-found new venue. With no social media to let punters know of the change of plan, the relocation of the event to Clapham became part of the enjoyment of the evening. Any punter who turned up at the original planned location was greeted by a wrecked venue and had to follow signage to locate the event's new home for the evening.

Michael has retained plenty of his contacts from those days and regularly has his friends Alex Paterson and Martin Glover in to DJ at the regular party evenings in the shop. Alex is in effect the Orb, being the only permanent member of the ambient music pioneers. Martin is better known as Youth the bass player of Killing Joke whose production and re-mixing credits read like a who's who of music artists. U2, Kate Bush, Texas, Depeche Mode and The Verve are just a few of the acts he has worked with.

Alex, Youth and Michael are regular DJs both in the shops and on their very own internet radio station, West Norwood Broadcasting Corporation (WNBC). Alex also hosts an event called Cake Lab on the first Sunday of each month. Lots of cake and good music is guaranteed. Shows are recorded in the shop on Thursdays at 12pm-6pm and Sundays 12-2pm. If you can plan a visit to coincide with one of the regular Open Decks Evenings you can bring down your own vinyl to be played. The shop has attracted some big-name DJs to play there. DJ Food, Mixmaster Morris and Jon More from Coldcut are just a few who have graced the decks.

The Book and Record Bar is not just a shop but a social hub. Michael is always happy to chat about books and records or the history of the Gipsy Queen over a cup of coffee

Brill *The owners surname is a description of the shop*
27 Exmouth Market, Clerkenwell, London EC1R 4QL
0207 833 9757
jeremy@clerkenwellmusic.co.uk; @Brillcafe
Monday-Friday 7.30am-6.00pm
Saturday 9.00am-6.00pm
Sunday 10.00am-5.00pm
Established 1999
Stock: Vinyl, CD, Coffee, Food, In-stores
Nearest station - Farringdon

Jeremy Brill was the drummer with 1980s ska band the Deltones. To supplement his earnings in the band he started working in the fondly remembered Wood Music record shop in Islington. As if that was not enough to keep him occupied, he was writing reviews for *Time Out*. One feature involved reviewing the record shops of the capital. Visiting these shops inspired him to open his own shop as he had been able to note down the best practices from each of them.

He found what he thought was a perfect location, filled hand-built wooden racks with 3,000 CDs and Clerkenwell Music opened for business. Unfortunately, 1999 turned out not to be the best year to open a record shop. Customers seemed to be merchants of doom, their conversations peppered with words such as "downloading", "file sharing", "Napster", "piracy" and the ominous phrase "you can get all your music for free".

After five consecutive profitless years, Jeremy had to find a way to improve takings. He tried selling DVDs and T-shirts, but neither improved the situation. His lightbulb moment came when he was sitting in Flat White, a coffee shop in Soho popular with visitors from Australia and New Zealand. They had turned the making of coffee into a theatrical performance and Jeremy was inspired to install a coffee machine.

He changed the shop's name to Brill, after his own distinctively positive name. What started off as a CD shop has now morphed in to a great café with a carefully selected range of vinyl and CDs. The bagels are baked in Brick Lane and, speaking from personal experience, the cakes are top class. Another four coffee shops have since opened in the same street, and although I have not tried them all, I will be amazed if any can beat the fantastic coffee served at Brill.

One thing I can guarantee is none of them have the atmosphere of Brill. Jeremy has an eclectic taste in music, so the shop will always be playing something stimulating to the ears. He has now introduced Vinyl Fridays. As the shop has an alcohol licence, it stays open late, serves tasty food, and plays vinyl giving the music fan visiting Clerkenwell the perfect reason to visit this great independent shop.

Casbah Records *The record shop that began on a magic bus*
320-322 Creek Road, Greenwich, London SE10 9SW
0208 858 1964.
casbahrecords.co.uk; casbahrecords80@gmail.com
Monday 11.30am-6pm Tuesday-Friday 10.30am-6pm Saturday-Sunday 10.30am-6pm
Established 2009
Stock: Vinyl, CD, Pre-owned, DVD, Books, Comics. Nearest station - Cutty Sark

Graham Davis started out on a stall selling records in Greenwich market and was an avid attendee of music festivals. He noticed at one festival that a big red bus had been converted into a café. It inspired him to look for a bus to purchase to sell records and CDs from. In those days to buy a vehicle you scoured the motor trade magazines. One day he came across just what they were looking for the only problem being the seller lived 230 miles away in in Hebdon Bridge. Convinced it was what he wanted he set off to Yorkshire and when the owner agreed to drive it down to Greenwich the deal was sealed.

The next few weeks were spent ripping out seats and painting the bus in a psychedelic style. After agreeing in advance with the market owners that he could station a bus there, Graham started trading. He named it The Magic Bus after the Who song. It proved immensely popular and became a tourist attraction for music fans. To supplement the income, the bus toured the UK turning up at festivals and universities. The first tour of universities took place in the late autumn with takings far exceeding expectations. A few months later they undertook the same tour again, but takings were far less than expected. Graham realised that on the autumn tour the students had just received their grants but by the winter the cash had run out. From then on, the Magic Bus tour would only hit the road at grant time. One thing Graham had not considered was that for security reasons he could not leave a bus full of records in Greenwich market, so he had to hire a lock-up which substantially ate into profits. The other negative was that the bus had to be at the market before all the other traders set up their stalls and could leave only after all the other traders had packed up. It was for this reason, Graham eventually decided to move to a bricks and mortar shop, which enabled him for the first time in years not to be up at the crack of dawn.

Naming the new shop Casbah Records, Graham was confident that vinyl sales would grow and make the gamble pay off. One feature of the store is the various mannequins and dummies all decorated with wigs, sunglasses and various music accessories. The shop also has a fine choice of vintage posters and produces its own range of button badges.

Casbah specialises in garage, psych from the 1960s, and cult TV and film soundtracks. Part of the joy of this shop is you are never sure what you will discover.

It is perfect for clothes shopping too, as within the same building is Retrobates dealing in vintage clothing and record players from the 1950s to the 1970s.

The shop describes itself as "small but perfectly formed" and is always looking at fun ways to promote itself. One of Graham's favourite promotions was when they had a tribute to the Rolling Stones when they were playing the nearby O2 Arena. The staff dressed up and played Stones records all day. The shop stocked an extensive range of Stones music and merch for sale and advertised it as Stoned Sunday. To judge from their faces, some of the customers that day interpreted the concept somewhat differently to the Casbah team.

A fond memory is of the enthusiastic young girl Graham took on to work in the shop. She was always keen to improve her music knowledge. One day she was processing some CDs and came across an unfamiliar name.

"Who is Holger Czukay?" she asked.

"He is in Can," Graham replied.

"Ooh, I do love the South of France," came the reply.

Graham explained that he was referring to Can the German group not Cannes the French holiday destination.

It is a great store for rarities and collectable items many of which festoon the wall. It is worth a visit just to admire the fabulous giant print of David Bowie which hangs above the counter.

Container Records *You won't be able to contain your joy*
49 Brixton Station Road, Brixton, London SW9 8PQ
07977 300074
containerrecords.com; info@containerrecords.com; @containeruk
Monday-Wednesday 11am-7pm
Thursday-Saturday 11am-8pm
Sunday 12-6pm
Established 2015
Stock: Vinyl, Pre-owned, Tickets, T-shirts
Nearest station - Brixton

Container Records is housed in a genuine shipping container in Pop Brixton where all the traders sell from old shipping containers. It is part of a community initiative that has transformed a disused plot of land into a ground-breaking space that showcases the most exciting independent businesses from around the Brixton area. It encourages new businesses by offering a substantial discount on renting the containers. It is a brilliant idea that more councils should start. It is home to 53 independent businesses including restaurants, retailers, street food traders, designers, digital start-ups, a community barbershop, a youth radio station and several social enterprises.

Although the shop is particularly strong on Afrobeat, electronic music, hip hop, world, grime, house and jungle, most genres are covered. Owner Jack Christie has a background in music, having traded records online, run his own Techno label and managed a nightclub in North London. In 2014 Jack started noticing a ringing in his ears and was diagnosed with tinnitus. It was time to move away from a career that involved working in an extremely loud environment. Due to Jack's condition you may notice the music is slightly quieter at Container than it is in some shops.

Jack always wanted his own record shop being inspired by memories of his school holidays visiting his grandparents farm house near Porthmadog in North Wales.

Those holidays involved his parents taking him to Cob Records. Having previously shopped at Our Price, Jack was blown away by the musty crate-digging, archive vibe of Cob. It left a lasting impression on him influencing his career choice.

Although not exactly the Sistine Chapel, the ceiling is brilliantly decorated, and it is by some distance the most atmospheric container you will ever visit. Jack stocks some eye-catching T-shirts. My favourites are Britain's Goth Talent, and one that lists the most whimsical names of local DJ's including Airdnb; Beatloaf; Ket Dealy; Pariah Carey; Eighth of Base; Niche Lorraine; Definitely Moby.

The shop had only been open a few weeks when David Bowie died in January 2016. Brixton, Bowie's birthplace, was suddenly full of news media. Jack received a phone call from Sky News asking if they could come and shoot in store with ex-Sex Pistol Glen Matlock. They asked if the shop had some David Bowie LPs in stock. The idea was for Glen to pick some out of the racks, take them to the counter were Jack would sell them to him. It was to be broadcast on the evening news. Jack agreed, but then realised he had nearly sold out of Bowie vinyl. Much to the dismay of his customers, Jack had to hide the Bowie selection. Sky News came and shot their story, although they didn't buy any of the records for real.

You can't fault Jack's commitment. He even has the Container Records logo tattooed on his leg. He also hosts regular punk gigs at local venue The Windmill. For those planning a visit on Record Store Day don't worry about the shop being too small. Jack hires out the container next door for the day.

Crazy Beat Records
87 Corbets Tey Road, Upminster, RM14 2AH
01708 228678
crazybeat.co.uk; sales@crazybeat.co.uk; @CrazyBeatTweets
Monday-Saturday 10am-6pm
Established 1991
Stock: Vinyl, CD, Pre-owned
Nearest station - Upminster

Owned by the legendary DJ Gary Dennis, Crazy Beat Records attracts soul, jazz and funk fans from all over the country. Gary is one of the most knowledgeable people in the country about soul music and still attracts big crowds for his DJ sets. A strong mail order section has ensured that the shop has survived through the bad times and has enjoyed a resurgence as a place for seeking out rare vinyl. There is a huge selection and if you are a collector of 12-inch singles, it is well worth a visit.

Crypt Of The Wizard *No need to get out of bed early to visit these shops*
324c Hackney Rd, London E2 7AX
cryptofthewizard.com; @CryptWizard
Tuesday-Sunday 11am-7pm
Established 2017
Stock: Vinyl, Cassette, Patches, T-Shirts
Nearest station - Bethnal Green

On Hackney Road you will come across two record shops, next to each other yet it is extremely rare for any customer to buy from both. Crypt Of The Wizard stock an unrivalled selection of heavy metal vinyl and tapes across the many subgenres. Not that owners Marcus and Charlie seem to care much about subgenres as the records are neatly stacked in alphabetical order. It is a mix of releases by smaller underground labels from around the world, together with self-released albums and the latest records from well-known bands.

"The Crypt is what I remember record shops being like when I grew up," says Marcus. "So I didn't know any other way to do it. The idea was to create a space where people could buy heavy metal records, but also somewhere where you can listen to the best metal music and discover new bands."

Marcus and Charlie first met via mutual friends at Muskelrock, a small heavy metal festival, dedicated to independent bands, in the middle of the dense Swedish forest. It was here that the idea of opening a record shop first took shape. "If they can organise this incredible heavy metal festival in the middle of nowhere, then we figured that we could open a heavy metal shop in London," Marcus says. It took a few years to turn the idea into reality, but since Crypt of the Wizard opened in 2017, the door has hardly been shut. Marcus and Charlie gladly spend time talking about the records to anyone and everyone, making recommendations and playing music for people to listen to. It's as far from the intimidating, old-school record shop as you can get. You leave feeling as if you met up with some old friends and, as it says on their tote bags: Metal Makes Us Strong.

Next door at 324d Hackney Road, is the bright and well-lit **Cosmos Records** a soul – jazz and funk specialist. Cosmos already has a branch in Toronto the first of which opened in 1998 and now has a UK outlet. Be warned though, neither shop opens early; Crypt Of The Wizard opens at 11am and Cosmos at 12 noon.

Eel Pie Records

44-45 Church Street, Twickenham, TW1 3NT
07817 756315
eelpierecords.com; kevin@eelpierecords.com; @eelpierecords
Monday-Saturday 10am-6pm Sunday 11am-6pm
Established 2016
Stock: Vinyl, CD, Books, Coffee, In-stores
Nearest station - Twickenham

The shop is named after Eel Pie Island a place with numerous musical connections situated a few hundred meters from the shop. In the 1960s it held many jazz and blues festivals, and Pete Townshend, who once owned a recording studio there, named his publishing company Eel Pie Music.

Based in the oldest street in the town, and certainly the most beautiful, Eel Pie Records is a haven. A local bylaw ensures that all the traders have hanging baskets, full of flowers displayed outside the shop. Eel Pie Records hangs them both at the front and rear entrance to the shop.

As well as ensuring the shop looks good from the outside, owners Phil Penman and Kevin Jones have used the natural brick and dark wood of the interior to create an atmosphere with many eye-catching features. A huge poster of John Peel adorns one wall, while gold discs are hung on others. I laughed at the sign saying No Hippies as well as the Paddy Roberts album on display titled *Songs for Gay Dogs*, a relic from an era when "gay" meant "happy".

The shop shares its space with an independent wine merchant and a Biltong, where pieces of dried meat are sold; everything you need for an evening of home entertainment in one place.

Flashback Records *The owner sold his house to buy more vinyl*
131 Bethnal Green Road, Shoreditch, London E2 7DG
020 7354 9356
flashback.co.uk; newvinyl@flashback.co.uk; @flashbacklondon
Monday-Saturday 10am-7pm
Sunday 12-6pm
Established 1997
Stock: Vinyl, Pre-owned
Nearest station - Bethnal Green

Mark Burgess is the Mystic Meg of record retailing. If he ever decides to sell up he could become a clairvoyant. After ten years of trading, his Islington record shop was losing money. While most people were getting out of the industry, Mark was convinced that the future lay in selling vinyl.

In 2006, he sold his own house in order to finance the takeover of an ailing record shop in Crouch End. His dedication is commendable and although he has been living in rented property for more than 10 years, his business is doing better than ever.

Mark has plenty of experience, having worked at two of the most famous UK pre-owned record shops: Music and Video Exchange and Reckless Records. He spent many years making money for other people before taking the plunge to go it alone. He opened in Islington originally selling vintage clothing in the basement and music on the ground floor.

His idea was to change the record shop experience from an intimidating run-in with surly cooler-than-thou members of staff into an enjoyable way to spend some time, knowing that the staff will be pleased to assist you, whether your interest is in Dean Martin or De la Soul.

The shop has had many famous musicians browse the racks but one who did not quite make it to the counter was Morrissey. Mark was delighted to see him walk through the door and was looking forward to engaging with the former Smiths singer about his musical taste. Before he had the chance, an assistant put a Smiths record on the deck to welcome him. On hearing the first notes, Morrissey did a U-turn and beat a hasty retreat from the shop.

In 2014, Flashback opened a new flagship branch in Shoreditch, the heart of London's vibrant, fashionable and most happening area. With both Rough Trade and Sister Ray having branches nearby, this area should be the first point of call for music fans visiting London. Flashback was voted 17th best shop in the whole of London in a recent *Time Out* survey (that's *all* shops in London, not just music shops). Mark recalls a record released on the Immediate label in 1969 called *Happy to Be Part of The Industry of Human Happiness*. It was a compilation album featuring the best of the label, Small Faces, Amen Corner, Humble Pie etc. The title sums up what he feels about running record shops.

Flashback has two other branches
50 Essex Road, Islington, London N1 8LR
144 Crouch Hill, Crouch End, London N8 9DX

Honest Jon's Records

278, Portobello Road, Notting Hill, London W10 5TE
0208 969 9822
honestjons.com: mail@honestjons.com; @HonestJonsLDN
Monday-Saturday 10am-6pm
Sunday 11am-5pm
Established 1974
Stock: Vinyl, CD, Pre-owned
Nearest station - Ladbroke Grove

Honest Jon's has made an outstanding contribution to modern music both as a record shop and record label. The original business was started by two friends Jon Clare and Dave Ryner, who rented a property at 76 Golborne Road.

As part of the preparations for opening, Jon hired a sign writer before he had decided on a name for the shop. He was still trying to make up his mind, when the exasperated fellow shouted down from the top of his ladder "What's your name?". Jon answered, and the sign was written: HONEST JON'S. It sounded a bit like a dodgy pre-owned car dealer. Jon liked it.

The original idea was to open the shop only on Fridays and Saturdays, enabling Jon to carry on with his lecturing work. To get the shop started, Jon and Dave put their own vinyl collections as part of the opening stock. They put up a sign advertising that they would pay cash for records. The shop started off as a second-hand record shop and, being based in Notting Hill, they soon started buying vast quantities of reggae from the local Caribbean community to compliment the already extensive jazz and soul range. Combining the shop with his lecturing career eventually proved too much for Jon, and he made the decision to leave lecturing and concentrate on record retailing. The pair opened more shops at other locations throughout London, the most successful of which was the branch on Chalk Farm Road in Camden Town. The original shop moved to the location on Portobello Road in 1979.

In 1982, Jon and Dave ended their business partnership. Dave took the Camden shop, renaming it Rhythm Records (since closed, sadly). Jon stayed on as the boss at

Portobello into the 1990s, when he left to paint, work in analysis, and run a B'n'B in Hay On Wye.

The current owners of Honest Jon's, Alan Scholefield and Mark Ainley joined the business in the mid-1980s as shop assistants and bought it in 1992. Borrowing off family members to purchase stock, Mark travelled over to America and went on a buying spree to ensure that when they reopened the shop as owners, it would be full of exciting and interesting product.

The shop was closed for a week for redecorations and a large queue waited outside the store on the wet Saturday morning of October 31, 1992, when the shop re-opened. The day is remembered affectionately for the "red shoes" incident (nothing to do with the Kate Bush album of the same name). The boys had painted the shop floor red, but unfortunately it had not dried by the time of opening. Anyone who visited that morning left with a novel souvenir of red paint on their soles.

For the first year, the shop enjoyed a honeymoon period during which business thrived, after which, slowly but surely, sales started to decline. One day, one of their regular customers came in and showed Alan a tiny hand-held device called an iPod. He told Alan that he now had his music collection on this little device and that this was the future. Alan was fascinated but did not realise how much this tiny device was going to hit sales, which were already in decline thanks to the boom in illegal downloading. Portobello Road is an expensive location to trade from so the boys knew that for the shop to survive they needed to diversify.

One of the shop's regular customers was Blur front man Damon Albarn, who was always looking for something different and interesting to listen to. Alan and Mark were always keen to turn their customers on to new music, and Damon enjoyed the world music they recommended to him, which inspired him to start playing and recording with many African artists. In 2000 Damon returned from a trip to Mali with some recordings he had made on cassette and suggested that they start their own record label.

Their first release on the Honest Jon's label was the fruit of Damon's trip to Bamako, *Mali Music*. The label has since gone from strength to strength, releasing eclectic and diverse recordings from as far afield as Lagos, The Bronx, Port of Spain, Algiers, Beirut, Baghdad, and East Africa.

I regard the Honest Jon's label as the bearers of the mantle of Alan Lomax, the great field collector of the 20th Century, who gathered recordings from all over the world. Lomax himself was carrying on the work started by his father John A. Lomax who became a famous folklorist and collector of recordings. During their careers, father and son made more than 10,000 historic recordings. Starting in 1937, Lomax recorded folk, blues and world music from all over the USA as well as venturing over to Britain, Ireland, the Caribbean, Italy, and Spain, using the latest recording technology to assemble a treasure trove of American and international culture. Today, these recordings are of incredible historical significance. Not only did Lomax record traditional songs, he recorded some of the most influential artists of the 20th Century such as Jelly Roll Morton, Woody Guthrie, Lead Belly, Pete Seeger, Sonny Terry and Muddy Waters. His recordings have been sampled by many DJs and performers, most notably Moby. Lomax passed away in 2002, but Mark, Alan and Damon have picked up his baton and are continuing to bring the world interesting recordings from all over the globe.

Like Lomax before them, Honest Jon's also releases music by musicians the public are already aware of. One of the most successful artists for the label has been Candi Staton, who is probably best known for her 1976 UK No.2 disco classic "Young Hearts Run Free". She was also the vocalist on the Source's dance classic "You Got the Love", which sold two million copies. Honest Jon's released the *Candi Staton* album in 2004, which was a wonderful collection of her early Southern Soul Recordings. In 2006, the follow-up, *His Hands*, was released, with Mark Nevers of Lambchop producing. The title track, written by Will Oldham, attracted a lot of attention. It was an enjoyable experience for Candi who, during an eventful life, had endured marital abuse and alcoholism. Now both her career and life were heading upwards again as she recorded the album, with her daughter Cassandra providing backing vocals and son Marcus contributing on drums. Her third album, *Who's Hurting Now?* released in 2009 found Candi going back to her gospel roots. Other successful releases on the Honest Jon's label have come from Trembling Bells and Damon Alban's super group Rocket Juice and The Moon which featured Flea from the Red Hot Chili Peppers, Tony Allen and Eryka Badu.

Former employees of Honest Jon's include Nick Gold, the man behind the World

Circuit record label which introduced the world to the Buena Vista Social Club, among others. Another former assistant was the influential DJ James Lavelle who in 1992 went on to form the critically acclaimed Mo' Wax label. Musicians and music fans throughout the world can be grateful to the contribution this record shop has made to music culture.

If Music *The record shop owner who is on the cover of an iconic jazz album*
12 D'Arblay Street, London W1F 8DUL
0207 437 4799 .
ifmusic.co.uk; info@ifmusic.co.uk; @ifmusiconline
Monday-Saturday 11.30am-7.30pm
Established 2003
Stock: Vinyl, CD, Pre-owned, Art, Bags, Books, Merchandise, Trainers, Turntables
Nearest station -Tottenham Court Road

If Music is unlike any other record shop I have visited. It is a centre for music, culture and design in the heart of Soho.

Located on the second floor of the building, you ring a buzzer to be invited in by the owner, the charismatic London DJ/producer Jean-Claude, who greets you warmly at the door. He invites you to hang your coat up and leave your bag at the reception area and is happy to make you a drink while you look through the shop's wares. The shop has a warm, welcoming vibe where customers are treated like guests in a private club. Indeed, Jean-Claude keeps the heating so high, that I felt like stripping down to my T-shirt even though the temperature outside was almost freezing.

The records are displayed in vintage wooden wine cases, a typically classy touch. The shop is an essential visit for DJs, with a strong selection of jazz, boogie/disco, techno/house, African, Brazilian and all types of world music. It helps that the knowledgeable Jean-Claude is behind the counter to guide you through what is new. His enthusiasm is infectious, and many customers leave with something they never intended to buy when they entered, thanks to Jean-Claude playing or enthusing about a new record. His mission is to help break acts and introduce the next generation of new talent to the established underground.

The walls are decorated with many interesting objects, including a picture of Jean-Claude – although you would be unlikely to recognise it as him. His father Cal, a photo-journalist, had been commissioned to take a photograph for the front cover of jazzman Charles Lloyd's debut LP. It was titled *Bizarre* – although, rather bizarrely, re-titled *Discovery* in the USA. On the front of the album cover, in front of Charles Lloyd, sits a six-year-old Jean-Claude wearing yellow shades.

The day of the photo shoot was memorable for young Jean-Claude as his mum had told him not to get dirty at school. So instead of playing British bulldog or stick in the mud with all the other children, Jean-Claude stood against the railings, not wanting to let his mum down. He grew up with a father who was addicted, not to alcohol or gambling, but to buying jazz music on vinyl. The result was an education in fine music that has stayed with him.

Jean-Claude spent six years running the famed Jazz Lounge at the dance record shop Release The Groove combining it with his DJ/production work as one half of the Amalgamation Of Soundz before starting his own business.

The shop stocks a beautiful collection of limited silk screen prints by Jules Mann, each one individually painted. It also displays and sells the work of Eddie Otchere, best known for his photographs of the rappers and DJs of the mid-1990s. His most celebrated works include portraits of Stevie Wonder, Isaac Hayes, Biggie Smalls, Blackstar, So Solid Crew, Goldie, Omar and many others. His work is on the covers of some of rap music's seminal albums.

My favourite Jean-Claude story concerns a 70-year-old woman who arrived in the shop with a beautifully hand-written list of all the records she wanted to sell. They included first pressings of albums by the Beatles, Pink Floyd, Led Zeppelin and more. She had listed all the extras that came with these albums such as posters and cards. She explained that they were all in pristine condition as she had only played each album once to record them on to tape.

Pride of place in this collection was a first pressing of the Beatles *White Album* which was numbered in the 90s. Ringo Starr had sold his copy of the *White Album* numbered 0000001 for $790,000 in 2015, so Jean-Claude was aware that this was worth a five-figure sum.

The woman explained that a local dealer had visited her house and offered her £500 for the collection. She felt it was worth more than that and refused. The next day he called back and offered £1,000. Again she turned it down. He then phoned with a "final offer" of £1,500, but his tone had become aggressive so she had stopped taking his calls and contacted Jean-Claude for a second opinion. Although he was tempted to make her an offer the old lady reminded Jean-Claude of his mum and he felt she needed protecting. He suggested that she box up the records and write a letter for her grandchildren to explain how special and valuable the records are. They were to be opened when she had passed away. The records would be an incredible inheritance. The lady thanked Jean-Claude for his words of wisdom and left. She later wrote him a nice letter. It was an admirable thing for Jean-Claude to do.

This shop is a stone's throw from other Soho record stores Phonica, Sounds Of The Universe and Sister Ray. If you are a fan of jazz, dance or world music, don't be intimidated. Ring the bell and step inside Jean-Claude's wonderful emporium.

Kristina Records

44, Stoke Newington Road, London N16 7XJ
0207 254 2130
kristinarecords.com; @kristinarecords
Monday-Saturday 12-8pm
Established 2011
Stock: Vinyl, Pre-owned, T-shirts
Nearest station - Rectory Road

Kristina Records is a well-designed store based in Dalston, an area of London quickly getting a reputation for all things cool. Bright and fresh with simple but refined furniture, it is the complete opposite of the traditional crate-digging model. They have used wood and chipboard to give it a distinct look. The shop's philosophy is to stock quality over quantity, specialising in independent and underground music. The shop is strong on all types of dance music with a good range of house, techno, disco and reggae.

Les Aldrich Music *The Kinks' local record shop*
98 Fortis Green Road, Muswell Hill, London N10 3HN
0208 883 5361
lesaldrichmusic.co.uk; lesaldrichmusic@gmail.com; @LesAldrichMusic
Monday-Friday 9.30am-5.30pm Saturday 9am-5pm Sunday 11am-4pm
Established 1955
Stock: Vinyl, CD, In-stores, Musical Instruments, Sheet Music
Nearest station - East Finchley

Les Aldrich Music was established in Muswell Hill more than 100 years ago, under the name Lester James. In 1955, Les Aldrich took over and renamed the shop after himself. He was the brother of the successful pianist Ronnie Aldrich who went on to become Musical Director of the *Benny Hill Show*.

The shop is associated with the Kinks. Ray Davies, the band's singer, was a regular customer in his youth. His sister Renee bought him his first guitar at Les Aldrich in 1957. I think the shop is missing a trick by not applying for a blue plaque to mark this historic event. In 2010, the BBC filmed a documentary on Ray's life titled *Imaginary Man* in which he paid a nostalgic visit to the shop that clearly held such happy memories for him. It was produced by Julian Temple and presented by Alan Yentob. At the time, Ray was promoting his album *See My Friends* and the shop was adorned with posters of the record.

Following the broadcast, Kinks fans from all over the world contacted the shop requesting posters. Many of them make pilgrimages to the shop to have their photo taken there. They often tie it in with a visit to the local pub The Clissold Arms where Ray and Dave Davis performed their first gig in 1957. The pub was the band's local and is full of Kinks photos and memorabilia.

The shop has always made an extra effort for their customers, and never more so than back in the 1970s when the miners had gone on strike, and in order to conserve coal supplies, the government allowed electricity to be used only three days a week. This meant that many businesses only opened for those three days. Not so Les Aldrich, who fitted his shop out with gaslights and lent torches to their customers to enable them to see the records.

One genre they don't have a large selection of is French music, much to the displeasure of one customer who had misread the shop's name as "les Aldrich", and assumed it specialised in Francophone records.

Les Aldrich Music is the second oldest shop in Muswell Hill, the oldest being Martin's, which sells freshly ground coffee with dried fruit. I am amazed nobody else has opened this kind of shop. The business model clearly works, as they have been trading for over 100 years. The secret is that they grind the coffee by the window and the aroma drifting from the shop makes it difficult to pass.

The current owner of Les Aldrich Music is Ian Rosenblatt who works at a city law firm during the week and serves in the shop at the weekend. Graham Coxon, the Blur guitarist, is a customer and the team describe him as charming. The first time he came in, the shop did not have in stock what he wanted, so they ordered it in for him. Unfortunately, the member of staff dealing with Graham – a classical expert with limited knowledge of Blur – got his name wrong and handed him a receipt made out to Brian Cox. Graham handed it straight back and explained that he was not the famous physicist.

This part of North London may be a bit of a wasteland for record shops, but if you are prepared to make the effort to travel there you will find a wonderful area with lots of interesting independent shops. With Cheeses of Muswell Hill (one of the UK's most famous cheese shops), a fabulous coffee shop, and a must-visit pub for music fans all nearby, it is a great place to while away a few hours.

Let It Roll Records
121 Kentish Town Rd, London NW1 8PB
0203 602 3917
letitrollrecords.com; gary@letitrollrecords.com
Monday-Saturday 11am-7pm
Sunday 12-6pm
Established 2018
Stock: Vinyl, Pre-owned, Coffee
Nearest station - Camden Town

When successful TV and film editor Kieran Smyth realized he no longer wanted to be a successful TV and film editor, he turned to the thing he'd always loved: music, and especially vinyl records.

"I've lived in Kentish Town since 2005 and had always thought it would be great to have a really good record shop within walking distance of my house," Kieran says.

"After 13 years of no-one coming up trumps, I decided I would have to do it myself.

I knew what I wanted the shop to look like and roughly what I thought we should stock. But I needed help from someone with experience in music retail."

Which is where Gary Robertson came in, a former employee of Sister Ray, with whom Kieran had spent many hours discussing music on his frequent visits to the shop in Soho.

"We're basically still the same music lovers we were when we first met over 20 years ago," Kieran says. "Between the two of us we've got all the genres in the shop covered. From indie-rock to dub reggae, thrash metal to banging techno, punk to jazz. We think we've created a cool environment for people who love their music to come and hang out."

Level Crossing Records   *Psychedelic counter made from recycled plastic bottles*
49, Sheen Lane, East Sheen, London SW14 8AB
markbuckle09@gmail.com
07759 080059
Established 2018
Stock: Vinyl, Pre-owned, Cake, Coffee
Nearest station - Mortlake

"We believe that much like a record spinning on a platter and the slow drip of an espresso, coffee and music are both best enjoyed in their most analogue forms." **Mark Buckle - Level Crossing Records**

Mark and Luisa Buckle's shop is named after the level crossing just 100 meters from the shop, which is less than a minute's walk away from Mortlake station. Mark is keen to point out just how much extra business the level crossing brings him. Six times an hour the barrier comes down creating an instant traffic jam. Many times, he has looked through his window and noticed drivers stuck in traffic looking at the shop while simultaneously typing details of the shop in to their phone.

Level Crossing Records has some wonderful features including an incredible counter manufactured from recycled plastic bottles that is lit by giant light bulbs. The location of the shop is in East Sheen village and, apart from a small Tesco, the rest of the road is all independent traders.

Mark is also a musician but it is a tough career to make a living from. He has now found a lifestyle he loves, enabling him to play and sell music, while also supplying the locals with a great place to meet and sample some quality coffee.

Lion Coffee and Records,

118 Lower Clapton Road, Hackney, London E5 0QR
0208 986 7372
lioncoffeerecords.com; lioncoffeerecords@gmail.com; @lioncoffeerec
Monday-Thursday 8am-5pm Friday-Saturday 8am-7pm Sunday 10am-6pm
Established 2014
Stock: Vinyl, Pre-owned, Books, Coffee, Food, Licensed, In-stores
Nearest station - Hackney Downs

Lion Coffee and Records was started by Chris Hayden former drummer with Florence and The Machine along with Mairead Nash founder of Luv Luv Luv records, a label dedicated to finding and discovering new talent. The third member of the team was entrepreneur Lee Rigg. The vision was to have a record shop that served great food and coffee and also provide an intimate live music venue. The trio have a wealth of experience in music, both playing and promoting, and have hosted many big acts including Courtney Love and Gruff Rhys.

As well as regular gigs and DJ nights they host a monthly open mic night, Clapton Unplugged, which takes place on the first and third Sunday of the month. They also hold a poetry and spoken word evening every other Thursday. They are the only record shop I am aware of who host supper club evenings.

The shop is magically lit with dozens of tiny bulbs illuminating the vinyl on the wall. The wooden floor and racking add to the old-world ambience. It is customer-friendly with new vinyl in the racking on the left as you walk in and pre-owned vinyl in the racking on the right. The walls of the shop are adorned with work from local photographers and artists

Make sure you check out the vinyl outside the shop, as the boxes are full of bargains with an offer of three-for-£15.

The team are proud of the fact that they are appealing to such a broad section of the community from local workers to discerning vinyl junkies all enjoying the intimate bohemian atmosphere. As well as selling food, coffee and vinyl, they also put on regular in-store events. All food is sourced from local traders, a great example of how independent businesses should be supporting each other.

Lion Vibes
Granville Arcade, 98, Coldharbour Lane, London SW9 8PS
07459 221925
lionvibes.com; lionvibes1@gmail.com; @lionvibes
Thursday-Sunday 11am -7pm
Established Unknown
Stock: Vinyl, Pre-owned, In-stores
Nearest station - Brixton

Lion Vibes owner Matt Downs has been trying to find out when his shop originally opened but has been told so many different tales that he is not sure himself. One local character insisted that "It's been here since records began". At one point, it was owned by the reggae singer Alton Ellis otherwise known as The Godfather of Rocksteady. His portrait still hangs proudly from the wall.

Matt has done a great job of designing the shop which features wood painted in traditional reggae colours, where green represents the land, black the strength of the people and gold the sunlight. Lion Vibe is also a record label releasing more than 30 7-inch singles. Matt imports pre-releases from Jamaica and has a vast selection of pre-owned reggae records.

Love Vinyl
5 Pearson Street, Hoxton, London E2 8JD
0207 729 8978
lovevinyl.london; love@lovevinyllondon; @LoveVinylLondon
Tuesday-Saturday 11.30am-7pm
Sunday 12-6pm
Established 2014
Stock: Vinyl, Pre-owned, T-shirts
Nearest station - Old Street

With a huge red and white logo (a heart entwined with a record) Love Vinyl is hard to miss. Describing itself as a mecca for dance fans the shop specialises in all forms of dance vinyl including house, techno, funk, soul, disco and anything that relates to the genre. From all their contacts in the club scene they have made DJs aware that they pay a good price for vinyl collections and have become the shop with a great reputation for purchasing dance vinyl. The shop has some brilliantly designed T-shirts and bags featuring the shop logo and name. It is well worth planning a visit to tie in with one of the shop's many guest DJ in-stores.

Matters Of Vinyl Importance *The record shop where you can learn to make pasta*
16, Hoxton Street, Hoxton, London N1 6PJ
07841 429885
mattersofvinylimportance.com; mattersofvinylimportance@gmail.com; @M-O-V-I
Monday-Friday 9.30am-6pm Saturday 9am-7pm Sunday 11am-4pm
Established 2017
Stock: Vinyl, Books, Cake, Cards, Coffee, Gallery
Nearest station - Hoxton

Matters Of Vinyl Importance is a joint enterprise owned by veteran A&R man Alan Pell and band manager and club promoter Ben Kirby.

They have created a quirky, vibrant space for the music community to hang out. You can enjoy a game of Hungry Hippos, Connect 4 or Snakes & Ladders while enjoying a coffee or bite to eat. You can even make your own pasta as the shop runs regular classes.

Alan Pell has a fascinating history in the music business. His introduction to the industry came through playing guitar in dodgy punk bands. When none of them troubled the chart, he started driving and tour managing equally dodgy punk bands. To earn a few pounds extra he reviewed their concerts for the now defunct music magazine *Sounds*. Soon the magazine was sending him out to review all sorts of artists.

Alan found himself working for the then independent Chrysalis Records, rubbing shoulders with artists as diverse as Wet Wet Wet and Five Star through to Sinead O'Connor and the Waterboys. He worked his way up to Director of A&R for the EMI-Chrysalis group, along the way working on albums with Texas, James, the Fall, Fun Lovin' Criminals, CSS and many more, including the Subways, managed by the aforementioned Ben Kirby who became his business partner.

Alan also moved into the film world in the role of music supervisor for many successful feature films including *Four Weddings and a Funeral*, *Mr. Bean* and the first *Bridget Jones's Diary*. His role was to select the music. If you enjoyed the soundtracks of these movies, Alan is the man to thank. Fast forward three decades and the work started to dry up. So what does a guy who has climbed the greasy pole of pop from tea boy to Managing Director, with a bunch of multi-platinum discs and his name on the credits of several blockbuster films do when he gets too old to be paid to rock and roll? Easy, he phones up his old mate, Ben Kirby, borrows 20 grand and opens a cool café.

The café hosts bands, album and book launches. The first one was with Creation founder Alan McGee.

Do check out their music-connection birthday and gift cards. My favourite is "Adele Boy", a card which features the most successful singer in the world dressed up as Derek Trotter from *Only Fools and Horses*. The shop is full of quirky items including lots of old recording equipment and ghetto blasters. They even sell cardboard record players. A wonderful feature of the shop is the toilets. The walls are made with wood from discarded pallets. See if you can spot the creepy glass eyeballs looking down at you as you are on the toilet? A bit disconcerting but very funny.

Alan and Ben have been asking themselves if what they have done is a shrewd business decision or a mid-life crisis. Show them they have made the right decision by checking out this delightful vinyl café.

Nightfly Records *Boris Johnson calls in during the Brexit referendum*
52a Windsor Street, Uxbridge, Middlesex UB8 1AB
01895 259369
nightflyrecords.com; david@nightflyrecords.com: @NightflyRecords
Monday-Thursday, Saturday 10am-5pm Friday 10am-6pm Sunday 11am-4pm
Established 2015
Stock: Vinyl, CD, Pre-owned, Books
Nearest station - Uxbridge

Windsor Street is opposite Uxbridge railway station. If you walk down the hill you will arrive at one of the most impressively designed record shops in the country. It helps that the owner David Hurst was the lighting designer for Merlin the theme park operator who owned Alton Towers, Thorpe Park and Madame Tussauds among others. Since he decided to pack it all in and do his dream job instead, life has been a bit of a roller coaster.

It is David's experience of working in lighting design that makes a visit to Nightfly Records so interesting. The shop is long and narrow with the counter area being like a DJ booth. It is here that David sits spinning the records. The shop is quite dark, evoking a cave like atmosphere, but carefully selected lighting highlights many items of interest. Situated next to the door are two comfy chairs so customers can chill out for a while.

Since opening the shop, David has discovered that there used to be a record shop on the very same site in the 1950s, where it traded for more than 20 years. Ex-staff and customers have all been delighted to come in and chat about the old times. The original shop had a listening booth upstairs and couples would often pop up, not just to listen to the records. One ex-member of staff recalled that he would hear the record upstairs stop and if the young teenagers did not come down he would have to rush upstairs to stop any hanky panky. Former customers have told David that they would listen to the tunes in the listening booth and then go and buy them in Woolworths as they were cheaper.

The debate on whether the UK should remain in the EU was of great interest in the town as the local MP was Boris Johnson. The BBC used the shop as a location to interview Boris. During the filming, David's son Jack pulled out some records that he thought would make a suitable backdrop, among them *Selling England by the Pound* by Genesis, "Should I Stay or Should I Go" by the Clash and "Don't Go" by Yazoo.

A customer came into the shop and asked "Do you have the Vanessa Paradis album *M&J* on CD?" David told him they hadn't got it, but he could order it for him from suppliers in either Germany or Italy. "I don't want it in German or Italian," the man replied, "Only in French." David reassured him the singing would still be in French, regardless of where he physically sourced the CD from. The CD was duly ordered and collected. The next time the customer came in, David asked him how he was enjoying the Vanessa Paradis CD. "I don't like it," he replied. "I can't understand what she is singing."

Phonica
51 Poland Street, Soho, London W1F 7LZ
0207 025 6070
phonicarecords.com; customerservice@phonica.com; @phonicarecords
Monday-Saturday 11.30am-7.30pm
Thursday-Friday 11.30am-8pm
Established 2003
Stock: Vinyl, CD, Accessories, Books, Bags, T-shirts
Nearest station - Tottenham Court Road

"Fads come and go but we still always sell good dance music." **Simon Rigg - Phonica**

Phonica has been at the heart of the vinyl revival and has been a huge boost to record shopping in the Soho area. To many observers it seemed a crazy idea to open a record shop in the middle of London in 2003 when vinyl sales had reached an all-time low. But time has shown that they were ahead of the game and Phonica has since influenced a new generation of record shops.

Founder Simon Rigg, who started his music career as a dance music buyer at Virgin, had a vision for a different type of record shop, stocking product that you could not get in the mainstream stores. In collaboration with FACT magazine and Vinyl Factory (who also had a pressing plant), Simon opened the shop in 2003 with Heidi (later to become a Radio1 DJ) and Tom Relleen (now part of the band Tomaga).

Phonica quickly gathered a reputation for carrying a particular kind of dance music that was becoming popular in the early 2000s, namely the German minimal sound embodied by the Kompakt & Playhouse labels, which nobody else was stocking at the time. Phonica captured this niche market and the later electro house movement, thereby establishing itself as the go-to shop for dance music, not only in the UK but worldwide. A large percentage of customers are DJs. The shop stocks all varieties of dance music: rare soul 7-inches, library soundtracks, big room house, techno 12-inch singles, and much more besides.

The customer can listen to records on one of the 10 Technics record decks in the shop before deciding what to purchase. The three-seater sofa at the front of the shop looking out on to a busy Poland Street is an ideal place for people watching. Another popular feature is tables that display the new CDs. Each CD is accompanied by an in-depth review, providing background information about potential purchases.

In 2008, Phonica started its own record label. With three out of the first four releases being by staff members, it soon became an important part of the business. In 2014, they released a triple-disc compilation, *Ten Years of Phonica*, featuring exclusive material from established DJs and producers. They now have five labels connected to the shop. The store is also renowned for its events, including its annual birthday party in such places as Fabric, Corsica Studios or XOYO. Such success is hardly surprising when ex-staff members include such notable DJs as Heidi, Hector, Anthea, Palms Trax (aka Jay Donaldson) and Nic Tasker (who runs the record label Whities and DJs on NTS radio).

Pure Vinyl Records
The Department Store
246 Ferndale Road, Brixton, London SW9 8FR
0203 598 5272
Hello@purevinylbrixton.co.uk, @PureVinylRecords
Monday-Wednesday 11am-6pm
Thursday-Friday 11am-7pm Saturday 11am-6pm Sunday 12am-5pm
Established 2015
Stock: Vinyl, Pre-owned, Merchandise, T-shirts
Nearest station - Brixton

"Reggae music is hugely responsible for keeping vinyl alive and is a massive part of the current vinyl revival." **Claudia Wilson - Pure Vinyl**

Located only a minute from Brixton tube station Pure Vinyl Records is owned by well-known local DJ Claudia Wilson. I guarantee anybody who visits this wonderful shop will leave in a happier frame of mind than when they went in. Claudia likes nothing more than talking music and playing customers the latest records she has discovered. She is especially supportive of the local Brixton music scene with her enthusiasm being so infectious that it is difficult to resist purchasing one of the records she will play you.

Claudia is a Brixton girl. Her parents moved from Kingston, Jamaica in 1958 with Claudia the youngest of their seven children. Her earliest memory is listening to a pile of Blue Beat singles her father kept in the Radiogram. By the age of five, Claudia had taken her first steps to being a DJ by learning to play the records herself. The house was always full of music as her older brother and sisters bought loads of records. Her brother would visit the legendary record shop Desmonds Hip City on Atlantic Road bringing back little brown boxes full of records. He would take out the titles he wanted and give the rest to Claudia to play. Her sisters were the ones who introduced her to soul and funk.

Her brother was a trained electrician and started building equipment in his bedroom in the 1970s. When he was away working she would go into the room herself to listen to artists such as Big Youth, Dennis Alcapone and U-Roy. They sang about things she understood and in an accent like those she heard in her community. It was a tense time entering the bedroom, not because her brother might catch her listening to his system, more from fear of receiving an electric shock from his home-made valve amps.

She practised her DJ skills with her friends and first started DJing at house parties in the 1980s. By the 1990s she was getting paid to DJ in bars at a time when few women were on the decks. It was during this period she met her partner Mark. He was running his Sound System RDK Hi-Fi, which he has continued to do for the past 30 years as well as establishing the record label Universal Roots Records.

The 1990s were a wonderful time for the couple. With young children in tow they toured Europe, where Mark and other DJ's would play their booming Sound System at clubs, festivals and parties. Claudia has fond memories of Rome, Pisa, Geneva and Salento. This was where she first started selling vinyl to help finance the tour, running a record stall as well as DJ-ing at some of the events.

Claudia also had a day job as a care worker, but her ambition was to open her own record shop modelled along the lines of the many reggae shops in the Brixton of her youth. Claudia had a residency at the now sadly closed Mango Landin bar which was at the hub of the Brixton scene. It was here that she played soul and reggae during a 10-year residence. She started an open deck night in 2011, naming it Pure Vinyl and is proud that she introduced many people to the joys of spinning vinyl.

At these events a constant stream of people kept coming up to her to ask where they could buy the records she was playing. She decided to bring a few boxes along to sell on the night. This proved so popular that she opened her own stall on Brixton market.

Claudia told me her story and her thoughts on the Brixton scene in general.

"It was in Brixton that I first realised the impact of gentrification. I knew Granville Arcade as a child and walked there holding my mother's hand. Now it had changed. It is Brixton Village. In the 1980s after the Brixton riots we watched as many of the Caribbean families we had grown up with left the area disillusioned with the lack of investment and the hardship of living here. Places like Granville Arcade had no investment and were no longer the vibrant markets of my childhood but now as I returned with my record stall in 2013 it had changed again.

Investment in the form of cheap rents brought in businesses from outside the area. Brixton Village was filled with brand new people. More and more people wanted to come here. Local businesses were closing or being forced away by rising costs. The Music Temple Record Shop was hugely important for me as I watched the markets change. As a working mother of four children, money was always tight and I wanted to buy records. To get to the record shop I had to walk through the new Brixton watching people eating food as I did my weekly shop in the market. I would get there and the record shop would be my sanctuary. I knew that I would find something that would make me happy and a place I knew I would be welcome even if I only had £2 left to spend.

I opened my own shop in Reliance Arcade. My aim was to have a local record shop that everyone could enjoy. Everything about it was amazing I built it from scratch with the help of family and friends and had inherited the space from the lady who had run the Holy Shop for the past 40 years.

I was an early pioneer of recycling as I noticed workmen removing windows from a local school and asked if I could have them. I found some wardrobes that had been thrown out and a friend, Mattias, made the boxes for the inside of the shop. The outside was built with the help of Mark and my friend Rex out of wood they took from skips and of course some I bought.

Reliance Arcade is truly the one part of old school Brixton that is untouched. The sense of community there is unparalleled in Brixton. Soon the locals found the shop. The collectors and the DJs came and, as word spread, so did everyone else. My Partner Mark, who has his own record label Universal Roots, joined me, and took over for a couple of days a week and quickly helped to soup up the Reggae selection.

For the black community of Brixton, the shop was especially important - for the elders and young people alike. For many people coming to Brixton has become alien. Except for using the market there are few places many people in the community can go. It is important to have somewhere to walk into that is welcoming and familiar where you are hearing music you love and bumping into people you know; the old-fashioned local record shop.

My shop wasn't built with lots of money behind it - none in fact - but what I was able to do was to make a space that would hark back to a time when the music mattered and where I could engage with people who were curious, happy or amazed to see vinyl return.

In 2017 while working in my shop I was introduced by a friend, Devon Thomas from the Brixton Neighbourhood Forum, to some architects who said they were about to open a record shop in their new building on Ferndale Road in Brixton across the road from me. They asked my advice about the current vinyl revival. I told them how vinyl had always been alive for collectors and DJs and that it was only the popular music industry that had completely abandoned it. Reggae, soul and rock collectors and DJs had never stopped buying vinyl. We talked about the quality of the sound and how having something that was tangible enabled you to feel more invested in the music and how I had designed and built my shop from scratch. Then something very strange happened. The architects came back and asked if I would like to move my shop into the new building. After the most difficult deliberation I have ever had to make…. here I am now!"

If you are coming to London for vinyl shopping Pure Vinyl is a must visit for anybody interested in soul or reggae.

Record Deck *The record shop that floats any vinyl lover's boat*
Summer: various locations and festivals on the canals and rivers of England.
Winter: various locations around London canals.
07579 964138
@therecorddeckuk
Opening Hours: Dry weekends
Established 2014
Stock: Vinyl, Pre-owned

After five years as a union rep at a college library in London, Luke Guilford was physically and mentally burnt out due to the constant conflict between management and employees.

He owned a boat, which he had been living on for 16 years, on and off. A record collector since the age of 12, he combined his two passions and came up with a seasonal, touring, record retail operation called The Record Deck. In the summer Luke travels to as many canal-accessible music festivals as possible and in the winter he retreats to the canal network of London, opening in different locations as and when the weather dictates. It can be like a treasure hunt trying to track him down. The best bet is to checkout his Facebook page: facebook.com/therecorddeckuk

Luke faces hazards unknown to other record shops. He somehow manages to fall into the canal at least once a year – on one occasion when carrying his portaloo, which thankfully held its integrity surprisingly well. It is not only Luke who has ended up in the drink. A couple of customers arrived at the shop by means of a rowing boat, which capsized on the journey back, depositing them and the vinyl they had just bought into the canal.

Travelling on the canals provides a great opportunity to visit shops, markets and car boots all over the country which provide a never-ending supply of stock. You are guaranteed to find Luke at the Cropredy Festival near Banbury, where he moors his boat on the canal near to the festival site. He always does a brisk trade in vinyl records by Fairport Convention, the organisers of Cropredy, as well as any other artist playing that year.

All the stock is displayed in wooden crates, so the term crate-digger applies to anybody who pays the boat a visit. Luke has managed to cram a lot in to a limited space. He keeps back-up stock at his Mum's house, so the racks are never empty. Look out for his blackboard sign on the towpath and the big red umbrella protecting his stock from the sun and the rain.

Reckless Records
30, Berwick Street, London W1F 8RH
0207 437 4271
reckless.co.uk
recklessrecordsuk@gmail.com; @RecklessRecords
7 days a week 10am-7pm
Established 1983
Stock: Vinyl, CD, Pre-owned, merchandise
Nearest station - Tottenham Court Road

One of the best second-hand vinyl shops in the UK Reckless Records is easy to spot with its bright red frontage. As well as second-hand records, the shop also stocks Record Store Day releases and a small amount of new vinyl. Reckless once had four shops – two in London and two in the USA – but these days just the branch in the heart of Soho survives.

Rough Trade East   *The record shop every music fan should visit once in their life*
Old Truman Brewery
91 Brick Lane, London E1 6QL
0207 392 7790
roughtrade.com; enquiries@roughtrade.com; @RoughTrade
Monday-Thursday 9.00am-9.00pm Friday 9.00am-8.00pm
Saturday 10.00am-8.00pm Sunday 11.00am-7.00pm
Established 1976
Stock: Vinyl, CD, Books, Cassettes, Coffee, Food, In-stores, Licensed, T-shirts
Nearest station - Aldgate East

Based in an area of London associated with Jack the Ripper, but nowadays better known as the best place in London to go for a curry, you will find the most renowned independent record shop in the world. Rough Trade has made a significant contribution to independent music for more than four decades. The story began in 1976, when Geoff Travis, a Cambridge graduate working as a drama teacher, took time out to visit America. In San Francisco, he discovered the well-known independent bookshop City Lights, which published the kind of edgy books that mainstream publishers steered clear of. It was a was a meeting place for poets and the art community.

The independent ethos and alternative spirit of City Lights made a considerable impression on Geoff. In those days, the exchange rate favoured visitors from the UK, and vinyl records were a good-value purchase. A committed music fan, Geoff took full advantage and brought hundreds of records back to England from the record shops he had visited on his travels, without any clear idea of what he was going to do with them.

With the help of a loan from the Bank of Dad, he opened his first premises with perfect timing in 1976 at 202 Kensington Park Road, Notting Hill. The punk revolution was starting, and the shop quickly established itself at the hub of the movement.

Like many record shops of that period, Geoff started his own label. The first release on Rough Trade was "Paris Marquis", a single by the French punk band Metal Urbain with the catalogue number RT001, quickly followed by releases by Stiff Little Fingers, Swell Maps, the Raincoats, and Cabaret Voltaire. The label quickly became a key influence on musicians and music fans alike.

Geoff has had an amazing career in the industry, having been involved in the signing and development of acts including Babyshambles, Belle & Sebastian, The Fall, James, the Libertines, the Strokes and, most famously, the Smiths.

Rough Trade originally specialised in US and Jamaican imports as well as being an outlet for the punk scene. It subsequently became a pilgrimage point for anyone buying or selling DIY new wave records and fanzines.

What followed was a period of swift international growth with branches of Rough Trade opening in San Francisco, Tokyo and Paris. When the decline in record shop retailing took hold, the shop closed down these global outposts and went back to its London roots. The shop and label businesses separated in 1982. Nigel House, Pete Donne and Judith Crighton, who were all Rough Trade employees, bought the shop and moved around the corner to 130 Talbot Road. Geoff, meanwhile, continued to run the record label.

In 1988, Rough Trade opened a second store at 16 Neal's Yard, Covent Garden - a hip courtyard just off Monmouth Street, which was full of quirky shops and cafes. In 2001, they celebrated their 25th anniversary with a series of gigs and the release of a commemorative 56-track compilation box set featuring artists such as the Smiths, Joy Division, the Buzzcocks and Nick Cave among many others. The same year, they received an award from *Music Week* in recognition of their unique contribution to the British music industry.

In 1996 Stephen Godfrey joined the business and was instrumental in launching the Album Club, a premium music recommendation service aimed at those people without the time or opportunity to visit a store who require an honest recommendation of exciting new music. The club came about after a gig by the Gotan Project at London's Festival Hall. Rough Trade had a stall and before the gig had even started they had sold out of all their Gotan Project CDs. This inspired Nigel to think that there must be thousands of people who love this type of music but can no longer purchase it, many would be ex-customers who had moved away from London and could no longer find the time to flick through record shop racks anymore. As people marry and have children, they often find they have less time, but this does not mean they have lost their taste for music. Each month, members receive a parcel through the post with the shop's recommendation. This is a perfect solution for music fans who wish to keep up with new music but can't make regular visits to the shop.

The criteria for music being chosen as an Album Club recommendation is simple. The staff must love it. The idea is to give exciting new music the chance to be enjoyed by people who appreciate something more stimulating than chart music. Customers choose what genres they like and decide if they want the release on CD or vinyl. Other benefits include exclusive goodies such as rare bonus recordings alongside invites to member-only gigs. To sign up, check out the website.

One innovation that is impressive at Rough Trade is their "counter culture". Piled high on the sales counter are a selection of CDs recommended by the staff. When a customer purchases a CD, the staff will often recommend a similar title that they feel the client would also appreciate.

2006 was a big year for Rough Trade - their 30th Anniversary, commemorated with the release of a double-album: *The Record Shop - 30 Years of Rough Trade Shops*. This was also the year they launched their digital store.

In 2013, Rough Trade fulfilled their international ambitions when they stunned the world of record retailing by announcing that they were opening a shop in New York at 64 North 9 Street, Brooklyn, NY11249.

This magnificent store is housed in an old film prop warehouse with more than 15,000 square feet of space which also houses the Brompton Café and Melville House bookstore. The shop is spread over two floors, in which old shipping containers are cleverly used as part of the design. The second floor houses a particularly quirky container which has been deployed as the Guardian Green Room. The room is fitted with touchscreen displays that visitors can use to read articles from the British newspaper. It would be intriguing to know what USA fans make of this innovation.

The building also houses a music equipment store, a lounge space, an installation gallery, (for temporary art exhibitions) and an impressive concert venue with a bar. The venue space will comfortably hold around 300 people.

Such is Rough Trade's reputation, the calibre of artist they can attract for in-store appearances is unrivalled. Bands that have played at Rough Trade in London include Arcade Fire, Belle & Sebastian, Blur, James, The Libertines, and Sufjan Stevens. Most days somebody is performing so check the website before you call in.

Rough Trade also has its own magazine which was first issued in 2015.The magazine is a cracking read for those wanting to know about new music. It has features on artists, labels, background to the shop's Albums of the Month and even runs a horoscope. One feature called Ask Jonathan gained cult status. Featured in the first 18 issues, it was written by musician Jonathan Richman, who answered questions sent in by fans. The only problem was Jonathan did not own a computer so Liv Siddall, the editor, would email the questions to Debbie Gulyas of Blue Arrow Records (Jonathan's label) who would ask Jonathan and email his answers back.

Rough Trade also has its own radio station where you can check out features, mixes and some chit chat with artists who have played in the shop or have records released. You can listen on iTunes or via SoundCloud at souncloud.com/rough-trade

Do not leave Rough Trade East without recording your memories of your visit in the shop's photo-booth. You can add your photo to the thousands displayed on the wall surrounding the machine.

Look out for Rough Trade pop up shops which can be found during the summer at the Green Man and End of the Road festivals.

In 2014, Rough Trade joined forces with the highly-rated Bristol-based chain Rise which had been started by Lawrence Montgomery. The first store opening was in Nottingham in the city's Creative Quarter at 5 Broad Street, NG1 3AL, 0115 896 4013.

December 2017 saw the opening of a Rough Trade shop at 3 New Bridwell, Nelson Street, Bristol, BS1 2QD. 01179 290383.The store is spread over 4,500 square feet and has a venue at the rear of the shop. Local band Idles performed on the opening evening.

If you have never been to a Rough Trade store, it is time to pay them a visit. If you are planning to open a record shop, make sure you visit Rough Trade for inspiration. You won't be disappointed.

Rough Trade has a smaller branch in London, known as Rough Trade West.
130 Talbot Road, W11 1JA,
01892 653451
I recommend you check out both East and West, but if you only have time to visit one

"go west" (to quote the Pet Shop Boys). The shop has been trading at the Talbot Road address since 1982 and has some amazing authentic posters of artists such as the Clash and the Sex Pistols. Don't think of it as a museum though. Rough Trade is still at the forefront of new music and the shop has a buzzy atmosphere.

Top tip - If you wish to read the full story of Rough Trade check out Neil Taylor's excellent book *An Intimate History of Rough Trade*.

Rye Wax *The most independent of independent record shops*
The Basement, CLF Art Café,133, Rye Lane, Peckham, London, SE15 4ST
0207 732 3176
ryewax.com; claire@ryewax.com; @Ryewax
Tuesday-Sunday 12am-8pm
Established 2014
Stock: Vinyl, CD, Pre-owned, Books, Cassettes, Coffee, Comics, In-stores, Licensed
Nearest station - Peckham Rye

Rye Wax is an independent record shop, bar and event space in the basement of the iconic Bussey Building, a 120-year-old multi-level warehouse space. From the stock it sells to its opening hours and ethos, this is a real independent shop which does what it wants to do. Don't expect to find releases from the major record companies.

I asked shop manager Claire Smith about its independent ethos.

"The music we stock has a local focus and we aim to showcase and represent local talent rather than all the latest releases. We're a hub for DJs and dance music but we stock anything we like from across the board. As well as being part of the new wave of South East London record shops, we're also recognised for nurturing local talent that has known international success. Siren is an all-female techno collective and club night that had its birthplace here at Rye Wax, and Cotch focuses on new underground urban music, exciting street music from around the world and road rap.

Generally, we like to represent cultures within music that we feel are underrepresented or marginalised in the current music scene, and countercultural movements rather than taking obvious routes. Our music in store reflects this ethos and also has a strong focus on local labels, local artists and friends of the shop. Additionally, this was the starting place of an annual event called The Run Out in celebration of local grassroots, independent music and vinyl culture which was intended as a response to the growing commercialism of Record Store Day. The Run Out has received widespread praise from the leading lights of the UK music press."

Claire makes an interesting point about Record Store Day, which does not cater for the dance market very extensively, as confirmed by the fact that many of London's top dance record shops including Cosmos, Kristina Records, and Rye Wax do not sign up to take part in the day.

Top tip – Turn up between 6pm and 8pm. When you have finished purchasing your vinyl, the bar does happy hour (or should that be happy two-hours?)

Sister Ray *The owner became a soccer coach because he knew the offside law*
75 Berwick Street, London W1F 8RP
0207 734 3297
sales@sisterray.co.uk; sisterray.co.uk; @SisterRayStore
Monday-Saturday 10am-8pm
Sunday 12-6pm
Established 1987
Stock: Vinyl, CD Pre-owned, In-stores Merchandise
Nearest station - Tottenham Court Road

Also, at 100 Shoreditch High Street, London E1 6JQ - Vinyl only

Sister Ray, named after the 17-minute track that closes the *White Light/White Heat* album by the Velvet Underground, has been a fixture of Soho and more importantly Berwick Street since the late 1980s. The owner, Phil Barton is one of music retail's great survivors. The shop, which was originally opened at 94 Berwick Street by Neil Brown, has seen three incarnations: a merger, a remix and now comes with a bonus site in Shoreditch. Phil has steered the ship through turbulent waters for nearly two decades and only now with the revival of vinyl are the retail seas slightly calmer.

As a kid growing up in South London, armed with a WH Smith tape recorder and a pile of blank BASF tapes, Phil developed an early, eclectic taste based on the Wombles, the Who and Elvis Presley. Moving to Whitstable in the mid 1970s broadened his diet somewhat and the Moody Blues, Colosseum and Judy Collins were lifted from his parents record collection. However, as with most teenagers of that time, it was the advent of punk rock and new wave that hastened his demise or salvation, depending on whether you were his parents or not.

A brief stint at Nottingham Trent Polytechnic led Phil to the door of Selectadisc, the iconic record shop owned by Brian Selby. Working as a singles buyer in the Bridlesmith Gate shop was a revelation. The gateway to music was opened and Phil stepped through enthusiastically embracing gigs, pop culture and the vinyl record.

Phil's was poached by Island Records where he became an area sales rep. At the age of 21 he was driving his mates round in a Volvo Estate crammed full of records, mistakenly believing that he could do anything. This explains a brief hiatus in the USA where Phil became a soccer coach based purely on his understanding of the offside rule.

Returning to London, he took a series of jobs in the Music Industry for MCA, Parlophone and Andrew Lloyd Webber. In every job he encountered leaders, ground breakers and pioneers who influenced him. John Walsh, Tony Wadsworth and Malcolm Hill at Parlophone. David Field at Capitol Records. Tris Penna at Really Useful and the indefatigable band members of China Drum, the band he managed and on whose behalf he negotiated record, publishing and merchandise deals on both sides of the Atlantic.

While working for IT Records, the in-house label for Andrew Lloyd Webber's Really Useful Group, Phil was promoting a tour by the newly signed band My Life Story. The tour had reached Brighton and he popped into Rounder Records, the town's leading independent store, and was offered the shop by the owner, who was seeking a quick exit. Phil accepted and went back to his retail roots.

Importantly, the knowledge gained from those early days at Selectadisc was still relevant. Dealing with reps, staff and red tape. Having learned how to buy overstocks from Selectadisc legend Jim Cooke, looking after customers and providing a great retail experience all helped Rounder Records thrive again. From there it was inevitable that the record retail Mecca that was Soho, would come calling.

Through a series of openings and closures the Sister Ray name is now proudly trading from 75 Berwick Street. There were tough times too, closing Rounder, buying and closing Selectadisc was both uplifting and demoralising. Phil recalls that the Selectadisc situation came at the wrong time. Record retail was carnage and he wanted to save Selectadisc, a shop so close to his heart. The truth was it was on its knees and the country was in recession.

There used to be 20 record shops on or near Berwick Street in Soho. There are now five. They are the tough guys and Sister Ray is one of them. I think of Phil Barton as the Rocky of independent record retailing. Like the Sylvester Stallone character, he has been on the ropes, many times, but came through the winner in the end.

A visit to Sister Ray will always start with a smile. Lovingly framed and prominently displayed in the window will be one of the worst album sleeves of all time, a feature which changes every month. On recent visits, they have featured "Diamond Lights" by Glenn & Chris, the former England footballers Glenn Hoddle and Chris Waddle (why not Hoddle and Waddle?) whose extreme mullet haircuts are a sight to behold. Another star of the series was the sleeve for "Hev Yew Gotta Loight Boy", the 1967 hit by the Singing Postman (aka Allan Smethurst) who may have influenced Slade with his approach to spelling, but not with his gormless postman image.

The shop itself is customer friendly, neat and well lit. Stencil graffiti adorns the wall with an impressive display of sprayed-on giant cassettes of albums by acts such as the Sex Pistols, David Bowie and Kraftwerk. These images would not look out of place in the Tate. Upstairs you will find new product, where key releases are displayed with the shop's review. Downstairs is the pre-owned and collectable stock. Many of the more valuable pieces are displayed on the wall.

In July 2014, Sister Ray opened a vinyl-only store housed in the Ace Hotel in Shoreditch. If you are a vinyl fan coming to London for the weekend, I cannot think of a better place to stay than a hotel with its own record shop.

Soul Brother *Backing singer stands in for Bobby Womack at PA*
1 Keswick Road, East Putney, London SW15 2HL
0208 875 1018
Soulbrother.com; LaurencePrangell@soulbrother.com @SoulBrotherRec
Monday-Saturday 10am-5pm Sunday 11am-5pm
Established 1991
Stock: Vinyl, CD, Pre-owned, In-stores
Nearest station - East Putney

Laurence and Malcolm Prangell were brought up in the 1960s in a large house in Watford. Laurence's first memory of music was courtesy of the next-door neighbours, a West Indian family, who played their reggae music very loud and into the early hours of the morning. This tended to annoy most of the neighbours, but not Laurence who lay awake enjoying the beats.

After leaving school Laurence went to Cambridge Technical College to train in accountancy. To earn a bit of extra cash, he started his own business, Record Enterprises. As well as studying, he bought and sold records wherever he could; at gigs, parties, college and eventually from a converted chicken shack.

Without references or paying money upfront he somehow managed to open accounts with all the major record companies. Studying during the day while working as a DJ and selling most evenings, Laurence realised he was working too hard when, at a gig at an American air base, he fell asleep in front of the enormous speakers.

After leaving college he found work with an office supply company but kept up his music related projects. He started a mail order service called Soul Brother, and in 1980 he sold Record Enterprises as he had got engaged to Doreen and the couple used the money towards their first flat. From then on, he concentrated on building up Soul Brother.

Laurence took the first of many trips over to the USA to purchase vinyl in 1992. The visit coincided with the first day of the Los Angeles riots. When he stepped off the plane, it looked like a scene from *Blade Runner* as plumes of smoke rose above the city, where an 8pm curfew was in force. He headed for the East Coast instead and, despite his initial problems, the trip was a success, perhaps too much so.

When the shipment arrived at his house in London, Laurence realised he had underestimated how much room the records would take up. His wife Doreen came home from work to find every bit of space in the house, including the bathroom, had been filled with records. Laurence needed to get selling. With the help of his brother Malcolm, he printed the first Soul Brother catalogue and posted it out to customers all over the world.

A couple of days later Doreen called Laurence and told him to get home as soon as possible. The phone had been ringing all day and they had taken more than 50 orders. When posting the catalogue to soul fans all over the world, Laurence had not taken into consideration the different time zones in which their potential customers were located. In those pre-Internet days, they soon found themselves receiving phone calls from customers in Australia at 3am.

After a family meeting, it was decided that the brothers would give up their day jobs, acquire suitable premises and, along with Doreen, devote themselves to selling records. In March 1994 Soul Brother opened for business and quickly established itself as the UK's best-known soul music shop. Malcolm was already writing for *Echoes* magazine, reviewing lots of the titles they were stocking and to obtain more publicity they started advertising on Jazz FM.

This brought in lots of new business and Laurence and Malcolm were asked if they would be the sponsors of Robbie Vincent's radio show and then, later, Johnny Hayward's show. Both DJ's were pioneers of the jazz, funk and soul scene. Jazz FM was available to more than 15 million people in the London Area. When Johnny Hayward was taken off the air the shop received nearly 100 complaints, many of them abusive, from listeners who assumed that Soul Brother were behind the decision. Many listeners assumed that, because the shop sponsored the show, they had some involvement in who was presenting it, which was never the case.

Soon people were queuing to get into the shop on Saturday afternoons. Laurence was going to the USA on regular buying trips. Customers would ask when the stock was being delivered, and before the shop opened there would be up to 30 soul fans waiting to look through the new stock.

Laurence had many adventures on his American tours. His trips would combine visits to wholesalers, record shops, dealers, record fairs and even meeting up with a bunch of taxi drivers in Washington who would fill up the boots of their taxis with records and meet him in the city. One record dealer known as Fat Tony was based in one of the less salubrious parts of Philadelphia where he ran an indoor market. Laurence was chuffed when Fat Tony said that he had something for him, assuming it was a piece of rare vinyl. Instead, Fat Tony handed him a gun, informing him that he would need it for protection in the neighbourhood. Laurence declined the offer, so Fat Tony kindly lent him his own personal minder for the visit.

At a record fair, one of the dealers suggested Laurence should pay a visit to someone known as The Count who had an amazing record collection. The directions Laurence was given were not clear, and Laurence found himself in a menacing, unlit area of town asking people on the street where he could find The Count. Eventually a group of youths pointed him in the direction of a three-story house. As he approached the door he noticed the house was lit by a deep red glow. He rang the bell and the door opened. Standing in the doorway, swathed in a big purple cape and looking like a version of Bela Lugosi, was The Count. "Come in," he beckoned. Laurence stood there for a few seconds wondering whether The Count was about to sink his teeth into his neck, before tentatively stepping inside.

The large room he entered had no furniture, no paint on the walls and was filled with records. Laurence presumed this must be the storage room. The Count summoned him to come upstairs. Again, the second floor was just records. Laurence guessed that the bottom two floors were used for storage and the top floor was where The Count lived. Imagine his shock when he reached the third floor and found it was the same. The Count had no TV, chairs or tables just three floors of records. Over the years The Count became a regular supplier for Soul Brother, but Laurence will never forget the first encounter.

Soul Brother has successfully brought international soul artists to England to promote their latest releases. They arrange gigs and signings in the shop. Laurence pointed out that while it was a lot of fun working with soul artists who are all extremely talented, organisation and timekeeping were often not their greatest strengths.

This was brought home to him after he arranged a signing session with singer and producer Leon Ware, who had worked with many top artists including Michael Jackson,

Marvin Gaye and Minnie Riperton. In the hours leading up to the signing Laurence had heard nothing from Leon and was beginning to get a bit worried. A queue was forming outside the shop, so Laurence drove to the hotel Leon was staying at. Sure enough, Leon had forgotten all about it. The two men rushed back to the shop and the story had a happy ending as Leon had a great time meeting up with his fans.

Not so successful was the occasion when soul legend Bobby Womack agreed to do a signing at a record fair held at the Hilton Hotel in Birmingham. Well over 100 fans turned up. But Bobby was feeling unwell and sent one of his backing singers to do the signing in his place. It was not a happy occasion for Laurence who had to explain to the people in the queue that the reason the person signing the albums did not look too much like Bobby Womack was due to her being a different sex. Bobby Womack had sent Alltrinna Grayson one of his female backing singers who seemed to be having a ball signing her name on the albums the fans had brought along for Bobby to sign.

According to Laurence, Jazz FM's rebranding to Smooth FM in 2005 was a major factor in the decline of the shop's sales at that time. The station's playlist changed from playing the music that Soul Brother sold to a more commercial sort of music that could be heard on other stations. This compounded the key problem for Soul Brother, which is a lack of media coverage for the music they sell. They receive support from *Echoes*, the black music magazine and numerous internet stations, but on national radio Gilles Peterson is the only DJ championing their sort of music. The station that has been the saviour of the shop is Solar Radio where Laurence has an extremely popular show that has been running for 18 years.

Soul Brother is a family business and a friendly shop with a great vibe. In Laurence, Johnny and Alex, who runs the mail order operation, you will not find anyone more knowledgeable or happier to share that knowledge. Sadly, due to health reasons Malcolm only works Sundays these days. Through the shop, gigs, mail order, the record label and Laurence's writings in *Echoes* the family work tirelessly to share their passion for soul music with the nation. If soul is your music, then make the pilgrimage to Putney.

Soul Proprietors *Look no further for Orville the Duck*
64 Elm Park, Brixton, London SW2 2UB
07532 492196
spbrixton@gmail.com; @soulproprietor1
Tuesday-Sunday 11am-7pm
Established 2017
Stock: Vinyl, Pre-owned
Nearest station - Brixton

To reach Nick Lucas' shop Soul Proprietors, was a bit of an adventure. Elm Park is opposite Brixton prison, where many buses stop. It is a lovely road full of nice houses and I was beginning to doubt there could be a record shop located here. Eventually a small parade of shops came into view one of which was Soul Proprietor. Outside it though was carnage: a knocked-down street sign, a smashed litter bin and a couple of flower boxes that had been obliterated, scattering soil and flowers on the pavement.

Nick explained to me that joyriders had crashed a car at 2.30am that morning and if it wasn't for the bin, the sign and the flower boxes they would have come straight through his window.

Nick had always been an avid record collector and while working in sales in Croydon would often daydream about opening his own record shop. He was a regular at the now defunct Wimbledon car-boot sale, buying for his own collection to begin with, but then to sell online.

He started specialising in original pressings of classical records. Many of these he sold in the Far East for sums in excess of £1,000. An offer of voluntary redundancy from his day job was the catalyst for him to look for a shop.

Through his contacts in the car-boot world Nick had established relationships with many people who arranged house clearances. One day he received a call asking if he was interested in clearing a house in the Isle of Wight of 20,000 vinyl records. Nick jumped at the chance, especially when he discovered that the asking price was just £1,200 for the lot. Clearly, they had not latched on to the beginning of the vinyl revival.

Nick hired a van and set off to the south coast. The sight that greeted him at the condemned property was mind-blowing. Records were piled up to the ceiling in every room. After numerous trips, all the records were transported back to the mainland. At the final count he had acquired 50,000 records – enough to stock the shop three times over - and surely one of the best vinyl bargains ever. Nick keeps the stock topped up through his regular house clearing contacts and, on his days off, scours the South in search of collectable classic vinyl.

Meanwhile, he has turned the back room of the shop into a new vinyl area.

One curiosity is the Keith Harris and Orville the Duck record prominently displayed above the counter of Soul Proprietors. This was acquired from a man who called in with a collection of records to sell. Nick was unimpressed both by the condition and the selection of stock and declined the offer. The man did not take this news well. "Surely you can sell Orville the Duck," he said. Nick took the record, to placate him, but his initial scepticism has been proved right. The record seems to have become a fixture in the shop and Nick has even become rather fond of it. However, if the price is right, it's yours.

Sounds Of The Universe *The home of the Soul Jazz label*
7 Broadwick Street, London W1F 0DA
0207 734 3430
soundsoftheuniverse.com; queries@soundsoftheuniverse.com: @SOTUSOHO
Monday-Saturday 11am-5.30pm Sunday 11.30am-5.30pm
Established 1993. Stock: Vinyl, CD, Pre-owned, Books, Clothing, Merchandise
Nearest station - Tottenham Court Road

The first thing you notice is the washing line hanging above the racks displaying the iconic T-shirts of Sounds Of The Universe. The shop is owned by Stuart Baker who also owns the London reissue label Soul Jazz Records. Starting off from a market stall 25 years ago, SOTU is now one of the must-visit record stores in the capital. The shop is particularly strong on grime, reggae, African, dubstep, funk and soul, Brazilian and hip hop. Upstairs you will find new product with plenty of listening posts to test out potential purchases. You will also find Soul Jazz bags for sale in 7-inch and 12-inch sizes, and a unique line in old-school vintage tracksuits.

Downstairs the basement is packed full of pre-owned vinyl, including some extremely rare albums and surprises. You would never expect to pick up a copy of *The Best of Lynn Anderson*, but I noticed a copy in the well-stocked pre-owned country section. Do make the effort to look in the boxes under the racking as plenty of well-priced stock is located there.

You will normally find the shop's main buyer Jonathan Burnip sitting in the corner behind the counter downstairs. He has a wealth of experience and is always pleased to recommend releases. The shop also has one of the finest selections of new and used music-related books I have come across. Gilles Peterson, Jamie Cullum and Martin Freeman are among the regular customers, but a big highlight for the shop was the day Prince walked in.

Sounds That Swing
88 Parkway, Camden Town, London NW1 7HB
0207 267 4682
nohitrecords.co.uk; nohitrecords@yahoo.co.uk; @NoHitRecords
Monday-Saturday 11am-6pm
Sunday 12-6pm
Established 1995
Stock: Vinyl, CD, Pre-owned
Nearest station - Camden Town

Located near the Dublin Castle, Neil Scott's shop Sounds That Swing is one of the best places in the UK to visit for fans of rockabilly and rock & roll.

Stranger Than Paradise

89-115 Mare Street, London E8 4RT
0203 745 2607
strangerthanparadise.com; info@strangerthanparadiserecords.com;
@StrangerThanParadiseRecords
Tuesday-Thursday 11am-8pm
Friday-Saturday 10am-8pm
Sunday 10am-6pm
Established 2018
Stock: Vinyl
Nearest station - London Fields

Ex-longtime Rough Trade employees Noreen McShane and Phil Adams used their experience to start their own shop. They named it after the 1984 cult film *Stranger Than Paradise* which starred Sonic Youth drummer Richard Edson and jazz saxophonist John Lurie, who also wrote the soundtrack. A vinyl copy stands proudly above the counter.

This is a vibrant, well-designed shop in a lively area. The shop is housed inside the buzzing, noisy Mare Street Market. It is easy to find thanks to the fabulous neon sign. The building is soundproofed, so all you hear when entering is the music they are playing. You could easily spend a few hours here as the market has plenty of cool options for eating and drinking. There are lots of quirky outlets to look round but none so quirky as this must-visit record shop.

Supertone

110 Acre Lane, Brixton, London SW2 5RA
0207 737 7761
supertonerecords.co.uk; info@supertonerecords.co.uk
Monday-Saturday 12-10pm
Sunday 1pm-7pm
Established 1983
Stock: Vinyl, CD, Pre-owned
Nearest station – Brixton

Supertone is a haven for reggae lovers. Every inch of wall space in Wally Bryan's legendary shop is covered in photos, posters and records. Although in places it looks like it could do with a lick of paint, this is a true, old school, atmospheric record shop. Mainly a second-hand shop, there is nevertheless a good selection of new imports and a superb selection of 7-inch and 12-inch singles. If visiting all the Brixton record shops, it is best to call here last, as it stays open till 10pm six days a week.

Tome Records
234 Graham Road, Hackney, London E8 1BP
0208 525 9857
tomerecords.co.uk; info@tomerecords.co.uk; @tomerecords
Monday-Sunday 11am-7pm
Stock: Vinyl, Pre-owned, Cassettes
Established 2015
Nearest station - Hackney Central

Originally opened in DIY Space for London in Bermondsey, the young enthusiastic owners Kevin Hendrick and Matt Estall recently moved Tome Records to Hackney, an area establishing itself as a vinyl heaven. It is located on a busy road, but within a minute's walk from the station. The boys are selective on what second-hand vinyl they purchase, resulting in a well curated choice of quality and collectable records.

Manchester

When people ask me where the best place in the UK is to buy vinyl, then Manchester would be my tip. The city has some legendary shops selling new vinyl and is the second-hand record shop capital of the UK. Head first for the square mile around Oldham Street, known locally as Vinyl Alley. Within a few hundred metres of each other you will find Piccadilly Records, Eastern Bloc, Vinyl Revival and Vinyl Exchange. Check out Afflecks, a beautiful building that is home to over 70 independent traders. Over the years it has had numerous record dealers housed there. Currently it is home to the wonderfully-named Vinyl Resting Place and Soundwaves, Here We Come. Both Empire Exchange and Clampdown Records are pre-owned specialists in the city. For information check out a brilliant website recordshopcity.co.uk. It contains reviews for all the record shops in the Manchester area and is a great help to anybody visiting the city on a vinyl-buying mission. It is a pity all cities in the UK do not have a website like this.

Eastern Bloc

5a Stevenson Square, Northern Quarter, Manchester M1 1DN
01612 286555
easternblocrecords.com; info@easternblocrecords.com; @Easternbloc1985
Monday-Friday 7.30am-6pm Saturday 9am-6pm Sunday 10am-4pm
Established 1985
Stock: Vinyl, Coffee, DJ events, Food, In-stores, Licensed Tickets

"We shift through all the rubbish, so you don't have to." **Jim Spratling, manager of Eastern Bloc**

Eastern Bloc was founded by John Berry and Martin Price, and quickly established itself as the must visit record shop for the dance music fans of Manchester. The shop was originally located in Afflecks, which it quickly outgrew, before opening larger premises in Oldham Street. The shop soon became an integral part of the Manchester music scene. Back in the late 1980s it helped to launch bands such as the Inspiral Carpets, while also hosting in-store signings with the Stone Roses and Happy Mondays.

The shop was responsible for breaking many of the new dance acts at the time, being a pioneer of importing dance music from around the globe. Eastern Bloc had heavy involvement in the early career paths of A Guy Called Gerald and K Klass, while the shop's co-founder Martin went on to become a member of the band 808 State.

The store was involved with some bizarre incidents involving the controversial Greater Manchester police chief James Anderton. In 1984, he ordered the shop to be raided. The front window was smashed, and police seized copies of records deemed to be obscene by bands such as Flux of Pink Indians, Crass and the Dead Kennedys.

Anderton was a polarising figure with many controversial views. He criticised church leaders for not offering moral leadership, was a vocal opponent of both gay rights and feminism and a supporter of corporal punishment. He launched a crackdown on late night drinking in Manchester, resulting in 24 nightclubs having their licences revoked. It was no surprise when he took out a private prosecution against Eastern Bloc for organising illegal raves.

The store has reinvented itself in recent years. In 2011, it moved to its current address and opened an in-store café with free wi-fi, making it the place to hang out for dance fans in Manchester. The timing was perfect. When they moved into Stevenson Square the area was quite run down, but now it is full of independent businesses. On Sunday the square has a market, making this the perfect time to visit to find some vinyl and enjoy one of the excellent breakfasts (I speak from personal experience).

The shop is on two levels, with the café downstairs and the vinyl floor upstairs. Look out for the traditional disco ball hanging from the ceiling. The shop has an extensive catalogue of dance music including jungle, dubstep, electronica, house techno, drum & bass. Since the move the shop has expanded the specialist sections, stocking more hip-hop, funk, jazz, reggae and African. With three decks for listening to vinyl, it is the meeting place for everybody connected with the Manchester dance scene.

Tom Houghton, who runs the upstairs, is one of the shop's DJs, along with Ben Marsden and long-term manager Jim Spratling. Tom makes an interesting observation. In most record shops people look through the racks, find what they want and bring it to the counter to purchase. At Eastern Bloc, many of the customers walk up the stairs, then go straight to the counter and ask the staff for recommendations. Tom informs me that the staff feel a great responsibility to get it right and suggest titles based on their knowledge of the customer. It is this system that has established such a loyal customer base.

On Fridays and Saturdays the shop is open until 11pm, as resident and guest DJs turn the evening into a dance party. Many of the events are warm-ups for the Manchester club crowd with the events often moving on to another venue after the shop closes. In the summer, it has even been referred to as the Manchester Riviera, as crowds spill outside on to the pavement. The team at Eastern Bloc have done a wonderful job of transforming themselves into a dance record shop with a quality café and DJ venue combined.

King Bee Records

519 Wilbraham Rd, Chorlton, Manchester, M21 OUF
01618 604762
kingbeerecords.co.uk; kingbee.records@yahoo.co.uk;
Monday-Saturday 10am-5.30pm
Established 1987
Stock: Vinyl, CD, Pre-owned

Owned by passionate Manchester City fan Les Hare, King Bee Records is painted an eye-catching, bumble bee yellow and set back among an unassuming row of shops. I called in not only to interview Les but to talk to the shop's most famous regular customer and great supporter of independent record shops, the guitarist Johnny Marr.

The shop was busy as I waited to talk with Les. It was a privilege to watch him in action. A regular customer purchased £180 worth of vinyl and, after much friendly banter, negotiated £20 off his purchase, leaving both parties happy. Another customer brought a huge collection of vinyl to the counter and Les sorted it out into records he can sell and records that the customer should try and dispose of at a car boot sale or give to a charity shop. Les offered £120 for the sorted lot and after much pleading from the seller eventually upped his offer to £125. The customer left happy. "The secret in this game is to always give a fair price" Les said. "That way people will come back."

Les Hare (who has no hair) opened King Bee in September 1987 (when he did have hair). His dad, Alan Hare, was a well-known jazz musician. As a teenager, Les was an avid collector of reggae and soul records with a particular passion for Northern Soul. While working at tractor company Massey Ferguson, he started selling records to his workmates. Before long, he began to supplement his wages by selling at local record fairs. Business was good, and in 1987 he handed in his notice and hired a stall in Chorlton Market, only a few hundred yards from where his current shop is. It was the kind of market that sold everything from knitting wool to tripe. Record collectors soon found him, and word spread about this great stall manned by a trader with a genuine knowledge and passion for music.

Les took on a young indie music fan called Rosie to help him out. On Wednesday afternoons, Les would leave Rosie in charge and take a tour around the other Manchester record shops to gauge the musical temperature and pick up a few bargains for himself. Left to her own devices, a mischievous Rosie would constantly play The Smiths album *Meat is Murder*. The record finishes with the disturbing sound of cattle on their way to the abattoir. Les would get back on Thursday mornings to angry complaints from the butcher's stall across the way. They would ask Rosie to turn it off but instead she would turn the volume up, alarming the old ladies queuing up to purchase their sausages and pies.

There was much celebration from the butcher, when Les moved to his current premises on Wilbraham Road. Although he had outgrown the market stall, Les did not have enough stock to fill the shop, formerly a grocery store, so he contacted T-shirt and poster suppliers to help him fill the gaps.

These days the shop attracts customers from as far afield as Japan, such is the shop's reputation for collectible vinyl. Smiths fans from all over Europe call in to check on the latest rarities by the band. Other customers include Bez from Happy Mondays and John Squire of the Stone Roses, while Derek Pringle, ex-cricketer and now sports journalist, always calls in when covering matches from Old Trafford. The legendary music producer Martin Hannett, prior to his death in 1991, used to sell his Joy Division rarities to Les.

A chap working as a painter and decorator in a newsagent a few doors away kept coming in and asking if Les had any Ricky Stevens. After doing a bit of research Les informed the gentleman he could obtain an EP, but it would cost £40. The man happily gave Les the money and Les told him he would get it in for him. Les asked him his name. "I'm Ricky Stevens," the man replied. Ricky was a successful singer in the early 1960s, best known for his recording of the pop standard "I Cried For You" released in 1961.

In true record shop tradition, Les and his assistant - the super knowledgeable Neil Barker - have secret nicknames for some of their customers. Mr. Chainsmoker, Everyday Steve, No Bag Jazz Man, Mr. Knocked The Turntable Over, Penny Farthing Face (who once parked his strange bicycle outside the shop), Girl With Black Hair Who's Going Through a Folky Phase, Blimey Charlie, and Mr. Any More Jazz Behind the Counter? The strangest of all was Purple Woman. Each day Les and Neil would see this strange woman walking past the shop, dressed from head to toe in purple. They would often discuss her, wondering where she was going and why she only dressed in the one colour. One day she came into the shop, pointed at a picture disc on the wall and said "I would like that record, please."

The record was "Purple Rain" by Prince and the price tag, a whopping £30. Purple Woman took it and has never called in since. She still walks past the shop and Les is on the lookout for more purple-related records to hang in the window in the hope of enticing her back in. So far no luck with "Purple Haze" by Jimi Hendrix or albums by

Deep Purple or the mod revival band Purple Hearts.

Records are merely a piece of plastic to the average person on the street, but to true collectors they are a matter of life and death. Witness the man who one day, frustrated that he could not afford a pricey 1960s record from the wall, in a moment of madness offered the keys to his motorhome parked outside the shop in exchange. Much as Les and Clare his wife would like to tour the country in their very own camper van, they declined his offer.

One unusual attraction at King Bee Records is the reggae auction held on an irregular basis, which draws more scary people than you can shake a stick at. There are wild-eyed chaps who communicate using a code constructed from old Blue Beat catalogue numbers and camel-coated characters who would seriously consider donating a kidney to obtain a copy of that once-in-a-lifetime Prince Buster gem "with original centre and no writing on the label." It is like Sotheby's during a Van Gogh sell off. Les takes phone bids, and there are weird twitches that signify bids and squabbling at the back over records that unexpectedly sell for hundreds of pounds.

Meeting the shop's most famous customer, Johnny Marr, reminded me of the Smiths song "This Charming Man". I could imagine happily spending an afternoon in the pub with the skinny, black-haired guitarist, who was happy to accommodate numerous requests from other customers to chat with him or sign a record. Indeed, Les sold almost every Smiths album he had in stock to customers keen for Johnny to sign them.

Johnny has never forgotten how independent record shops supported the Smiths when they started out. It is no coincidence that the Smiths signed to Rough Trade - a label which also had a record shop. When Johnny and drummer Mike Joyce called into the Rough Trade warehouse and met the owner Geoff Travis, they greeted him with words that have become folklore: "Will you listen to this? It's not just another tape." The full story can be read in Johnny's excellent autobiography *Set The Boy Free*.

Johnny, who appeared in the film of *Last Shop Standing*, and has championed independent shops in the past, is a massive vinyl fan and, more recently, has taken part in a BBC radio programme on the subject. He has also visited many of the record shops that I have written about.

"A new reason to love records I think [is that they are] the alternative to the experience of listening to an mp3 - not just from a sonic point of view [but] from the actual experience of it. If I put on an album and I'm answering the emails or reading or something - you experience twenty odd minutes of Roxy Music or whatever it is and you're engaged with the musicians who made that record. And then you go over and flip it over."

Johnny spoke with great nostalgia about his early days of buying T. Rex and David Bowie records and purchasing the *Spiral Scratch* EP by the Buzzcocks, a record that had a profound influence on him. Weekends were spent trawling the record shops of Manchester building up his collection. "When I was young, record shops were meeting places where you learned about music, clothes, style and clubs. Everyone in my town who was interesting was in the record shop at some point."

He expressed contempt for councils and greedy landlords who had priced so many record shops off the high street. This applied not just to record shops, but to many shops run by enthusiasts, whether they related to music, clothes or photography. Johnny wrote a blog on his website about the importance of record shops. Of all the people I have interviewed, he best understood the role of the record shop in supporting new artists and introducing us to different music.

"There's so much talk about the death of vinyl versus the download boom as if we all fled away from records because we love our iPods too much, but that isn't exactly the whole story," Johnny said. "The experience that I've had with the younger people I know, fans and my kids and mates and stuff, it's like vinyl's this like amazing version of the CD. It looks better, it's nicer to own. Some people I know in Portland, say they grew up with their Elliott Smith CDs, but the vinyl, they treasure it, it's like a deluxe version of this crappy little thing.

"All through the 1990s, stores that were rented and run by enthusiasts of say, photography and cameras, as well as music, got totally priced out of their premises and livelihoods, and our culture, by councils and landlords with the next quid and Starbucks dollar in their eyes. It wasn't all the fault of the megabyte and pixel, and now what's left? High streets that are so expensive to rent that only the richest, and therefore blandest of commercial giants can afford to ride out the recession there. Bad news for us, especially if you want a great piece of cultural art, which is what a record actually is.

"If record shops were able to function as commercial premises on our streets, then the stuff they sell would flourish. And that doesn't mean ditching our beloved iPods. It just means owning a great piece of work by our favourite band with a piece of real art on the cover, and something that actually sounds good too. Not bad for the price of two Lattes."

Piccadilly Records

Smithfield Buildings, 53 Oldham Street, Manchester M1 1JR
01618 398008
piccadillyrecords.com; mail@piccadillyrecords.com; @PiccadillyRecs
Monday-Saturday 10am-6pm
Sunday 11am-5pm
Established 1978
Stock: Vinyl, CD, Merchandise, Tickets, T-Shirts

Piccadilly Records prospered in the post-punk 1980s, selling a mixture of rock, pop, indie and alternative music. In 1990 the current management took over and continued to build upon its reputation as one of the world's best independent record shops. In 1997 the shop moved to its current location in the vibrant Northern Quarter area of Manchester.

Known for its passionate support of new music and especially the local scene, Piccadilly Records started life as Edwin P. Lees, a white goods retailer selling fridges and washing machines, with a chain of shops throughout the North West.

In 1978, they opened a record department in the Manchester branch based in the Piccadilly Plaza and the Piccadilly Records brand was born.

As the record department established itself, they started employing the store's most knowledgeable customers to work there. That is how the current owners Laura Spencer and Darryl Motorhead, came on board. Laura nearly didn't start at all. She had a dental appointment before she was due to start work on her first day and, while the dentist was working on her teeth, he dropped a file, which Laura swallowed. She was packed off to casualty to get the piece of metal removed from her stomach. After an x-ray, Laura was informed that the file would come out naturally when she went to the toilet, and no operation was necessary. On her next visit to the dentist, she noticed he had a file attached to a finger chain.

In January 1983, the Edwin P. Lees chain closed, making all the staff redundant. The staff took out bank loans, signed on to the government-based Enterprise Allowance Scheme, which provided valuable financial support, and re-opened Piccadilly Records in a new location on Brown Street.

One of the first things they did was to change the antiquated filing system used in the old shop. Most record shops would file records under the band or artist's name. But for some reason Piccadilly had always filed records by catalogue number. This system only worked smoothly when the customer brought the record to the counter. If somebody asked for a record by its title or the name of an artist, the staff would need to look up the catalogue number for a record they had filed away. If anyone needs to know the catalogue number of an independent record from the mid-1980s, ask the team at Piccadilly. Hundreds of the numbers are ingrained in their memories. Should any of them appear on *Mastermind*, Catalogue Numbers of 1980s Records would be their best bet for a specialist subject.

The mid 1990s was a booming time for the shop. At the height of the Madchester scene, it was common for them to order around 750 copies of a new 12-inch single by the Stone Roses. Nowadays they would deem a new release a good seller if it sold 10 copies.

One of the successes of this period was the "Cool as Fuck" T-shirts and hoodies produced by the band Inspiral Carpets. At the band's peak the shop would sell around 20 a day. The only problem was that they were popular with shoplifters, so a decision was made to hang them from the ceiling out of reach – from most customers, but not all. The legendary basketball stars Harlem Globetrotters, who were in Manchester for an exhibition match, called in, and effortlessly reached up to pull down the hoodies. The whole squad bought one, which made for quite a sight as they walked out of the shop.

The saddest day in the shop's history was June 15,1996. A red and white Ford truck was parked on Corporation Street, outside the Marks & Spencer store. CCTV footage showed the truck abandoned on yellow lines by two hooded men. Within three minutes a traffic warden had issued the vehicle with a parking ticket. At 9:43 a.m. Granada TV Studios received a telephone call claiming that there was a bomb in the car that would explode in one hour. The caller had an Irish accent and gave a code word so that police knew the threat was genuine. Thousands of people were evacuated including the staff and customers of Piccadilly Records. They were moved to King Street where they watched the events unfold.

The bomb disposal unit arrived and estimated that the truck contained a 3,000lb bomb. They attempted to defuse the bomb using a remote-controlled device, but they ran out of time. The bomb exploded at 11.17 a.m. initiating an estimated £1 billion damage. Marks & Spencer and the iconic sky bridge connecting it to the Arndale Shopping Centre along with neighboring buildings were destroyed. Piccadilly Records was one of the businesses badly damaged, all the windows being blown out. Due to structural damage caused by the bomb it was two weeks before the staff were allowed back to survey the damage. It took another two weeks for the shop to get up and running again.

As is often the case, the insurance company policy did not pay them as much as expected and in a double whammy their premiums more than doubled. The team took stock of the situation and decided to move to a cheaper part of town. They found suitable premises in Oldham Street in Manchester's Northern Quarter where they have remained to the present.

Stocking an across-the-board variety of genres including indie, disco, funk, house, Balearic, psych and everything in between, Piccadilly has a wealth of undiscovered music available on both vinyl and CD. Though this could be a daunting prospect, each release features an entertaining, informative and occasionally insane review by a different member of staff, intended to guide you towards your new jam. And if you're still not sure, you're welcome to give anything a spin on the in-store listening decks.

With an emphasis on friendly, knowledgeable and enthusiastic service, the Piccadilly staff enjoy nothing more than across-the-counter conversations about long-forgotten janglers, recommending their latest obsessions or naming that "one dance tune you heard in the club last week." This fervour for new music is reflected in their annual *Best of Year* booklet, an essential compendium of their favourite LPs, compilations, reissues, box sets and singles.

The Piccadilly team can be proud of their efforts, because despite some stiff competition they are the city's most famous independent record shop and a must visit for any vinyl fan heading to the North West.

In recent years, they have been voted Best Independent Record Store at the prestigious *Music Week* awards and Best Record Store at Gilles Peterson's Worldwide Awards. They have also featured in *The Observer*'s World's Best Shops, *The Guardian*'s Best Record Shops and at No.1 in *The Independent*'s Top 50 UK Independent Record Shops.

Top tip - If you would like to know the full story behind Piccadilly Records, pick up a copy of *The Piccadilly Records Book,* by Michael and Gwen Riley Jones, an excellent account which was published to celebrate 25 years of the shop. It is on sale in the shop.

Static Records

53 Mesnes Street, Wigan, Greater Manchester WN1 1QX
07913 061976
staticrecordswigan.co.uk; paulstatic@hotmail.com; @StaticRecords
Tuesday-Saturday 11am-5pm
Established 2012
Stock: Vinyl, Pre-owned

In a town more famous for rugby league than record shops you will find Static Records, an emporium that does not live up to its name thanks to the hordes of vinyl fans forever on the move, digging through its racks. Owners Paul Dolman and Martin Dutton were avid vinyl collectors and felt Wigan was a place that needed an independent record shop. Over the years both Music Zone and HMV have closed, leaving Static as the only port of call left for vinyl fans. Check out the shop's website, where you will find the extremely funny "Sleeve Face" feature, where customers pose with album sleeves in front of their face. And watch the videos of Record Store Day at Static on YouTube – they are hysterical. I have yet to find a more bonkers record shop in the UK.

If you are a Whitesnake fan, then you will have a lot of fun here. Anytime somebody asks for something by the 1980s rockers, Paul pulls out from behind the counter a giant rubber white snake saying, "Will this do?"

Owner Paul will even draw your portrait for you. Furthermore, if you are good at darts, then this is the shop to visit. At Christmas, customers have the chance to become the shop's "Ace of Spades". The competition originated after a customer left a large new spade in the shop for safe keeping, which he never returned to pick up. After six months they decided to use the spade as a trophy for the shop's Christmas darts tournament. Ask to see it when you call in.

Before he was a mega-star, comedian Peter Kay would frequent X-Records in Bolton. If he ever decides to write a Phoenix Nights-style comedy based on a record shop, then I suggest he pays a visit to Static Records, a mere 12 miles from Bolton. There is enough comedy here to make a six-part series. Static is a shop that you are likely to leave with a bag of vinyl and a beaming smile on your face.

Tasty Records

25 Regent Road, Altrincham, Trafford, Greater Manchester WA14 1EJ
07876 722500
tastyrecordsaltrincham@gmail.com; @tasty_records
Monday-Saturday 10am-5pm
Established 2013
Stock: Vinyl, Pre-owned, Turntables

"Vinyl holds a reaction in people that no other format does, and I love it. I wanted to be a part of that, I'm not a digital man, I like face to face, I like tangible. That's what my shop is about." **Ben Molesworth – Tasty Records**

Ben Molesworth's well named shop (yes, you will find some tasty bargains) is located close to Altrincham's iconic market. Ben told me a tale about the effect that vinyl shopping can have on you. "I recently had a gentleman collapse into diabetic shock in the shop," Ben said. "He was a very tall, healthy-looking, well-built bloke. This form of diabetic shock involves the person being unresponsive, but rolling around on the floor and thrashing out uncontrollably. I noticed his open insulin kit, so I immediately phoned an ambulance and told them the situation. Within a few minutes an ambulance arrived, and we had to get this dude to stop rolling around and kicking record browsers while the paramedic gave him some medication. No easy task. Thankfully he recovered almost immediately, we sat him up and all nervously had a laugh together about him nearly dying in my shop, as we were picking up various bits of knocked-down furniture. He kept unnecessarily apologising and told us that this has happened before – but only in a record shop."

Vinyl Exchange

18, Oldham Street, Manchester, M1 1JN
01612 281122
vinylexchange.co.uk; mailorder@vinylexchange.co.uk; @vinylexchange
Monday-Saturday 10am-6pm Sunday 12-5pm
Established 1988
Stock: Vinyl, CD, Pre-owned, DVD

Manchester's Northern Quarter is home to Vinyl Exchange, one of the largest second-hand record shops in the UK. Set over two floors, the shop is owned by James Zeiter and Richard Farnell, who had been working there for several years when in 2008 they were offered the chance to purchase the business. At that point Vinyl Exchange had two shops in the city, but the pair shrewdly *merged the business back into the larger and more vinyl orientated shop.* It was a gamble, as record retailing was in crisis at this point. But James and Richard supported vinyl in the belief that sales of the format would grow. Time has proven them right.

The shop was originally all pre-owned, but in 2014 they started selling new vinyl. This came about after James did some consultancy work for Warners Records. The company encouraged them to stock new vinyl and ever since then, the proportion of new vinyl stocked in the shop has increased at a rapid rate.

If James appeared on mastermind, though, his specialist subject would be New Order. He has seen them more than 30 times and has an encyclopedic knowledge of the band. *He has worked as a consultant on recent releases by the band and is currently working on a large box set project for them.*

Vinyl Exchange is strong on dance, hip-hop and especially techno.

Vinyl Revival

5 Hilton Street, Manchester, M4 1LP
01616 616393
vinylrevivalmcr.com; vinylrevival@btinternet.com; @VinylRevivalMcr
Monday-Friday 9am-5.30pm
Saturday 10am-5pm
Established 1997
Stock: Vinyl, CDs, Pre-owned, Memorabilia, T-shirts

Owner Colin White probably has the best collection of Factory Records product of any record shop. The shop is decorated with original Factory posters and has a great selection of T-shirts and other Factory memorabilia. Most of the vinyl is second-hand, with some new stock. They have an excellent selection of Manchester-associated artists, with over half the floor space dedicated to local bands from the 1960s to the present day.

Colin has been selling music since the age of 10 when he used to help his dad Bill on the markets. When he left school, he became a windscreen fitter, which he combined with playing in a band. He had always been a vinyl fan and thought up the idea of opening a record shop that celebrated the Manchester scene. For months, he toured flea markets, car boot sales and charity shops to build up his vinyl stock.

He is helped in the shop by his friend Russ Taylor, who has spent his life wheeling and dealing in records around the North Wales coast. Colin is grateful for Russ's ability to spot famous faces in the shop, such as Ryan Adams and snooker legend Steve Davis, both seen browsing through the racks. This should be the first port of call for anybody looking for music connected with Manchester.

X-Records

44 Bridge Street, Bolton, Greater Manchester BL1 2EG
01204 384579 xrecords.co.uk; xrecords@xrecords.co.uk; @xrecordsbolton
Monday-Saturday 10am-5.30pm Sunday 10am-4pm
Established 1986
Stock: Vinyl, CD, Pre-owned, Cassettes, Merchandise, Tickets

It is only a 40-minute drive from Manchester to X-Records in Bolton, owned by Steve Meekings. As well as a huge selection of music, the store has a Scalextric track, an impressive collection of boxing magazines and lots of music memorabilia such as T-shirts, music figures and mugs. To give you an idea of how extensive his collection is, this is the merchandise he has in stock from one of his favourite bands, Kiss: Kiss baseball caps, Kiss baseball bats, Kiss coffee, Kiss flasks, Kiss beach towels, Kiss figurines, Kiss guitar straps, Kiss guitar hero faceplates, Kiss perfume for girls and Kiss aftershave for men, Kiss cycling jerseys, Kiss polo shirts, Kiss fridge magnets, Kiss photos, Kiss fanzines, autographed Kiss books. The shop also has the largest collection of cassettes I have ever seen. Steve explains that his is one of the few shops still to retail them, and he sells them for £1 each. They have a huge second-hand section and keep over 70,000 units in stock, while listing another 70,000 items on the X-website

Steve is a likeable chap and it is clear he has tried everything to keep the business going in difficult circumstances. As well as organising rock and punk gigs in Bolton, he promotes poetry readings. Displayed in prominent positions by the counter are releases by local bands. Steve constantly plays them in the shop, enthusing about each one to the store's regular customers. He even tried to launch his own record label, but it proved to be a huge drain on the shop's resources as all the bands he signed lost money. He had high hopes of the rock band Dirty Tryx, who had created a real buzz in the industry. Steve pressed their record to coincide with the band's UK tour. Unfortunately, due to "musical differences" the band split up on the eve of the record's release.

Like many record shop owners, Steve started by buying and selling at record fairs before taking the plunge and hiring a table inside an alternative clothes emporium called Xstatic. He didn't have any racks, just tables held up by beer crates. In 1986, he opened his own shop in a converted post office next to Bolton College. It was a great location as Steve would experience an influx of students at lunchtime as well as in the early evening.

A rock & roll moment occurred at the shop when one of Steve's customers tripped and fell head first into the poster rack. Steve rushed over to help the man who had seemingly got himself wedged. It turned out to be 1960s pop star PJ Proby, and Steve was relieved to see that his trousers showed no signs of ripping, as they had so often on stage in his heyday. Another regular visitor was Ian Brown of the Stone Roses, who used to deliver the band's T-shirts for the shop to sell.

X-Records is the only record shop to be sponsored by a pasty company: local independent company Carrs Pasties can be seen handing free pasties out to the queue outside the store on Record Store Day. Once inside, record collectors could pass away many hours, as Steve has so much stock to look through. The shop offers surely the best vinyl deal of all time: a perfect starter for anybody wishing to start a vinyl collection. They have a £1 second-hand vinyl section, where you can choose 20 records for £10. If you are planning to visit this excellent record shop, my suggestion would be take a packed lunch, as you may be there a long time.

Merseyside

For a city with such an incredible music history, the 2015 Liverpool record shop scene was in a sorry state. The three key independent shops in the city - Probe, The Musical Box and 3b Records - had 150 years of record retailing between them. But it was time to give the long-established shops some competition, which arrived in the shape of two excellent new shops: 81 Renshaw Street and The Jacaranda, both housed in historic buildings that played a part in the city's musical past.

The city still lags behind its rival Manchester when it comes to quantity of record shops to visit, but due to other music-based attractions, Liverpool makes a superb weekend break for vinyl fans. My suggestion would be to combine visiting the record shops with a trip to the British Music Experience as well as The Beatles Story Exhibition. If you still need more Beatles, then there is the A Day in The Life Beatles bike tour that takes you out of the city to visit the landmarks associated with the group. For accommodation, there is the Hard Day's Night hotel, or you can stay in a real Yellow Submarine, moored at the Albert Dock. Do ensure you leave time to take a ferry across the Mersey over to Birkenhead, to call in at Skeleton Records.

3b Records
5, Slater Street, Liverpool, L1 4BW
0151 343 7027
3brecords.co.uk; info@3brecords.co.uk; @3btickets
Monday-Saturday 10am-5.30pm
Established 1989
Stock: Vinyl, CD, DJ Equipment, Tickets, T-Shirts

3b Records is Liverpool's dance specialist, formerly also a successful record label. In 2009 the label and shop became separate businesses. The label produced four records that have made the top 40 singles charts by Aaron Smith (featuring Luvli), Afrojack, Steve Aoki (featuring Miss Palmer) and Agnes. The team behind the counter are all experienced DJs, producers and industry stalwarts. It is the place to go in Liverpool for fans of house, techno, disco, nu-disco, soul, funk and electronica.

81 Renshaw Street, Liverpool, L1 2SJ
0151 707 1805
81renshaw.co.uk; info@81renshaw.co.uk; @81Renshaw
Tuesday-Sunday 12-11pm
Established 2016
Stock: Vinyl, Second-hand, Coffee, Food, In-stores, Comedy Club and Arts
Venue, Licensed.

Located in the basement of the building that housed the offices of Bill Harry's legendary and influential Merseybeat magazine is 81 Renshaw Street, a store named after its famous address. Upstairs houses a bar and venue, which hosts live music, comedy, improv theatre, musical open mic evenings and even life drawing classes. It is also home for Neil Tilly, the shop's owner, who lives in the flat above.

It is a vibrant and happening place in the heart of Liverpool's music scene that has made a big impact.

Neil has always been an entrepreneur and landed himself in hot water when as a schoolboy with the help of his chemistry set, he manufactured his own fireworks. Amazingly, they worked. Neil sold them at school and then went one step further. He produced some flyers for Tilly's Fireworks. After handing them out at school he pasted them around town, including on the Liverpool buses. He made one crucial error: he put his contact details on the flyers. That curtailed his first venture.

Next, he produced Tilly's Top 30. Each week he would ask his classmates at school for their current favourite three records. He would then compile a sheet with the results neatly typed out. He recalled the excitement of having his favourite record by X-Ray Spex at No.2 in Tilly's Top 30 while it was only just in the Top 20 in the national chart, proving to him that his classmates had better taste than the public.

The young entrepreneur then went on to produce his own comic, which included music-related articles. It was his success with this that later led to him starting his own Liverpool music magazine titled *Breakout*.

Upon leaving school he found work in a shipping office. It was here that the plans for *Breakout* formed. One of his work colleagues was Tim Wildy who played in a local band called Twisted Nervz. Tim was passionate about Liverpool music and when he was not playing gigs he was checking out other bands in the Liverpool scene. He started introducing Neil to bands such as OMD, Echo & The Bunnymen, the Teardrop Explodes and Wah! Heat. The music that Neil had been enjoying up until then was by big, inaccessible acts, but in Liverpool he could not only buy the records but could go out and see these artists playing in the city. He concluded that Liverpool had many fine bands who were not getting the attention they deserved.

Neil started to interview local bands and soon had enough material for the first issue. He had no money for printing but, luckily, the shipping office was equipped with an industrial-sized printer, which Neil took advantage of. He printed 1,000 copies of the magazine which he hand-stapled before delivering to record shops and venues across the city.

The magazine was an instant hit and demand was such that he felt it was too risky to continue to use his employer's printing machine. Instead, he outsourced the printing to a company in Diss, Norfolk. This arrangement involved a monthly 480-mile round trip in a van to collect the magazine from the printers. Incredibly, despite the cost of the van hire and petrol, it worked out far cheaper than having it printed in Liverpool.

He did have one scary moment at work when his boss enquired about the magazine. His boss's son was enthusing about the magazine one evening while reading it at home. His dad noticed that the editor was one Neil Tilly, the enthusiastic music fan who seemed to have spent a lot of time near the company printer. Luckily, by this point Neil was no longer using the work printer as part of his chain of production.

By issue No.6 Neil decided to leave the shipping office and make *Breakout* his career. In 1984 he added a short-lived record label. The only release on the Breakout label was "Wise Up!" a single by the local band Foundation. The record became a cult classic and was recently on sale on Discogs for £293. The magazine ran till 1986, when Neil decided he needed a more stable job as by now he had married Jan and had young children. Over the years *Breakout* did a fantastic job of promoting the north-west music scene. As well as interviewing many Liverpool bands Neil also met Tears For Fears, the Stranglers, the Damned, Steve Harley, Stuart Copeland, John Foxx, Bill Nelson and, most famously, Paul McCartney.

The Macca meeting came about after Neil received a phone call from Bernard Doherty, Paul's press officer, asking if Neil could send some back issues of *Breakout* to Paul, who wanted to read them. Neil was delighted, cheekily asking "Any chance of an interview?" Bernard laughed and Neil thought nothing more of it. A few weeks later Bernard was on the phone again, offering him the chance to interview Paul at Air Studios in London. Neil could not understand why an artist of his status would choose to give his first interview in three years to a small Liverpool magazine.

Now that Neil has had time to reflect on it, he suspects it was down to the aftermath of John Lennon's death, when Paul did an interview and was upset with what was printed, feeling that what he had said had been taken out of context. For the next three years Paul refused all other interview requests, but evidently felt he could trust Neil, an enthusiastic, 20-year-old journalist from his home city, to report exactly what he said.

When he entered Air Studios and introduced himself, Neil was asked to sign a document saying he must not ask any questions about John Lennon, nor report on anything Paul might say about his fellow Beatle, a condition he was happy to agree to. Paul walked in and greeted Neil warmly. The initial conversation was about Liverpool, given that both came from the same part of the city, Paul from Speke and Neil from Garston. Both had even been regular visitors to Garston Library. Paul then brought tales of John Lennon into the conversation. After half an hour Neil was beginning to get worried that he was not going to have any content for his interview. So far, the conversation had revolved around John Lennon, which he could not use, while the story of how they both went to Garston library was hardly a scoop. Fortunately, the conversation turned to Paul's new album, *Pipes of Peace*. Neil's interview lasted longer than an hour and he found Paul charming. He even invited Neil and Jan to the premier of *Give my Regards to Broad Street*.

The next day back in Liverpool, Neil had visits from three national newspapers, all wishing to do a feature on the young journalist who had scooped an interview with Paul McCartney. The *News of the World*, the *Sunday People* and the *Sunday Mirror* all asked him questions, then wanted a photograph. They thought it would be a great shot for him to be holding a Beatles album. Unfortunately, Neil only owned cassettes of the band, so the photo did not quite work. They went instead for a picture of him looking serious while writing. The issue of *Breakout* featuring the interview with Paul McCartney quickly sold out of all 20,000 copies. Neil has never used the part of the interview where Paul spoke about John Lennon. He hopes that one day he will be able to publish it.

There were two interviews he did that were never used at all. The first was with one of his heroes, Andy Partridge of XTC. Neil had decided to do no more issues as he had obtained a job with a wholesale metals company. Soon after he took the decision he received a call from Andy (whom he had been chasing for ages), agreeing to an interview. XTC were one of his favourite bands, so even though he was not going to use it, he travelled down to Swindon to interview Andy for the feature that never was. Neil recalled he spent most of the interview answering questions from Andy about his McCartney interview.

Ever the entrepreneur, Neil left the wholesale metals company to start his own business, manufacturing and supplying plastic tubing, which he called Peninsular Plastic. The business did well and in 1995 Neil launched a new magazine called *Reverb*. The tag line was Scandal-Music-Theatre-Comedy-Soaps-Filth. He was years ahead of his time, as this was a free paper, funded by adverts. The first issue, in October 1995, featured the Charlatans, Cast and TV soap *Brookside*. It attracted some quality writers including ex-*Melody Maker* journalist Penny Kiley, John Robb and Liverpool playwright and author Ian Salmon. *Reverb* only ran for nine issues but captured the culture of those times.

Just before he closed *Reverb*, Neil was asked if he would interview a new five-piece girl band Virgin Records had signed. That was the Spice Girls, another scoop that has never seen the light of day.

In 2016 Neil took over 81 Renshaw Street. At the time it was just a café, but he has turned it into one of the most exciting places in the north west for fans of culture, art and music. His favourite customer is Single Man, not a reference to his marital status, but in recognition of the fact that he has bought three 7-inch singles nearly every day since the shop opened. The shop has thousands of these, on offer at 40p each or three for a £1. Single Man has always gone for the bulk deal. One day he even bought six for £2.

The work Neil has done promoting Merseyside music through his magazines is not dissimilar to the most famous occupant of 81 Renshaw Street, Bill Harry, a name synonymous with Liverpool music, who helped launch The Beatles. John Lennon was one of his best friends, when both were studying at Liverpool Art College along with Stuart Sutcliffe (original bass player in the Beatles) and Cynthia Powell (later Lennon, John's wife).

Frustrated by the lack of media coverage of the Liverpool music scene, Bill started his own *Mersey Beat* magazine. Based on the top floor at 81 Renshaw Street, with the help of his girlfriend Virginia - whom he had met at the Jacaranda club (now another Liverpool record shop) and who later became his wife - he produced and printed 5,000 copies of the first issue which hit the streets in July 1961.

It was a huge success and soon became the street music bible for Merseyside youngsters. Thanks to Bill's contacts with The Beatles, the band featured heavily in *Mersey Beat*. Bill was able to obtain many scoops and featured sketches by John Lennon in the magazine. Indeed so much Beatles material featured that the magazine was sometimes jokingly referred to as *Mersey Beatles*.

The magazine's circulation grew to 75,000 and its popularity was instrumental in moving the hub of the music industry from London to the north west. Instead of bands routinely moving south to London, the industry A&R men came north to Liverpool to check out and sign many of the hundreds of bands on the scene.

Neil told me about the only time Bill had witnessed John Lennon in tears. John kept all his sketches in a drawer on the top floor. During the move downstairs, his sketches went missing. John was distraught. They were never found. Nobody knows if they were stolen or thrown out. Neil is tempted to remove the floorboards in 81 Renshaw Street just in case they have slipped down the cracks.

In his own way, Neil Tilly has continued the great work done by Bill Harry.

Top tip - Find yourself a window seat in the café and look out for all the Beatles tour groups who stop outside the shop to hear tales and take photos. Keep an eye out on the Indian restaurant at No.83 called Indian Legend. You will see many people having their photograph taken outside. This is because Liverpool City Council have produced a "Walking Guide to the Beatles". It has the background and photos of sites around Liverpool connected with the band. Unfortunately, instead of taking a photograph of Neil's record shop at No.81, they took a photo of the restaurant next door. Neil reckons it has cost him quite a few customers as many people go there for a curry, thinking they are eating in a building connected with the Beatles.

Defend Vinyl *The record shop helped by the kindness of Liverpool music fans*
150, Smithdown Road, Liverpool, L15 3JR
0151 306 7121
defendvinyl@gmail.com
Monday-Saturday 11am-7pm
Established 2016
Stock: Vinyl, Pre-owned

It was a joy to come across a record shop whose owner has the same name as myself, Graham Jones. There is a lot of love for this little record shop, which was opened with the help of a crowdfunding appeal. Launched on September 30, 2016, the fund raised £1,890 in just 28 days, with 73 people making contributions. Graham offered incentives such as mugs, T-Shirts and an invite to the launch party. To attend, you had to pledge £50 - the perk being you had free drinks all night. In hindsight, Graham wonders if he made any money on that last perk, as the party was drunk dry.

Graham has spent most of his life either playing in bands or being unemployed but now has found his true vocation. The shop has attracted some colourful characters such as the Giant Nutella man who walked in with the biggest jar of Nutella Graham had ever seen.
Giant Nutella man: "Would you like to buy this giant jar of Nutella for £10?"
Graham: "We are a record shop."
Giant Nutella man: "OK, £8?"
Graham: "We sell records."
Giant Nutella man: "Boy you drive a hard bargain. Make it £6."

Graham was not tempted, being dubious of the spread's origin. Graham also proved why record shop owners would make great detectives through this real-life conversation:
Woman: "Have you got that record?"
Graham: "Which one?"

Woman: "You know, that band who are always on the radio."
Graham: "Can you tell me anything more about them?"
Woman: "Yes, they are massive."
Graham: "Any more clues?"
Woman: "The singer is a girl with blonde hair."
Graham: "Blondie?"
Woman: "Not her, a different blonde woman."

After six more questions the woman walked happily out of the shop, having been sold a copy of Fleetwood Mac's *Rumours*. Sometimes record store staff deserve a medal for patience.

The shop was formerly a tattoo studio, so Graham has endless former clients from that business coming in to ask for a touch-up on their last tattoo or with an idea for a new design, somehow not noticing the tattoo shop now stocks thousands of vinyl records. Although Defend Vinyl is a little way out of the town centre it is worth getting the 86 or 87 buses to support Graham's shop.

Top tip – If you are thinking of opening a record shop, I would highly recommend you use crowdfunding. Not only does it help raise funds for you to buy stock, it establishes a community of people who will support you and spread the word about the shop.

Jacaranda *Referred to as The Jack by locals*
21-23 Slater Street, Liverpool, L1 4BW
0151 708 2942
jacarandarecords@gmail.com; @jacarandalpool
Sunday-Thursday 1pm-10pm Friday-Saturday 10am-2am
Established 1958
Stock: Vinyl, Pre-owned, Coffee, Cake, Licensed, Memorabilia, Venue

Spread over three floors, Jacaranda is not just a record store, but a café and bar housed in a venue historically tied to the Beatles. It was opened by Alan Williams, the band's first manager who became known as "the man who gave the Beatles away". John Lennon, Paul McCartney and the group's first bass player, Stuart Sutcliffe, were regular customers and soon started pestering Alan for a gig at the club. Taking advantage of the situation, Alan persuaded John and Stuart to paint the basement, in return for which the band could use it for rehearsals. Eventually he agreed to give them a gig when house band, The Royal Caribbean Steel Band, had a Monday night off. The Silver Beetles, as they were then called, performed their first-ever gig in the club in May 1960, and were paid with a soft drink and a snack. Over the next couple of years, Alan lined up dozens of gigs for the band before they left for an ill-fated (for Alan) residency in Hamburg. After an argument over his 10% commission for setting up the trip, he resigned, famously advising his successor, Brian Epstein: "Don't touch them with a f****g bargepole." Epstein ignored his words of wisdom.

Bands can now follow in the footsteps of The Beatles as the basement is still rented out for rehearsal space, although offers to paint the basement, as payment, are no longer accepted. The Jacaranda offers 10 slots a week, free of charge - a great example of supporting local music. The club closed in 2011, but reopened after a major refurbishment in November 2014. The venue is managed by Graham Stanley, who has a long history in the Liverpool club scene, and the record shop is run by Danny Fitzgerald, who also compiles world music compilations for Island Records.

The basement, with its alcoves and wooden benches, has lots of nooks and crannies to sit in and with a replica Beatles drum kit on the stage, it is not dissimilar in appearance to the original Cavern. You can see live music there from Thursday to Sunday, starting at 8pm. The ground floor is now an atmospheric pub with a traditional wood-panelled bar and lots of Beatles memorabilia on the walls. Check out the wooden plaque on the wall celebrating the meeting between Alan Williams and the Beatles.

Both the ground floor and basement have beautiful Wurlitzer jukeboxes installed, full of 7-inch singles from the 1960s and later. They are popular with customers and at peak times you may be waiting a long time to hear your selection. Upstairs is now home to Jacaranda records. It allows the opportunity to choose a second-hand record from the racks to play on the vinyl record players sunk into the tables, while sitting in six-seater listening booths. They have a good selection of Liverpool bands on vinyl, not forgetting local superstar, the much-missed Ken Dodd.

Coffee, cake and cocktails are served until late. Try the Fab Four Shots or a Strawberry Fields cocktail. Pride of place goes to an original 1948 Voice-O-Graph machine, which allows customers to cut their own two-minute record. Looking like a phone booth, they have recently attracted much media attention after both Jack White and Neil Young made records in them. Young recorded his 2014 album *A Letter Home* in the Voice-O-Graph at White's Third Man studios. It is incredible that Jacaranda still has one of these fabulous machines, making it a must-see for visitors to Liverpool. Jacaranda is set to become a major tourist attraction, so pay it a visit before the crowds descend on a record shop with a unique and fascinating history.

In the summer of 2018, Jacaranda launched a pop-up store in Seel Street. Called Phase One, it is part-record shop, part-bar, part-live venue and part-restaurant. It contains four listening booths built from converted garden sheds. It is another welcome addition to a city that is transforming itself for vinyl buyers.

Kaleidoscope Records
30 Westfield Street, St Helens, Merseyside, WA1D 1QF
01744 454190
krecords.com; greg@krecords.com
Monday-Saturday 10am-5pm
Established 1984
Stock: Vinyl, Pre-owned, Tour programmes

If you are planning a record shopping trip in Liverpool and Manchester, travel down the A580 between the cities and stop off at Kaleidoscope Records. Greg Duggins swapped total silence for non-stop loudness when he left his job as a librarian to open his own record shop upstairs in St Helens Market. Business was so good that he moved to his current location. The shop is strong on psychedelia, classic rock and krautrock and a must visit for anybody looking to purchase tour programmes, of which Greg has a vast selection.

Musical Box
457, West Derby Road, Liverpool, L16 1BL
0151 263 3845
musicalbox@hotmail.co.uk
Monday-Saturday 9am-5pm
Established 1947
Stock: Vinyl, Pre-owned, CD, 7-inch singles

The Musical Box started off as a shop selling toys, model railways, 78-rpm records and music boxes. It has always been in the Cain family. Current owner Diane Cain started helping her parents out in the early 1950s. They had bought the business from their Uncle Jack for the sum of £500, and the family lived above the shop. How Diane wishes she had kept some of the thousands of Dinky toys they sold back then. These days, Diane works in tandem with her son Tony Quinn, who was born in the room above the shop. They are a great combination, with Diane being an expert on country music and nostalgia, while Tony's field is rock and pop. Like most Liverpudlians they have a great sense of humour and if you spend any time there you may not buy something, but you are guaranteed laughs as mother and son take the mickey out of each other. The shop reminds me of the corner shops of my childhood in which people shopped for their groceries. The Musical Box always seems to have a steady stream of regulars popping in for a cup of tea and a gossip, and the shop has a warm and friendly atmosphere.

Diane sold her first record aged 13. She fondly recalls how in the 1950s the store would stay open until midnight on Christmas Eve to capture all the men who staggered out of the pubs at closing time, needing a last-minute present. At about that time records started taking up more space in the shop and fancy goods were phased out. The shop established a reputation for being the best country music shop in the north west. Many of their customers were American GIs based at Burtonwood Airfield near Warrington. One week several airmen came in and asked for material by a new vocalist called Elvis Presley. Diane and her mother, Dorothy, had never heard of him and presumed he was a country and western singer. The next week they noticed on their new release sheet a single by Elvis called "Heartbreak Hotel" and decided to purchase a boxful, as there was such a buzz about this record. On a sunny Wednesday afternoon their new releases arrived, and Diane could not wait to hear this hot new singer. They put the single on the turntable and could not believe what they were hearing. "This is rubbish!" exclaimed Dorothy. Diane agreed and couldn't understand what the fuss was all about. They firmly agreed that this Elvis chap had no future. Diane also recalls serving the Beatles in the shop. At the time, she didn't think they were the best band in Liverpool, never mind the world.

In 1959 the Musical Box opened a second shop, which Diane managed in Liverpool's Old Swan district, whilst her parents continued to run the West Derby branch. While the 1950s were exciting times, running a record shop in the 1960s in Liverpool was something else. For Diane, the 1970s was a golden period, as she loved the disco music of the day. The shop has survived through an ever-changing music scene, and Diane puts their longevity down to the fact that her mum was shrewd enough to buy the property, so they have no rent to pay and as the store is far enough out of the city, people can park outside free of charge. Being in the industry for so long, Diane has a wealth of anecdotes which she is happy to share with customers over a cup of tea, my favourite being:

Customer: "Have you got anything by a guy called Beethoven?"

Staff: "Yes, we have lots of titles. Do you know what recording you are looking for?"

Customer: "Tell you what, just give me his latest album."

A visit to the Musical Box is an absolute delight. Although a few miles out of the city centre, you can pop on the number 12 bus, which drops you off right outside the shop.

Probe Records

1, The Bluecoat, School Lane, Liverpool, Merseyside L1 3BX
0151 708 8815
probe-records.co.uk;probe-records@btconnect.com;@ProbeRecords
Monday-Saturday 9.30am-6pm
Sunday 12.30pm-5pm
Established 1971
Stock: Vinyl, CD, Pre-owned, 7-inch singles, T-Shirts

Only Brian Epstein and John Peel have done more to promote music in Liverpool than Probe Records. The shop was founded in 1971 when Geoff Davis took out a loan, found cheap premises in Clarence Street, and filled the place with pre-owned records. He stocked the shop with music that he liked, so along with progressive rock he purchased new vinyl records by blues, jazz and folk artists. On the first day of trading he took £47, but word soon spread about this friendly record shop where you were encouraged to hang out and the proprietors were happy to play anything you requested.

Geoff was quick to spot trends before they became mainstream and was soon importing rare records from America and reggae from Jamaica. This meant a weekly journey to Liverpool's Speke airport (now John Lennon airport) to collect the records. He also imported music he heard on his travels further afield, and Probe offered wide-ranging collections of Middle Eastern and North African music, well before the term "world music" became popular.

The raw sound of the Ramones from New York made an instant impression on Geoff, and provided an early introduction to punk rock. In 1976, with the help of his then wife Annie, Geoff moved Probe Records to a more central location at Button Street, just off Mathew Street and less than a minute's walk from the celebrated nightclub Eric's. The club, run by Geoff's friend Roger Eagle, and Probe Records became the hub of a vibrant local music scene that gave birth to scores of Liverpool bands. With the punk movement taking off, Probe became a meeting place where the new music could be listened to and talked about.

The shop also became an unlikely tourist trap as people took a detour to gawp at the brightly dressed crowd with their Mohican hair-dos gathered around the entrance. During this period record shops were springing up all over the country to cater for fans of the punk rock movement. The people who worked behind the counter at Probe included Julian Cope of the Teardrop Explodes, Pete Wylie of Wah!, Paul Rutherford of Frankie Goes to Hollywood and, most famously, the late Pete Burns who found fame as the singer with Dead Or Alive.

In 1981 Geoff set up his own record label, Probe Plus. The first release was a self-titled EP by local band Ex Post Facto. Geoff was soon inundated with bands wishing to release records on his label. He recalled the day Nigel Blackwell, the frontman of Half Man

Half Biscuit, came into the shop with his demo tape. Geoff looked at the back of the cassette and it was full of tracks such as "The Len Ganley Stance" and "Venus in Flares". "If the songs are half as good as the titles, we'll do it," he told Nigel. They were, and it was the beginning of a successful partnership that is still going strong today.

After receiving a test pressing of the Half Man Half Biscuit album, John Peel rang Geoff to tell him that the group was brilliant and to book them for the first of 12 sessions that they would record for his radio show over the next few years. Peel described them as "the best band in the land". Their debut album *Back in the DHSS* became the best-selling independent album of 1986, while their single "Trumpton Riots" was the best-selling independent single. If you enjoy whimsical lyrics and have not heard HMHB, you are missing out. As well as having the band on his label, Geoff also manages them and introduces them at gigs.

In 1986 the Probe business split up, with Geoff taking the record label and Annie the shop. In the early 1990s Annie relocated Probe to Slater Street, and once again the shop found itself in the right place at the right time. Probe was now just around the corner from Cream, which was to become one of the most famous nightclubs in the dance scene.

In August 2010 Probe moved again, to its current premises at The Bluecoat on School Lane. The Bluecoat is an established creative centre for modern art and music, and also the oldest extant building in Liverpool city centre - and grade one listed to boot, hence no signage on the exterior. I strongly recommend a visit. Probe is not just a record shop but part of Liverpool's cultural history. Beautifully designed by Annie, the shop now has a whitewashed interior with art on the wall. Above the entrance is an arched window, where you can often see music fans having their photo taken. Annie still runs Probe with her long-serving members of staff Bob Parker and John Atherton.

Top tip - Steve Harman and Nick Dawes are two amateur cyclists who set up The Half Man Half Bike Kit Place Name Challenge. They have resolved to visit every British place name mentioned in a Half Man Half Biscuit lyric. They have been doing it for five years and, so far, have visited 115 places. They only have another 224 to go. Keep up with their progress at halfmanhalfbikekit.com.

Skeleton Records
1st Floor, 11 Oxton Road, Birkenhead, Merseyside CH41 2QQ
0151 653 9003
skrecs@hotmail.co.uk
Monday-Saturday 11am-5.30pm
Established 1971
Stock: Vinyl, CD, Pre-owned

"We must be the only shop in the country who has Hawkwind as their biggest-selling band."
John Weaver - Skeleton Records

Any vinyl fan visiting Liverpool should make the effort to take the ferry across the river to visit the legendary music institution known affectionately as Skellys. As a 13-year-old schoolboy, growing up in Bebington, I would get the bus each weekend into Birkenhead to visit Skeleton, a magical and mystical experience. The shop had no window and to enter you walked along a dark corridor. The throbbing sound of progressive rock could be heard coming from the end of what seemed like a cave, while the air was filled with the heady smell of joss sticks and patchouli oil.

Time has not dimmed the memory of my first visit. I recall entering a dimly-lit world where anyone with less-than-perfect eyesight would struggle to read the sleeve notes of the LPs on sale. At the counter sat a man with long black hair and a droopy moustache. This was my introduction to the owner John Weaver. He looked like Frank Zappa's younger brother and referred to everybody as "Man". I am pleased to say he is still going strong 40 years later. The long hair is a now grey and shorter, the moustache has gone. But he still refers to you as "Man".

I found that the shop had moved. The directions I received from a passer by were: "Just stay on this road till you see the Recession Bar [surely the most depressingly named pub in the land]. Opposite there is a road. Turn down there and Skeleton is between Mr. Yummy's kebab shop and the funeral parlour."

Although the shop still has no window, a huge mural of a skeleton is painted on the exterior with a gigantic red arrow pointing to the shop's doorway. I would be interested to hear the funeral director's opinion of the mural, which cannot be great for their business. You enter the doorway and climb the stairs, which are decorated with classic LP sleeves and posters promoting local gigs.

The shop itself is divided into two rooms, one for new product, the other for second-hand. The floor is covered in piles of collectable magazines such as *Q*, *Mojo*, *Record Collector*, *Kerrang!* and *Blues & Rhythm*. If you are a collector of *Blues & Rhythm*, get in touch with John, because the issues he has for sale go back as far as 1972.

John lives above the shop so he can sleep late every morning. His commute consists of a mere twelve steps. John has spent his life in Birkenhead as his family owned a chain of bookmakers. It was "odds on" that he would start work there when he left school. Instead he started work in what he called the "Toytown Savings Bank" better known as the TSB. Although he was good at his job, John was keen to work for himself. Spotting a gap in the market thanks to Birkenhead's lack of a proper record shop, he packed in his job to fulfil his dream.

Finding cheap premises next door to a printer's, he opened Skeleton Records in August 1971. As well as dealing in second-hand records, he also sold posters, books, underground press, incense, costume jewellery, joss sticks and patchouli oil. He took the name from a line in the Syd Barrett song "If It's In You", from his 1970 album *The Madcap Laughs*, in which Syd sings "Skeleton kissed a steel rail".

Although they bought new stock, Skeleton was mainly a pre-owned emporium, selling reasonably-priced stock. In the 1970s, I thought it was the best record shop on the Wirral, and nothing has happened to change my view. Every week I would purchase from John and if I didn't like what I bought I would take it back and he would let me trade it in. Many people preferred to sell their records to him for cash. I was always impressed that no matter how dark it was in the shop, John would be able to pick up any scratch on an LP that someone was looking to sell, giving him the opportunity to knock them down on price. If you took records to sell to him he would inspect them and divide them into three piles.

If he raised his eyebrows and uttered the sound "ermm!" you knew you had given him something of interest. A second pile of records was the "OK" pile, where John made out he was doing you a favour to take them off your hands. The third pile was stuff that John didn't want clogging up his racks, and would elicit a look which said "How come you brought me this crap?"

One Christmas I had been given a Ronco compilation album. Although it had the odd song I liked such as Blackfoot Sue's "Standing in the Road", most of the stuff was easy listening such as The Carpenters, Middle Of The Road and Sammy Davis Jnr, singing "The Candy Man" (a song now played constantly by Chris Evans on Radio 2, still sounding as bad as it did then). Although somewhat disappointed with my present, I took solace in the fact that I could take it to Skeleton and swap it for something decent. To this day, I have never forgotten the embarrassment of handing over my brand-new copy of *Ronco's 20 Greatest Hits* LP to John and hearing him saying, in front of a crowded shop, "Sorry man, even I can't sell this."

In 1976 John started promoting gigs in and around the Birkenhead and Liverpool area by acts such as Motorhead, the Jam, Fairport Convention and the Dead Kennedys. He must be the only man to have booked the Sex Pistols three times and, even though every gig was cancelled, managed to make a profit. On the first two occasions, the band cancelled, but each time John was able to rearrange the gig. For the long-awaited rearranged concert, John hired out a large cabaret club in Birkenhead called The Hamilton. Recent artists who had played there included Tom O'Connor, Tony Christie, Stan Boardman and the Grumbleweeds. It was a place that served chicken in a basket and would have a raffle after the first act had performed: hardly a venue where you would expect to find the most controversial band in the country performing. On the day tickets went on sale, the shop had more than 80 people queuing outside. Tickets quickly sold out for what was to become the most anticipated gig in the history of Birkenhead.

The Hamilton Club started getting pressure from both the council and the police to cancel the gig, something they had never experienced when putting on Tom O'Connor.

With stories dominating the tabloid press to the effect that the band were corrupting the youth of the nation, the owners of the club met with John and told him that with much reluctance they were going to have to cancel the gig. John braced himself for hundreds of fans coming in to the shop to claim a refund, but the rush never materialized. Only a trickle of fans came in to ask for their money back. John made an £800 profit on the gig because fans preferred to keep the tickets as a souvenir of a Sex Pistols gig that

Haydn Pugh of the wacky and wonderful Haystacks, Music & More in Hay-on-Wye.
Check out his medallion made from a 7" single.

Bella Union in Brighton. This shop is wonderfully designed with some intriguing features. It only sells music by artists on the Bella Union label. Bhodi, the shop's dog, can often be found behind the counter.

This brightly coloured Vinyl Revolution in Brighton. Pictured outside are owners Simon and Rachel with Treacle the dog, who is often found resting under the racks.

Alan and Chrissie Rowett from the Vault in Bournemouth. Their first shop was once a slaughterhouse.

Matt Davies of Tangled Parrot in Carmarthen whose shop was saved by fund-raising from the local community. Check out the shop's collection of parrotphernalia.

Ewen Duncan of Europa Music in Stirling modelling one of his many multi-coloured jumpers.

Mark Stubbs of Black Slab in Redcar who sourced many of the shop's features from the town's closed down steel mill.

Owner Ewan Hood standing outside his striking graffiti covered shop, Rarekind Records in Brighton.

The dynamic duo of Ant & Dec who you will find behind the counter at Vinyl Tap in Huddersfield.

Don't ask for Max Bygraves, Adam Faith or an all day breakfast at
Henry's Records in Burton-on-Trent

Owner Andy Haddon with musician and producer Ethan Johns outside Left For Dead following
Ethan's in-store performance.

Richard Churchyard owner of Raves From The Grave in Frome.
Photo by Jameson Kergozou www.jamesonkergozou.co.uk

Vod Music in Mold. The smallest record shop in the UK.

One of London's newest record shops. Level Crossing Records in Mortlake.
Check out the counter top manufactured from recycled plastic bottles.

never happened, rather than claim a refund. And who knows what one of those tickets is worth now?

One of the earliest punk gigs John promoted was Siouxsie & the Banshees. On the day of the gig he was surprised to receive a phone call to ask if Siouxsie could not only borrow the support band's equipment but also go on stage first. It turned out the band could not afford to hire a van, so they had purchased some cheap day return tickets for the train instead. The problem was that the last train back to London was at 10.30pm. The punters who decided to give the support band a miss that night witnessed a performance by local band the Accelerators who couldn't believe their luck, playing to a sell-out crowd.

The most pleasing gig John put on was Elvis Costello. He received a phone call from Elvis's management, asking if he could promote a gig in the Birkenhead area. The only problem was that John was not allowed to advertise it or put up posters. Clearly this would not work as he could only make money if people attended. He need not have worried, because he found a venue in New Brighton and through word of mouth alone, more than 400 people turned up to see Elvis play. It was only during the encore that the reason became apparent why Elvis had wanted to play the low-key gig: he had brought his mum, who lived locally, onto the stage to sing her "Happy Birthday". With a packed venue, it was a great atmosphere and something his mum would never forget.

John formed the Skeleton Records label in 1978, releasing records by Attempted Moustache, Afraid Of Mice, Wayne Hussey (who went on to find fame with The Mission), Windows, The Relations, Geisha Girls, Instant Agony and This Final Frame. Both Instant Agony singles reached the top ten of the indie charts. He also passed up the chance the chance to release the first ever single by Orchestral Manoeuvres in the Dark. He had seen the band perform at Eric's, the famous Liverpool venue, and was so impressed by their electronic sound that he offered to release their debut single. OMD had decided to release a song called "Always" but John persuaded them that the B-side "Electricity" was a better track. He had booked a holiday to America and when he came back he was disappointed to discover that OMD had gone for a deal with Factory Records. "Electricity" became a cult classic helping OMD to become one of the most successful chart acts of the last 40 years.

John's financial position didn't improve as none of the label's releases were making him a profit and he lost his Christmas trade after the shop closed during that crucial trading period, due to a flood. As is often the case, the insurance company paid him a lot less than the value of the stock and business he had lost. Debts were piling up and John was advised to go bankrupt. He was warned that the receivers would come and confiscate all his stock, so he devised a cunning plan. John hired a van and drove down to the Record Exchange in London. He offered to take as much stock off them as possible if it was priced at 10p or below. The Record Exchange were delighted to clear out thousands of unsellable records and John drove back to Birkenhead with probably the worst music collection ever.

Back in Birkenhead, John arranged with a mate who ran a pub to store all the good stock from the shop. John then replaced the empty racks with the stock he had bought from the Record Exchange. What he didn't count on was the receivers turning up so early, as he was still transferring the quality stock over to the pub. He allowed himself a smile when the receivers commented that it was no wonder he went bust, "selling this crap". Due to the stress of going bankrupt, John took a bit of time out to recover before starting again at the address he still has today under the name Skellys. He waited a few years for the fuss about his bankruptcy to die down before reverting to the shop's original name Skeleton Records. I am glad to say this avid Tranmere Rovers fan and legend of record retailing is still delighting music fans of The Wirral and it is worth a visit just to see the Skeleton painting on the wall outside the shop.

Norfolk & Suffolk

There are plenty of opportunities in this beautiful part of England for anybody thinking of opening a record shop. Great Yarmouth, Diss, Thetford, Kings Lynn and Lowestoft have all had record shops in the past. With the vinyl revival in full swing, they have the potential to sustain a new record shop.

Norwich was once a great city for vinyl retailing, but now only Soundclash takes part in Record Store Day from that city. It is well worth the journey to Holt to visit Holt Vinyl Vault, one of the quirkiest record shops in the UK.

Compact Music

91 North Street, Sudbury, Suffolk CO10 1RF
01787 881160
compact-music.co.uk; sales@compact-music.co.uk
Monday-Saturday 9am-5.30pm
Established 1988
Stock: Vinyl, CD, Musical Instruments

This is a one-stop shop for anything musical, based in the centre of Sudbury. There is an excellent selection of classical and jazz. The owner, James Morgan, does a great job on Record Store Day, organising a live event in Sudbury with lots of bands playing in the town square.

Holt Vinyl Vault *It may not be a post office any more, but it still delivers*

1 Cromer Road, Holt, Norfolk, NR25 6AA
01263 713225
captainfm247@gmail.com; @Holtvinylvault
Monday-Saturday 10am-5pm (Sundays in school summer holidays)
Established 2010
Stock: Vinyl, Pre-owned

Situated in an area sometimes dubbed the North Norfolk Rivieria, Holt Vinyl Vault began life as a record shop based inside a working post office, where customers could browse the LPs while sub-postmaster and proprietor Andrew Worsdale served the queue of customers posting parcels or wanting their passport applications checked.

Queuing in most post offices is a chore. You're bombarded with adverts from a TV screen while waiting for a booming voice to direct you to "Cashier number 12, please". It was a lot more relaxed at the Vault, where Andrew played classic rock or reggae while you waited to tax your car or buy your stamps. Soon, following rave reviews in *Record Collector* and *The Guardian*, customers more interested in Graham Bond than premium bonds began travelling from all over the country to visit this unlikely emporium.

After leaving university, Andrew worked in London in the civil service while his wife Jane was a teacher. The couple would spend weekends exploring the beaches of England's east coast, and eventually took the life changing decision to relocate to the seaside town of Sheringham. Jane remained in teaching and the couple bought a post office in the town for Andrew to manage. The building had plenty of spare space and, inspired by the record fairs he frequented, Andrew filled it with pre-owned records. This proved extremely popular and soon attracted plenty of local publicity.

After he had been trading from the premises in Sheringham for three years, Post Office Limited decided to close Andrew's branch. Undeterred, Andrew moved his vinyl operation and his postmaster's datestamp to a post office in the nearby market town of Holt where in 2010 he opened Holt Vinyl Vault. The shop is much larger than the Sheringham branch, and he filled the extra space with lots of new as well as vintage vinyl.

The Vault became famous worldwide after it was featured in the Tim Burgess book *Vinyl Adventures from Istanbul to San Francisco* (a bit more glamorous than *Vinyl Adventures from Istanbul to Holt, Norfolk*, I presume). The book is the story of how Tim, the Charlatans singer, goes on a journey to track down vinyl recommendations suggested by his famous friends such as Johnny Marr, Paul Weller and Iggy Pop. Andrew is proud to have had in stock three of the albums Tim's friends had asked him to obtain.

Tim Burgess had been living in Holt for a while before writing the book. He would pop in to the shop to collect record-shaped packages sent to him in the post and often came up to the counter with a selection of vinyl from the racks under his arm. Andrew was keen to engage Tim in conversation but, being so busy with post office duties, it was months before he had the chance to introduce himself. From then on whenever Tim paid the shop a visit the two of them would discuss music and vinyl. Tim featured one such chat - about Dexys Midnight Runners - in his book to illustrate the way old-school record shops bring people together to share their love of music in all its variety.

Another of Andrew's less famous customers was a shy young man known as Bobble Hat, since you could always rely on him to have his woolly hat on whether it was sunny, rainy or snowy on the North Norfolk Riviera. He came in several times a week, investing most of the wages he'd earned as a kitchen porter on mountains of vinyl, which he'd carry home in various teetering boxes to his bedroom in his father's house down the road.

It took Andrew a while to become attuned to this customer's needs. It was clear that Bobble Hat did not have much money, so Andrew was keen to help his limited funds go as far as they could in building a credible, and reliably curated, record collection. Naturally shy, Bobble Hat would creep up to the post office counter and whisper a band or artist's name, such as Simple Minds. This was Andrew's cue to explain that he was once a big fan of Jim Kerr's band, and that although he had albums from throughout their career in the Vault, Bobble Hat might consider not carrying forward his stake in the band beyond 1982's *New Gold Dream* LP, after which, in his considered opinion, their cold wave deftness and wistful angularity of sound gave way to stadium rock bombast.

"Trust me," implored Andrew, seeking to build a solid bond in the record-buying heart of Bobble Hat, as he recalled witnessing the first flush of the band's painful, though undeniably lucrative, decline "from ballet to ballast", while hanging dejectedly from the balustrade at Hammersmith Odeon in 1983. That said, the indicators had already been there in the shape of their release *Sparkle in the Rain*, which in his view was the worst-produced album ever released in the UK.

Alas, Andrew's impassioned advice went unheeded. Bobble Hat was revealed as a Simple Mind-ed completist and continued to assemble his Kerr and co. vinyl collection before moving on, with unerring alphabetical logic, to Simply Red where the same scenario unfolded. Before long, he was targeting Rod Stewart, at which point the public servant ethos of the self-styled spinning subpostmaster compelled Andrew to offer Bobble Hat the view that after some classic early albums, Rod's *Smiler* album was the dividing line between "divine rock god Rod" and "dreadful, dad-dancing, disco lothario Rod". Again, Andrew's advice fell on deaf ears as Bobble Hat wanted, quite simply, to own every Rod album in the known world.

Next, breaking the alphabetical sequence it was Everly - Don and Phil, in every known singularity or combination, then Everett. Which Everett, though? It turned out that it didn't matter: Betty, Roy, Vince, even Kenny - Bobble Hat bought every record he could find in the Vault with Everett on the label or sleeve. Next, he moved on to artists featuring the word "everything". He quickly purchased all the Everything But The Girl records, before making a request that was somewhat premature: he wanted everything by media darlings Everything Everything, who hadn't actually released anything on vinyl at the time.

The shop also had its own JR Hartley moment. Anybody who watched TV in the 1980s will immediately recall the fictional character who appeared in an advertising campaign for Yellow Pages. The advert showed an elderly gentleman asking in several pre-owned bookshops for *Fly Fishing* by JR Hartley. No bookshop had it in stock, and the old man goes home dejected. His daughter, sympathising, hands him the Yellow Pages, a pre-Google phone book publication, listing all the different businesses in the area. After phoning numerous shops without success, he finally locates a copy. He is delighted. The shopkeeper asks for his name, and he responds "My name? Oh, yes, it's JR Hartley." The advert was voted one of the best of all time.

Fast forward nearly 30 years and one Ian David, a charismatic gentleman who had enjoyed a short-lived pop career, had been searching the UK's record shops for a copy of his 1989 single „I Must Just Leave A Kiss". His search had been fruitless, but he was determined to obtain a copy to prove to his daughter that he once had a pop career. One day he called in to Vinyl Vault and asked Andrew if by any chance, he had a copy of his record. To his amazement, Andrew replied he might. A few days earlier a man had come in wanting to sell a vinyl collection that had belonged to a recently deceased BBC producer. Among the records in that collection Andrew remembered seeing a sleeve image that could have passed for the face of the man now standing before him, 28 years after the picture on the sleeve had been taken. I have a theory that record shop owners would make great detectives, because they are so good at tracking things down. This was a great example. Sure enough it was the long-forgotten single that his customer was looking for. Everybody won. Ian David was over the moon. His daughter was delighted to receive a record sung by her dad and Andrew was chuffed to dispose of a record he thought he was unlikely to sell.

In addition to some singular customers, Holt Vinyl Vault has many unique features, one of which is the shop's mascot, Jonny Record created by Andy Ward, who adorns a plethora of postcards, badges and flyers. Andrew still uses the original wooden counters from the post office, and the back room has a two-way mirror, originally used so the postmaster could keep his eye on his staff. The shop also has two large safes, so Andrew has no problem storing the day's takings - although on a dark, cold, winter's day in Holt, a piggy bank might suffice.

Sadly, for post office fans, Andrew was forced by yet another reorganisation of the post office network to relinquish that side of the business at the end of 2016, and to concentrate on being a stand-alone record shop. At least this means he is no longer plagued by jokers asking for post-office related records, such as "Return to Sender" (Elvis); "Please Mr. Postman" (Marvelettes, Beatles or Carpenters); "Signed, Sealed, Delivered I'm Yours" (Stevie Wonder); and "Telegram Sam" (T. Rex).

The shop still looks like a post office from the exterior. However, the original, lit-up Radio 1 ON AIR sign and various Jonny Record-related posters in the window give the game away. Inside, it looks as if a designer with a penchant for bees has been let loose. The long-suffering post office carpet has been ripped up and everything - floors, walls, even chairs - is painted black and yellow.

In 2009, Andrew published a novel *FM247: This Is Radio Binfield!* written with his best friend Rob Spooner. It is the sort of book most music fans will enjoy (myself included). It tells the story of The Emperor, a DJ from the community radio station, Radio Binfield, who experiences a mental breakdown during the search for his childhood friend, The Captain, whom he betrayed. The Emperor presents his all-time favourite 100-song countdown. The songs are presented as vignettes in the style of his favourite DJs from his youth, who used to broadcast on the fictional Radio Fun from the 1960s to the 1980s: Tony Sideburns, Simon Mates, Johnnie Talker, Steve Trite, Mike Lead and the legendary John Zeal. The songs eventually come together to tell the whole story. Buy a copy from the shop and help Andrew reduce his stockpile. You won't regret it.

One of the most rewarding responses to my own book, *Last Shop Standing,* was that of the many vinyl fans who subsequently kept in touch by informing me of how many of the 50 record shops featured in the book they had visited - rather like soccer fans attempting to visit all the football grounds in the country. Some asked the shop owners to sign my book. Anybody trying to do something similar with this book will find that Holt Vinyl Vault is located many miles away from any other record shop. My tip would be to visit the area on a sunny weekend. Look through the shop's wares and buy one of its iconic Punk Office T-shirts, along with a copy of Andrew's book. Spend the rest of the day on the beach and return for one of the regular Saturday-evening events, when the shop is transformed into a nightclub with Norfolk legend DJ Trevor Half Nelson behind the decks playing reggae and Northern Soul. Later in the evening Andrew, in the guise of Postmaster Flash, magically takes over playing music by anyone from Sun Ra to his personal hero Prince. You may be lucky enough to catch a set by one of the guest DJs such as funkmeister Sugar Beat, disco don Hitman Hawkins or indie expert Shelia Take A Bow.

These are nights when cheap booze and classic music combine to heady effect, and are popular with visitors and locals alike. North Norfolk has golden beaches and a classic record shop, so it is a trip you won't regret.

Soundclash

28 St Benedicts Street, Norwich, Norfolk NR2 4AQ
01603 761004
soundclash-records@virginmedia.com; @SOUNDCLASH
Monday-Saturday 10am-5.30pm
Established 1991. Stock: Vinyl, CD, Pre-owned, Books, Merchandise, Tickets

Paul Mills, the owner of Soundclash, has spent his life in record shops since he left school. He was even in a record shop when he should have still been at school, as he would skip lessons to hang out in Backs Records in Norwich. Paul became as much of a fixture in the shop as the record racking, and upon leaving school they offered him a job.

When punk came along in 1976, the major record companies froze like rabbits caught in the glare of oncoming headlights. The anti-establishment ethos of punk rendered record companies unfashionable. They wanted to be part of the action, but did not know how to harness the emerging movement's youthful energy. Suddenly, anybody who could play an instrument could be in a band and make a record. Hundreds of bands were formed, many releasing 7-inch singles on their own label. These records would be self-financed or paid for by local music entrepreneurs. Without a major record deal, the only way they could recoup the money spent was by selling the record at gigs and asking the local independent record shop to stock the record on the band's behalf. The band would then return on a regular basis to collect the money from the copies sold.

The major record companies signed the bands who were being written about in the pages of the influential music magazines of the time, among them the Sex Pistols, the Clash, the Stranglers and the Damned. At the same time, John Peel would be playing dozens of new records on his Radio 1 show every night, championing obscure bands from all over the UK, and often the only way you could obtain these records was via the local record shop in the town they were based.

In order to address the situation a group of independent distributors mainly based in record shops formed a cartel to promote independent record releases in their area of the country. The members consisted of Probe in Liverpool, Rough Trade in London, Backs in Norwich, Red Rhino in York, Revolver in Bristol, Fast Forward in Edinburgh and Nine Mile in Leamington Spa. The cartel offered pressing and distribution deals to small labels that would reach all the shops in a region. Shops preferred to deal with only a handful of distributors and so the small distributors also agreed to distribute each other's stock, segregating the market by the geography of the shops, rather than by the content or labels. Pooling their resources in this way allowed them to compete with the larger distribution operations of the major record labels and to gain access to the larger chains of the time such as HMV, Virgin and Our Price. Among the most successful acts they distributed were Joy Division, the Buzzcocks, the Smiths and Depeche Mode.

The youthful Paul Mills was delighted to be a cog in the mighty wheel of UK independent record distribution. At that time, Norwich had eight music outlets selling records. The shops would contact Backs by phone with a list of the records they required. At the end of each day, Paul would load up a sack trolley (a trolley with two handles for transporting goods normally contained in sacks) with boxes of records which he would deliver to the other record shops of Norwich.

In between his distribution work Paul would serve behind the counter of the shop enjoying a musical rapport with his regular customers. One of these was John Peel — a big supporter of the Norwich music scene and an avid buyer of records – who would happily travel the 38 miles from his home in Stowmarket to visit the shop. Many people would assume that John would receive enough records sent to him in the post, free of charge, to satisfy his constant search for new music. But this was clearly not the case.

Paul would wonder where John found time to fit everything in to a schedule which included his regular BBC radio show in London, the John Peel roadshow (gigs normally in universities or colleges where John would play music and introduce bands), his TV appearances, supporting Liverpool FC, and spending time with his family. Clearly, he was a man who did not waste a second of his life.

Paul interviewed John on a local radio station but never thought to ask him about his schedule. His memory of the event is hazy, but he recalls after the interview John advising him "Don't talk so much". John was, doubtless, referring to a radio broadcasting scenario. But in a general sense, it is fair to say that Paul has ignored John's advice. He will chat about music all day.

In 1991 Backs hived off its retail operation to concentrate on distribution. Paul took over the shop and renamed it Soundclash. His timing could not have been better as the acid house, rave and techno scene had just taken off. He embraced the culture, racking the shop out with 12-inch singles and establishing it as the place to go in Norwich for dance music.

From day one, Soundclash has been a vinyl shop. Despite booming sales of 12-inch records in the 1990s, Paul noticed with growing dismay that the major record companies were not releasing certain albums in the vinyl format, a severe blow to his business. Many other record shops felt the same way, so the Save Vinyl Campaign was launched for the purpose of lobbying record companies to continue to release albums on vinyl.

Pre-internet, you could not organise an online petition or send the record company an email. Everything had to be done with a pen and paper, and Paul spent a lot of time writing to record companies suggesting albums that Soundclash could sell if released on vinyl. He encouraged all his customers to write in, and passed his opinions on to the record company sales reps who visited the shop.

Sadly, the Save Vinyl Campaign's efforts were in vain as the industry remained deaf to the appeals of vinyl fans and blind to the long-term revenue opportunities of selling vinyl alongside CD. Instead, the industry could smell the money that could quickly be made by forcing vinyl fans to buy their record collection again in the CD format. Some record companies actively did all they could to shift buying habits away from the vinyl LP towards the CD. Traditionally, record companies would help shops with unsold stock by allowing the shops to return a percentage of unsold stock – a system known as "percentage returns". In the 1980s record companies would generally accept returns of up to 5% of a shop's turnover. But as the CD took over, the terms for these agreements started to change. The percentage return allowed for CDs was increased, while for vinyl it was reduced and, in some cases, withdrawn altogether. If a shop did not sell a CD, it could generally return it and get a credit. But if it stocked vinyl that did not sell, it was stuck with the stock which it would eventually have to offload at a substantially reduced price, often losing money in the process.

Pre-vinyl revival days were tough for Soundclash. But, just as he had done with dance culture, Paul embraced the growing hip-hop scene and Soundclash became the place to go in Norfolk for followers of the genre.

In 2016, the shop was involved in the 40 Years of Punk celebration whereby 40 bands played at 40 venues and 4,000 punk photographs were on display. Paul has kept the spirit of punk alive in Soundclash and intends to do so for a long time to come.

Vinyl Hunter
56 St Johns Street, Bury St Edmunds, Suffolk, IP33 1SN
01284 725410
vinyl-hunter.co.uk; info@vinyl-hunter.co.uk; @Vinyl_Hunter
Monday-Friday 9am-5.30pm
Saturday 9am-6pm
Sunday 10.30am-4pm
Established 2014
Stock: Vinyl, Pre-owned, Coffee, Food

Record buyers have long associated Bury St Edmunds with the Andys record chain. Andy Gray, the chain's founder, still runs his successful Beat Goes On re-issue label from the historic market town. At one point the Andys chain had more than 30 shops, but the chain went into administration in 2003.

The man who filled the subsequent void in Bury St Edmunds was Will Hunter, who must be the youngest record shop proprietor in the UK. Will was just 19 when he opened Vinyl Hunter in 2014 with support from his mum Rosie and ex-HMV manager Ross Alderdice. They have made the shop a great space to while away a couple of hours.

To prepare for opening the shop, Will volunteered his time to Rough Trade and learnt about running a store. They have created a meeting space where music fans can eat locally-sourced food. All the cakes are baked by Lilie who lives above the shop. The coffee is roasted by local merchants Butterworth & Son. They spent time sourcing soft drinks from suppliers who share similar values ensuring they are organic but fair-trade (check out the John Lemon lemonade). Not only do they sell juice to drink, but if you have run out of juice for your phone or laptop, you can chill and charge using the shop's coffee table chargers, a great innovation.

In a nice touch, Andy Gray was one of the first customers through the door on its opening day, delighted that at long last somebody was taking over his mantle. Budding DJs of East Anglia should note that each month the shop hosts an open-deck DJ event. Each DJ gets a 20-minute set to play whatever music they like.

The shop's most memorable customer was the girl who asked if Fleetwood Mac were named after McDonalds.

They also run their own Vinyl Hunter VIP club where members receive a clubcard entitling them to various benefits such as:
Free vinyl every time total points exceeds 250
Special offers exclusive to VH VIP members
Bonus points when you start
Exclusive access to Record Store Day list & queue
Club points reward for every purchase

In 2016 Vinyl Hunter opened a second shop at:

Allens Farm, Tye Road, Elmstead, Essex, CO7 7BB
Thursday-Friday 10am-5pm Saturday 11am-6pm Sunday 11am-4pm
It is not easy to find so check website for directions.

Wells
4 Queen Street, Southwold, Suffolk IP1 86EQ
015027 23906
wellsphoto@live.co.uk
Monday-Saturday 10am-5.30pm (closed 1-2pm) Sunday 2pm-4pm
Stock: Vinyl, CD, Art, Books

Southwold is a beautiful seaside town, famous for its beach huts, Adnams Brewery and the best pier I have ever visited. Inventor and engineer Tim Hunkin has built a unique collection of utterly bonkers machinery where you can walk a metal dog, get the mother-in-law frisked and „whack-a-banker". Other attractions include lending a hand to grandma on „Mobility Masterclass" and trying to get her across the road with a Zimmer frame in one piece. You can even manhandle plutonium rods into your own nuclear reactor.

If you are a vinyl fan on a day trip to the resort and you have done the brewery tour and visited the pier then the only place to get your fix is at Richard Wells' shop.

It was opened by his father John and is unique in that it is the only record shop I know that combines selling music with a photographic service (although Boots offered this service until the 1990s). Richard is a renowned photographer who specialises in photos of the town that are outstanding. The shop has the best selection of folk CDs in East Anglia while the vinyl section encompasses jazz, blues, folk, country and world music.

Richard highlights two problems that have had a severe impact on independent retailers. As well as records and CDs, the shop does a good business selling books. Recently, a new competitor opened in the town, a beautiful, quaint shop called Southwold Books which blended with the various independent shops on the picturesque high street. All was not quite as it seemed, however. Although branded in such a way as to help them integrate with the local community, Southwold Books is in fact owned by Waterstones, and thus able to benefit from economies of scale that the truly independent traders, like Richard, cannot compete with. Imitation is the sincerest form of flattery, but it is not a trend that the true independents would wish to encourage. With Waterstones apparently planning to open more of these pseudo-local shops, it will be interesting to see if, in the future, a new national chain of record shops tries to pull off the same trick.

If a national competitor in disguise is not enough, independent businesses in Southwold have also had to absorb an average 177% increase in business rates in recent years. This is a nationwide problem that has had a severely negative impact on independent record shops. This tax is killing the high street, while simultaneously handing online retailers an unfair advantage. It urgently needs to be reformed.

Northern Ireland

The record retail landscape in Northern Ireland is dire. Back in the late 1980s when I first travelled there, my biggest problem was being stopped by the army to enquire what I was up to. They were always suspicious of the black case that I carried my CD samples around in. Nowadays my biggest problem is finding enough record shops to visit to justify the cost of going there. Record shop numbers have never been so low.

Belfast suffered the closure of both Sick Records and Head Records in 2017, leaving a huge gap. No record shop in Belfast took part in Record Store Day. Hopefully somebody will pick up the independent record shop baton as record retailing in the province is in poor health. If you need a vinyl fix in Belfast, then Belfast Underground Records, 33 Upper Queen Street, BT1 6EA is good for lovers of dance music, while Dragon Records, 58 Wellington Place, BT1 6GF is best for pre-owned. For new vinyl head to HMV. The city does have several other excellent second-hand record shops including Octopus's Garden, Timeslip Records, Top Sounds and Young Savage. A couple of them stock a limited selection of new vinyl. Surely one of them will grasp the nettle and get involved in RSD next year.

The four shops in Northern Ireland that participated in RSD in 2018 are featured below.

Armagh Music

3c Dobbin Street, Armagh BT61 7QQ
028 3752 5452
armaghmusic@gmail.com
Monday-Saturday 10am-5.30pm
Established 1989
Stock: Vinyl, CD, Pre-owned, T-shirts

Armagh Music was formerly known as The Tape Deck. It is understandable that they changed the name. The shop has an impressive selection of signed memorabilia.

Bending Sound

59, High Street, Bangor, County Down BT20 5BE
07902 032048
steven@bendingsound.co.uk; @BendingSoundNI
Sunday-Thursday 12-5pm
Friday 12-8pm
Sunday 12-5pm
Established 2017
Stock: Vinyl, In-stores

With no Belfast record shop taking part in Record Store Day 2018, vinyl fans had to trek out to the coast to visit Bending Sounds, the nearest participant to the capital. Steven Boyd's store is easy to spot with its bright yellow sign, standing out like a belisha beacon. The shop chose the busiest day possible to open; their first day was Record Store Day 2017.

Cool Discs *The shop which has seen off bombs, bullets, Virgin and HMV*
6, Lesley House, Foyle Street, Derry BT48 6AL
Monday-Thursday 9-7.30pm
Friday 9am-8pm Saturday 8.30am-6pm Sunday 1pm-6pm
lee@cooldiscsmusic.com; @cooldiscs
Established 1996
Stock: Vinyl, CD, Pre-owned, In-stores

Before opening his own shop, Lee worked in another record shop, Caroline Music, for close to 10 years. Late in 1995, Virgin opened a huge shop in a nearby shopping centre and the owners of Caroline Music, believing they could not compete, closed the shop early in 1996.

Lee's world was turned upside down. "I couldn't understand the decision to close," Lee says. "The guys I worked for were wealthy people, the shop was still doing really good business, even with the arrival of Virgin. But it turned out to be a blessing in disguise."

A Derry man born and bred, Lee decided to fight back. Armed with a decent business plan he approached his bank. The manager thought he was mad trying to take on Virgin, but was still happy to loan him £3,000. Whatever happened to bank managers like that?

When he opened Cool Discs, the shop received fantastic support from local suppliers and the music community of the city. All profits were ploughed straight back in to expanding his stock. Soon after opening, an Irish rep from one of the big record labels came in and told Lee that he had just been in Virgin where one of their senior staff members had told him "Cool Discs will be closed in two or three months."

Whenever things got tough, Lee would think of those words for inspiration. At the time of writing, he has been open 32 years and two months, and I expect him to be there for a long time to come.

Lee tries to support fellow independent local traders when he can. Don't expect to see him with a cup of coffee from a well-known coffee shop in his hand. This is a community record shop and when I visited the place it was buzzing with customers chatting to Lee about music, politics, football and all things local. Lee informs me I am the only sales rep from UK mainland who has taken the trouble to come and visit him so far.

In 2003, with the news that HMV were on their way to Derry to compete with Virgin, Cool Discs expanded to twice its original size. Lee was pleasantly surprised at just how loyal his customers proved to be.

"We could not compete with the marketing machine of these two giant multiples, but we could compete with them in terms of knowledge and being able to change prices every day if we wanted," Lee says. "The toughest times for the shop were the Christmas periods when the only festive footfall we picked up was when people could not get what they wanted elsewhere, and had to walk the 100 yards down the street to us.

"Some of the prices these guys charged at Christmas was out of order and they got away with it for years because they could. That was frustrating for us. The expansion lasted three years and we downsized to our original unit once again. One thing I have learned in business is never be afraid to take a chance, but also if it doesn't work, cut the cloth accordingly. But hey, we are still here doing what we do, and I'm proud we are the only local record shop in Derry."

Cool Discs are champions of local music. The shop has a whole rack dedicated to fine local artists and bands. In 2013 when Derry was the city of culture, Cool Discs paid tribute to the best local music around and produced a CD that customers got for free when they bought an album by a local artist.

The vinyl revival has delighted Lee, but he has strong opinions on the prices some record and charity shops are now charging for second-hand vinyl. "Let's all be honest, since vinyl become popular once again a lot of these places are charging inflated prices for used vinyl," Lee says. "Why would you pay £20 and more for a used copy when you can buy it brand new for £15 or less? There are exceptions, I know, but I have seen a lot of people getting ripped off. Do your homework, as we always say. Don't get mugged."

Away from Cool Discs, Lee has promoted many gigs. In the early days of the shop he got behind Irish band the Frames led by Glen Hansard who went on to win an Oscar for his song "Falling Simple" from the film *Once*. Behind the counter, high out of harm's way, there sits a vinyl album *For the Birds* by the Frames with a message from Glen Hansard that says: "Lee, you are doing a great thing, giving us a voice, thanks for the support – Glen Hansard".

Thousands of music fans in Derry and Northern Ireland would echo those sentiments.

Top tip – Vinyl fans should check out Ben Allen's cleverly-named **Abbazappa Record Shop**, The Yellow Yard, Palace Street, Derry, BT48 6PS. Although a vintage shop, it is located in an old shirt factory which is full of independent businesses selling vegan food, vintage clothes, arts and crafts, and a bookshop. It is well worth a couple of hours of your time to explore.

Fairhill Records

3, Hill Street, Ballymena, County Antrim BT43 6BH
02825 641795
fairhillrecords@gmail.com
Tuesday-Saturday 10am-5pm
Established 2017
Stock: Vinyl, Pre-owned

Fairhill Records used to be known as Track Records. Jonathan Holmes, who was a regular customer at Track Records while working full-time as a production scheduler for Michelin Tyres, built up his record collection over many years. And after buying some job lots in 2013, he began selling vinyl himself, online and at record fairs. When Michelin closed the plant where he worked, Jonathan took voluntary redundancy. Still too young to re-tyre(!), he used the money to buy out the owner of Track Records which he re-opened as Fairhill Records in November 2017.

The shop stocks a wide range of vinyl records, CDs, books and "associated ephemera". Record collections are bought and sold.

Oxfordshire

In 2012, the UK's two most famous university cities Oxford and Cambridge did not have a single independent record shop that sold new vinyl. Fast forward six years and the situation has vastly improved with Cambridge having three shops and Oxford two. You can certainly visit the record shops of the county in a day. It is worth travelling to Witney to visit Rapture. Although under the same ownership it is a completely different shopping experience to visiting Truck their sister store in Oxford. Rapture is more mainstream and Truck more cutting edge. Do try and fit in a visit to the ancient market town of Wallingford to call in on local DJ and personality Richard Strange at The Music Box.

Blackwell's Music Shop

51, Broad Street, Oxford OX1 3BQ
music.ox@blackwell.co.uk
Monday-Saturday 9am-6.30pm
Sunday 10am-4.30pm
Established 1879 (as a bookseller)
Stock; Vinyl, CD, Books

Being a famous bookshop, Blackwell's is not a place a vinyl fan might think of visiting. But since the closure of HMV in the city centre, the shop has built up a good stock of vinyl records. Blackwell's Music has had a presence in and around its flagship store on Broad Street since it opened its doors in 1879. Until 2013, Blackwell's was solely a classical music specialist but has since widened the range to incorporate every genre of recorded music. Its shops in Edinburgh and Cambridge also stock music, but only in CD format. As part of Oxford's most famous bookshop and with a Café Nero upstairs, Blackwell's is a great place to while away a few hours.

Blackwell's took part in Record Store Day for many years, but the shop was removed in 2017 because, it was argued, as a bookshop and part of a chain it did not meet the necessary criteria. The big losers were the customers who turned up on RSD only to find that the shop had been denied access to the vinyl promotions that HMV and independent stores were able to offer. The same happened to Foyles, the famous bookshop that opened in 1906, located at 107 Charing Cross Road in London. Despite having an excellent record department, the fact that they are part of a chain of seven bookshops meant they were excluded from the event. My sympathies are with Blackwell's and Foyles. If there have to be exclusions to RSD, it would make more sense to review the position of the dozen or so second-hand record shops who buy hardly any new vinyl other than Record Store Day product.

In The Groove Records

14 Reading Road, Henley-on-Thames, Oxfordshire RG9 1AG
01491 579167
inthegrooverecords.co.uk; andy@inthegrooverecords.co.uk @In-TheGroove
Monday-Saturday 11am-5pm
Established 2006
Stock: Vinyl, CD, Pre-owned, 7-inch singles, Photography, Turntables

In The Groove Records, formerly known as Henley Records, is well worth a visit, not only for its collection of music but also to check out the interior. The shop, owned by Andy Tucker, features a giant egg chair and retro sofa with Tamla Motown cushions for you to sit on while listening to the music. The walls are adorned with fabulous photographs of Morrissey and the Smiths taken by Andy's friend Stephen Wright, who became a famous photographer, taking pictures of many bands of that era. Among them is the famous shot of the Smiths outside Salford Boys Club. Prints are for sale, making this a must-visit shop for fans of the Smiths. Another wall features a magnificent collage of the Miles Davis album *Bitches Brew*.

Andy's own music career started in 1978 in Cardiff where he hung out with Reptile Ranch, one of a host of local bands that would play in the city's Grassroots Café Bar. On Andy's suggestion, the band approached other bands who played there with the idea of releasing a compilation album to highlight the talent in the Cardiff music scene. Each of eight bands received an allocation of six minutes on the album and, in return for a payment of £200, they each received 25 copies to sell at gigs. Andy and Reptile Ranch built a temporary studio at the back of the café where the songs were recorded for the album *Is the War Over?* distributed by Rough Trade. It became a cult success, best remembered for the fact that Rough Trade signed one of the bands featured, Young Marble Giants, to their label.

Andy threw himself into more music-related projects, including joining the band Puritan Guitars, but was unable to replicate that early success and dropped out of music. For 25 years he worked at the Rank Organisation in Ealing, a job he did not enjoy. When offered voluntary redundancy, he jumped at the opportunity. He volunteered to work at his local Oxfam shop, where he enjoyed pricing and selling the records and CDs the public donated so much that he bought Henley Records.

His enthusiasm had clouded his judgement and he quickly realised he had bought a shop full of terrible stock. Only two customers bought anything on his first day's trading, and business only got worse after the stock market crash of 2008. Andy's redundancy payment enabled him to survive a tough period of initial trading. Slowly but surely things improved and with the vinyl revival taking off in 2014, he moved to larger premises further down the road. Most of the stock is second-hand and their 3 LPs-for-£10 offer is worth investigating, as well as the 10,000 7-inch singles in stock. Andy also stocks the largest collection of second-hand vintage record carrying cases that I have seen. The shop hosts a regular pop quiz at the local Bird In The Hand pub.

Music Box

14 Market Place, Wallingford, Oxfordshire OX10 0AD
themusicbox.net; richard@themusicbox.net; @themusicboxose
Monday-Saturday 10am-5.30pm
Established 1997
Stock: Vinyl, Pre-owned

Richard Strange's first week as owner of Music Box was memorable for two reasons. On the day he opened, one of the biggest hit singles of the 1990s "Wannabe" by the Spice Girls was released. And his son Robert was born. Better to be an absentee record shop owner than an absentee new father, and luckily the previous owner stepped in to help out while Richard took a week off to be at home.

Combining his work as a well-known DJ in the Oxfordshire area with running the shop, Richard traded successfully for many years until a pre-Christmas burglary forced the store to close. The thieves took £30,000-worth of stock leaving him little time to restock. Showing impeccable taste, the intruders left only one CD in the racks: the latest album from gardening guru Alan Titchmarsh. With few exceptions, the record companies acted like Scrooges, the majority of them turning down Richard's requests for extended credit to help replace the stock.

To plug the gap, Richard bought his CDs from Tesco. Through December to February he spent a staggering £75,000 with the supermarket chain. His logic was simple. Tesco concentrated on selling the chart CDs and sold many for £6.99 each. At the time the record companies charged him on average around £8.50 inclusive of VAT for the same titles. Richard took on Tesco in David and Goliath style. Tesco had two large shops in the area, one in Wallingford and one in Didcot. Richard would call in late on a Friday evening with a group of friends and family. Between them they would clear the shelves of the chart CDs that he required. As Tesco did not get CD deliveries at the weekend, they would have no stock of many of the key chart titles over the busy Saturday and Sunday.

Richard took delight in hearing customers who had come in to his shop to buy CDs, declare that they had been to Tesco but they had sold out, so they would buy from him in future. The problem was that, for all his efforts, Richard could not make any money on these CDs. He could price them only a little bit higher than Tesco or else he would get a reputation for being too expensive. His one consolation was that his friends and family had a hell of a lot of Tesco Clubcard points to spend in January.

Although Richard's trips to Tesco kept the shop going for a while, the pay-out from the insurance company, when it eventually came was only £15,000, about half of what he was expecting. Richard struggled on for a few more months, before reluctantly closing the shop in September 2006.

Thanks to the vinyl revival he opened Music Box again in Wallingford in 2014 as a vinyl specialist.

The shop has a contender in the daftest customer award.

Customer: "Are you taking part in Black Friday?"

Staff: "Yes, we will have lots of titles in."

Customer: "Is it next Saturday?"

Rapture

Woolgate Centre, Witney, Oxfordshire OX28 6AP

01993 700567

rapturewitney.co.uk; info@rapture-online.co.uk; @RaptureWitney

Monday-Saturday 9am-6pm Sunday 10.30am-4.30pm

Established 2004 Stock: Vinyl, CD, DVD, Coffee, In-stores

Owned by ex-Our Price manager Gary Smith, Rapture is typical of the independents that have survived the drastic changes in the industry over the last 20 years. Gary is an experienced retailer, who comments below on the changes he has witnessed and his thoughts about the future:

"After 14 years owning record shops and selling rock'n'roll to the masses, what has changed? Am I jaded? Have I gone from being a new kid on the block to curmudgeonly old fart? Well a lot has changed, and nothing has changed. It is still the best job in the world – that is certain.

I'll admit that the sheer excitement of running a business has levelled off somewhat, but my enthusiasm for new music and seeing new releases arrive in store is undimmed. How RSD has saved us has, I'm sure, been written about extensively elsewhere. But a mention should also go to the rise of DAB radio and particularly BBC Radio 6 Music for helping keep our customers enthused about new stuff.

So, the resurgence of vinyl has saved the industry? Well it's certainly kept many independent shops in business, although it's still not easy. Retail in general is in the doldrums. At the time of writing, there are a dozen or more household names that are facing severe restructuring or in some cases extinction. On top of the normal threats to retail, we face the occasional hostile action from the very people who are helping keep us alive.

The music retailer and record company relationship has always been a slightly awkward one. I was buying for a chain in the early 2000s and one of the contributors to the awkwardness was the importing of cheaper chart CDs from Europe. We had to do this to stay in the game because of the supermarkets taking chunks of the business. I remember being at a leading record company bash and the sales director making a speech about how delighted he was that their latest new act's album had gone straight to number one. The problem was, he said, that the chart sales for the first week were more than the UK record company had shipped – cue an audience of slightly sheepish retailers.

In recent years, the relationship has been much better with us all working together to keep up interest in the physical product. The relationship has been more open and honest from both sides. Although I do think there is a danger that we are heading for the old days – for example one of the major record companies has its own website selling exclusives. If we return to the dark days this time, there will be no format resurgence to save us."

Gary's last point is so important. Record companies have two choices. Work with the the shops by supporting *them* with exclusive product. The alternative is what is beginning to happen now. Selling the exclusives through their own or artists' websites. If they choose the latter, then I believe the independent record shop is facing another long, steady decline. It is time for the industry to wake up and see the damage it is inflicting on independent record shops. This time there is no vinyl safety net.

The record companies have a network of more than 200 record shops that are potentially an all year-round marketing machine for them. These shops are hubs where music fans meet and discuss, with loads of wall space and ear space to promote whatever they like. So, it's strange that a lot of exclusives are produced to sell direct themselves or via artists' websites where solitary purchases are made. You're not going to discover a new artist on the U2 website.

Truck Store *The shop that had a Prime Minister and a Jedi as customers*
101 Cowley Road, Oxford, OX4 1HU
01865 793866
truckmusicstore.co.uk; info@truckmusicstore.co.uk; @TruckMusicStore
Monday-Friday 9.30am-6.30pm
Saturday 10am-7pm
Sunday 11am-6pm
Established 2014
Stock: Vinyl, CD, Pre-owned, Cake, Coffee, In-stores, Tickets

Gary Smith (of Rapture in Witney) is also the owner of Truck Records, which has undergone a transformation in recent years. Oxford has long punched above its weight in terms of local music. Radiohead, Supergrass, Foals, Ride and Stornoway are the standard bearers of a vibrant and varied scene based around several great venues. The city is home to many independent record labels, promoters, and a monthly music magazine called *Nightshift*. The annual Truck Festival was considered by many to be the first boutique festival. All Oxford lacked was a great independent record store, and Truck filled the gap, though initially as a pop-up shop. They were the official festival ticket outlet for the festival and ran the on-site merchandise stall. They then converted 101 Cowley Road, a recently-closed video rental store, into a temporary record store and were met with such a great response from Oxford music lovers that in February 2011 they made it a permanent fixture, taking the name Truck Store in recognition of the festival's ethos.

Under manager Carl Smithson's leadership, the shop has become a cultural hub for Oxford's music scene and beyond. The vinyl revolution is alive and well in Oxford. As with most record store staff Carl feels he could be a detective if he did not work in a record shop, due to his skill in deciphering the strange requests he gets. One such case involved a request for a CD by the soul singer "Phil Willis". Carl worked out that the man wanted Pharrell Williams's "Happy".

Live music is also an integral part of the store, with its tiny stage hosting more than 250 acts to date, including Beth Orton, Wedding Present, James Vincent McMorrow, Guillemots, Willy Mason, Augustines, Johnny Flynn and countless local acts. They also host regular exhibitions of work by local artists.

It is probably the only shop to have had a Prime Minister (David Cameron) and a Jedi (Daisy Ridley) as customers, although not at the same time.

Scotland

Scotland has some of the best independent record shops in the UK. The well-designed Assai record shops in Dundee and Edinburgh are a welcome addition to the independent scene. Following the closure of One Up Records in Aberdeen in 2015, the city was left without an independent record shop. Aberdeen has gone from famine to feast with the recent openings of three completely different types of record shop: Chameleon, Maidinvinyl and Spin.

Dundee always had one of the best second-hand record shops around, Grouchos, but for many years had no independent record shops selling new vinyl. Now three new record shops have opened there, making it a must-visit destination for vinyl fans. When travelling between Dundee and Aberdeen, it is worth making the detour to Mo' Fidelity in Montrose. For the more adventurous, take a trip over to Orkney to visit Groove Records, one of the most magnificent and exciting record shops in the UK. It may seem a long way to go, but you will be rewarded with fabulous scenery and, if you plan your visit to coincide with one of Orkney's many music festivals, a wonderful weekend is assured.

Assai Record Shop

241 King Street, Broughty Ferry, Dundee, Angus DD5 2AX
01382 738406
assai.co.uk; keith.Ingram@hts-scotland.com; @Assai_UK
Monday 9.30am-5.30pm Tuesday 10am-4pm
Wednesday-Saturday 9.30am-5.30pm Sunday 12-4.30pm
Established 2015
Stock: Vinyl, In-stores, Merchandise, T-shirts, Turntables

Also at 1, Grindlay Street, Edinburgh EH3 9AT

Assai Record Shop on the outskirts of Dundee, is one of the most aesthetically pleasing record shops in the UK. The all-wooden interior gives it a spacious, clean look.

The owner Keith Ingram, who grew up in the area, worked at HMV before starting the successful online music retailers HTS Scotland Ltd. He had been sitting behind a screen since 2004, running an online business when he met up with Andy McLaren, who had been working in the iconic Groucho's Record Store of Dundee for the previous 13 years. Groucho's only stocks second-hand vinyl, and Keith realised that there was a demand for a shop in Dundee to sell new product.

Keith opened Assai in 2015, with Andy as manager. The shop complements rather than competes with Groucho's. Assai does a brisk business with its own branded record decks, an idea I am surprised more stores have not adopted.

In 2017 Assai opened a new branch in Edinburgh in the building that formerly housed the McAlister Matheston classical music shop.

Barnstorm Records

128 Queensberry Street, Dumfries, Dumfries and Galloway DG1 1BU
01387 267894
gmbarnstorm@googlemail.com
Monday-Saturday 9am-5pm
Established 1998
Stock: Vinyl, CD, Pre-owned, DVD, Tickets

Barnstorm Records has a superb selection of second-hand vinyl. The owner Gordon Maxwell is a stalwart of promoting and selling recorded music. He has fond memories of Calvin Harris (then known as Adam) coming in to the shop after school.

Big Sparra Vinyl

7 New Bridge Street, Ayr, Ayrshire KA7JX
01292 737520
bigsparravinyl@gmail.com; @bigsparravinyl
Monday-Saturday 10am-5.30pm
Established 2010
Stock: Vinyl, CD, Pre-owned, Cassettes, Tickets, T-shirts, Turntables

Owners Robert McKain and Ian Wallace describe Big Sparra Vinyl as a little store with a big heart. Originally, they rented space within a studio in Glasgow, before moving to Ayr, again renting space, this time within the local post office. This unusual arrangement worked surprisingly well. Vinyl fans in Ayr were delighted to have a retail outlet for the format, even if it was in a post office. It was not long before Big Sparra had four shelves to display their wares, but demand soon outstripped display space and the duo rented a shop with a beautiful view over the harbour.

Since then Big Sparra Vinyl has thrived. Record Store Day is a good barometer of the improvement. When they opened the door on RSD 2015, the first year that they participated, the queue consisted of four people. In 2016, the queue was up to 14, and in 2017, 140 people were waiting outside. By 2018, the queue was too big to count.

Robert and Ian are committed to the local community, championing unsigned local bands whose records they sell without taking a cut.

In 2018 Rob opened the Big Sparra Music Café ,137a Glasgow Road, Dumbarton, G82. The shop/café sells new vinyl along with coffee and food.

Chameleon
162 Union Grove, Aberdeen, AB10 6SR
01224 467892
chameleon.scot; design@chameleon.scot; @ChameleonABZ
Tuesday, Wednesday, Friday 10am-5.30pm
Thursday 10am-7pm
Saturday 10am-4pm.
Established 2014
Stock: Vinyl, Pre-owned, Art, Furniture

One of the most unusual record shops in the UK, Chameleon stocks new vinyl alongside the very best in designer Scandinavian furniture, contemporary lighting, glassware and art prints. You can pick up an £8,000 sofa or the latest indie vinyl release. The shop is located on the outskirts of the city centre, where it gets little passing trade while still attracting curious vinyl fans from all over Scotland.

Coda Music *Scotland's premier folk and Celtic shop*
12 Bank Street, Edinburgh EH12LN
0131 622 7246
codamusic.co.uk; mail@moundmusic.co.uk; @CodaMusic
Monday-Saturday 9.30am-5.30pm
Established 1990
Stock: Vinyl, CD, In-stores

Coda Music's co-owner, Dougie Anderson started his career in Bruce's Record Shop in Edinburgh, back in 1970. He worked there for two and a half years and found it an education in business. He then took a job with Virgin Records, at a tiny shop in Thistle Street, and after a while became manager. Virgin was great in those days. Richard Branson and Nik Powell were a joy to work for, with a huge sense of adventure, and the shops were innovative.

Dougie's partner, Rose Norton started her career in a local Portsmouth record shop in 1972. After eight years she moved onto Virgin Records when they opened their megastore at the Tricorn Centre in Portsmouth. She too has fond memories of the early Virgin days, when the staff felt they were part of a special company. Until circa 1988 when, according to Rose, the people who had made Virgin the great brand that is was were swapped for financial advisors.

For many years, Virgin was not only successful, but also the most fashionable chain of record shops in the country. Virgin grasped the ethic of punk long before many other record companies. Richard Branson signed The Sex Pistols, and the shops continued to do well.

In 1983, Dougie was promoted to Virgin area manager for Scotland and the North of England. With the help of Rose, who had moved to Virgin Edinburgh and been appointed the assistant area manager, he and their team of managers lowered overheads and increased sales dramatically. But, having been instructed to open as many shops as quickly as possible, they were disillusioned to discover that Virgin's plan was to sell them all off to Our Price as soon as the expansion was complete.

Dougie and Rose left Virgin to set up their own shop. With a £4,000 payoff and a bank loan, they set up Coda Music in Edinburgh's Waverley Shopping Centre. The shop was successful straight away, and they quickly paid off the loan. A second shop was soon opened in Glenrothes, Fife, which also did well and soon they opened a third shop in Livingston, West Lothian. The plan was to start an independent chain where the public would receive quality service by staff that knew about music. It seemed to work.

They opened a small, specialist folk music shop – also called Coda Music - on The Mound overlooking Princes Street in Edinburgh, which quickly established itself as the best place to buy traditional music in Scotland. At this point, they were the largest independent music retail chain in Scotland.

Over a period of 15 years, the supermarkets and internet retailers were gradually hitting all record shops and business at Coda Music started to slump. Dougie and Rose felt badly let down by the record companies, who they found to be unhelpful, if not actively hostile. Regrettably, they were forced to close their three mainstream shops.

Fortunately, they had established the folk music shop as a separate company, and were able to carry on trading there. Realising that vinyl was the future, in 2013 they opened a room within the shop dedicated to vinyl of all genres. Dougie remembers seeing a Japanese tourist listening on headphones, but looking puzzled. He glanced at the turntable to see which of the vinyl albums she was listening to. The answer was none. She had put the needle on the rubber mat and was nodding along to the sound of a stylus getting completely wrecked. It was odd to find that, for many people, putting a needle on a record is a completely new experience.

Dougie and Rose enjoy support and are now friends again with most of the major record companies and all independent labels. They support self-releasing artists and stock many albums by local musicians.

After nearly 50 years in the business, the pair still enjoy opening the doors every day and learning about and listening to new music. They've lived through the ups and downs of the record business. LPs, cassettes, 8-tracks, CDs, downloads and back to vinyl. It all comes around again.

Concorde Music   *The shop named after a plane, but which has lasted longer*
15 Scott Street, Perth, Perthshire PH1 5EJ
01738 621818
concordemusic.com; info@concordemusic.com
Monday-Saturday 9am-5.30pm
Established 1967
Stock: Vinyl, CD, Pre-owned, DVD, Merchandise, Turntables.

If it was in the USA, Concorde Music would be known as a Mom and Pop record shop. A family business, the shop is owned by Garry and Hazel Smith with their son Craig working there too, and caters for everything a music fan could want.

The shop was purchased by Garry's parents Rena and Norman from Sir Jimmy Shand, who owned it with his family. Jimmy, an accordion player, was known as The King of Scottish Dance Music. His most famous composition was "The Bluebell Polka". Richard Thompson, the English folk musician who wrote "Don't Sit on my Jimmy Shands" on his 1991 album *Rumor and Sigh*, was a big fan. Under the Shand family's ownership, The

Music Shop, as it was then known, was primarily a musical instrument shop. Rena and Norman transformed it into a record shop. They renamed the shop Concorde, after the supersonic aeroplane, which was deemed the future of travel. If you named a record shop on the same principle today, it might be called Driverless Car Records. Or maybe not. It is ironic that Concorde Music has lasted longer than the then-futuristic plane it was named after.

With the retirement of his parents, Garry took over the running of the shop. He attributes Concorde Music's survival to the family's willingness to diversify and try something different. During the punk era, they stocked bondage gear and converted part of the shop into a changing room. It could be a bit of a shock for some of their more conventional customers, coming in to buy a classical record, to be confronted by a spikey-haired punk, emerging from behind a curtain, trying on his tartan bondage trousers.

Garry recalls the golden age of record retailing in the 1980s when, for winning a sales-based competition with the record label Pye Records, he and Hazel were flown out to Cannes where they stayed in The Carlton for a luxury weekend. In those days, he might have up to seven sales reps from the record companies in his shop on a Thursday afternoon, all vying for business. How times change. In the last two years, according to Garry, only one rep from a record company has ventured up to Perth: yours truly, as part of my day job for Proper Music Distribution.

Over the years, Garry and Hazel have had plenty of competition in Perth, but have managed to outlast HMV, Our Price, MVC, Virgin, Goldrush, Menzies and The Poparound. They can be proud of being, literally, the last record shop standing in Perth.

Europa Music *The shop saved by the generosity of Scotland's vinyl buyers*
10 Friars Street, Stirling, Stirlingshire FK8 1HA
01786 448623
europamusic@btinternet.com; @Europa_Music
Monday-Saturday 9.30am-5.30pm Sunday 12-5pm
Established 1976
Stock: Vinyl, CD, Pre-owned, Merchandise, In-stores

Europa Music was originally opened by Adrian Wightman at the height of the 1970s punk boom, when it was one of seven music retailers in the small town of Alloa, Clackmannanshire. Adrian named the shop after his Lotus Europa car. The current owner, Ewen Duncan, acquired the shop in 1982.

Ewen is one of music retailing's great survivors. When he took on the shop, business had already started to decline due to the impact of the miners' strike of 1974. The Central Lowlands of Scotland depended on the coal industry and the pit closures had a devastating effect on the local economy, which suffered a further blow with the closure of the nearby Carsebridge Distillery in 1983. In 1992, Ewen moved Europa Music eight miles west to the much bigger town of Stirling.

Ewen was ahead of his time. While hundreds of record shops were reducing the space given to vinyl at this time, he opened a specialist vinyl room attached to the back of the shop. In October 1995, Ewen was awoken in the night by a phone call from the police, informing him that the shop was on fire. The front of the shop survived, but the vinyl room was destroyed. The insurance did not cover the stock, a significant omission, given that its retail value was £250,000.

Arson was suspected, but nobody was arrested for it. The people of Stirling rallied round, and a campaign was launched to save the town's record shop. With the help of local builders, family and friends, the vinyl room was rebuilt and an appeal went out through local media for donations of vinyl. Dozens of people called in to donate their vinyl records, including one gentleman who drove up from Edinburgh with a magnificent collection which included an original copy of the *White Album* by the Beatles. Ewen was incredibly touched by such support, which showed how much a record shop can be appreciated as part of the local community.

By 2006, business had improved so much that Ewen advertised for an extra person to work in the shop. More than 200 local youngsters applied. Ewen whittled it down to a shortlist of 10 who were then all entered in a music quiz to decide who should get the job. Ewen included one trick question: Name the members of Girls Aloud. Anybody who got all five correct had their application automatically turned down! The standard of the candidates was higher than Ewen had expected, and he ended up taking on three of the applicants, two of which, Alastair and Ali, still work In Europa Music today.

The shop has made the most of the vinyl revival. "On Record Store Day, we took more money than during the whole month of December," Ewen says.

With more than 10,000 pieces of vinyl on sale in the vinyl room, Europa Music should be the first shop on your list, if you are a vinyl fan in Scotland. This wonderful shop does not get the publicity it deserves. You can take a virtual tour of the shop via a video on YouTube: type in "Europa Record Store Walking Tour 24".

Feel The Groove *Paolo Nutini conducts an in-store proposal of marriage*
48 Causeyside St, Paisley, Renfrewshire PA1 1YH
01412 581990
info@feelthegroove.co.uk; @ftgpaisley
Monday-Wednesday 10am-6pm Thursday 10am-8pm
Friday-Saturday 10am-6pm
Established 2016
Stock: Vinyl, CD, Pre-owned

Feel The Groove, formerly Apollo Music, was owned by legendary music retailer Mike Dillon who had been trading since 1986. On his retirement in 2016, the shop was bought by Gavin Simpson, who had previously worked at the record labels Jive and Mercury. He changed the name to Feel The Groove and combined running the shop with working as a lecturer. The combination was more taxing than he had anticipated, and the shop was not taking the money he had hoped for. Paisley-born singer-songwriter Paolo Nutini, who had been a regular customer for many years, offered to do a free gig to help.

The shop only had space for 60 fans, so the idea was that each £5 spent in the shop earned the purchaser one ticket in a raffle. Each ticket pulled out of the raffle allowed two people to attend. When details of the gig were made public, sales went ballistic. Fans travelled from all over the world to spend small fortunes at the shop in the hope of being one of the lucky winners.

One man determined to win a ticket was Jonty Murdoch, so much so that he spent more than £200 in the days leading up to the raffle. The draw was held live on Facebook, and when his number – 450 – was pulled out, Jonty was ecstatic. His partner, Sarah, was a Paolo Nutini superfan and Jonty decided he would propose to her during the concert. Paolo performed a specially-choreographed version of his song "Better Man" after which Jonty went down on one knee and proposed. A huge cheer went up, after which Paolo offered his services as best man.

It was an occasion that will always be remembered by every person who was there. What a magnificent gesture by Paolo, who is a global star and a true supporter of independent record shops. I wish more major artists were prepared to do similar.

Flipside Vinyl & CDs
Kilmarnock Indoor Market, 65-75 Titchfield Street,
Kilmarnock, Ayrshire KA1 1QS
07473 116015
hugh@flipsidevinyl.co.uk
Tuesday-Friday 10am-5pm Sunday 12-4pm
Established 2017
Stock; Vinyl, CD, Pre-owned

Any vinyl fan traveling by train between Glasgow and Ayr should make a detour to Flipside Vinyl & CDs, a little shop located a minute's walk away from Kilmarnock station. Owner Hugh Fee is a local blues DJ, so the shop has an excellent selection of that genre. Hugh worked as a paramedic for 31 years before deciding to open his own shop. He has gone from having people dial 999 to secure his services with a first aid kit to selling records by 999 and First Aid Kit.

Local bands should get in touch. Hugh has a wonderful scheme whereby if you leave your stock with him and set a price, he will give you 100% of the proceeds from all sales.

Grooves *The UK's most northerly record shop*
17 Albert St, Kirkwall, Orkney, Northern Isles KW15 1HP
01856 872239
orkneymusic.co.uk; neil@groovesrecords.co.uk; @_theoldlibary
Monday-Saturday 10am-6pm
Established 1990
Stock: Vinyl, CDs, Pre-owned, Art Gallery, Books, DVD, Coffee, Food, Licensed Music Venue, Toys

Visiting Grooves, the most northerly record shop in the UK, is an adventure. It involves flying to Aberdeen before changing to a much smaller plane for a short flight to Kirkwall. I was told it could be a bumpy, turbulent flight and was advised to take a travel sickness pill. Should I take the ferry then, instead? "Oh no, that is 10 times worse."

After a pleasant, not-at-all turbulent flight, passing over many of the smaller islands, I landed at Kirkwall airport, an experience as far removed from arriving at Heathrow as I could imagine. The luggage was placed on the runway - no queuing at the baggage carousel - and as I walked to the terminal, I noticed a double rainbow in the sky. What a welcome.

The bus journey into town was an ornithologist's delight. The island was teeming with seabirds and geese, and a flock of swallows flew in a V-formation overhead. The bus contained even fewer passengers than the plane. The driver asked why I was visiting. I said I was there to meet the owner of the most northerly record shop in the UK. "Oh, that will be Neil Stevenson then," he replied.

I stopped for a coffee in an Italian café called Lucanos. The only other customer was a gentleman named John Ross Scott who turned out to be the editor of the local newspaper. I told him I was there to meet the owner of the most northerly record shop in the UK. "That must be Neil Stevenson," he said. By the time I left the café I had been told so many tales about Grooves by John and the café owner Francesco that I almost felt I had enough material for this part of the book without a contribution from Neil!

Grooves has moved location seven times in its 27-year history, though I am confident they have now found a permanent home.

Neil's two great passions as a young man were music and film. Although there had been many record shops which had come and gone in Kirkwall, none had catered for his own taste in heavy rock. He recalled one shop that, when you ordered a record from them, would commit the sacrilege of writing the customer's name on the record sleeve.

Neil incorporated a video hire business into his record shop. He had been hiring videos from a shop in the town which charged a membership fee and closed at 5pm each day. Grooves allowed customers to rent without having to join a club, and stayed open until 8pm. Soon enough, business was booming.

Over the years, videos were replaced by DVDs and Neil discontinued the rental business to concentrate instead on selling product. Every few years the shop would run out of space, and each time Neil would find larger premises slightly nearer the centre of town. By his sixth such move, the business had hit an upward curve. Even so, many people thought he had lost his marbles when he chose to move into a shop next door to Woolworths, his main rival for selling music and DVDs.

It turned out to be a shrewd decision. Woolworths purchased all their stock through a buying team based in their Head Office, which was then scaled out to all the branches in the country. Neil matched Woolworths on price on whatever promotion they were doing and although on some lines he was hardly making a profit, he soon established a reputation for never being undercut by the chain. And being an independent gave him the freedom to do his own promotions which Woolworths, as part of a chain, could not match. Not only was the local population naturally supportive of a local business, music fans had no reason ever to buy music from Woolworths. Neil was not on the Woolworths management's Christmas card list.

Neil had long been aware that Kirkwall lacked venues for young bands to play and an independent gallery for local artists to showcase their work. So in 2016, he took a gamble and bought the historic Old Town Library, which had closed down, and boldly added a music venue, an exhibition space, a café and a toy shop to Groove's core activities as a music retailer. Although there were plenty of excellent places to eat in the town, Neil thought it would be fun to include a licensed, record-themed café where fans of music and art could chill out for a while. As for the toy shop, Neil wanted to revive the happy memories of his childhood when visiting a toy shop did not involve a journey to a huge warehouse on a soulless trading estate.

The concept of Grooves is magnificent. I wish there were similar places on the UK mainland but sadly, right now, this place is unique. Perhaps somebody reading this, will recognise that their town has an unused historic building that could be transformed into an arts and entertainment centre, based around a community record shop. I was the first music sales rep to visit Grooves in 27 years of trading, but I can guarantee it is worth a journey to Orkney to be inspired.

KCC Vinyl
Unit 1, Olympia Arcade, Kirkcaldy, Fife KY1 1QF
01592 329964
kcvinyl@gmail.com;@kingdomvinyl Tuesday-Saturday 10am-4.30pm
Established 2017. Stock: Vinyl, Pre-owned

KCC Vinyl began when Tony McPhee started selling records from a small corner of his brother's shop Kingdom Comics and Collectibles (KCC). When his brother needed the space back, Tony took his vinyl collection and found his own premises where he continues to trade as KCC Vinyl - although you won't find any comics there.

According to Tony's former workmates, packing in a secure job as an aircraft engineer to embark on a long-held desire to own a record shop was sheer folly. There are days when he is running KCC Vinyl, that Tony thinks they might be right. But when such doubts surface he selects some uplifting music from his stock, sticks it on the turntable and blasts it out extremely loud. It reassures him that there are worse ways to spend your day.

Le Freak Records
159 Perth Road, Dundee, Angus DD2 1AR
07539 473932
lefreakrecords@gmail.com
Tuesday-Saturday 11am-8pm
Sunday 12-5pm
Established 2017
Stock: Vinyl, Pre-owned, In-stores, T-shirts

"Le Freak's soul and disco collection could melt the most frozen of hearts," says Jack Le Feuvre, who co-owns the shop with his brother Tom. Named after the 1978 hit by Chic, Le Freak Records is housed in a bright yellow building which some would call eye-catching, others garish, but none would fail to notice.

Love Music
34 Dundas Street, Glasgow, G1 2AQ
01413 322099
lovemusicglasgow.com; lovemusicglasgow@gmail.com; @LoveMusicGlasgo
Monday-Saturday 9am-6pm
Sunday 12-6pm
Established 1996
Stock: Vinyl, CD, Pre-owned, Tickets, In-stores

"Without Record Store Day, I don't think we'd be here. It came along at a very good time and it is a very big part of getting the vinyl revival going. It made people appreciate collectability and taught a new generation the excitement of coloured vinyl or a picture disc."
Sandy McLean – Love Music

Love Music is the first shop to visit in Glasgow, as it is only a 30-second walk from Queen Street station. As well as all the latest new releases and classic back catalogue you will find a fine selection of records by Scottish bands.

Despite his Scottish name, the owner Sandy McLean is originally from Nova Scotia in Canada. He came to Scotland on a gap year nearly 40 years ago, landed a job in a record shop and has spent his life in music retail.

Sandy is a champion of new music. He took over what was previously the Glasgow branch of Avalanche Records and changed the name to Love Music. He has survived the bad times and describes the days when three independent record shops a week were closing as "a whole industry just going down the plughole; a case of rearranging deck chairs on the Titanic." Luckily, the independent record shops were thrown a lifeline in the form of Record Store Day.

"Without Record Store Day, I don't think we'd be here," Sandy says. "It came along at a very good time and it is a very big part of getting the vinyl revival going. It made people appreciate collectability and taught a new generation the excitement of coloured vinyl or a picture disc."

Love Music has embraced Record Store Day from the beginning and is always looking to do something different on the day. Pride of place in the shop is a working pinball machine which customers are welcome to use. On Record Store Day, Sandy set out to find Glasgow's own Pinball Wizard. He invited three-time Scottish Pinball Champion Eric Ridley down to the shop to compete against budding pinball participants. Anybody who beat him received a special RSD prize.

Sandy goes the extra mile for RSD, setting up a stall with complimentary tea and cake and even providing a bag-minding service, so customers do not have to carry around their purchases all day.

LP Records
11, Park Road, Glasgow G4 9JD
01413 395270
lprecordsglasgow@gmail.com; @LP_Glasgow
Monday 12-6pm
Tuesday-Saturday 11am-6pm
Sunday 12-5pm
Established 2015
Stock: Vinyl, Pre-owned, In-stores

LP Records, owned by Lorenzo Pacitti, is popular with students. Located near the University, outside the city centre, the look of the shop is minimalistic with a high ceiling that contributes to the shop's good acoustics. With the initials LP, Lorenzo was always destined to open a record shop and has now started his own label which supports local music. LP Records is strong on new indie vinyl. Unlike many record shops in the city, parking is available outside the shop.

Maidinvinyl Records
Rosemount Viaduct, Aberdeen, AB25 1NE
07864 547203
maidinvinyl.co.uk; robertgabruce@yahoo.co.uk
Tuesday-Friday 10am-6pm
Saturday 11am-5pm
Sunday 12-4pm
Stock: Vinyl, Pre-owned

Maidinvinyl Records owner Robert Bruce was delighted to move from the shop's old premises located inside a gym, thus putting an end to the many jokey requests for records such as "Pump It Up" by Elvis Costello, "Physical" by Olivia Newton-John and "Stronger" by Kanye West.

The shop moved to larger premises in Aberdeen, close to the Central Library in 2016.

Robert is a professional singer and is not always at the shop. You are more likely to meet Liz and Aileen, as well as the shop's beautiful, musically-named dogs Mojo and Lemmy. Effervescent Liz is a whirlwind of enthusiasm, ensuring that few people leave the shop without making a purchase.

Mixed Up Records
18 Otago Lane, Glasgow G12 8PB
0141 357 5735
mixedup98@gmail.com; mixeduprecords.com; @mixeduprecords
Monday-Saturday 10am-6pm
Established 1998
Stock: Vinyl, CD, Pre-owned, DVD

Mixed Up Records, located a stone's throw from the university in the West End of Glasgow, is easy to spot thanks to its distinctive, sky-blue frontage. The shop, owned by Pete Ashby, sells mainly second-hand vinyl and with bargains starting at £1, it can cater for students on the tightest of budgets.

Mo Fidelity Records
128 Murray Street, Montrose, Angus DD10 8JG
01674 675379
neilmcl.afc@gmail.com; @MoFiRecords
Tuesday-Saturday 10.30am-5.30pm
Established 2017
Stock: Vinyl, CD, Pre-owned

Situated in the beautiful seaside town of Montrose, Mo Fidelity Records is worth a diversion for anybody travelling between Dundee and Aberdeen. The shop owned by Neil McCloud is easy to find thanks to its bright yellow and black design.

Neil took voluntary redundancy after working for more than 20 years as a Welfare Officer. It was love that inspired his career change. He had been a regular customer at Love Music in Glasgow for many years. Love's owner Sandy gave Neil the opportunity to work part-time in the shop. When Neil's partner Lyndsay McMillan's work took her to Montrose, he joined her there. Lyndsay combines her own therapy practice with helping out in the shop. The apprenticeship Neil had served with Sandy gave him the confidence to open his own shop and he has not looked back.

Monorail Music
97 Kings Street, Kings Court, Glasgow, G1 5RB
01415 529458
monorailmusic.com; info@monorailmusic.com; @Monorail_Music
Monday-Saturday 11am-7pm
Sunday 12-7pm
Established 2002
Stock: Vinyl, CD, DVD, Pre-owned, In-stores, Merchandise, Tickets

"I think the future for vinyl's amazing just now, there's never been so much coming out, I've been doing this for twenty-two years now and it seems better than it's ever been." **Dep Downie – Monorail Music, Glasgow**

Monorail Music is one of the best record shops in the UK, an idyllic musical sanctuary in which to while away the hours. While you are unlikely to find records by chart bands, you will discover the best in new and indie vinyl. It helps that the Mono building is situated under a railway arch, and that there is a superb vegan café, called Mono, within the arch (I can highly recommend the Banh mi, a baguette filled with crispy tofu, salad, basil and chili) and an in-house microbrewery. These added attractions make Monorail Music the perfect place for fans to meet. Who cares if your friend is late when you can wait for them in such a superb environment?

Glasgow has always been an energetic music city, but Stephen McRobbie, Dep Downie and John Williamson felt it was missing a great record shop, which they set out to provide. Both Stephen and Dep had spent time working in fondly remembered record shops in the city, Stephen at John Smiths and Dep at Missing Records. Stephen is guitarist and singer with the Pastels, one of the most influential Scottish bands of the last 30 years thanks to albums released on three of the most credible labels: Creation, Rough Trade and Domino.

The three men shared the belief that the future was vinyl and time has proved their judgement to be sound. Their idea was that the shop would not be a strictly retail experience and that by taking a more community-based approach, they would make people feel part of it.

With Stephen at the helm, Monorail Music was always going to have close relationship with the local music community. Teenage Fanclub, Belle & Sebastian, Mogwai and many others have all supported the shop. They have a close relationship with Mono next door, and often the two businesses collaborate on events. As well as a fabulous selection of indie music the shop is the place to go for fans of metal. Russell Elder is the shops resident metal expert ensuring they stock a comprehensive range of the genre.

The shop has organised a monthly film club at the Glasgow Film Theatre and has invited famous names including Alex Kapranos from Franz Ferdinand and Vic Godard to pick out their most treasured cinematic gems. I attended one enjoyable evening and was left with the impression that many people attend the Film Club purely on the reputation Monorail has for picking out interesting films.

Monorail is a beautifully-curated shop with wooden browsers run by a group of passionate music fans who want to share their love of new music. There is a consistent theme running through the internet reviews for Monorail: time and again, people say, "Great service".

Record Shak
69, Clerk Street, Edinburgh, EH8 9JG
01316 677144
Wednesday-Saturday 11.30am-6pm
Established 1983
Stock: Vinyl, Pre-owned, CD

Record Shak is a crate diggers paradise. The owner, David Gass, keeps the shop incredibly tidy but it is like an iceberg. Out front is just a small part of what he has for sale. A vast amount of stock is kept behind the counter, so it is worth asking if you can't see what you want. I have called in on more than one occasion to think the shop was empty, only for Dave to pop out from behind one of the boxes that are piled high around the counter.

Record Shak was once a chain with three branches in the unusual locations of Edinburgh, Newcastle and Kirkwall in the Orkney Islands. The original owner Shaki (who named the shop) had relatives in all three places, but eventually found it was too difficult to keep such a thinly-spread chain going and sold the business. His longtime employee David bought the Edinburgh branch.

Record Shak is an old school record shop with an excellent range of jazz and classical records. Dave does not bother with the internet. If you need information on a record he is stocking, he is likely to come up with it quicker than a google search.

Some Great Reward   *A must visit for Depeche Mode fans*
520, Victoria Road, Glasgow, G42 8B
01414 234141
hello@somegreatreward.scot; @SGR_RecordCafe
Wednesday-Sunday 10am-5pm
Established 2018
Stock: Vinyl, Cake, Coffee

Glasgow's Southside has a rich musical heritage with musicians such as Fran Healy, Bobby Gillespie, Jim Kerr, Charlie Burchill and Creation Records founder Alan McGee all growing up there. Despite these illustrious connections it has always been a weak link in the record retailing landscape of Glasgow. I am delighted to report that Some Great Reward has changed all that. A bright, new, airy vinyl café, it is named after the owner Olly McFadden's favourite record, the fourth album by Depeche Mode, released in 1984.

Olly bought his flat from Norman Blake of Teenage Fanclub, who was leaving to go to Canada, and who kindly left his piano behind. A few weeks later Olly was cleaning up when, tucked away in a cupboard, he found a bundle of test pressings of Teenage Fanclub's album *Songs from Northern Britain*. That was some great reward.

Top tip - Check out the vegan raspberry cake.

Spin Records

10 Littlejohn Street, Aberdeen, Aberdeenshire AB101FG
01224 649114
info@thetunnels.co.uk
Monday-Sunday 10am-11pm
Established 2016
Stock: Vinyl, Pre-owned, Coffee, Food, Licenced

Spin Records has a fabulous selection of used vinyl and the longest opening hours of any record shop I know. The owner, Jim Sandison combines running the first-floor shop with a café and late-night bar below. Jim opened the shop when he was 65. Retirement did not seem to appeal to him.

This Way Up

85b Perth Road, Dundee, Angus DD14HZ
07874 340554
thiswayupdundee@gmail.com; @thiswayupdundee
Monday-Saturday 9am-6pm
Sunday 10am-6pm
Established 2017
Stock: Vinyl, Pre-owned, Books, Cassettes

This Way Up boasts an excellent selection of pre-owned books and vinyl, and one of the best selections of world music vinyl in Scotland. It also does a good trade in cassettes. The owners Matt Stokey and Angelina Pendova experimented with a pop-up shop in the George Orwell pub before opening their own small shop.

Underground Solu'shn

9 Cockburn Street, Edinburgh, EH11BP
0131 226 2242
undergroundsolushn.com; info@undergroundsolushn.com; @Usolushn
Monday-Wednesday,Friday-Saturday 10am-6pm
Thursday 10am-7pm
Sunday 12-6pm
Established 1995
Stock: Vinyl, Pre-owned, Books, DJ equipment

Underground Solu'shn is the best place for dance music in Edinburgh. Starting out in a dingy old town basement on Cockburn Street, before relocating to overground premises further down the same street, it began as an "underground" record shop selling house, techno, disco, hip-hop, funk, soul, jazz and drum & bass on vinyl. The vinyl format is still an important part of the business, but embracing new technology they have expanded by stocking the latest DJ and music production equipment including turntables, mixers, CD decks, midi controllers, computer DJ systems, software and speakers.

VoxBox Music
21 St Stephen Street, Edinburgh, EH3 5AN
01316 296775
voxboxmusic.co.uk; voxbox@live.co.uk; @VoxBoxMusic
Wednesday-Friday 12-5pm
Saturday 10.30am-5pm
Sunday 12-4pm
Established 2011
Stock: Vinyl, CD, Pre-owned

VoxBox Music was opened by retired teacher George Robertson and a former junior doctor Darren Yeats. George had been dealing in used records as a sideline for 25 years and owned a second-hand vinyl stall in Edinburgh. Darren had become one of his best customers, and the pair became firm friends despite the father–son sized age gap.

George wanted to wind down the amount of record fairs that he attended, while Darren wanted a break from the stress of being a doctor. They bought the premises together and got the venture off the ground. In 2014 Darren bought out George, after which he extended the opening hours. He has also installed an original Dansette record player on which customers are welcome to play any of the records stocked in the shop.

Running a record shop is easy compared to the long hours and burden of responsibility he shouldered as a junior doctor. "Work has never been so much fun," he says.

Shropshire

For vinyl fans in Shrewsbury it must seem like all their Christmases have come at once. In 2014, they had no independent record shop in the town selling new vinyl. The HMV store was no longer stocking the format. Fast forward a few years and now HMV has an extensive range and the town has three independent record shops.

Cave Records

The Parade Shopping Centre, St Mary's Place, Shrewsbury, Shropshire SY1 1DL
07772 225651
caverecords.co.uk; caverecords@gmail.com; @Caverecordsshrewsbury
Established 2013
Stock: Vinyl, Pre-owned

Cave Records is tucked away in an arcade and named after its owner Joseph Cave. Joseph is also a musician who jokingly describes the shop as "a much cleaner time capsule of my teenage bedroom." Stock is mainly second-hand but the shop takes part in Record Store Day.

Left For Dead

14 Wyle Cop, Shrewsbury, Shropshire SY1 1XB
0174 324 7777
leftfordeadshop.co.uk; left-for-dead@outlook.com; @LeftForDeadshop
Monday-Saturday 10am-5.30pm
Established 2013
Stock: Vinyl, CD, Books, In-stores

Andy Haddon, owner of Left For Dead, has been working in record shops for almost 25 years, managing shops across the UK for HMV, Fopp and Rise. The idea for Left For Dead was born in the back of a camper van with his wife Jenny somewhere in Western Australia during a year-long career break in 2012.

The name Left For Dead was inspired by a phrase shouted out by Ryan Adams at the end of the opening, spoken-word sequence on his 2000 debut album *Heartbreaker*, produced by Ethan Johns. Andy felt that "left for dead" was a good description of how the music industry had treated record shops. Years later, in 2016, Andy persuaded Ethan Johns - a notable supporter of independent record shops - to do an in-store event, and was able to thank him, in person, for the inspiration.

Andy opened Left For Dead in 2013 in Birmingham, at a development known as the Custard Factory, but struggled to make a profit until he moved to the current premises in Shrewsbury in 2015. It is part of the longest row of independent shops in the UK situated on a beautiful historic hill called Wyle Cop. The shop runs a successful loyalty card scheme, offering regular cardholders a 10% discount. As well as prize draws, it offers priority to people wishing to attend the shop's many in-store events.

Andy discovered an unlikely source of income thanks to the sun and the town's most famous resident naturalist, Charles Darwin. When the shop was based in Birmingham he would display the new vinyl releases in the window. Upon moving to Shrewsbury, he adopted the same policy, but to his dismay he discovered that the sun melted the vinyl in his window display. He had recently purchased a selection of books on Darwin, which he put in the window instead. It turned out that tourists could not get enough of books about Darwin. For any record shop to survive these days it must have more income streams than just selling recorded music, as the margins are so low. Thanks to Darwin, Andy has one of the more unusual alternative sources of income.

One thing Left For Dead will not stock is cheap record players. For Andy, this is a major bone of contention, and his argument is backed up by most record retailers. So many young people have latched onto the vinyl revival now that the format is viewed as fashionable. Music fans argue that vinyl gives you a superior sound quality, but this argument falls flat on its face when the record is played on the wrong sort of deck. The problem is that many music fans are playing their vinyl on cheap record players that have flooded the market and been heavily promoted by the supermarkets and chain stores. In 2015 it was announced that the record player was the most popular Christmas present, but most of these were record players retailing at less than £50. Does coffee taste nicer in a plastic cup? Does anybody look smart wearing a suit and trainers? Does vinyl sound good on a cheap record player?

When the budget record players first appeared on the market, independent record shops embraced them. These shops promptly became disillusioned as so many customers were returning them, disappointed by the sound quality. The hassle of giving refunds and, most of all, losing customer goodwill, resulted in many shops stocking more expensive and higher quality models, or not stocking them at all. Although budget record players give an initial boost to vinyl sales (you need some vinyl to play on it, after all) in the long term it leaves its customers with the view that vinyl does not sound superior, and the danger is that the industry loses another long-term vinyl customer.

Although you will not see any pictures of Andy next to a budget record player, you can see lots of images of him, as he is known as the record retailer of a thousand faces. Check out the shop's Facebook page, where you will find Andy promoting his latest recommended albums. The album's sleeve is held next to Andy's face, always wearing a comical expression. He should make a collage of them all. The one expression you always get from Andy is a smile, as he likes nothing better than to chat with fellow music fans.

"More and more people are beginning to appreciate independent businesses and I think this is a reaction to the characterless and soulless identikit shopping malls and coffee houses on our high streets, Andy says. "I think the resurgence of the vinyl record is like the resurgence we've seen in the book industry; it's an appreciation of something that is tangible and a reaction against the disposable digital media and eBooks.

"Independent record shops have adapted and changed too: in the past they were often dingy grottoes stuffed with musty cardboard boxes and staffed by miserable old men. They were exclusive to the point of extinction. Nowadays, your thriving indie record shop is a brightly lit destination store, often with a cafe and bar attached, with space for live performances. The new release records hang artfully from every wall and every week there's a smorgasbord of great new artists and groups to discover.

"I am quietly optimistic about the state of the bricks and mortar indies, although I have worked in the industry long enough to know that there isn't another industry on the planet as short-sighted and self-sabotaging as the music business. I think that like most trends, the vinyl revival will plateau. Records aren't cheap and the age-old argument about vinyl's superior sound quality means nothing when kids are wrecking their records on cheap-ass record players."

Tubeway Records
Unit K12, Lower Level, Pride Hill Centre, Shrewsbury, Shropshire SY1 1BY
01743 588890
tubewayrecords@hotmail.com; @tubewayrecords
Monday-Saturday 10.30-4pm
Sunday 9am-4.30pm
Established 2015
Stock: Vinyl, CD's, Pre-owned cassettes

Gary Numan fan Aden Horne named his shop after Gary's band Tubeway Army. If you are a Numan fan, you will find a fantastic range of items here. This is a family business with Aden's wife Carol and film-making son Alex also working in the shop. Star of the show is youngest son eight-year-old Zac, who loves being in the shop, chatting to customers and pulling a few items out of the rack. After a few minutes "work", he normally returns to his Lego set. You can always tell if Zac is in, as he loves listening to "Mr Blue Sky" by ELO, "Cars" by Gary Numan and Monty Python records. The shop also sells autographs of musicians.

Somerset

Bath has proved a graveyard for record shops. In recent years Nesher's Music Store, Milsom & Son, Replay, Bath Compact Disc, Rival and Music Matters have all closed. And if top music retailers such as Fopp and Raves From The Grave can't make it work here either, who can? It is the last place I would recommend anybody to open a record shop. Most closures are blamed on the high rent and rates. Compared with other cities Bath does not have an independent shop ethos. With its heavy traffic congestion and high parking charges it is not a great shopping experience.

The government and councils should support and encourage the opening of more independent shops. Why not introduce a two-tier rating system? If a person owns three or less stores they should be liable for a lower rate than chain stores and bigger companies who are able to employ experts to ensure they keep their tax contributions to a minimum. Without extra support for independent traders our city centres will become increasingly homogenised.

Currently Bath has no record shop that takes part in Record Store Day but if you are in the city and need a vinyl fix it is worth a trip to Resolution Records, Green Park Market, BA1 1JD, which has a fine selection of second-hand stock. It is owned by Mark O'Shaughnessy who writes a regular column in Long Live Vinyl magazine.

Covers Vinyl Record Store
10 Catherine Hill, Frome, Somerset BA11 1BZ
01373 472175
coversvinyl.co.uk; info@coversvinyl.co.uk; @coversvinyl
Tuesday-Saturday 10am-5pm Established 2016 Stock: Vinyl

Frome is the town for vinyl fans in Somerset. It has two record shops selling the format: Raves From The Grave and the more recently opened Covers Vinyl Record Store (CVRS). Howard Phillis, the owner of CVRS, started selling vinyl online in 2013, specialising in new indie and alternative music, which he combined with a day job in advertising. Eager to escape the London rat race, he moved to Frome. Within a week he came upon an empty unit on the town's historic Catherine Hill. A steep, cobbled hill dating back to the 15th century, when it was at the centre of the local wool trade, the area is now a haven for independent shops and has proved the perfect home for CVRS.

The shop is small and spotless, yet stocks a vast range of vinyl. The secret is the pull-out drawers, featuring genres such as jazz, blues, hip hop, reggae and electronica which are installed underneath the vinyl racking. Star of the shop is an extremely friendly pug dog called Poppy, who has become popular with the town's music fans. She even has her own Instagram account, @poppypuglet.

Frome is one of the best independent retailing towns in the country and my tip is to plan a visit to coincide with the monthly Frome Independent Market which is held on the first Sunday every month from April to December. The town is buzzing with music, street theatre, hands-on activities and tasty street food. Spend the Saturday visiting the record shops and Sunday at the market. "Vinyl is the perfect antidote to hectic modern life," Howard says. "Take things slow."

"To gauge the worth of a town's record shop, see if they've a section devoted to the trailblazing art rock band Pere Ubu. I ran the test here and instantly decided to move to Frome."
John Harris, The Guardian

Raves From The Grave

20 Cheap Street, Frome, Somerset BA11 1BN
01373 464666
ravesfromthegrave.com; raves@btconnect.com; @RavesGrave
Monday-Saturday 9am-5pm
Established 1997
Stock: Vinyl, CD, Pre-owned, Cassettes, DVD, Merchandise, 7-inch singles, In-stores
Also at 5 Weymouth Street, Warminster, Wiltshire BA12 9NP

Raves From The Grave is situated in the old town of Frome on a medieval street full of interesting retail outlets. I am confident it is the only record shop in the world that has an open leat (artificial watercourse) running in front of the store. It is the kind of shop you remember from your childhood, with records, CDs and DVDs piled everywhere. It never ceases to amaze me that the staff seem to know where everything is, a staggering achievement given that, between the two shops, they stock 80,000 CDs, 75,000 LPs and 10,000 DVDs. Fans of cassettes should pay them a visit too, as they sell them at 4 for £5.

The owner, Richard Churchyard was a shop manager at WH Smith in Notting Hill Gate when he decided that corporate life was not for him. Looking for a town with no record shop, he settled on Frome. After his first day's trading, when he took only £13, he began to think there was a reason why Frome did not have a record shop. Luckily it was not long before he started receiving support from the local community. He has never regretted the decision to move to Frome, and despite being skint, he has never been happier. By 2010 he had so much stock that he opened a second shop, which is run by his wife Debbie.

A great example of what fantastic customer service independent record shops provide is highlighted by the following story. The day before my visit, Richard was disappointed that he could successfully fulfil only three of four difficult requests.

Customer one: "I am after a box set of EastEnders videos."
No problem. Richard found one.
Customer two: "I am after any recordings of the Ffestiniog railway."
No problem. Richard found a 7-inch single in Holland and ordered it in.
Customer three: "I am after any cassette singles of Steps or S Club 7."
No problem. Richard had some in stock.
Customer four: "I am after a DVD of Caroline Clipsham, live at Leatherhead Village Hall. It was a gig I attended about seven years ago."
Richard: "Leave it with me for a couple of hours."
After searching the internet and the artist's website, Richard could find no trace of this DVD. Two hours later the customer returned.
Customer: "Did you get it?"
Richard: "Sorry I could find no trace. When you were at the concert did you notice the performance being filmed?"
Customer: "No. But you never know. I thought I would check."

Raves From The Grave is so full of stock that there is no space for bands to play inside, and it is the only shop I know of that does in-store events outside (out-stores?). Artists such as World Party, Tom Robinson and Billy Bragg have been happy to play outside (their performances can be viewed on YouTube). Billy Bragg describes it as "A record shop that has too many records in it for the space it occupies." In 2017, Raves From The Grave celebrated 20 years in business and threw a big party in the town. Tom Robinson was among the musicians who played on that memorable evening.

In recent years the shop has had a vinyl stall at the Glastonbury festival.

Spaced Out Records
169a High Street, Street, Chard, Somerset, BA16 0ND
07722 906366
info@shiftys.org
Tuesday-Saturday 10am-5pm
Established 2017
Stock: Vinyl, CD, Pre-owned, Memorabilia

If you are a fan of shoes and music, then the village of Street is the place for you. Located three miles from Glastonbury, it is the home of the famous Clark family who started manufacturing shoes in the 17th century. Production stopped in 1993 and the giant factory was turned into Clarks Village, a shopping outlet. Sadly, none of the 90 stores there sell vinyl. Fear not, though: just a few hundred yards away is Chris Sheldon's shop Spaced Out.

The shop changed its name from Shiftys in 2018. I can understand why, as Shiftys for me conjures up an image of a Del Boy-type character, which is the complete opposite of Chris. I asked him what inspired the new name. "It came from the feeling of how music carries you into a spaced out state of mind," Chris explained. "You forget your problems and nothing else matters but the music."

Chris Sheldon's dad was an avid vinyl collector and bought the format throughout his life. He passed his love of records on to his son and between them they had a massive collection. When his dad passed away, Chris re-evaluated his life. He had been working in construction for many years but with the vinyl revival in full swing, he opened his own record shop. He opened accounts with record companies for new stock and had a large second-hand section which he acquired having spent previous weekends touring the car boot sales of the south west. Chris combines selling records with working in music production. He offers affordable, basic mixing and mastering services, so if you are a musician based in the area it gives you another reason to visit the shop. Backing onto the shop is a laundrette with a large back yard. If you visit on a weekday it is full of washing hanging out to dry. The laundrette is closed of a weekend, and in summer months Chris hosts local bands there, combining it with a barbeque. Unlike the laundrette, Chris is not cleaning up, although his quality of life has never been better.

Staffordshire

Staffordshire is one of the most disappointing counties in the UK for record shops with only four shops taking part in Record Store Day. In the past, towns such as Lichfield, Uttoxeter, Stafford, Leek, Tamworth, Newcastle-Under-Lyme and Cannock have all had a record shop. For somebody looking to open a record shop selling new vinyl, these are places worth considering.

Fish Records
Unit 2, Crown Couryard, Crown Street, Stone, Staffordshire ST15 8UY
01785 282839
Fishrecords.co.uk; info@fishrecords.co.uk; @FishRecordsUK
Established 1999
Stock: Vinyl, CD

Fish Records was founded by Neil Pearson in 1999, trading online in folk, acoustic and singer/songwriters. When Neil moved into artist promotion and development, Pete Morgan took on the business and expanded its activities and base, particularly into Americana and alternative country. Pete has now taken the plunge and opened a bricks and mortar store. As you would expect the shop is strong on folk, but all genres are stocked. Pete combines his shop work with working as a booking agent and arranges gigs. The shop also has a stall at the Shrewsbury Folk Festival. Be careful when googling the shop or you are likely to end up with listings of the heaviest pike caught in the UK.

Global Groove *The shop manager who was making "records" as a four-year-old*
Global House, 13 Bucknall New Road, Hanley, Stoke-on-Trent,
Staffordshire, ST1 2BA
01782 215554
globalgroove.co.uk; mail@globalgroove.co.uk
Monday-Friday 10am-6pm
Established 1992
Stock: Vinyl, New & Pre-owned

Global Groove has an excellent reputation for its mail order service and is managed by local DJ Pete Bromley. He started making records at the age of four. He was not a child singing prodigy, but he had a talent for cutting cardboard circles from Dairylea soft cheese boxes, then colouring the middles in to look like his own singles. He soon graduated to a kid record player that played nursery rhymes on 5-inch singles before starting to buy his own records, independently, from the age of eight.

After leaving school, Pete started as an apprentice electrician, while spending his spare time and money DJing and hanging out at Lotus Records in Hanley where he put together a weekly dance chart for the shop. He was soon advising them on which dance 12-inch singles to purchase, and when a job became available Pete was the obvious choice. Although three-and-a-half years in to a four-year apprenticeship, and despite strong opposition from family and friends, he took the job. After 28 years of working in record shops it is clear he chose the right path.

Pete worked at Lotus Records for 18 months and established it as the dance specialist shop of The Potteries. A fellow DJ and friend known as Tes offered to finance a shop for Pete to manage and Global Groove was born. Pete ran the record shop during the day, and by night established himself as a top DJ, sharing events with dance luminaries such as Judge Jules, Boy George, Pete Tong and Carl Cox.

Around 2008 things got tough for Global Groove and for a while it was a hand to mouth existence. Many other dance specialist shops were closing down. But Pete and his staff adopted their own catchphrase: "We will keep doing this till we have to get a proper job." Pete believes that many dance record shops gave up too quickly during this period. He is glad to have proved that, with sufficient determination and passion, you could survive.

A turning point came when the local HMV stopped stocking vinyl. Pete changed Global Groove from a dance specialist to a vinyl specialist with a fantastic range of dance music. If you are a fan of dance or vinyl in general, and in The Potteries, this place is for you. The shop is closed on Saturdays.

Henry's Records *Don't ask for Max Bygraves or an all-day breakfast*
17, Station Road, Burton-on-Trent, Staffordshire DE14 1BX
01283 510110
henrysrecords.co.uk; henrysrecords@postmaster.co.uk
Tuesday-Saturday 9.30am-4pm
Established 1996
Stock: Vinyl, CD, Pre-owned, Memorabilia

When visiting Henry's Records, the first of your senses that you become attuned to is smell as opposed to sound. This somewhat eccentric establishment is located in front of the town's brewery. Outside, the smell of the brewery dominates the streets. But inside Henry's, the smell of incense hangs in the air, reminding me of the record shops of my youth.

The shop is full of the most fascinating memorabilia, including original posters of Morecambe and Wise, James Bond and Carry On films. Behind the counter stands a life-size cardboard cutout of Dolly Parton. The shop's owner John Brisbrowne informs me she is his assistant...but only works 9 to 5!

You could easily spend hours here as there is so much to see. The music that is played while you browse is a soundtrack of classic 1960s and 1970s songs. The shop is named after John's middle name. He thought Henry's sounded better than John's. Always a great collector of vinyl, and having records stored in every room of his home, he took a short-term lease on the shop, with the idea of closing as soon as he had sold his collection. However, he enjoyed serving customers who were delighted a record shop had opened in the town, and could rarely resist the record collections that he was offered to purchase. Over the years he has begun to lose patience with some of the characters who come in describing some of them as "bloody nutters".

There was the occasion when John noticed a man pulling vast quantities of CDs out of the racks and stacking them on the floor. John did not pay much attention, assuming he was going to be buying big. After about two hours, the man approached the counter. John was perplexed as he did not have any CDs with him and the pile stacked high on the floor was no longer there.

"No need to pay me, I just did it to help you out," the man said.

"What do you mean?" John asked.

"Well, I noticed that lots of your CDs were in the wrong section. You had John Lennon under L and Joni Mitchell under M. To help you, I moved them to the J section. I have done the same in all your CD racking from A to Z".

The look on John's face was enough to convey to the man that his efforts were not appreciated and he beat a hasty retreat. It took John the rest of the day to put the titles back into their correct alphabetical sections.

Another bizarre encounter involved a family group of mum, dad and son who came up to the counter, walking past thousands of records in the process, for mum to ask:

"Do you have three All-Day Breakfasts?"

"Are they a band?"

"No, three all-day breakfasts to eat. We are starving."

At this point dad decided to take over, clearly thinking his wife had not got the message through:

"Are you not open?"

"Yes, I am open, but I am a record shop which does not cook all-day breakfasts."

"Would you cook one for us?"

"No! Look around. I have no tables, chairs, crockery or cutlery; just records."

"Oh, OK. Is there anywhere in Burton that does all-day breakfasts then?"

"Try B&Q", John said, sarcastically."

"OK. We will go there then."

And off they went to annoy the staff at the builder's merchants.

Another problematic customer was the woman who enquired if John had "anything by Max Bygraves". Having found the old crooner a hard act to sell, John had accumulated quite a few Max titles over the years. But some were in the shop, some in a lock-up and others in a garage. "Fantastic," said the woman, "I will take everything you have. I will come down Monday to collect them". John pointed out that he was normally closed on a Monday but would open especially for her. He spent all of Sunday searching his stock and came up with more than 20 items. Next day, Max's biggest fan turned up and John proudly presented all the stock he had dug out.

"Oh, my mother will be so disappointed," she said. "There are no DVDs. All she wants is DVDs".

"You said that you will buy anything by Max Bygraves."

"What I meant was that I would take anything on DVD."

"But you did not say that."

"I know, but that is what I meant. I have come all this way for nothing. My mother will be heartbroken."

"Take this LP. You can have it. Why not go back to your mother and if she is half as thick as you, wave at it up and down in front of her face? Perhaps she will think she is watching a DVD."

John's all-time worst customer was a local man he christened Tamworth Bottle Glasses (TBG) due to him wearing glasses with lenses so thick that John reckoned he could see Jupiter through them. Their paths first crossed when John was doing some filing under the counter and he heard a voice say to him.

"My wife has left me."

"I'm sorry to hear that."

"My wife leaving me isn't the worse news though. She scarpered with my record collection, so I'm down here to replace it."

John was sorry to hear about his marital problems, but delighted he had visited him in order to re-purchase his collection. John wondered, optimistically, how big his collection had been. Two hours later TBG returned to the counter, carrying two albums.

"Is that it – just two records?"

"No. I am after one other record."

"What is it?"

"I heard Adam Faith sing it on TV last night but don't know what it is called."

Luckily, John had watched the programme and knew the song TBG was talking about: Adam Faith's 1959 No.1 hit "What Do You Want?".

"It's 'What Do You Want?'."

"Yes, I do want the song from the programme."

"It is Adam Faith singing 'What Do You Want?'."

"Yes, I want the song that Adam Faith sang on the programme last night, but I'm not sure what it's called."

"The song from the programme last night that Adam Faith sang was 'What Do You Want?'!"

"Yes, that is what I want, the song from the programme."

At this point, John took his hand and marched TBG to the Adam Faith section and thrust the record into the hands of another satisfied customer.

John dreads rainy days. Because the shop is so close to the railway station, people take refuge whenever a downpour occurs. Often it can be jam-packed with many people pretending to be looking, but hardly anybody buying anything. John observes from the counter through gritted teeth as they drip water over his beloved vinyl. On the plus side, if you are planning a visit, take the train and within a minute of arriving you can be looking through the racks of a great Burton institution.

Music Mania

3-6 Piccadilly Arcade, Hanley, Stoke-on-Trent, Staffordshire ST1 1DL
01782 206000
sales@musicmaniauk.com; @musicmaniastoke
Monday-Saturday 9am-5.30pm
Established 2001
Stock: Vinyl, CD, Pre-owned, Tickets

Music Mania owner Ian Gadsby is a fan of new music, and has noticed that more of his customers are coming in to buy records they have heard on BBC 6 Music or read about in music magazines which they cannot get in the supermarkets. He has embraced social media and keeps his followers informed of the music that the shop staff are enjoying. The result is that the average age of his customer is younger than it was ten years ago. When the shop opened, it sold exclusively second-hand CDs. These days it is a mixture of both new and used stock. Music Mania has a great vibe and more than its fair share of eccentric customers. These include:

Rammstein Tooth, who only buys Rammstein albums and has one fearfully protruding front tooth.

Vicky Onions, who pops her head through the door, shouts "YOU GOT ANY NOWS?" (*Now That's What I Call Music* compilations) and leaves without waiting for an answer.

Frankenstein Hipster, who lumbers in like Mary Shelley's creation to buy the latest Yacht rock compilation.

The Thrash Brothers, who ask for thrash metal bands no one has heard of. Nephew, who comes in to ask "Have You Seen Uncle Darren?" To this day no one in the shop knows who Uncle Darren is.

Strand Records

19 The Strand, Stoke-on-Trent, Staffordshire ST3 2JF
07592 908319
strandrecords@hotmail.co.uk; @StrandRecords
Monday-Saturday 10am-5.30pm
Established 2013
Stock: Vinyl, Pre-owned, CD, DVD, Badges, Cassettes, Mugs

Strand Records is based inside the Longton Market. Although the shop is small, the owner, Kendall Trigg, has managed to cram a lot of stock in while keeping it neat and tidy. The shop has an excellent £3 pre-owned vinyl section, and prices in general are among the lowest I have come across. Don't leave without purchasing one of the shop's distinctive mugs and bags.

Those Old Records

The man who went out to buy a chicken dinner and ended up with a record shop
Brewery Shopping Centre, Rugeley, Staffordshire WS15 2DY
07795 548242
thoseoldrecords@btinternet.com; thoseoldrecords.co.uk; @thoseoldrecords
Tuesday, Thursday-Saturday 9am-4pm
Established 2005
Stock: Vinyl, Pre-owned

"I went to Rugeley to buy a chicken for dinner and ended up buying a record shop," says Chris McGranaghan, owner and manager of Those Old Records. On his way in to the historic market town Chris, who up until then had been selling vinyl on eBay, at record fairs and on his own website, spotted a small retail unit at Brewery Street Shopping Centre. Despite being warned that it was madness to open a record shop in Rugeley, he took the unit on for a three-month trial. The town, which was severely run down in the aftermath of the pit closures of the 1980s, has more recently seen its fortunes revived thanks, ironically, to the arrival of Amazon – the shop's main competitor - who moved in to a giant warehouse nearby.

Chris feels that many record shops act like drop-in centres for people to meet their mates. He runs his shop like a business, with every record having to earn its space in the racks. Records come in and out with speed. Nothing is "under the counter". He doesn't sell on eBay unless the record is unusual and unlikely to sell in the shop. All records he tries to sell in the shop first as he always wants his customers to come back. Their stocking policy caters to a wide and growing customer base, with a philosophy that today's kids are tomorrow's adults with money in their pocket.

In 2013, Chris started his own TOR record label, which has been a big success. Many of the early releases on the label have become collectable. TOR specialises in limited vinyl pressings that nearly always sell out. Chris is one of the handful of independent record shops who sell new vinyl who have opted out of Record Store Day.

"We opt out of RSD primarily because I feel that what was a great initiative has now been taken over and controlled by the larger record companies," Chris explains. "It has moved away from the promotion of independent record shops into a means for companies to shift more stock. It has become a greed-fest for folk who would never come near the shop for the rest of the year, and I don't run the business on that basis. We are in for the long haul, and that means keeping and maintaining regular customers. I don't need RSD and I really don't need the greed and avarice associated with it. These days we still close the shop and take a bunch of regulars for a pint in Wetherspoons. They seem to like that."

Although I disagree with Chris, it is good to hear a different perspective. One of the great things about independent record shops is they are all different and have no head office to answer to.

Top tip – The shop holds a live acoustic session on the third Saturday of the month. These are filmed and can be viewed on YouTube.

Surrey

It is surprising to find that the two most populated towns in the county - Guildford and Woking - don't have traditional independent record shops. Both towns would be high on my list of places to open one. Guildford boasts the specialist shop Dance 2. It is also the location of one of the best second-hand record shops in the UK: Ben's Collectors Records, 5 Tunsgate GU1 3QT, although as Ben's only does second-hand, I believe Guildford would be the perfect location for a Record Café selling new vinyl.

101 Collectors Records *The shop that was nearly called ARSE Records*
101 West Street, Farnham, Surrey GU9 7EN
01252 734409
101collectorsrecords.co.uk; andyhib101@hotmail.com; @101andyhibberd
Monday-Saturday 10am-5.30pm
Established 2002
Stock: Vinyl, CD, Pre-owned

101 Records is a gem. The owner, Andy Hibberd, previously worked for a jewellery business which took him on regular sales visits to Tokyo, where he would tour the shops in his spare time, When in the Far East he would purchase Japanese vinyl records. He picked up many pieces of rare collectable stock which came in handy years later when he took over 101 Collectors Records. The Japanese are meticulous, and albums produced there were always pressed on virgin vinyl, unlike the rest of the world where recycled plastic was often used, resulting in a slightly inferior sound.

Back in Guildford, Andy would spend his lunch hours in a second-hand record shop called Ben's Collectors Records. The shop still trades today and is one of the UK's finest second-hand record shops. Ben had another shop in Farnham, which he sold to Andy, who felt it would be best to change the name from Ben's. He ruled out the obvious name of Andy's because, even though the big record shop chain of the same name had just closed down, he suspected it could still create problems.

He toyed with the idea of calling the shop Andy's Record Selling Emporium - or ARSE for short. He imagined it would be a lot of fun asking people to make out cheques to ARSE and coming up with a suitable logo to match. He quickly came to his senses and settled with ended 101 Collectors Records – after the shop's address in West Street - an astute choice, since most companies list businesses in numerical order then alphabetical. Andy found his shop at the top of everybody's list to contact. Record companies would ring him up with offers before phoning other shops. It is good business sense not to call your company something beginning with Z.

Andy remembers closing the doors at 6pm at the end of his first day, as a relief in more ways than one. The shop had been so busy that he hadn't been able to leave the counter for a moment all day. He found that his training in jewellery retail adapted well to working in a record shop. It had always been drummed into him that if you treat the customer well, they will return. Andy now has hundreds of loyal customers, many of whom he regards as friends.

Although Andy had a good knowledge of music, he tended to err on the side of caution when pricing stock he had bought. One enthusiastic customer would always want to look through all the new stock that Andy had purchased. It took Andy six months to realise that this "great customer" was a rival dealer who was taking advantage of his low prices.

Andy prides himself on giving everybody a fair price and always does business with a smile. Sometimes his honesty has backfired on him, though. A man called by, explaining that he was clearing a house out and was on his way to the tip with a van full of rubbish, among which was three boxes of old records. He had seen the shop and called in to see if Andy would give him any money for them. It was clear that the man knew nothing about music but, recognising that he had some very collectable titles and wanting to be fair with him, Andy offered £300. The man was gobsmacked but, seconds later, so was Andy, when the man told him that as they were worth so much, he'd better take them around the other record shops to get a second valuation. It took all of Andy's charm to persuade him that his offer would be the best and to sell him a collection that 20 minutes earlier, was on its way to the tip.

The type of customer Andy finds frustrating is the person who imagines he is in possession of a much sought-after collectable or who comes in with a tatty copy of *Sgt. Pepper* with a torn cover expecting him to pay a fortune for it. He gives the example of the man who came in with a Japanese picture disc by Culture Club, for which he had paid £20 back in 1984. Expecting Andy to offer a fortune, he was gutted when Andy offered him a couple of pounds explaining that there isn't much demand for records by Culture Club these days. All record shops will be able to relate to that.

Dance 2 Records
107, Woodbridge Road, Guildford, Surrey GU1 4PY
01483 451002
dance2.co.uk; ln2dance@hotmail.com
Monday-Saturday 10am-6pm
Stock: Vinyl, Sound & Light Hire

Dance 2 Records is a dance music specialist who stock an amazing amount of DJ gear and turntables. They will transfer your vinyl on to CD. They take part in Record Store Day.

Record Corner   *No power, no lighting, no problem. We gave the customers torches*
Pound Lane, Godalming, Surrey GU7 1BX
01483 425739
recordcorner.co.uk: herald@therecordcorner.co.uk: @RecordCorner
Monday-Friday 9.15am-5pm Saturday 9am-5.30pm
Established 1958
Stock: Vinyl, CD, Classical, Sheet Music, Tickets

Record Corner was founded by the husband and wife team of Tom and Sue Briggs and is managed by Danny Cornell. The shop is tucked away down a cul-de-sac off the high street. With no passing trade, it relies on a small portable sign placed on the high street to direct people towards them. It is to the shop's credit that it is still trading after 60 years.

The store is divided into a jazz/classical room which is a haven of tranquility, and an altogether noisier rock room.

The Christmas of 2013 could have been a disaster, due to the storms which meant the shop had no power for a while. It was noticeable that, on that Christmas Eve in Godalming, the only shops to continue trading were the independents. The resourceful staff at Record Corner provided a batch of torches, so customers could still purchase stock in the dark. They even brought their original, manual cash till, from 1958, out of the shed and put it to use. Each time it opened, a little bell would ring providing much amusement among the customers.

The shop has an extremely good selection of classical music and a thriving mail order division.

The Rock Box

151 London Rd, Camberley, Surrey GU15 3JY
01276 26628
mailorder@rockbox.co.uk; rockbox.co.uk
Monday-Saturday 10am-5.30pm
Established 1987
Stock: Vinyl, CD, Pre-owned, T-shirts

If you mention the town "Camberley", people in the music industry expect the next three words to be "The Rock Box". Owner Ken Dudley was an avid music collector whose break into the music industry came when a promoter at the local Farnborough Technical College asked him to undertake some fly-posting. Ken travelled all over the country a few weeks in advance of a band touring, putting up posters on walls and windows of any closed-down shops. It was an exciting job – illegal in fact, which meant that Ken had to spend a fair amount of time and energy dodging the police. He would dress as a painter to give the impression he was on his way to work and put up his posters in the early hours of the morning. Although the police pulled him in many times, he was only arrested twice and fined £20 for his first offence rising to £100 for the second.

Ken loved the work which brought him closer to the bands he loved. His favourites over the years included Iron Maiden, Hawkwind and the Groundhogs - the British blues band led by Tony McPhee, which he saw more than 30 times. One band which caused him an uncomfortable morning was the Sex Pistols. The band had appeared on TV the previous evening, being interviewed by Bill Grundy. The interview was the talk of the nation as Grundy had baited the band to swear and be as obnoxious as possible. Ken knew nothing of this as he had been at a gig the night before and was taken aback by all the abuse he was receiving from members of the public as he was putting up Pistols posters. How he now wishes he had kept some of those posters from that tour. It also pains him to think that he did not keep back any posters from the Led Zeppelin tours that he put up. Ken has stopped looking at eBay to see their worth today, as it upsets him so much.

In 1980, after purchasing a job lot of second-hand books, Ken took out a small unit in Aldershot market. After displaying the books, the unit still looked a bit threadbare, so Ken put out a few boxes of his own records. The records proved far more popular than the books and so he concentrated on selling vinyl. He opened his stall three days a week, combining it with the fly-posting work, eventually moving to Camberley - where the shop has since been based – to concentrate on selling music full-time,

Ken has a chuckle when telling me about the weekly visits he used to receive from what he christened The Biggest Waste of Time Buying Team. These were a group of four young women employed by a record promotion company to go into record shops and buy records that the sales rep had left free of charge, to hype them up the chart – a common practice for decades in the music industry. At the same time every week, the women would come in, each buying the same records. Ken was meant to enter the catalogue numbers of the records purchased into the Gallup machine on his counter which report the data back to Gallup to be used in the compiling of the charts in the pre-digital age. Ken was happy to take the free records, but never entered a single number in his machine. He laughs about the thousands of records he was given, and how he misses those weekly visits by the time-wasting team.

In 2016 Ken decided to close the shop. He was so overwhelmed by the reaction of his customers, who were dismayed by the idea, that he decided to keep the shop going until he could find a buyer. In 2018, Mark Nightingale, a man who never forgot the days when he worked at Our Price Oxford, bought the business. He is delighted to be back in the world of record retailing.

Sussex

The city of Brighton once rivalled Manchester and London as the best place to spend a day vinyl shopping. In recent years it has fallen behind and has seen the closure of two big independents in the shape of Borderline Records and Rounder Records. In 2017, HMV in Churchill Square closed following a proposed rent rise. Brighton is still home to Resident Music, one of the best UK independent record shops, and the seaside town has a thriving collection of second-hand record shops

Bella Union Vinyl Shop & Coffee

13, Ship Street Gardens, Brighton, East Sussex BN1 1JA
012732 45287
bellaunionvinylrecordstore@gmail.com;@bellaunion
Wednesday-Sunday 12-6pm
Established 2016
Stock: Vinyl, CD, Art, Cassettes

Hidden away in The Lanes, Bella Union is not the easiest shop to find in Brighton. You approach it via a narrow alley and my initial impression was that surely there is not a record shop here. I was pleased to be proved wrong.

Inside it is a feast for your eyes with so many interesting and quirky things to see you are not sure where to focus. The counter is completely circular. Co-owner Abbey Raymonde explained to me that when she first bought records while living in New York she found some of the staff intimidating. Abbey wanted people to come in to Bella Union and feel welcome. The circular counter ensures that Abbey never has her back to the customer. The shop has a cozy atmosphere where there is no pressure to buy. Abbey serves free coffee to customers and you can sit and admire the art while listening to the latest releases from the shop's own Bella Union label.

The shop has a sky-blue neon Bella Union sign, the biggest David Bowie poster you will ever see and a section where you can purchase test pressings of Bella Union artists (how cool is that?). These are discs produced to check the quality of manufacture and often have plain white labels on them. They can become highly collectable.

With virtually no passing trade the shop relies on its reputation as one of the UK's best independent record labels, promoting via social media plus word of mouth to attract customers. The label is home to artists such as John Grant, Father John Misty, Beach House, Jonathan Wilson, Ezra Furman and many others. It is the place to go in Brighton if you are a fan of any of the artists on the label as often they have exclusives and signed copies.

The Bella Union label was founded by Simon Raymonde, who worked at Beggars Banquet record shop before going on to become a member of the Cocteau Twins, one of the most successful independent UK bands of the 1980s and 1990s. Following the band's split in 1997, Simon formed the label, initially releasing Cocteau Twins product and his own solo work. He soon started signing artists and produced many of the early releases himself. Independent record shops can be grateful to Simon for his contribution to their business. The Cocteau Twins were the sort of band you bought in an independent record shop as opposed to Woolworths or the supermarkets. It is a similar case with the Bella Union label. The artists it represents are huge sellers in independent record shops, with many citing Bella Union as their best-selling label.

Simon and Abbey met at a music conference in Montreal and their first date was record shopping. If there is a better way to spend a first date I am unaware of it. Soon the couple were discussing opening their own shop and it was not long before Abbey relocated to the UK, settled in Brighton and started to look for a location. While out walking in the town she came across the building the shop is now housed in and the couple quickly did a deal. What the duo did not know was the history of the building. It had previously been a jewellery business but before that was home to Impure Art, who claimed to be the UK's best erotic art gallery. Abbey's mum certainly got a shock when she googled the address of her daughter's new business.

The shop offers some excellent incentives. If you sign up for their loyalty card, after you have purchased six records the seventh is free. They also offer a 15% discount to students. Bella Union is the only shop which takes part in Record Store Day, but does not purchase any stock. Abbey points out that the record shops of Brighton support their label throughout the year, so they have no wish to take any sales away from them – a magnanimous gesture. It is still worth popping in on the day, as surprise events are hosted there.

Bella Union records always boast very high-quality artwork and packaging.

"Quality packaging is something that is being appreciated by the vinyl fans and collectors," Simon says. "Because the costs of making vinyl are still prohibitively high, the runs are generally quite small and therefore even more collectible. The irony is that it isn't really the desire of the labels to make collectible vinyl, per se, it is the restrictions of the marketplace that dictates that.

"Coloured vinyl is now the norm, but I am sure that fad will pass. Certainly, the more extravagant your colouring, and the blend of those colours, the more you run the risk of the audio being slightly inferior. A year or so ago, people were telling us that often they don't open the vinyl they just like to keep it perfect and pristine. They listen to the music on Spotify but like to own the vinyl, unopened.

"I think we've moved into a different phase now where those who have either just got into vinyl in last few years, or returned to it are upgrading their hi-fis again, and the knock-on effect is that vinyl is being opened and listened to but the packaging, sleeve art, liner notes, etc. are being enjoyed in as deep a way as was happening in the 1970s."

Are their any particular headaches involved in running both a label and a record shop?

"None," Simon declares. "It is for me the dream combo."

Simon's dad, Ivor was a musician, producer and arranger who co-wrote the Dusty Springfield hit "I Only Want to be With You", later to be a hit for the Bay City Rollers, the Tourists, and Samantha Fox. With Abbey Raymonde running the record shop and Simon the label, the family name continues to bring music worthy of attention to the world.

Top tip – In the right-hand corner of the shop is a wall-mounted 1980s phone booth. Pop your head inside. There is an iPod with a set of headphones where you can listen to many of the label's artists.

Fine Records

2 George Street, Hove, East Sussex BN3 3YB

01273 723345

finerecords.co.uk; mail@finerecords.co.uk

Monday-Saturday 10am-5pm

Established 1973

Stock: Vinyl, CD ,Pre-owned, Cassette

No vinyl-buying trip to Brighton & Hove would be complete without a visit to Fine Records to witness owner Julian Pelling in action. At the age of 74, he has lost none of his passion and enthusiasm for music, and is one of the most charismatic people I have met. His use of the English language is a joy even if, at times, he can make the Queen sound common.

Sitting proudly behind the counter of the shop is an award for being runner-up in the 1999 Hove Business Personality of the Year. I think Julian was robbed, as it is hard to imagine anybody with more personality than him. I would like to meet the personality who won.

Fine Records is an old, traditional record shop, and in the decades I have been popping in it has hardly changed a bit. This is not the place to visit if you are after the latest Metallica or dance release. But if you are looking for classical or jazz music on vinyl, Fine Records is just fine.

Music's Not Dead

71 Devonshire Road, Bexhill-on-Sea, East Sussex TN40 1BD

01424 552435

musicsnotdead.com; richard.wortley@live.co.uk; @MusicsNotDead1

Monday-Saturday 9.30am-5.30pm

Sunday 12-4pm

Established 2011

Stock: Vinyl, CD, Pre-owned, Books, In-stores, T-Shirts

Music's Not Dead is not just a record shop. It is a mission statement that the owners Rich Wortley and Del Querns live by. The duo were longtime employees of Powerplay, a chain of record shops on the south coast. The owners had decided to close the business down, telling the boys that record retailing was dead. They were not convinced and decided to start their own shop, choosing the name as an act of defiance. When both their wives announced that they thought it was a terrible name, they knew they had to go for it.

People told them it was crazy to open a shop in Bexhill. There is a saying about the town: "People retire to Bexhill to live out their last days, and then forget what they went there for." Accordingly, it is home to the highest percentage of people over the age of 100 anywhere in the UK. The biggest danger when walking from the station to the record shop is that of being run over by one of the numerous mobility scooters driving around the town.

Del and Richard believed that they could offer something for the young people of the town. Although the shop is small, it is beautiful and offers chairs, magazines and freshly brewed coffee.

The shop puts on gigs and the walls are decorated with posters of artists they have promoted. One poster they were not thrilled about was put up by a man who asked Del if he had any Blutack. "Sorry we don't", Del replied, "but next door sell it". "It's OK" said the man, "I will cope". It was only a few weeks after the event had taken place that Del discovered the World's Meanest Poster Man had stuck the poster up using chewing gum.

The greatest coup for Music's Not Dead was getting local lads and record shop supporters Keane to play in the shop, an event which prompted one fan to fly in from Canada specifically to see the band.

Pebble Records   *The classiest looking UK record shop. It has chandeliers*
14, Gildridge Road, Eastbourne, East Sussex BN21 4RL
0132 343 0304
pebblerecords.co.uk; pebblerecords@btconnect.com
Monday-Saturday 10am-6pm
Sunday 11am-4pm
Stock: Vinyl, CD, Pre-owned, Record Players, Tickets
Established 2013

Be amazed as you go down the steps and enter this shop. The sight that catches your eye is a pair of a beautiful crystal chandeliers. The shop is clean, neat and airy, with both vinyl and record players well displayed. Owner Michael Kearton started out selling vinyl online and the shop still does well with its internet trade. It felt a natural progression to open a bricks and mortar store. "I will be looking to buy lots of vinyl for the shop next week, as the money from my divorce has come through," Michael told me.

Rarekind Records
104 Trafalgar Street, Brighton, East Sussex BN1 4ER
01273 818170
rarekindrecords.co.uk; music@rarekindrecords.co.uk; @RarekindRecords
Monday-Saturday 11am-6pm
Sunday 12-5pm
Established 2003
Stock: Vinyl, Pre-owned, T-shirts

Rarekind Records is easy to find thanks to the fabulous mural painted on the wall above the entrance. Originally opened as a graffiti gallery by David Samuel with the help of a grant from the Prince's Trust, it sold paint, customised clothing and a few records. The shop featured in an episode of the TV programme *Faking It*, where David's task was to turn a fine art student into a graffiti artist, something he succeeded in doing with aplomb.

Current owner Ewan Hood was a local hip-hop promoter and regular customer. He offered to help develop the vinyl section, and thanks to his knowledge it soon became a focal point of the shop. When the building next door became vacant the landlord offered Ewan a very favourable rent to enable him to expand the record side of the shop. David picked up some school tables at the local wood recyclers for £2 each which gave the building a very minimalistic look: bricks, tables and records.

In 2006 Rarekind Records moved to its current location in Trafalgar Street. David swopped records for the skilled labour of his carpenter and plumber friends to help renovate the dilapidated building.

A couple of years later David called time on the graffiti gallery and moved to London, leaving Ewan to take over the whole building. No longer just a hip-hop specialist, Ewan has expanded into other genres in recent years. He gives credit to Record Store Day for bringing people into the shop who may not have checked out Rarekind otherwise.

Rarekind has an extensive range of hip hop, funk, soul, jazz, afro and reggae and lots of 7-inch vinyl. The prices for second-hand items are extremely reasonable. If you are in Brighton, the shop is worth a visit just to admire the mural.

Resident Music

27-28 Kensington Gardens, Brighton, East Sussex BN1 4AL
012736 06312
resident-music.com; info@resident-music.com; @residentmusic
Monday-Saturday: 9am-6.30pm Sunday 10am-6pm
Established 2004
Stock: Vinyl, CD, Tickets, In-stores

Owned by Derry Watkins and Natasha Youngs, Resident Music is one of the world's best record shops. It was winner of England's Favourite Independent Record Shop in a poll organised for Record Store Day. It's a far cry from the day before they opened, when Natasha, perched halfway up a ladder painting the shop, heard a man shouting at her "This is the last thing Brighton needs, another record shop. I guarantee you will be closed in six months."

Derry, who was born in Horsham, West Sussex, has spent his life working in music And up until the birth of his son, he was also an avid gig goer, seeing up to four bands a week. The first gig he attended was Motorhead, who made a huge impression on him – and his ears, which were ringing for days. The gigs he attended afterwards all seemed incredibly quiet. He has never forgotten the UK Subs gig he attended as a teenager in Crawley. In those days, it was not unusual for fights to break out at venues, but this gig was different. After a fracas started, the band jumped into the crowd to join in. The fight turned into a mass brawl and as he looked around, Derry seemed to be the only person in the room not fighting.

Derry only ever wanted to work in a record shop, and his first job was at Our Price in London's Tottenham Court Road. The Our Price chain was later bought out by WH Smith, so Derry took the opportunity to move to the Virgin Megastore. The laid-back atmosphere at Virgin was a bit of a shock compared to the corporate Our Price. His job title was Roots Buyer and his training consisted of the manager showing him the Roots section and saying "Here you go, fill it up." Derry made an instant impression, increasing sales rapidly as he brought in the professional stock control methods he had used at Our Price. His efforts did not go unnoticed, and he was soon promoted to work in the Virgin Head Office as a Chart Manager, responsible for key releases. It was through his work here that he rubbed shoulders with the aristocracy of rock, leaving him with lots of great memories, including talking to Robert Plant about football for hours in a hotel bar in Istanbul (they had a common bond as they both supported underachieving teams, Wolves for Robert and Leyton Orient for Derry). Earlier in the day he had witnessed Jimmy Page bartering over the price of a fake Rolex on the street outside (apparently it was a great bargain, although I am sure Jimmy had enough loose change to buy an original).

The most memorable in-store event at Virgin was Oasis playing a midnight gig to launch their second album *(What's the Story) Morning Glory*, at which Noel goaded Liam into walking out so that he (Noel) could play the solo show he had wanted to do in the first place. Although he enjoyed working for Virgin, Derry felt they were losing direction. He found it frustrating that music no longer seemed important to the company, which was concentrating its efforts on other aspects of the business such as airlines and phones. Following a restructuring of the company, Derry worked on the V-phone project which turned Virgin record shops into mobile phone stores. While working on this project he met Natasha, who had worked her way up the company. The duo shared a vision of opening their own, great record shop as opposed to changing other people's into phone shops. Soon they were an item and Derry moved to Brighton to live with her.

Accepting the offer of voluntary redundancies from Virgin, Derry and Natasha took off to tour the world for six months. Evenings were spent in exotic locations sharing bottles of wine as they planned to open their record shop.

Resident Music opened in 2004. Initially the shop only sold CDs but they quickly responded to customer requests for releases on vinyl, putting in a vinyl rack which now accounts for a major percentage of the shop's turnover. There is a low counter, so the staff don't appear intimidating. This is a great feature. So many record shops of the past had high counters that separated the staff from the customers. I recall shops that looked like a coconut shy where you could only see the heads of the staff above the counter, which certainly created a barrier.

Resident have incorporated many appealing design elements. The shop is neat, clean and browser friendly. The racks are full but not overcrowded, with reviews added to the covers of all new releases. The shop has also worked hard to capture the attention of the student population. Each year they give away fresher's packs consisting of posters, samplers, badges and a welcome letter providing useful information about the city. Resident embraces social networking and makes regular use of Twitter, Instagram and Facebook, including a daily Album of the Day feature. The shop sells tickets for more than 250 local events, a great way of getting people into the store. Resident also has a weekly mailout to more than 15,000 customers. The Resident team are happy to offer musical guidance to anybody looking to discover new music. They even guarantee cheery smiles.

The XX, Laura Marling and Mumford & Sons have all played in-stores at Resident Music to help promote their debut albums. The most memorable day was when Jarvis Cocker, a champion of independent record shops, worked behind the counter at the time his *Further Complications* album was released. He was supposed to stay for an hour but had such a great time that he stayed for more than four hours, serving and chatting to more than 200 customers.

I have a lot of admiration for what Derry, Natasha and the team at Resident Music have achieved. They opened the shop at a time when more than 100 independent record shops a year where closing. The golden days of music retailing were over, the free stock had stopped arriving and record companies had switched their promotional support to supermarkets and online retailers. People thought they were mad to open a new shop at such a time. But Derry and Natasha have proved that if your model is correct, if you are prepared to work hard, if you are innovative, if you support local music and the community and if you offer great customer service, then you can succeed.

Resident Music's achievements have been recognised by the music industry. The shop has won the title Best Independent Record Shop in the UK three times (2011, 2014 and 2015). It was also voted Best Indie Shop In The Country both times that Record Store Day organisers ran a public poll. In the lead-up to RSD in 2016, BBC 6 Music's Lauren Laverne broadcast live from the shop and included a DJ set by local musician and record shop supporter Norman Cook.

Derry and Natasha can be proud of their achievement, proving all the doubters wrong and thoroughly deserving the awards the shop has received.

The Record Album   *The oldest record shop owner in the UK*
8 Terminus Road, Brighton, East Sussex BN1 3PD.
01273 323853
george.therecordalbum@btinternet.com
Monday-Saturday 11.30am-4.30pm
Established 1948
Stock: Vinyl, Pre-owned

88-year-old George Ginn is a true record retailing legend. His shop offers as good a selection of second-hand TV soundtracks, film scores and musicals as you will find anywhere. George has always been vinyl mad and questions whether CD stands for "Clinically Dead", claiming that the best use for the silver discs is to scare birds away from your garden. The sign in the window sums the shop up well: The Record Shop for Connoisseurs. Make sure you bring plenty of cash, as George does not take credit cards. You must admire his spirit, as it was not so long back that he took out yet another five-year lease on the shop.

The Vinyl Frontier
35 Grove Road, Little Chelsea, Eastbourne, East Sussex BN21 4TT
01323 410313
shop@recordsuk.co.uk; @RecordsUK
Monday-Saturday 10am-5.30pm
Established 2012
Stock: Vinyl, Pre-owned, Cake, Coffee

Chris King is a former music journalist, DJ, band manager and promoter, who owns The Vinyl Frontier with fellow DJ and fellow former journalist Rhyddian Pugh. As you enter the shop, the smell of fresh coffee hits you. With its wooden floors and café at the rear of the store, the duo have created a pleasant, atmospheric meeting place for music fans of the town. The filing system is simple, with all the new vinyl in the right-hand racks and second-hand vinyl on the left. The shop has an incredible selection in the £1 vinyl section, and it is not unusual to see customers purchasing bundles from there. I asked how they keep the stock topped up. Chris took me down to the basement where he had thousands of albums waiting to go in the £1 section. The boys are happy to buy job lots and collections, no matter how large, to keep their regular customers for second-hand vinyl happy.

Chris and Rhyddian recall some of the craziest requests they have had.
Customer: "I am after a vinyl LP."
Staff: "Any genre?"
Customer: "It needs to be modern." Then, pointing to the wall. "I will take that."
Staff: "It is a T-shirt, sir."

Other classics include the elderly woman who came in for a DVD for her grandson, *Harry Potter and the Chamber of Commerce;* the man who informed the shop owners that they would do well, as he had heard that music is coming back; the man who asked if they sold YouTubes; and this memorable exchange:
Customer: "Do you buy records?"
Staff: "Yes, we do. What sort of era are we talking?"
Customer: "They're from the Chas & Dave era."

Union Music Store

1 Lansdown Place, Lewes, East Sussex BN7 2JT
0127 3474053
unionmusicstore.com; stevie@unionmusicstore.com
Monday-Saturday 9.30am-5.30pm
Established 2010
Stock: Vinyl, CDs, Pre-owned Merchandise, Musical Instruments, Tickets

Except for legendary broadcaster Bob Harris, I can think of no one who has done more to promote the genre of Americana in the UK than Stevie Freeman, co-owner of Union Music Store. She is 2018 chair of the Americana Music Association and was the force behind organising the official Americana chart. She arranges an annual conference and travels to Nashville each year to keep up with what is happening in the world of Americana.

Union Music Store has used a wooden floor and wooden racking to give it a western feel. The furniture was all hand-made by Stevie and her partner Jamie Freeman, who is a singer, songwriter and leader of the Jamie Freeman Agreement. It is the only record shop I know that stocks lozenges for singers with throat problems. As well as promoting gigs for bands touring the UK from the USA and Canada, the shop has its own Union Music Store record label. Police Dog Hogan has been the label's biggest success and while Jamie Freeman received critical acclaim for his album *Spiral Earth*.

The shop has a loyalty discount card which offers cheaper prices in the shop and a discount in the coffee shops across the road.

In June 2018 the couple sold the business to Del Day a well-known journalist and promotor and Danny Wilson lead singer with the excellent 'Danny and the Champions of the World'.

Top tip - If visiting the area, check out the Union Music Store website, as almost every Saturday at 3pm they have a performance in the shop. If planning to visit the record shops of Brighton on a Saturday, do it in the morning and then travel out to Lewes for the afternoon gig and to browse through this gem of a shop.

Viva-Vinyl *Please support this wonderful and worthy enterprise*
63, Queen Victoria Avenue, Hove, East Sussex BN3 6XA
07900 191324
andy@viva-vinyl.com; @vivavinyl
Monday-Saturday 10am-5pm
Established 2017
Stock: Vinyl, Pre-owned, Coffee, Food, Memorabilia (including art produced from vinyl records)

Brian and Julie Rosehill have opened a wonderful vinyl café in a residential area of Hove. It is the last place you would expect to discover somebody selling vinyl. The shop itself though is hard to miss. With a window full of vinyl curiosities, it stands out like a beacon.

The reason for the unusual location soon becomes clear. Co-owner Brian has Parkinson's disease and the shop is only 80 meters from his house, so his wife, Julie, is able to push him the short distance in his wheelchair.

Brian and Julie are a couple of amazing characters and you have to admire their entrepreneurial spirit and resilience. Life has not always been kind to them but what they have achieved is remarkable.

After his diagnosis 26 years ago, Brian was forced to give up his job in health care. The couple decided to set up their own business working from home selling gift vouchers, and within a few years The Voucher Shop was a staple name in the incentives industry. They sold the business a few years ago for a six-figure sum, and Brian has since been investing some of those profits into expanding his already enormous vinyl collection.

The couple started selling some of Brian's surplus vinyl at record fairs and dealing on eBay. By now Brian had too many records to accommodate in the house so he hired a lock-up. While chatting with a local estate agent, who told them that he had an empty shop to let for only £50-a-month more than cost of the lock up, the idea for Viva-Vinyl was born.

Brian and Julie decided to make the shop a meeting place for the community by creating a vinyl café. Julie has created a unique and quirky atmosphere by incorporating a range of vinyl related products including vinyl design cushions, bowls, magazine racks, cake stands and clocks.

You will find an extensive selection of Leonard Cohen vinyl as he is Brian and Julie's favourite artist. They are such fans that they once planned a holiday based on the hope of bumping into him.

Over 40 years ago they decided to holiday in the Greek islands with the idea of travelling over to Hydra where Leonard lived, in the hope of bumping into him. Hydra is a tiny island that does not even allow cars. Upon arrival, they headed to the nearest taverna where, to their amazement, they found Leonard sitting at a table feeding his baby beside him in a pram. Brian and Julie ordered some food and waited for an ideal time to introduce themselves.

Suddenly, Leonard started to leave, Brian and Julie quickly paid the bill and followed him out. They were too shy to go up and speak to him, so as Leonard pushed the pram through the winding streets of Hydra, Brian and Julie followed at a distance. Leonard became aware he was being followed, but each time he turned around to check, Brian and Julie would look away pretending they were not stalking him. Leonard upped the pace, clearly wanting to get away from this couple, and on this extremely hot day Julie and Brian were virtually jogging up the hill to keep Leonard in their sights. Leonard turned off the path into his house, leaving the duo frustrated they had not spoken to their idol, but pleased that they had at least seen him.

In 2013, Leonard was playing the Luca International Blues Festival in Italy and Brian and Julie had booked into a top hotel nearby. They were waiting to take the lift to their room and when the doors opened, Leonard Cohen was standing there. "It's you," exclaimed Julie. Leonard indeed confirmed it was him. After all these years "Hallelujah" – they could finally chat to him. Leonard could not have been nicer and was happy to pose for a photograph with the couple, which is now a treasured possession.

Viva-Vinyl is a lovely shop with a welcoming atmosphere. If in the Brighton and Hove area do make the effort to visit. A percentage of the shop's profit is donated to the Parkinson's Society to assist their work in finding a cure can be found for this awful disease.

In 2017, Brian took a nasty fall while delivering flyers to advertise the shop. He spent six months in hospital recovering. Afterwards, his surgeon admitted that he did not think Brian would pull through. By opening this shop, and surviving a life-threatening fall, Brian has proved that even Parkinson's can't defeat his spirit and determination to offer vinyl lovers a place to visit in Hove.

Wow And Flutter
Trinity Street, Hastings, East Sussex TN34 1HG
01424 439859
wowandflutterhastings@gmail.com; wowandflutterhastings.com
Established 2014
Opening hours Tuesday-Saturday 11am-5pm
Stock: Vinyl, Pre-owned, Books, Comics, Coffee, Food, In-stores, Tickets

Wow And Flutter, a well-designed shop with wooden floors and artistically decorated walls, is named after the shops owners Tim Scullian and Susan McNally's favourite song by Stereolab. Tim was a BBC producer with a stressful life in London before the couple moved to the calmer environment of Hastings. Their life-changing moment came about at a car boot sale where the couple had gone to sell some of their vast collection of vinyl records that they no longer played. They soon found out they were both natural salespeople, selling most of the vinyl while thoroughly enjoying chatting to like-minded vinyl fans.

They discussed the idea of opening a vinyl record shop. Tim remembered how intimidating some of the shops he used to visit could be and the couple resolved to open a friendly record shop where they would do all they could to create a happy vibe. To make the shop stand out they make regular trips to Japan to purchase vinyl, comics and anything they think will be of interest to customers.

With Susan's background in art, this is not just a record shop. You will discover no end of quirky things. It is the only record shop I have visited which sells sick bags. Airlines are missing out by supplying just boring plain sick bags. Here the sick bags are adorned with art from a local artist. The shop also sells sticker packs and no end of nostalgic merchandise that will bring back memories of years gone by.

Like all record shop owners, they are delighted by the interest shown in vinyl by the younger generation. Not all of the younger customers, though, are aware of just what a vinyl record is, as illustrated by the girl who came in and asked what the "small plastic things" are (7-inch singles). Many shop assistants have had similar experiences of young people finding novel ways of asking for records, including:

"What's the name of the black giant CDs?"

"Can you transfer those big black round things onto CD?"

"Do you stock those plastic things that sound like CDs?"

Tim and Susan have achieved what every new record shop should aim for: a shop with a warm and welcoming atmosphere, which has become a hub for the local music and art community.

Vinyl Revolution

33 Duke Street, Brighton, East Sussex BN1 1AG
03333 230736
simon@vinyl-revolution.co.uk; www.vinyl-revolution.co.uk; @vinylrev
Monday-Saturday 10am-6pm Sunday 11am-5pm
Established 2016
Stock: Vinyl, Second-hand Record Players, Art, Clothing, Posters, Home Stuff, In-stores

"We want to save the world from a soul-less shopping experience. Records do not belong in supermarkets." **Simon Parker, Vinyl Revolution**

Imagine if Salvador Dali, Andy Warhol, Tracey Emin and Jamie Reid decided to open a record shop. They would end up with something akin to Vinyl Revolution. With its dayglow yellow and pink design this is a shop you need to be wearing shades to enter. Is the garish colour scheme a touch of genius or utterly bonkers? I guess it is a bit of both. It has adopted *The Simpsons* method of design. The reason the cartoon characters in the TV series were bright yellow was to catch the attention of channel surfers. It is the same with Vinyl Revolution. Before going in, watch the people around you for a couple of minutes and marvel at how many of them look at the shop. The shop has become a focal point of conversation among the vinyl fans of Brighton.

Before setting foot in the shop, check out the window which is full of quirky merchandise. You will also find four brightly-coloured mannequins which draw attention from passing shoppers. On the day I called in they were modelling bikinis made from 7-inch singles.

The previous day the mannequins had been laid out in glorious sunshine on music-designed beach towels on the pavement outside. It made a very funny sight until the shop was asked to remove them in case somebody tripped over them. It is hard to believe that anyone would fail to notice dayglow mannequins lying on equally bright beach towels, but Brighton is a very "health and safety" type of place.

One thing that stands out as you enter the shop is the header boards that separate the different genres and artists of vinyl. They are a luminous yellow giving an eerie glow to the racks. I have never seen anything like them.

Co-owner Simon Parker has been around the music scene for a while. He narrowly avoided success in the 1990s with the indie bands Colourburst and Fruit Machine, and his book *Road to Nowhere* provided a witty account of the trials and tribulations of a musician who nearly hit the big-time.

Simon established himself as one of Brighton's leading promoters, introducing bands such as Kasabian, Keane and Bat For Lashes to the local scene. He lectured at Brighton's Institute of Modern Music (BIMM). He had his own radio show on Radio Reverb and continues to make music with his current bands Villareal and Lightning Dept alongside his work as a DJ. I struggle to understand how he finds the time to run a record shop.

In 2015, Simon moved to Oxford to help Truck Records set up a new vinyl division, live music venue and coffee shop at their store in Witney. His time spent there reignited his desire to start his own record shop. In October 2016 he and his partner and co-founder Rachel Lowe launched Vinyl Revolution as a pop-up shop in Tunbridge Wells. After a successful three months there, Vinyl Revolution moved into its first permanent shop in Brighton in July 2017.

Simon and Rachel had been closely watching the resurgence in the vinyl format and had realised that was moving back into the mainstream. Schoolchildren were buying singles with their pocket money, teenagers were shunning Spotify to gather with friends around their newly-bought turntables, and parents and grandparents were rescuing their record players from lofts and rediscovering the joy of vinyl while sharing it with their children and grandchildren. This was creating a new type of buyer, who was not only embracing vinyl records but also rock and pop culture in all its forms. The young buyers in particular were relishing ownership of something tangible, whether that be a new album in coloured vinyl with a beautiful gatefold sleeve or a Rolling Stones poster.

Out of this realisation Vinyl Revolution was born. A shop created for vinyl collectors old and new, those with music knowledge and those without. Those seeking rare, new wave, 7-inch singles and those lusting after the latest album by Taylor Swift.

It also caters for those wanting to celebrate rock and pop culture without a record player. Vinyl Revolution created its own range of art prints, clothing and goods for the home featuring quotes from music icons. There are eco-friendly T-shirts, babygros, mugs, and, being based at the seaside, even a range of beach towels.

My favourite is the Boy George teapot emblazoned with the quote "Sex? I would rather have a cup of tea".

The amount of Vinyl Revolution-designed, music-related merchandise is impressive and includes:

Art prints, both framed and unframed, with quotes from music icons

Clothing, which is both carbon neutral, organic and ethically produced including hoodies, t-shirts and babygros

Mugs, beer glasses, aprons, tea towels, teapots, beach towels, slip mats along with recycled records turned into coasters, wine racks and bowls.

You could easily spend a happy thirty minutes here reading the amusing quotes from rock stars that feature in their own-designed art prints that cover the walls of the shop. The basement is where they sell the new vinyl from and often you will find the stairs down a bit cramped as customers linger there reading the quotes on the pictures.

Look out for their friendly dog Treacle, who you will often notice lingering under the vinyl browsers.

Simon is also updating *Road to Nowhere*. His story of a life spent in pursuit of musical dreams is funny, heartfelt and full of lists of bands you had forgotten or never heard of in the first place. If you are a music fan you will laugh out loud. And the new edition will also recount the trials and tribulations of opening a record shop.

No doubt the shop will soon be selling it. Another reason to visit the wonderful and wacky world of Vinyl Revolution.

Teesside, Tyneside & Northumberland

Not much has changed in the North East over recent years with few new shops opening and not many older shops closing. The area is extremely strong for rock music. JG Windows is worth visiting as it is in the most beautiful location of any UK record shop. It is worth a trip to Stockton to visit the subject of the film Sound It Out. Not only are you likely to meet Tom Butchart the shop's owner but if you are lucky you might bump in to one of the customers who featured in this charming documentary. Incredibly for a university city, Durham does not have a shop which takes part in Record Store Day. For fans of 7-inch singles, RPM Discs at 7a The Shop, Front Street, Wingate, Durham, TS28 5AA keeps more than 40,000 in stock.

586 Records

Commercial Union House, 39 Pilgrim Street, Newcastle upon Tyne, NE1 6QE
0789 4071892
586records.com
Tuesday-Friday 10am-6pm
Saturday 10am-3.30pm
Established 2014
Stock: Vinyl, Pre-owned

586 Records is a vinyl-only store owned by Peterlee-born Antony Daly, a longtime promoter and DJ. Antony had always been an avid record collector and was not overly impressed with the record shops in Newcastle. He therefore decided to open his own.

It wasn't easy, but with his own collection supplemented by donations of vinyl from friends and family he managed to get the business up and running. He has received support from the Pinetree Trust that works to promote the disabled and disadvantaged in establishing small businesses. This worthy venture is well worth your support.

Beatdown

Unit 1, Clarendon House, Berwick Street, Newcastle upon Tyne NE1 5EE
01912 618894
info@beatdownrecords.co.uk; beatdownrecords.co.uk; @beatdownncl
Monday-Saturday 10am-5pm
Stock: Vinyl, CD, Pre-owned, T-Shirts

"Compact Discs are not compact enough for kids who just want to play things on their phone, and you can't display them on your wall." **Nick Wrightson, Beatdown**

Beatdown Records is a record shop and online store close to the Central station. It is owned by ex-HMV employee Nick Wrightson and ex-Steel Wheels employee Paul Donley. Steel Wheels was one of the best-known second-hand record shops in Newcastle. When it was put up for sale, Paul hooked up with Nick, bought the stock, and Beatdown was born.

Beyond Vinyl
88, Westgate Road, Newcastle upon Tyne NE1 4AF
07496 351309
beyondvinyl.co.uk; info@beyondvinyl.co.uk
Monday-Saturday 9am-6pm
Established 2018
Stock: Vinyl, CD, Pre-owned, Coffee, Cake, In-stores

Located near the O2 Academy, Dave McGovern describes his shop as a Record Café hangout. That sums this shop up well as it is the perfect place for music fans to meet and at the same time purchase music. If you are planning a tour of Newcastle record shops this is the perfect place to stop halfway through for refreshment. With low prices you are likely to find a bargain too.

Dave is well known to the music buyers of the North East having managed JG Windows record department for many years. It is rare that you won't find Dave without a smile on his face and is never happier than talking music. The odd occasions he is not smiling is usually down to men of a certain age coming up to the counter asking for a massage.

The shop was previously a Chinese massage parlour and Dave finds it incredible that men walk through the shop past all the vinyl on display to enquire about a massage.

Hot Rats Records
38 Stockton Road, Sunderland, Tyne and Wear SR1 3NR
01915 672099
marty.hotrat@ntlworld.com
Monday-Saturday 10am-5pm
Established 1993
Stock: Vinyl, CD, Pre-owned, Tickets

Hot Rats Records is owned by Marty Yule, a former drummer in punk rock band the Toy Dolls. This is not quite as impressive as it first sounds, as it seems like every musician in the north east has played in the band. Formed in 1979, and still going strong, the Dolls have gone through 14 drummers and 12 bass players. Although best known for the UK No.4 hit single "Nellie the Elephant", released in 1982, it would be unfair to class them as one-hit wonders. The band has released 15 albums with many songs becoming cult classics. The band has a witty sense of humour, expressed in songs such as "James Bond Lives Down our Street", "Yul Brynner was a Skinhead" and "Neville is a Nerd". If you are a fan of Half Man Half Biscuit, you will enjoy exploring the band's back catalogue. Marty was also drummer with Martin Stephenson and The Dainties for three years.

Marty named his shop after the Frank Zappa album, released in 1969, on which all but one of the tracks were instrumentals. He is delighted by how many young customers come into the shop to buy vinyl, but was surprised by how many were bringing records back, complaining that they sounded funny. He now finds it best to explain to them that singles play at 45rpm and LPs at 33rpm.

JG Windows
1 Central Arcade, Newcastle upon Tyne, NE1 5BP
0191 232 1356
jgwindows.com; info@jgwindows.com; @jgwindows
Monday-Friday 9am-9pm Saturday 9am-7pm Sunday 11am-5pm
Established 1908
Stock: Vinyl, CD, Musical Instruments, Turntables

JG Windows has been at the heart of the north east's music scene for a century and its flagship store in Newcastle is one of the UK's longest established music stores. Opened in 1908 by James Gale Windows, it is the most famous record shop in the north east. Located in the beautiful Central Arcade, it covers three floors, selling musical instruments, studio and DJ equipment, live sound PA systems and printed music, as well as CDs, DVDs and vinyl.

Many of the north east's most famous musicians shopped at JG Windows. Bryan Ferry bought his first records there. He was a regular in the shop's listening booths. As a teenager he had a Saturday job at Jackson the Tailor in Northumberland Street, and ended up spending a lot of his cash in JG Windows. The first record he bought was by the Charlie Parker Quintet, featuring Miles Davis. At that age, jazz was his big passion and certainly influenced his work, none more so when in 2012 he released *The Jazz Age*, an album of his classic recordings played as instrumentals in an early jazz style. Another local musician who frequented the store on a regular basis was AC/DC and Geordie frontman Brian Johnson. Dire Straits guitarist Mark Knopfler would also visit the store as a young lad. His dad bought him his first guitar from the shop, a twin pick-up Hofner Super Solid costing £50.

In 2006, the company was purchased from the Windows family by three current and former employees and long-time associates, and they have since driven the company forward, opening a second branch in the Metro Centre in 2009 and a third in Darlington in 2011. To prove that the vinyl revival is being embraced by people from all walks of life, none other than legendary Australian megastar Barry Humphries - aka Dame Edna Everage - has recently been in the store to buy a record player. You could hardly describe Barry as a regular, but the staff had fond memories of his last visit, 20 years previously. He arrived dressed in full Dame Edna regalia, stayed for more than half an hour entertaining the customers and departed after purchasing a large collection of classical CDs.

The staff have been amazed by the vinyl resurgence, although they smile when customers that binned their vinyl 20 years ago come back in and buy the very same records they bought when they were kids. Many say the same thing: "If I had kept my original copy of this it would be worth thousands."

Pop Recs Ltd

27 Stockton Road, Sunderland, Tyne and Wear SR2 7AQ
01915 652150
poprecsltd@gmail.com; @poprecsltd
Established 2014

Pop Recs Ltd is a record shop, a coffee shop, an art space and live music venue run by the band Frankie & the Heartstrings. If you want to browse vinyl record collections, admire paintings, drawings and sculptures by local artists while enjoying a coffee then this is the place to visit. It also hosts regular live music gigs which have included shows by Badly Drawn Boy, Maximo Park, Edwyn Collins and James Bay. Mainly second-hand vinyl but they take part in Record Store Day.

RPM Music

4 Old George Yard, Newcastle upon Tyne, NE1 1EZ
01912 210201
contactrpm@gmail.com; @RPMmusic
Monday-Friday 10.30am-5.30pm
Saturday 9.30am-5.30pm
Established 1988
Stock: Vinyl, CD, Pre-owned, Vintage audio equipment

RPM Music has changed focus over the years and is now one of the best places in the UK to buy a vintage record player. They have a good selection of second-hand vinyl and owner Marek Norvid and ever friendly manager Richie Lattimore are always good people to chat with about music. Look up when you enter, as the shop is festooned with washing lines with dozens of 7-inch singles threaded through them.

Reflex

23, Nunn Street, Newcastle upon Tyne
01912 603246
reflexrecordshop.com; info@reflexcd.co.uk; @REFLEX-CD-VINYL
Monday 8:30am-6pm
Tuesday-Wednesday 9am-6pm
Thursday 9am-7pm
Friday-Saturday 9am-5:30pm
Sunday 11am-5pm
Stock: Vinyl, Pre-owned, CD

With its distinctive turquoise front, Reflex has a reputation for some of the lowest prices for CDs and vinyl in the country. The shop works on the principle of high volume and low margin, constantly striving to offer the best value. Owner Alan Jordan has been working in the record shops of the north east for 30 years and has had a colourful career. After abandoning his university course to become a DJ, he has been behind the counter at music retailers such as Volume, Virgin and Our Price, using the experience he gained there to help him start Reflex.

The concept of an independent record shop can sometimes be a stereotyped image of a lazy old place where people work just to hang out and listen to music, but the truth at Reflex is very different. Alan has never stood still, committing firmly to the high street, while embracing every possible avenue for the continuing profitability of his business. He was one of the first UK sellers on Amazon marketplace and still today they have a thriving online presence.

The shop has increased the space it gives to vinyl from two metres in 2009 to six metres now. Yet Alan is keen to emphasize that in his view, the CD is far from dead. It is still the biggest-selling format sold at Reflex. Alan has been elected to the Board of Directors at the Entertainment Retail Association, at which he is also Chairman of Operations.

Sound It Out *The subject of an award-winning documentary*
15a Yarm Street, Stockton-on-Tees, County Durham TS18 3DR
01642 860068
info@sounditoutrecords.co.uk; sounditout@yahoo.com; @-sounditout
Monday-Friday 10am-5pm
Saturday 9am-5:30pm
Established 1996
Stock: Vinyl, CD, Pre-owned, Books, Cassettes

Sound It Out was the subject of a hit worldwide documentary *Sound it out* in 2011 (see feature in Chapter 4, record shop movies). Since then Tom Butchart's shop has gone from strength to strength and now employs seven staff, with a dedicated online and finance department run by Kelly Laybourne and Chris Smith respectively, aided by Graham Seaman and newest recruit Dan Briggs. At the front of house, the shop has Tom along with Stuart Willoughby, who has worked there for seven years and recently wrote a book about his musical hero, Prince. The youngest member of the shop team is Natalie Chapman. Each member of staff brings a unique strength to the business, and as a unit they are a formidable team. Year-on-year profits are up and Sound It Out wins new customers every day.

The shop has free in-store gigs on Saturday afternoons. Recent acts to perform there include Public Service Broadcasting, Ethan Johns, TV Smith, Charlie Simpson from Busted (who pulled the largest crowd ever seen in the shop), Maximo, Claire Hamill and Cattle & Cane. Tom was surprised and honoured when 150 copies of Goat's *World Music* album were specially pressed on never-to-be-repeated coloured vinyl by the band's label, in recognition of Sound It Out selling more copies of the album than any other shop in the country.

From time to time rarities have turned up in the shop, including letters handwritten by U2 guitarist The Edge in 1980; the world's rarest Status Quo single, worth £5,000; and a signed Beatles album that eventually made £22,000.

The *Sound it out* documentary film features lots of the shop's charismatic regulars. Not featured was Graeme, who comes in once a week and only buys records by Stock Aitken and Waterman artists, along with Simple Minds and Hugh Cornwell. He asks Tom to order stuff online for him as he doesn't trust the internet and thinks the government is spying on him. He always takes 10 minutes to say goodbye and writes letters to Hollywood film studios with suggestions for new *Star Trek* and *Terminator* films. None of his suggestions have yet been taken up. Another customer who calls himself Paul McCartwheel, believes he is the son of Paul McCartney and spends his time re-arranging all the Beatles albums in the shop. He despises Sting, and hides singles by the Police in random locations throughout the shop. Then there's Dennis, aged 68, who collects Italian dance music and 1980s disco. He only buys CDs and often pays hundreds of pounds for one CD, which they order online for him on a weekly basis.

Located behind a pub and a job centre, Sound It Out is an oasis of culture in a desert of charity and pound shops. The shop doubled in size in 2013 and stocks around 70,000 records. Sales are currently at an all-time peak, which is good news as none of the staff want to go back to a proper job.

Vinyl Guru   *Fans of David Bowie should check out this shop*
69 Westgate Road, Newcastle upon Tyne, NE1 1SG
01912 420430
vinylguru.co.uk; info@vinylguru.co.uk; @VinylGuru
Monday-Friday 10.30am-5pm (and first Saturday of the month)
Stock: Vinyl, Pre-owned, Accessories, Books, Turntables

Situated in a Grade II listed building which forms part of the Newcastle Arts Centre complex, Vinyl Guru benefits from a host of supporting businesses on site including a live music venue with fully licensed bar, jazz cafe, art gallery and outdoor courtyard with seating area.

Vinyl Guru incorporates a large stock of new and second-hand vinyl, alongside new and vintage turntables, hi-fi and accessories. Also, on the premises is the Vinyl Gallery selling framed vinyl album cover art prints and vintage jukeboxes. And there is a specialist Bowie Shop, stocked with Bowie rarities and merchandise, including signed prints.

Wales

You can have an action-packed vinyl weekend in Wales as so many shops are situated within a few miles of the M4. Day One would be a chance to visit the long-established music retailers including Diverse in Newport, Spillers in Cardiff and Derricks in Swansea. Stay overnight in the charming seaside town of Tenby. Day Two: stay in Tenby and pop in to see the Welsh record retailing double act of Laurie and Richie at Dales. Drive on to Terminal Records in Haverfordwest and finish the day by calling in to Slipped Discs and Tangled Parrot both in Carmarthen. The Tangled Parrot is based within a venue so time your visit to coincide with a band playing or a comedy evening.

Opportunities for opening a new shop are limited though Bridgend along with the seaside towns of Barry and Llandudno are worth considering.

Alun Hughes Film, Music & Nostalgia

Unit 1, 7 Bank Street, Wrexham, LL11 1AH
01978 355577
poralun@aol.com
Monday, Friday, Saturday 9am-5pm
Tuesday-Thursday 10am-5pm
Established 2006
Stock: Vinyl, CD, Pre-owned, Cassettes, DVD, Memorabilia

Alun Hughes and his daughter Sarah have owned and run Alun Hughes Film, Music & Nostalgia since 2006. They have surfed the wave of vinyl resurgence, but also offer a fabulous range of products. Alun is proud to say that his shop is the least cutting-edge record shop in the universe. It is certainly one of the few which still sell spool tapes and cassettes. He is happy to stock everything.

Alun started his retailing career selling his own records at a stall in Mold market in Flintshire. He opened Rabbit Records in Mold in 1977 when his stock included 10,000 7-inch singles. The focus was the rock, indie and disco music of the day. He closed Rabbit in 2001 and a year later opened the iconic Phase One Records on King Street, Wrexham.

These were the days when record companies were generous with their promotional budgets and Phase One won the competition for the best window display in respect of the movie *Hi Fidelity*. The prize was a trip for two to Chicago, but three days before he was due to fly out, Alun watched in horror as the news reports showed two planes crashed into the World Trade Centre in New York on September 11, 2001. He never went to America and ended up receiving a weekend in York instead.

In 2005, like many hundreds of other record shops, Phase One closed but Alun soon bounced back and, following a couple of relocations, his Film, Music & Nostalgia shop continues to trade in a two-floor shop off the centre of Wrexham.

Andy's Records

16 Northgate Street, Aberystwyth, Ceredigion SY23 2JS
01970 624581
andys-records.com; shop@andys-records.co.uk; @RecordsAndys
Monday-Tuesday 12-6pm
Thursday-Saturday 12-6pm
Established 1985
Stock: Vinyl, CD

"Record Store Day is an incredible boost for me reaffirming to me that we do have a future in business and why I still bother, after 43 years, to ride the sonic waves as an Octave Doctor."
Andy Davis – Andy's

Not to be confused with the discontinued Andys chain, Andy's in Aberystwyth is the last Andy's standing. When customers ask the owner Andy Davis about any connection between him and Andy Gray (the owner of the now defunct Andys chain), Andy Davis tells them "He is richer than me, but I am better looking, and I still have a record shop." According to Andy, "The shop [in Aberystwyth] has stayed afloat thanks to loyal local support and healthy tourist trade. But without the cultural shift started by *Last Shop Standing*, Record Store Day and the collectors' website Discogs, the retail panorama in the UK might look significantly less healthy than it does today."

Andy Davis started his career in the Stirling branch of Scotland's Bruce's Records, in 1975. Having managed record departments for WH Smith's and Debenhams, in 1985 he began trading in his own right from the basement of a local music shop. Steadfastly declining to spend his time rooting through people's dusty, old, unwanted vinyl, he opted to work on the cutting edge of music and sell only new product. He realised that trading used items requires a different skill-set from interpreting current trends and staying abreast of the constant changes in dance, rock and indie which dominated the scene at that time. Today, playing to his strengths means curating a varied balance of the classic and the current, and being a little bit different and daring with the selection available.

Although Andy's is off the beaten track, if you are travelling to this part of Wales it is worth the effort to call in.

Cob Records

1-3 Britannia Terrace, Porthmadog, Gwynedd, LL49 9NA
01766 512170
cobrecords.com; cobrecords@cobrecords.com; @cobrecords
Monday-Saturday 9am-5pm
Established 1967
Stock: Vinyl, CD, Pre-owned

Located in an area of outstanding natural beauty, Cob Records began inauspiciously in 1967 when Brian Davies started selling ex juke box singles at 1/6d (7½p) to bring in extra income to what was then a thriving cafe. Brian was ahead of his time, as it is only in the last 10 years, that the idea of the Record Shop Café has taken off.

With no record shop in the area, it soon became apparent that there was a demand for new LPs and singles. Accounts were opened with the record companies and the basement of the cafe was fitted out as a record shop. Although LPs were only 32/6d (£1.62) in those days, they were still not affordable to many, so they offered a service of "any three of your old LPs for a new one of ours", and before long they had a large selection of used LPs along with the new stock. They still operate a similar service, but in today's more complex market they now offer a part-exchange price against the new items required.

Cob Records began to advertise internationally, offering new LPs at discount prices. This proved to be such a success that they closed the cafe and concentrated solely on the record business, moving up from the basement to acquire more space.

By 1971 business was booming. Cob Records were mailing, on average, about 7,000 LPs per week to some 25,000 customers in more than 50 countries worldwide and employing about 25 staff members. Shortage of space again became a problem, so they bought and fitted out a warehouse directly opposite and moved the mail-order operation in, separating it from the shop sales. The bulk of mail-order sales was, and still is, to private individuals – with some notable exceptions. They can remember sending three orders of cassettes, each worth £1,000, to a store in Port Stanley for the troops during the Falklands War.

The shop is located opposite the Ffestiniog station, on one of the most scenic railway routes in the UK, so if you are a train and a vinyl fan then you will be in paradise. As well as the railway, the Italian style village of Portmeirion built by Sir Clough William-Ellis, and used as the location for the cult TV programme *The Prisoner*, is close by. The shop is perfectly placed for anyone visiting this popular tourist attraction or attending the *Number 6* festival, which takes place each September.

Dales Music

High Street, Tenby, Pembrokeshire SA7 OHD
01384 842285
laurence.dale@tiscali.co.uk
Monday-Saturday 9am-5.30pm
Established 1947
Stock: Vinyl, CD, Pre-owned, Badges, Cassettes, DVDs, Merchandise, Videos

Dales Music has been trading for more than 70 years in the Welsh holiday resort of Tenby. The store started off as a piano retailer run by the current owner Laurie Dale's father. As a teenager, Laurie was always spending his pocket money on 78rpm records, so he persuaded his father to start stocking them in the shop to compliment the piano sales.

Laurie and the shop manager Richie Westmacott are colourful characters who are well-known to locals. Laurie is a singer and actor while Richie is guitarist in one of Wales's premier blues bands Elephant Gerald. The band has played with Dr Feelgood and Albert Lee among others. Richie always looks as if he is about to go on stage, as you never see him without his beloved bandana on his head.

Laurie and Richie are like a double act bouncing banter off each other and their sheer enthusiasm for music creates a happy atmosphere. In the summer months, Laurie can often be found sitting, shirtless, on a stool outside the store. He engages holidaymakers in conversation, encouraging them in to look through this treasure trove of a store. The decor is old-fashioned, and the racks are jammed with too much stock, but this adds to the character of the store. When entering the store, look up at the ceiling which resembles a rock & roll version of Michelangelo's Sistine Chapel.

There are literally thousands of CDs and DVDs displayed above head height, reaching right up to the ceiling, and it is impossible from floor level to see all the titles. Richie and his customers are constantly climbing a stepladder to view them.

Laurie takes great pride in having many customers who first visited the store as teenagers in the 1960s, who now visit the shop with their own children and grandchildren. It is satisfying to see three generations of Dales Music customers all in the shop at the same time.

The shop has an interesting in-store music policy. Six days a week, the shop features the choices of Richie, which tend to be rock and blues, while Sunday is designated Easy Listening Day and there is a much more relaxed feel to the store as Laurie chooses records by his favourite crooners. Laurie is now aged 89 (despite looking 20 years younger). He is the oldest record retailer in the UK and loves the business so much that retirement is still a faraway prospect.

Derricks Music *The unluckiest record shop owner in the world*
221 Oxford Street, Swansea SA1 38Q
01792 654226
derricksmusic.co.uk; info@derricksmusic.co.uk; @DerricksMusic
Monday-Saturday 9am-5.30pm
Sunday 11am-4pm
Established 1956
Stock: Vinyl, CD, Tickets

Derricks Music was started in Port Talbot by Derrick, the uncle of current owner Chris Stylinaou, as an electrical store that stocked a few LPs. Like other shops in the 1950s and 1960s, they found that selling records was more lucrative than selling electrical goods, so the family opened a second shop in Port Talbot selling only records, which was said to be the first record shop dedicated to pop and rock music in Wales.

In 1968, Port Talbot was being re-developed and one of the Derricks shops was due to be demolished, prompting the family to move their record retailing business to Swansea. Like many stores which have survived the recent downturn, a fundamental reason why they are still standing is that Chris owns the building which they trade from. One of his shrewdest moves was to rent out space for a cash machine, which is neatly embedded in Derricks front window, making it super-convenient for customers who have just acquired a bunch of crisp new notes to spend some of them in the shop.

Derricks is also kept in business thanks to sales of concert tickets and the success of Swansea Live, an event organised by Chris which takes place in the city centre every August. With more than 20 bands playing across three stages, it attracts large crowds to the city and gives up-and-coming local bands the chance to play to a large audience. This is what record shops do: they support the local music community.

Chris inherited the record shop after Derrick passed away in 1985. He has been ably assisted over the years by his longtime assistant Sian. It is worth a visit to Derricks to hear the banter between the two of them, even if you have no plans to make a purchase. Chris has several claims to fame including being Welsh Junior Surf Champion. He can often be seen surfing the waves off the Gower Peninsula. Many years ago, Elizabeth Taylor cooked him chips one evening when he visited his friends Alan and Richard, the sons of the late Graham Jenkins who was Richard Burton's brother. Richard and Elizabeth were visiting, and the Oscar-winning actress cooked the evening meal.

One claim to fame Chris wishes he did not have is that of being the unluckiest record shop owner in the world. His run of bad luck started in 1998 when he was the victim of a violent robbery. At 8.00am he was preparing the shop for opening when he heard a knock on the back door. When he opened the door Chris was confronted by two men brandishing a gun. They attacked Chris, tied him up and then cleared out what money he had in the till. They then dragged him up the stairs which resulted in a serious wound to his leg as a metal strip ripped open his shin. The burglars threatened to shoot Chris unless he revealed the code to access the safe. After emptying the safe they locked him in the cupboard. With blood pouring from his wound Chris knew that he needed to get to a hospital soon. The cupboard he was locked in was where he kept his tools. He managed pick up his saw and cut through his ties. He then used his hammer to smash his way out of the cupboard and called the police.

After visiting the hospital, Chris spent the next day being questioned by the police about the break in. His leg-wound took a long time to heal leaving him with a large scar that reminds him of the awful experience. Sian demonstrated her supreme sales skills, even under such troubling circumstances. While the shop was shut that day, she sold CDs to the police investigating the crime, some of whom still come in to the shop to this day.

More bad luck occurred not long after. During a heavy storm the drains blocked, and the shop was flooded. The floor was ruined along with the vinyl kept in boxes under the racking.

On another occasion, when scaffolding had been erected to enable repairs to the building, another gang of burglars gained access to the shop by climbing up and smashing the upstairs window.

Disaster struck again when Chris became violently ill after eating a meal of prawns. He was sick for weeks and lost all the hair on his body except for a small patch on the back of his head which turned from black to white. He had suffered mercury poisoning and is still being treated for the effects of it to this day.

Things could hardly get any worse. Or could they? In 2014 Chris's neighbours started building an extension on their house. When their builders dug into the ground it caused the foundations of Chris's house to drop, making the whole structure unstable. Huge cracks appeared in the walls and ceilings. The council, fearing that the house could collapse at any point, ordered Chris and his family to leave immediately. For the last few years, they have lived in temporary accommodation while builders are trying to secure his house. He is beginning to wish they had knocked it down and he could start again.

In January 2018, I wrote to Chris to ask if he minded me referring to him as "the unluckiest record shop owner in the world." I did not hear back for a week. He finally called to apologise for the delay in replying. He had been laid up in hospital, following a heart attack.

A week later there was an earthquake in the UK. The epicenter was in Swansea. My immediate thought was that it was bound to have struck underneath Derricks. Thankfully, the shop had been left unscathed – by the earthquake, at least. However, the builders had left a tap running over the weekend and the house had flooded. And his wife Vicky had just written off her car in a crash.

I am glad to report Vicky was unhurt. And that Chris has made a full recovery from his heart attack. Through all this misfortune, Chris remains philosophical and has never lost his enthusiasm for running the shop as it evolves with the times. "Music is not life and death," he says. "It is here to make the bad times better – and the good times even better."

This hard-working man deserves some good fortune. Fingers crossed for the future, Chris.

Diverse Music *The record shop that featured in an episode of Dr Who*
10 Charles Street, Newport, NP20 1JU
01633 259661
diversevinyl.com; orders@diversevinyl.com; @DiverseMusic
Monday-Friday 9.30am-5.30pm
Sunday 10am-4pm
Established 1988
Stock: Vinyl, CD, Pre-owned, In-stores

Diverse Music is a record shop side which is housed with two sister companies at the same address: Diverse Vinyl, a mail order company; and Diverse Records a vinyl-only record label. The business is owned by Paul Hawkins and Matt Jarrett.

Matt spent many years working at WH Smith. Dissatisfied with the range of music stocked there, he would spend his lunch breaks hanging out and buying records at Diverse. Eventually, Paul persuaded him to join him at Diverse.

The mail order department was set up in 1995, at a time when vinyl was in its darkest days. Many major new album releases were on CD only, and import pressings were thin on the ground as many independent record stores stopped stocking the format. Contrary to popular belief however, vinyl was still alive, and Diverse Music continued to stock all new releases on vinyl. As the company's reputation grew, they started to receive phone calls from customers all over the UK, desperately searching for new vinyl releases which their local stores were not stocking. With the launch of the internet, the stock became readily available to vinyl junkies all over the world, and their site becoming a major portal for analogue fans worldwide.

Meanwhile their own vinyl label, Diverse Records, went from strength to strength, and now numbers many fine albums by Alison Krauss, Richard Thompson, Rickie Lee Jones, Frank Black, Dr John and others among its catalogue.

Now that the rest of the world has caught up with the vinyl revival, Diverse are reaping the rewards of being a longtime vinyl specialist. In 2013 the company launched their own limited-edition turntable to celebrate the 25th anniversary of the shop.

Further celebrations for the quarter century milestone saw them taking over Newport's Le Pub venue for a weekend of live music. They brewed their own beer for the occasion in collaboration with local comedy rappers Goldie Lookin Chain. Goldie Lookin Ale proved so popular that it completely sold out and continues to do so whenever the brewers, Tiny Rebel, stick a barrel on.

In 2006, the shop was invaded by a BBC crew for an episode of *Doctor Who*. They hired the shop for three days. The whole of Charles Street got an enormous lift with the visit of the Doctor played by David Tennant. He turned out to be a music fan, particularly of Scottish bands the Proclaimers and Franz Ferdinand.

While the shop is a window for the vinyl mail-order business, it still sells CDs and remains passionate about supporting Newport bands. Diverse has lived up to its name by stocking a varied range and establishing a database of worldwide vinyl fans. They also sell at specialist Hi-Fi shows, recognising that anybody in the market for new stereo equipment is also likely to want to purchase vinyl.

Have a look at the walls when you visit the shop. They are covered in cult posters and cartoons about record shops. On the right, you will see a collection of framed and signed album sleeves by indie darlings Laura Marling, Cowboy Junkies, Idlewild, Gretchen Peters and others. On the opposite wall, are framed album sleeves by artists of a more traditional bearing, including Isla St Clair, Lionel Blair and Mary O'Hara.

The shop does exceptionally well with its Staff Picks section of releases recommended by the staff. One trusting customer comes in each week and buys nearly every title on the list - a pile of vinyl that usually costs him around £120. He seldom complains of buying anything that he has not enjoyed.

Another trusting customer is Mr. Any. He always asks for an album by a particular artist – Led Zeppelin, for example. When Matt asks him which particular album by Led Zeppelin he would like, he invariably replies "Any." Matt reckons he is replacing his CD collection with vinyl, and nowadays as soon as Mr. Any announces the name of the band he is looking for, Matt will dig out the album he thinks he will enjoy most.

Paul and Matt have been joined behind the counter at Diverse Music by Vaughan, who covers them for days off, when he is not touring the seedier pubs of South Wales and beyond with his glam punk band the Sick Livers.

Haystacks Music & More *The record shop that was raided by the police*
Backfold, Hay-on-Wye, Powys HR3 5EQ
07512 7298199
Monday-Sunday 9.30am-4.30pm
Established 2013.
Stock: Vinyl, CD, Pre-owned, 78s, Books, DVD, T-shirts, and all manner of oddities

The wellington boots filled with flowers standing either side of the doorway are a sign of what lies within this delightful record shop. To approach the racks of vinyl, you must pass a diverse array of distractions; pink wigs, psychedelic dresses, lava lamps, wildlife paintings, a large sign declaring, "Turn Off, Re-Tune and Drop in" and a copy of an Andy Warhol print of the Beatles, to name but a few.

With this build up, you except the owner Haydn Pugh to be a character and he does not disappoint. Dressed in a shirt with dozens of vinyl records printed on it and a medallion made from a 7-inch single, he soon starts enthusing about the unusual items he has in stock.

The shop achieved notoriety after a police raid in 2016 following a complaint about a poster at the entrance to his shop featuring a vinyl disc, a CD and a book in a clear bag underneath the words "Legal highs sold". Also hanging from the ceiling are coloured vinyl records with slogans such as "High on Music" printed on them. Haydn is referring to getting high on music as opposed to drugs. The story featured in the local press and in the national red-tops, *The Sun* and *The Daily Star*.

The police were not the only ones confused by Haydn's poster and its mischievous reference to the mood-enhancing qualities of music and literature. A straggly looking man came in and asked "Any dope?"

"Only the one I am looking at," Haydn replied.

Vinyl fans paying a visit to the annual Hay Festival of Literature & Arts will be well rewarded by a visit to this fascinating shop.

Moonlight Records

27, Bridge Street, Wrexham, LL13 7HP
01978 361756
Bryandavies11@hotmail.com
Monday-Tuesday, Thursday-Saturday 10am-5pm
Wednesday 12-5pm
Established 1987
Stock: Vinyl, Pre-owned, CD, DVD

Moonlight Records is owned by Bryan Davies. The stock is nearly all second-hand but the shop does stock Record Store Day releases.

Red House Music

9, The Indoor Market, Aberdare, Rhondda Cynon Taf CF44 7EB
01685 268162
redhouseaberdare@hotmail.com
Monday-Saturday 10am-4.30pm
Established 2001
Stock: Vinyl, CD, Pre-owned, Memorabilia, Merchandise

"What I love about owning a record shop is that I always get first dibs on the records that come in."
Laura George - Red House Music

Expect to hear loud music on a visit to Red House Music. The charismatic owner, Laura George loves her customers, greeting them as they enter like long lost friends but attracts her fair share of eccentrics. There was the man who said "Can I have a fireman's lift?" Laura asked him if that was the name of a band. "No," replied the customer. "I have a bad pain in my knees and being lifted off the ground relieves it." The man was tiny, so Laura picked him up and slung him over her shoulder.

Laura is very popular with her customers. At Christmas and on her birthday she receives many gifts although some of them, such as a used Ladyshave, half a pasty and a voodoo doll of herself, left her underwhelmed.

Despite the shop being called Red House Music it is painted inside in a shade of paint called Purple Haze. Laura told me that as soon as she noticed that shade she knew it would be perfect for the shop. She has kept the red painted door.

On all my travels around record shops I have never seen vinyl albums so cheap. Laura has a 20p section which contained artists such as the Shadows and Shirley Bassey. When

I pointed this out to Laura, she told me she had an even cheaper section. Sure enough, outside the shop she had her "Please save these albums from landfill" section. These albums were all free and people were welcome to take them away.

Red House Music has a strong selection of blues, vinyl and vast quantities of 7-inch singles. And no shortage of characters and an atmosphere of happiness.

Slipped Discs

Carmarthen Indoor Market, Carmarthen, Dyfed SA31 1QY
0126 723 0479
slipdisks82@gmail.com
Monday 11.30am-3.30pm
Tuesday-Saturday 9.30-4.30pm
Established 1982
Stock: Vinyl, CD, Pre-owned

Carmarthen has two excellent record stores. Tangled Parrot caters for an alternative market while Slipped Discs is a more traditional store, catering for all tastes. A lot of the shop's business is in sales of second-hand vinyl, and as well as buying from her customers, the owner Oonah Crawford treks through the local car-boot sales on a Sunday searching for collectable stock.

While looking through a pile of old classical albums, one title caught her eye: Leonid Kogan playing Tchaikovsky's First Violin Concerto. It was the old printed label on the record that enticed her to buy it for £1. Normally, Oonah would put the record in the racks, but she had a gut feeling that it might be special, and put it on eBay instead. When she checked its status she was astonished to find that the bidding had already passed £200. The album was eventually sold to a gentleman in Hong Kong for a staggering £1,047.

Oonah points out that selling vinyl to China and Korea has become a lucrative part of her business. This is something other shops should consider.

Spillers Records *The oldest record shop in the world*

27 Morgan Arcade, Cardiff, CF10 1AF
02920 224 905
www.spillersrecords.com; info@spillersrecords.com; @spillersrecords
Monday-Saturday 10am-6pm
Established 1894
Stock: Vinyl, CD, In-stores, Merchandise, Tickets

Spillers is no ordinary shop. A two-part documentary, *The Oldest Record Shop in The World,* broadcast on ITV in 2008, told the incredible story of this legendary retailer and its latterday battle to keep trading after a huge redevelopment in the Cardiff area led to colossal rent hikes.

The shop opened in Queens Arcade in 1894. It was founded by Henry Spiller and Joe Gregory, who were quick to recognise that there was money to be made in the recorded music business. Originally, they sold wax phonograph cylinders and shellac phonograph discs. In the late 1920s they added musical instruments to the range of stock and in the 1940s the shop relocated to its longest-lasting premises (so far) on The Hayes. It remained in the Spiller family until 1962 when they sold the shop to a consortium of local businessmen. The shop changed hands again in 1986 when it was bought by Nick Todd, who had been its manager since 1975.

Nick's daughter Ashli now owns the shop, working seven days a week, not for the money, but for the joy of introducing people to music they have not heard. "Even though everything is supposedly accessible on a computer at the end of your fingertips, nothing beats the buzz of meeting somebody face to face across the counter and saying 'Hey, have you heard this?'" Ashli says. "A real-life recommendation beats any algorithm! We're really just sharing happiness all day. You can't get sick of it. Sick of music, sick of life."

As well as its longevity, the store is famous for its iconic T-shirts. If you attend any music festival you are bound to see someone wearing the distinctive design with the red vinyl disc on a black background. Customers are encouraged to send in photos of themselves wearing the T-shirt from the most obscure parts of the globe.

In the early days of their career the Manic Street Preachers seemed to spend half their leisure time at Spillers. If they were not in the shop buying records, they would be outside busking in the street. Their singer, James Dean Bradfield, included the Spillers Records logo as part of the sleeve artwork of his 2006 album *The Great Western*.

In 2006, the shop faced a review of its lease after a major new development, St David 2, was built on the site opposite. Spillers could not absorb the substantial increase in rent that was being demanded, but Nick Todd wasn't prepared to let the shop fold. With the help of Hywel Thomas, a loyal customer who happened to be Plaid Cymru's press officer for the Welsh Assembly, he organised a petition to save Spillers.

The response from the public was amazing. More than 20,000 people signed the petition, including stars such as Bob Dylan, Bruce Springsteen, Justin Timberlake, Beyonce and, of course, the Manic Street Preachers. The petition attracted publicity from all over the world in the music and national press, and earned the store a reprieve.

In 2016, Spillers made a remarkable gesture, after hearing of the plight of a man called Geoffrey Harris from Neath in Port Talbot, about 40 miles away, who suffered from depression and panic attacks that had left him unable to visit Cardiff for many years. Inspired by the PM programme's "Take a Leap" feature on BBC Radio 4, Geoffrey had made great progress in overcoming his condition, but getting from Cardiff train station to Spillers was beyond him at that time. Through the offices of PM, Spillers let Geoffrey know that if he ever felt up to making a visit to the shop, they would come and meet him from the station. It wasn't long before PM were arranging for the presenter Eddie Mair to bring Geoffrey to Spillers, where they were welcomed with tea and Welsh cakes. Now Geoffrey makes a few trips each year to the Welsh capital to partake in a spot of lunch and, of course, a stop off for tea and records in the shop.

Spillers is now located in the exquisite Morgan Arcade adjacent to The Hayes. For Ashli who is now the sole owner, the business is full on as she spends all of her waking hours working on its demands. Her motivation and inspiration is the joy of introducing people to music they have not heard before and the special place Spillers has earned among the music community of South Wales and beyond during its unrivalled tenure.

One of her proudest memories from her 22 years behind the Spillers counter was the undying gratitude she received from Terry, a regular customer for several decades, after she noticed his sudden weight loss and urged him to see his GP. He reported back a few months later that he had been diagnosed with diabetes. After suffering serious complications, Terry now manages his condition and is still a frequent face at the counter.

Spillers has proudly participated in every Record Store Day, but the 2018 celebrations will last in the memory for many years to come. To celebrate the occasion, Lauren Lavern showed up to broadcast her BBC 6 Music show from the Spillers counter the day before. With a staff and customer base who are all avid 6 Music devotees, the event was an enormous honor.

Ashli has joked that one day she would like to open a record shop in a warmer climate. It would be a great loss for Cardiff, but no music fan in Wales would begrudge one of the most-hard working women in the music industry a life in the sun. She took the shop on during the most difficult period in music retailing and has battled hard to keep Spillers as one of the best record shops in the UK. Wherever Spillers is based in the future it will never lose its charm and character and remains the first port of call for music fans visiting Wales.

Tangled Parrot *The original Apple store now selling parrotphernalia*
32 King Street, Carmarthen, Dyfed SA31 1BS
01554 890231
tangledparrot.com; tangledparrot@gmail.com; @tangledparrot
Monday-Saturday 10am-5pm
Stock: Vinyl, CD, Pre-owned, Badges, Clothing, In-stores, Parrotphernalia

Also, at Lion Street, Hay-on-Wye, HR3 5AA.

Matt Davies was so short of money when he opened Tangled Parrot, that after purchasing his initial stock he had no money left for racking. A local orchard solved the problem by selling him crates that had previously been used to store apples. Many customers enjoyed the aroma of the new shop, but the problem was that any record that did not sell quickly soon picked up the smell of apples from the boxes. It was funny for Matt to sell records on the Apple label which smelled of the fruit.

The shop picked up its unusual name through a frustrating Christmas present Matt bought for his daughter Maia. It was a parrot constructed of wood and fishing wire which 5-year-old Maia loved. By pulling on the wire the parrot flapped its wings. The problem was that Maia constantly snagged the wire up resulting in Matt repeatedly having to disentangle it. When his friend called around and asked if Maia was enjoying the present, Matt explained that she was, but he had christened it the tangled parrot. His friend commented that it would make a great name for a band. As Matt was opening a record shop and not joining a band he thought it would be the perfect name for his new business.

Matt deployed his daughter's talents to draw the shop's mascot, a tiny, colourful parrot that is still festooned all over the shop's racking. You will also find lots of "parrotphernalia" for sale. They have stuffed plastic and wooden parrots as well as T-shirts, badges, beer mats, harmonicas with parrots on, and even parrot food (not a great seller). I am pleased to say that the original tangled parrot still hangs from the shop's ceiling, with Matt willing to demonstrate the curious device to any customer that asks.

Matt has always been a great supporter of the Carmarthen music scene but was disappointed when two local venues closed. When a local pub was put up for sale

Matt mortgaged himself to the hilt to purchase it. He turned the downstairs into a café and bar which hosted bands and comedians during the evenings, and moved his record shop upstairs.

He called the business The Parrot. It soon became the social hub of the town with events taking place there at least three days every week. Unfortunately, music retailing was going through a difficult period. With the added pressures of the interest on his loan, Matt was struggling to keep the business afloat.

In 2011, he reluctantly took the decision to close the business – but the story did not end there. After hearing the news of Matt's impending closure, a group of artists and musicians formed the West Wales Music Collective. The aim was to keep the project open. They approached Matt and informed him that they had started a crowdfunding campaign to raise enough money to keep him going. Through fundraising events and pledges they had soon raised £2,000. They crashed through the £5,000 barrier soon after, thanks to an anonymous benefactor who donated £3,000 to the fund. A rumour spread that it was the comedian Rhod Gilbert who was born in the town. When approached by the BBC and asked if he was the mystery benefactor, Rhod dryly replied "I am not the mystery benefactor anymore."

Thanks to the publicity generated by Rhod's generosity, the fund topped £11,000.

Matt was so touched by the warmth of the town towards him that he had no choice but to re-open and has not looked back. The shop is the thriving centre of the Carmarthen community. Try and combine your visit with seeing a band playing and enjoy some of the local craft beer sold in the bar. Matt, a man who has done so much to bring good music, culture and art to South Wales, deserves your support.

Terminal Records

Unit 25, Courtyard Shops, Old Bridge, Haverfordwest, Pembrokeshire SA61 2AN
07796 987534
terminalrecords5@gmail.com
Monday-Saturday 10.30am-4.30pm
Established 1980
Stock: Vinyl, CD, Pre-owned, Cassettes

I have sold music to Martin Thompson at Terminal Records for many years, and during the period of record shop decline when 540 record shops closed in just 4 years (between 2005 and 2009), I was sure that Martin was going to add to that statistic. This was due to his habit of answering the phone with the words "Hello, Terminal decline". I am delighted to say he not only rode out the storm, but after 36 years of being inside Haverfordwest market he has moved to a stand-alone record shop.

Although Terminal Records stocks all genres, it is primarily a shop that sells rock music with all its sub divisions. Martin describes Terminal as "A haven of tranquility, safe from pestering sales staff." He is happy for people to browse as long as they like, and is always delighted to recommend records he thinks you will enjoy. "I feel a warm glow when somebody comes back to the shop and says, 'I love that record you recommended to me'," Martin says. A regular customer recently said to him "In all the years I have been coming here, you have never given me a bum steer." Martin feels it's one of the nicest things anybody has said to him.

Martin's path to the world of record retailing has been varied and at times somewhat smelly. His first job on leaving college in the 1970s was at the local cheese factory. If he thought the smell was bad there, it was nothing compared to the fumes that wafted over from the local sewage works close by. Things got worse. He landed a job at a Hide and Skin merchant, where he had to wade ankle-deep through the blood and guts of animals recently separated from their skin. There was no refuge; they even displayed a sheep's head by the canteen door. "A truly offal job", as Martin put it.

He switched to more agreeable conditions at Haverfordwest museum before, in 1980, taking inspiration from an old college friend Hag Harris, who had successfully opened Hag's Records, a couple of years earlier, 50 miles away in Lampeter. (Hag's Records lasted until 2016, and Hag even enjoyed a spell as Mayor of Lampeter.)

Martin borrowed £1,500 from the Bank of Dad (an institution that seems more popular than ever these days) and bought some stock. He started selling at three Welsh markets: Haverfordwest, Fishguard and Pembroke Dock. The market in Pembroke Dock was open to the elements and in the winter, could be freezing. Martin described it as a "blue hand job", which sounds like something sexual, but merely referred to the colour of his hands after spending a day working there. In 1982, he was offered a permanent place at the indoor Riverside Market and blue hands became a thing of the past.

For a record shop located in a town the size of Haverfordwest (population 13,367 in 2001) Terminal Records has seen off a surprising array of competitors over the years, ranging from Swales Music Centre to AW Jazz, the wonderful jazz specialist shop run by Andrew Fuller, which closed in 2017.

There was also the unlikely challenge of a Sam Goody store which had strayed a long way from its roots on New York's 9th Avenue. Sam Goody was once the largest music retailer in the USA, at one point having 880 outlets. The stores were named after the chain's founder who started off selling discounted vinyl by mail order, before branching out to selling from bricks and mortar stores. The chain was incredibly popular, and they rolled out the model in the UK in 1990. At one point, they had 22 shops in this country, but UK music buyers never really took them to their hearts and when the going got tough for record retailers they pulled the plug on their UK venture. By 1999 all the UK shops had been sold to a variety of other UK-based retailers. In America, disaster followed as the chain passed through different companies who each disposed of hundreds of stores until by 2012, there was only one shop left - in San Diego - trading under that name. By the end of that year the Sam Goody music retailer was no more.

Terminal is the only record shop I know where, if you ask nicely, you can get your purchase wrapped in a paper bag with a hand-drawn illustration. Martin's friend, Roy Conolly used to help in the shop sometimes and, when the mood took him, he would draw record shop-related pictures on the brown paper bags. Some of Martin's favourites adorn the shop and there are many examples of Roy's talented and frequently hilarious artwork on the Terminal Records Facebook page.

In 2016, after years of uncertainty, the traders at Riverside Market were given six-months notice to quit. It was the end of an era. Many of Martin's fellow traders packed it in after the market closed. But Martin found a new trading location, 30 yards from the market building, and business is, once again, going well. No longer in terminal decline, Terminal Records have a bright future ahead of them.

Terry's Music
8 Church Street, Pontypridd, Rhondda Cynon Taf CF37 2TH
0144 340 6421
terryreece@btconnect.com; @Terrysmusicshop
Monday-Wednesday 9am-5pm
Thursday 9.30am-1.30pm
Saturday 9am-4.30pm
Established 1997
Stock: Vinyl, Pre-owned, CD, In-stores, Merchandise, Musical Instruments

Terry's Music first opened for business at the Open Market in the village of Treorchy in the Rhondda Valley in 1997. It was something of a roving record shop in the early days, moving to Aberdare, then Tonypandy, before settling in the outside market in Pontypridd. In April 2014, the owner Terry Rees finally moved into a shop in Church Street, which has enabled him to expand the range of high quality musical instruments and other items on offer and to provide a supportive hub for the local music community.

Hard Lines *They will deliver your vinyl by bicycle*
Castle Emporium, Womanby Street, Cardiff CF10 1BS
07051 37082
team@outpostrecords.co.uk; @HardLinesCoffee
Monday-Friday 8am-5pm
Saturday 10am-6pm
Established 2016
Stock: Vinyl, Coffee, Food, Licensed

Over coffee in Barcelona, two young entrepreneurs Matt Jones and Sophie Smith dreamed up the idea of opening a coffee shop selling vinyl in Cardiff. They tested out the venture with a pop-up shop at street festivals, markets and craft breweries, where they found a warm welcome which gave them the confidence to open a permanent shop.
   Hard Lines is based in the Castle Emporium, a haven for all things independent including an art gallery, a comic book store and numerous clothing retailers. The shop was originally named Outpost, but it was "hard lines" for Matt and Sophie when they discovered another company had the exclusive rights to that name.
   Hard Lines has gained a reputation for serving some of the best coffee in the city.
   Matt and Sophie are music fanatics and enthusiastic supporters of Welsh artists. If you live in the Cardiff area, they will even deliver your vinyl by bicycle.

VOD Music *The UK's smallest record shop*
28 Newton Street, Mold, Flintshire CH17 1NZ
07904 688739
vodmusic.co.uk; enquiries@vodmusic.co.uk; @VODMusic1
Wednesday-Saturday 10.30am-4pm
Established 2009
Stock: Vinyl, CD, Pre-owned, Merchandise

VOD (Vinyl On Deck) Records is owned by Colin Trueman, who has spent many years organising record fairs around North Wales. Formerly an ice cream parlour and measuring just 67 square feet, VOD Music is the UK's smallest record shop. Colin has converted the serving hatch into a counter and created the record shop equivalent of the Tardis.

Big isn't always best and VOD Music is worth a visit if only to marvel at how much Colin has managed to cram into such a small space. He has had great support from the local community and runs the shop while continuing to organise record fairs.

West Midlands

As the UK's second largest city, you'd expect that Birmingham would be home to a plethora of independent record shops. Instead, the city punches well below its weight and it is only a handful of long established stores such as Swordfish, The Diskery and Polar Bear that fly the flag. Some new stores have not lasted long, with both Milque & Music and Left For Dead abandoning their home in the Custard Factory. Milque & Music are now selling online while Left For Dead moved to Shrewsbury where the shop has thrived, leaving behind a city that's crying out for some new blood in the world of record retailing.

Walsall is the place to go for new record shops, with two opening within a month of each other in 2017. But music fans visiting the area should also not miss Pete and Julie Chambers' wonderful Coventry Music Museum at 74-80 Walsgrave Rd, Coventry, CV2 4ED, 07971 171441. Although it covers the history of music from the Roman times, the star attraction is the 2 Tone Village. Here you will find great memorabilia and a selection of vinyl and CDs from that exciting period during the late 1970s and early 1980s in British music, as well as a café.

Leamington Spa is worth a visit as it is home to Seismic Records and the recently re-opened Head Records. It also has one of the best classical record shops in the UK, Presto Records located at 11 Park Street CV32 4QN.

Eclipse Records

Unit 4, Victorian Arcade, Walsall, West Midlands WS1 1RE
01922 322142
pete@eclipse-records.co.uk
Established 2017
Stock: Vinyl, CD, Pre-owned

"Listening to Lauren Laverne talking about Record Store Day changed my life." **Pete Holland, Eclipse Records**

Pete Holland had been working in transport for more than 20 years, but his love of the job was beginning to wane. One day on a three-hour drive to a meeting, he was listening to Lauren Laverne on BBC 6 Music interviewing the team at Vinyl Tap in Huddersfield about what was happening in the shop on Record Store Day. Pete recalled how happy and enthusiastic everybody was, with the staff emphasising how much they loved working there. It was the kick up the backside he needed to change his life. He sat through a two-hour "crap meeting", but his heart was not in it. His head was full of ideas about starting his own record shop. By the end of his three-hour journey home, he had a plan.

Pete experimented with a pop-up shop in a local pub, The Fountain Inn, where the combination of popping in for a pint and buying vinyl proved to be a winner. It gave him the confidence to find his own premises in Walsall town centre, just seven months after hearing the radio interview. He will never forget the date of the interview that changed his life – April 21, 2017 – and he is looking forward to paying a visit to Vinyl Tap to thank the team for inspiring his life change.

Frank Harvey Hi Fi Excellence
163 Spon Street, Coventry, West Midlands CV1 3BB
hifix.co.uk; kevin@frankharvey.co.uk
Monday-Saturday 9.30am-5.30pm
Established 1982
Stock: Vinyl, Hi Fi Equipment

Frank Harvey Hi Fi Excellence is a hi-fi shop that also stocks new vinyl and takes part in Record Store Day. The three-storey showroom where the shop is housed dates to the early 1500s. You are unlikely to find a more historic place to browse vinyl, in a street lined with Grade II listed 16th century buildings. Number 163 was dismantled and relocated to Spon Street from another part of Coventry after it survived heavy bombing in World War II.

Head
Lower Mall, Royal Priors, Leamington Spa, Warwickshire CV32 4XU
Monday-Saturday 9am-6pm
Sunday 10.30am-4.30pm
Established 2007
Stock: Vinyl, CD, Pre-owned, DVD, In-stores

Simon Dullenty was employed as a senior manager at Head, the music retail chain which opened its first branch in Leamington Spa. The aim of the shop is to offer a complete record-store experience to all walks of life: the young, the old, the dedicated music fan and the casual punter.

Simon started his record retailing career at HMV, holding various buying positions, and managing stores, before he joined Head. Having been a vinyl buyer at HMV Manchester he believed that the Head shops should be stocking the format. Not all the staff agreed so, as an experiment, he brought all the albums from his own, personal collection into the shop and displayed them in an old T-shirt rack. Within a week, most of the LPs had been sold. Simon had proved his point and from then on, Head embraced vinyl.

In 2018, the Head chain went into liquidation and all five of its shops in England and the Republic of Ireland were closed. Social media was inundated with customers saying how sad they were.

Simon, who came up with the brand name to begin with, reopened the Leamington shop, as his own independent venture, in July 2018. Many people in the industry thought he was bonkers, but he is determined to prove the doubters wrong.

Ignite Records
Level 2, Oasis Indoor Market, 110-114 Corporation Street, Birmingham, B4 6SX
0121 233 4488
igniterecordstore@hotmail.co.uk,@Ignite_Brum
Monday-Friday 10am-5.30pm
Saturday 10am-6pm
Established 2010
Stock: Vinyl, T-shirts

When the popular Tempest Records sadly closed its doors a few years ago, Rich Perry who was the buyer there, decided to set up a much smaller affair within the Oasis Indoor Market. It certainly is an oasis of joy for vinyl fans in the desert that is Birmingham's record retailing. Although it is a small unit, Rich uses every inch of space, including the floor, to cram in as much vinyl as possible. The shop specializes in indie, metal, hardcore, punk, industrial and goth.

Oldies Unlimited
89 Darlington Street, Wolverhampton, West Midlands WV1 4EX
01902 313668
oldiesvinylrecords.com; oldiesunlimited@btinternet.com; @OldiesUnlimited
Monday-Saturday 9am-5pm
Established sometime in the distant past!
Stock: Vinyl, CD, Pre-owned, 7-inch singles, Merchandise, T-Shirts

Oldies Unlimited is one of the most mysterious record shops I have visited. It used to be a chain with a thriving mail order business based in Telford which advertised 7-inch singles in the music press. They also would supply merchandise to shops by providing a spinner rack full of 7-inch singles. Even the current owner, Simon Malpas, does not know when the shop opened. If you know, drop me a line.

Polar Bear Records

10 York Road, Birmingham B14 7RZ
01214 415202
stevepolarbear@hotmail.co.uk
Monday-Saturday 10am-6pm
Established 1991
Stock: Vinyl, CD, Pre-owned, T-Shirts

Although the sign on the frontage of Polar Bear Records says "Compact Discs bought and sold", vinyl has been the growth area in recent years.

A small independent record store situated in the Kings Heath area of the city, Polar Bear specializes in jazz, classic rock, metal, prog, kraut rock and folk. It is the place to visit if you are interested in Bob Dylan, as the owner Steve Bull is a huge fan.

Steve makes a thought-provoking comment regarding the double-vinyl Dylan album *Blonde on Blonde*. One of his customers told him that when the album was released in 1966 it cost 59/- (shillings) which was just less than £3 in today's money. He had just started work and that was nearly a day's wages. So, even if you are paying £20 for a vinyl album today, it is still a comparative bargain, and claims that the format is expensive are just not true.

There is some fabulous memorabilia decorating the walls of Polar Bear Records, including the largest Sex Pistols poster I have ever seen.

Revolution Records & Vapes   *The owner sold his vinyl collection to save his life*

16 Park Place Shopping Centre, Walsall, West Midlands WS1 1NP
01922 620895
david@revolutionrecords.uk
Established 2017
Stock: Vinyl, Pre-owned, E-cigarettes

Revolution Records & Vapes is owned by music journalist David Hughes and his friend Chun Pala. In 2010, David was diagnosed with an inoperable brain tumour and given just nine months to live. It was either make a bucket list or find alternative treatment.

Dave discovered a new, state-of-the-art treatment called CyberKnife, in which tumours are removed using robotic radiosurgery. The treatment, which was not available on the NHS, would cost him more than £20,000. For decades he had amassed a fabulous vinyl collection, and much as it pained him he was forced to sell it to pay for the life-saving procedure.

The operation was a complete success, and these days CyberKnife is available on the NHS. Dave, however, was still plagued with other health problems which resulted in him having a stroke. He recovered from this too, although his left thigh is still so numb that you could stick a fork in it and he would not feel it.

He has spent the years since then writing and re-building both his life and his vinyl collection. He successfully started trading vinyl online and, when his friend Chun Pala invited him to sell vinyl from the Vape Shop he owned in Walsall, Dave jumped at the chance. Noting that other shops have successfully marketed themselves selling combinations such as vinyl & pies and vinyl & craft beers, the pair have created the world's first vinyl & vape shop. Working with his old friends has given Dave a new lease of life.

"We sell music not data," says the shop's manager Mark Burns, who used to run the fondly remembered Sundown Records in Walsall, which closed in 2005. Mark has many happy memories of his time at Sundown, especially the day Ozzy Osbourne spent four hours in the shop signing copies of his album *Bark at the Moon*. To prepare for the event the sales rep from Sony had filled the window with sleeves of the album and done further displays within the shop. After a couple of hours Mark noticed the stock was not selling as quickly as he had thought it would. He then noticed that Ozzy seemed to be signing more sleeves than albums. He looked in the window and it was bare. Fans had cleared it of sleeves, getting Ozzy to sign them rather than purchasing the album. Mark has a saying: "I have more vinyl than sense."

Seismic Records
Spencer Street, Leamington Spa, Warwickshire CV31 3NF
01926 831333
seismicrecords.co.uk; info@seismicrecords.co.uk; @seismicrecords
Monday-Saturday 10am-5.30pm
Established 2005
Stock: Vinyl, CD, Pre-owned, Merchandise, T-shirts

Stuart Smith's charming shop is located in the Assembly venue in the Old Town, which is south of the river. It makes perfect sense to time your visit for when a band is playing.

Stuart started Seismic Records after leaving his former employer Fopp, who had taken the short-sighted decision to stop stocking vinyl.

Seismic Records has won critical acclaim with articles in *The Guardian*, *The Independent* and *The Observer*. It has also appeared in *The Guardian Shopping Directory 2007* a selection of the UK's best independent shops. The shop has a reputation for excellent service with good prices. Check out Seismic if you are buying online.

S T Records
165 Wolverhampton Street, Dudley, West Midlands DY1 3AH
0138 423 0726
Strecords84@gmail.com
Tuesday-Thursday 9am-5pm Friday 9am-7pm Saturday 9am-5pm
Established 1984
Stock: Vinyl, CD, Pre-owned, DVD, T-shirts

With its brick frontage and grey metal door it would be easy to miss S T Records. If you are a fan of rock/metal this would be a mistake, as this unassuming shop specialises in these genres. Owner Steve Thornley is a rock expert who started the business as a mail order operation which he turned into a shop after four years.

Steve has made some great business decisions over the years but there is one move he regrets. That was not to close up the day 600 English Defence League members marched outside the shop. Most of the shops in the town had closed that day, but business was not great, and Steve did not want to lose out on his Saturday trade. But, as EDL supporters and Unite Against Fascism protestors hurled bricks back and forth outside the shop while the poor police attempted to keep the sides apart, Steve resorted to locking his customers in for their own safety. The Clash's "White Riot" was the perfect musical accompaniment as they sheltered from the chaos outside.

Swordfish Records
66 Dalton Street, Birmingham, B4 7LX
0121 200 1521
Swordfish.co.uk; swordfishrecords@gmail.com; @SwordfishBham
Monday-Saturday 10am-5.30pm
Established 1979
Stock: Vinyl, CD, Pre-owned, Merchandise, T-shirts

Mike Caddick and Gareth Owen opened their first shop, Rockers, on Hurst Street, Birmingham in the summer of 1979, selling punk, post-punk and, later, New Romantic records. Rockers was more of a place for music lovers and local bands to hang out than a business. Soon after, they started a record label releasing records by bands they enjoyed, the most famous being by the Lilac Time. In 1995 they moved on to Needless Alley, a street of many trades with a watch repairer, a needlewoman, a stamp collector and a chip shop as neighbours. With these esoteric new premises, Rockers was renamed Swordfish Records and business picked up as CD sales soared. In 1996 more redevelopment of the city brought another move to new premises in Temple Street, and with the Britpop boom, times were good, with CD sales reaching an all-time high. Ten years on, with the music industry in turmoil, Swordfish was on the move again, this time to Dalton Street. The boys have certainly done their bit to support the local independent removal companies.

The shop is part of the Independent Birmingham scheme which gives customers 10% off all used vinyl and CDs in the shop. The scheme should be rolled out across every town and city in the UK. Membership costs only £12 and offers discounts at more than 80 of Birmingham's independent shops.

The Diskery

99-102 Bromsgrove Street, Birmingham, B5 6QB
0121 622 2219
thediskerymusic@gmail.com; thediskery.com
Monday-Saturday 9.30am-6pm
Established 1952
Stock: Vinyl, CD, Pre-owned, In-stores, Memorabilia

In 1952, Morris Hunting started a small jazz specialist shop The Diskery in Moor Street. It is the only shop I know of which was started as an act of revenge. Morris regularly purchased his 78-rpm records from a Birmingham record store called Mansell's until one day when, in front of a crowd of customers, the owner of Mansell's challenged him to open his coat. "Why?" Morris asked. "So that I can see how many records you're trying to steal," the owner responded. Morris was so angry that he vowed never to set foot in the store again. Not only that, when he came into some money – as compensation for being the innocent party in a road accident – he set up his own record shop as a direct competitor to Mansell's with the express intent of showing the customers of Birmingham how a store should treat its customers. The point was well made and while Mansell's is long gone, The Diskery continues to thrive.

In 1972, The Diskery moved to its current location on Bromsgrove Street. With an ever expanding and diversifying range of music and with new records imported directly from the USA, the shop went from strength to strength and soon became a popular haunt for local musicians to explore music and exchange ideas, including Robert Plant, UB40, Slade and Ranking Roger of the Beat. Many other artists have popped into The Diskery over the years, including ELO, Chaka Khan, Steve Winwood, Black Sabbath, Paul Barber, Joe Cocker, Jimmy Page and Winston Edwards.

Morris Hunting passed away in 2012. "Morris was a real legend in music in Birmingham," said the shop's manager at the time, Jimmy Shannon. "I do not think that the Birmingham music scene would have been anything like it became without this shop." Jimmy retired himself in 2015, whereupon the current owners Lee Dearn and Paul Dearn appointed Jimmy's assistant Liam Scully as manager.

"This has got to be the longest-ever stint as an apprentice," said Liam, who has worked at the shop for 44 years. What began as a part-time trial job when he was starting out as an art student looks like it is going to end as a life sentence.

I associate Liam with promotional T-shirts. You never see him wearing anything else. Back in the 1970s and 1980s, record company sales reps gave them away like confetti to record shop staff in order to curry favour. When the supermarkets started selling music, the record companies switched their promotional budgets to them and the T-shirts dried up. For some reason Liam didn't get the memo, and whenever I call into the shop his opening line is always "Got any T-shirts?" Although I seldom get given any to hand out these days, whenever I do, I always save one for Liam.

Posters from a bygone era adorn the shop's walls, including original Beatles, Elvis Presley and Eddie Cochran material, and the shop has an amazing collection of memorabilia, including wind-up gramophones, copies of *Melody Maker* dating from 1947, Matchbox cars and photographs from the *Carry On* movies. It stocks more than 100,000 vinyl records, of which 12,000 are 78s, with 7 inch discs starting from 10p. If a vinyl fan cannot find something to buy here, they are probably best advised to take up another hobby. To top it off, an endless supply of free tea entices customers to stay and browse for hours in this wonderful record shop. Since Lee and Paul have taken over the business, they have dramatically increased the amount of new vinyl they stock, and have started to host gigs in the shop. Named as one of the five most treasured record shops in the UK by the BBC, The Diskery is a must-visit destination.

Vinyl & Vintage
5a Cleveland Street, Wolverhampton, West Midlands WV1 3HL
07760 168972
vinylandvintage.net
Monday-Saturday 10am-5pm
Established 2012
Stock: Vinyl, Pre-owned, CD, 7-inch singles, Autographs,
Cassettes, Memorabilia, T-Shirts

Claire Howell has been selling vinyl and memorabilia for more than 30 years, starting out at record fairs and online at the birth of eBay. She found selling via the internet lacked the personal touch, so took the bold move of opening her own shop, before moving to a larger location in 2018. If you're on the hunt for that long-forgotten format known as the laser disc, then this is the shop for you.

Wiltshire

A few years back, Sound Knowledge was the only independent record shop in the county. Recently a whole host of outlets have opened on the back of the vinyl revival. For Elton John fans, a must-visit is Vinyl Collectors & Sellers in Salisbury, where the selection of recordings by this legendary singer is unrivalled.

Red House Records (inside Holmes Music)
21, Faringdon Road, Swindon, Wiltshire SN1 5AR
01793 5263972
redhouserecords.co.uk; info@redhouserecords.co.uk; @Red_RecordsUK
Monday-Saturday 9am-5.30pm
Established 2013
Stock: Vinyl, Pre-owned, Musical Instruments

A vinyl obsessive, who was eager to expand his family's musical instrument business Holmes Music, Paul Holmes opened Red House Records after HMV announced the closure of its Swindon branch. HMV unexpectedly reopened soon afterwards, but according to Ian, Red House Records remains "a cocoon of vinyl warmth" for the connoisseur with a distinct but complementary identity from the musical instrument superstore in which it is housed.

Sound Knowledge
22 Hughenden Yard, Marlborough, Wiltshire SN18 1LT
01672 511106
@SoundKnowledge_
Monday-Saturday 9am-7pm
Sunday 11am-4pm
Established 1995
Stock: Vinyl, CD, In-stores

Roger Mortimer, owner of Sound Knowledge, is a Wiltshire lad, born in Melksham in 1959. He tuned into music at a young age, having an older brother and sister, and spent his early years listening to their musical purchases, including the Beatles, the Stones and Otis Redding. The listening habit developed during summer holidays spent at his hippy sister's village house, where he had access to a huge record collection to while away the time.

On leaving school he pursued a career as a thatcher in the New Forest and started an apprenticeship in the summer of 1976, one of the hottest on record. Thatched roofs were burning down all over the forest, so work was plentiful. Roger loved the job and could picture this as his future career, but there were problems. One was the distance he was travelling each day on his trusty moped. Secondly, on the apprentice wages of £11 per week, it proved difficult to make ends meet.

Roger found himself constantly clashing with his boss, a grizzled west country yokel who didn't appreciate his laid-back, hippy attitude. Roger began to think that thatching wasn't for him. The final straw (forgive the pun) was when his moped broke down, leaving him stranded in the middle of nowhere.

He landed a new job at Wessex Records, an independent shop in Bath which was later bought out by Rival Records, and more recently became a Fopp store. The shop at that time was run by two elderly women Mrs Gallop (who was the wife of the mayor) and Mrs Gumption. While both of them knew their Elvis, neither of them knew much about the cutting edge of music, so young Roger brought a bit of youth and enthusiasm to the shop. Both women were chain smokers and Roger remembers having to peer through a misty haze to see the far end of the shop. The two women never quite grasped punk, and Roger recalls Mrs Gallop removing a youth from the shop after he asked if she had the Snivelling Shits: not a medical malady, as she evidently thought he meant, but the punk band fronted by Giovanni Dadamo, who later became a respected music journalist.

Bath as a city had yet to embrace punk and the shop received a visit from the local constabulary shortly after displaying a copy of the Sex Pistols album *Never Mind the Bollocks* in the window. The day Elvis died, Roger recalls the women in tears for most of the day. His relationship with them was not improved after Roger made the observation that the King's current single "Way Down" was a suitable epitaph, as that was where he was heading. A year or so later, Roger resigned as the daily commute to Bath (by now on a Suzuki 120, not much more reliable) was becoming tiresome, and he took up an invitation to take an extended holiday to the USA.

Upon his return Roger worked in a flat-pack furniture manufacturing company called Dreamscape, a place he describes as not a dream but a nightmare. He spent a lot of his wages in the local record store, PR Sounds, where he got to know the owner Pete Randall who suggested could have a job vacancy coming up. Roger took some more time out for travelling. After two years doing a variety of odd jobs in France, he returned to Wiltshire and paid a visit to PR Sounds, where he was greeted with the words "Are you still interested in that job?"

Pete started immediately and in due course Pete appointed him manager of a new shop that he was preparing to open in Devizes about 20 miles east of Bath. Pete and Roger spent weeks getting the store ready, purchasing stock and preparing for the shop opening. As the big day approached a hard blizzard and sub-zero temperatures hit the county. Pete arrived at the new shop opened the door and saw a bunch of LPs floating out on a torrent of water. The pipes had burst and the men spent the first day working in freezing conditions, trying to repair the damage and sort out an insurance claim.

Roger thought things could not get worse, until he received a call from his landlord to tell him that the pipes had also burst in the house he was renting. Furthermore, the landlord was holding Roger responsible for not having kept the flat warm enough, and summarily evicted him. He refused to give Roger his deposit back, saying he was keeping it to pay for the damage. Pete graciously allowed Roger to stay in the room above the shop in Devizes until he got himself sorted out. He stayed working in the shop and living above it for the next 15 years.

Pete eventually opened his own record shop in Marlborough, the town with a famous college once attended by Nick Drake, where some of his earliest songs were written. The opening day was an improvement on the disaster that struck the previous shop in Devizes, but not by much. With the store due to open at 9am, he was delighted to see a gentleman already eager to come in. Roger opened the door and proudly informed him that he was the shop's first customer. "I'm no customer," the man replied. He was in fact from the Performing Rights Society (PRS) and had come to check there was a licence to play music at the premises. Roger had to pay up before he had played or sold a single record. The next visitor was an elderly chap who approached the counter to tell Roger that the shop was doomed. "This part of town has had so many failed businesses, they should change the name from Hughenden Yard to Grave Yard," he said. Roger thanked the merchant of doom and asked how he could be of assistance.

"Oh, I've not come down to buy anything," he said. "I thought I would just let you know that your business has no chance of succeeding here."

Mr. Happy couldn't have got it more wrong. Sound Knowledge has thrived. The shop has become a firm favourite with the students at Marlborough College. It has been trading for more than twenty years and become a gathering place for music lovers far and wide. Punters travel from miles around to attend the free in-store events and personal appearances which they regularly put on. These are held in the café/bar next door to the shop, and the small stage there has been graced by Ed Sheeran, Newton Faulkner, Tom Odell (plus baby grand piano), Scouting for Girls, the Pretty Things, Ethan Johns, Turin Brakes and the shop's favourite Nick Harper. They do brisk business with signings after the performances.

Located in a market town in the depths of Wiltshire, the shop seldom picks up the publicity it deserves. If it were based in London, it would be a media favourite. Sound Knowledge is the perfect independent record store.

Top tip - When entering the shop, it appears as if it is all on one floor. In the far-left hand corner is a beautiful spiral staircase that leads up to a loft studio space that is full of vinyl.

Vinyl Collectors And Sellers *Note for Elton John: call in when in Wiltshire*
Unit 11, Cross Keys Arcade, Salisbury, Wiltshire SP1 1EY
01722 410660 info@vinylcollectorsandsellers.com;
vinylcollectorsandsellers.wordpress.com; @vcands
Monday-Thursday 9am-5.30pm Friday-Saturday 9am-6pm Sunday 10am-4pm
Established 2016
Stock: Vinyl, CD, Pre-owned, Books, DVD, Memorabilia, Posters, T-shirts

The first thing I noticed when walking into Vinyl Collectors And Sellers is the large black sign painted on the wall proclaiming, "We Love Vinyl". However, the owner Paul Smith needs to change it to "We Love Vinyl and Elton John". No other record shop in the world can have such an incredible collection of Elton-related product and memorabilia. Besides vinyl and CDs, the shop sells Elton-themed posters, concert programmes, T-shirts, photographs, 8-track cartridges (once a rival to cassettes), stamps and scarves. Pride of place goes to four large-size, 70-page books in which Paul keeps all the press cuttings he has collected of Elton since he became a fan, at eight years-old, after watching him perform on the Royal Variety Show. These books are a great read. If you ask Paul, he will be delighted to let you look through them as he is always happy to share his appreciation of Elton.

Paul's personal Elton collection extends to more than 400 CDs and 300 pieces of vinyl. This includes many alternative versions of the same titles, either pressed in different countries, or bearing slightly different track-listings. The rarest item is a CD recording from 1990 of a private concert on a boat called The Siran which Elton gave for his family and friends. Only 50 copies were manufactured, each of which was numbered. Paul has copy No.9.

Paul has been to more than 70 Elton concerts, including twice flying out to New York to see him play at Madison Square Garden. As well as running a Facebook group, Paul was the subject of an episode of the TV programme *Collectors' Lot* where he displayed items from his Elton collection. He is also an expert on Elton's early recording career, which involved the superstar-to-be singing on many budget compilation albums such as the *Chartbusters*, *Hot Hits* and *Top of the Pops* series, featuring Top 40 hits re-recorded by nameless soundalike performers. These albums were called "budget compilations" for good reason. They were cheaply produced, cheaply recorded, and cheaply sold, displayed on early-1970s spinner racks in shops like Boots for 49p each.

The first budget compilation, *Hits 67*, was released on the Music for Pleasure (MFP) label. In 1968 the first of the *Top of the Pops* cover version albums was released, a series that became almost as well known for its notoriously naff glamour model artwork, as for the clunky cover versions of the songs. MFP responded by changing the name of its series to *Hot Hits*, and hiring its own scantily-clad models. The standard of the covers varied greatly. Some were laughable, while others sounded impressively like the original versions. Elton's covers were generally among the best.

These budget compilation albums sold in massive quantities. Three of them made it to No.1 in the UK album chart in 1971 alone. And they caused immense disappointment to children of my generation. I recall waking up on Christmas Day to discover I had been given one of these albums. I excitedly opened it and rushed downstairs to put it on the record player. My disappointment upon hearing the songs I loved to hear on the radio reduced to a low-grade karaoke experience, was no doubt repeated thousands of times up and down the country as parents and older relatives bought these records for children, thinking they were purchasing the original versions.

Thankfully, the plug was pulled on the budget labels in 1972 when Arcade and K-Tel began licensing original songs from the record companies, and issuing them on TV-advertised compilation albums. Arcade's *20 Fantastic Hits* and K-Tel's *20 Dynamic Hits* both went to No.1. The public clearly preferred the original versions of songs.

This practice belied a staggering incompetence on the part of the record labels which, instead of releasing their own product themselves, were licensing it out to third parties. It took more than 10 years before the penny finally dropped with the launch in 1983 of the *Now That's What I Call Music* series. Since shortened to *Now*, it has become the most popular compilation series in the history of recorded music, even spawning its own TV channel where you can watch videos of the songs featured on the albums.

Elton John's cover versions were compiled for an album titled *Chartbusters Go Pop*. I am sure you can purchase a copy from Paul, who is such an expert on this subject that he once did a two-hour radio show talking about the album and playing tracks from it.

There is a good chance that when you walk in to Vinyl Collectors And Sellers, Paul will be playing *Tumbleweed Connection*. He rates this album, released in 1970, as a masterpiece even though it contains no hit singles. *Rolling Stone* magazine shares his view, rating it at No.458 in their Greatest Albums of All Time list. Paul has sold dozens of copies just by playing it in the shop. Customers who ask him what is playing are almost certain to end up purchasing a copy, once they have been exposed to Paul's passion for the record.

Vinyl Collectors And Sellers is not *all* about Elton John. Paul has an excellent range of stock with the vinyl elegantly displayed in wooden crates. Painted white, the shop looks clean, bright and airy. Paul likes nothing better than chatting about music with his customers. He is also a natural salesman. On my last visit there, the postman called in to drop off some mail and left a few minutes later having purchased an album.

Paul's background is in construction, but he was always an enthusiastic record collector. He packed in his job to open his own record shop in 2016 and has not had a moment of regret since.

Elton John has been a massive supporter of record shops all his life, and used to work at One Stop Records in London during the 1960s. In 2017, Elton was appointed as Record Store Day Ambassador. If there is one record shop that would appreciate his attention more than any other, he will find it tucked in between TK Maxx and the Skate Shop in an arcade in Salisbury.

Vinyl Realm

52 Long Street, Devizes, Wiltshire SN10 1NP
07502 332327
Tuesday-Saturday 9.30am-5pm
Established 2018
Stock: Vinyl, Pre-owned, Turntables

After 20 years, I am pleased to report the historic town of Devizes has a record shop again. Pete and Jackie Bennett are the owners of Vinyl Realm which specializes in second-hand vinyl records including, rare, deleted and collectable records across a wide range of genres. They recently converted the basement to enable them to stock more vinyl.

Yorkshire

Sheffield once had a thriving independent record shop scene. But from the 1990s onwards it has suffered a steady decline, leaving the legendary Record Collector to fight the good fight on its own. The city is however returning to its former glories with a host of new shops opening in recent years. The long-established shops in Leeds, Crash and Jumbo, are two of the best record shops in the UK.

The county still has many towns that could accommodate a new record shop. Bridlington and Whitby are places where a vinyl café could thrive. A two-day trip around the county incorporating the shops of Leeds and Sheffield, including detours for refreshments at Muse Music in Hebden Bridge and The Record Café in Bradford, would be a perfect weekend break.

Bear Tree Records

Unit 13-16, The Forum, 127 Devonshire Street, Sheffield, South Yorkshire S3 7SB
01142 751309
beartreerecords.com; blackestrainbow@googlemail.com; @beartreerecords
Monday-Tuesday 10am-5.30pm Thursday-Friday 10am-6pm Saturday 10am-5pm
Sunday 12.30pm-3.30pm
Established 2015 Stock: Vinyl

Joe Blanchard had worked at two of the most famous record shops in the UK, Nottingham's Selectadisc and Sheffield's Record Collector, before deciding it was time to open his own shop. His approach at Bear Tree Records is to keep the stock fresh and to support new music. His biggest problem, to begin with, was lack of space.

When the shop next door, which was three times the size, became vacant, Joe launched a crowdfunding project to raise the funds necessary to expand into it. A £5 contribution was rewarded with a random record; £20 got you a T-shirt; and for greater amounts there was a subscription scheme whereby customers would receive a record every month at a discounted rate. A contribution of £100 was worth 10% off all purchases for a year. Joe raised £2,000 in less than 48 hours and achieved his £4,000 target in less than a week, a result which reaffirms how much love the public have for record shops. In the summer of 2018, he relocated again to an even bigger shop.

Black Slab Records

22 Milbank Terrace, Redcar, North Yorkshire TS10 1ED
07590 590735 blackslabrecords.com;blackslab@protonmail.com
Tuesday-Saturday 10am-5pm Sunday 11am-3pm
Established 2016 Stock: Vinyl, Pre-owned, Art, Footwear, Menswear
Also, at 20, Baker Street, Middlesbrough, North Yorkshire TS1 2LH

Black Slab Records is part-vinyl record shop and part-fashion shop, incorporating some fabulous memorabilia from the Teesside steelworks. Closed in 2015 with the loss of 4,000 jobs, the steelworks were the town's major employer. Founded in 1917, the steel was used in the construction of the Tyne, Sydney Harbour and Auckland Harbour bridges.

Mark Stubbs, a postman at the time of closure, felt it was important to keep the memory of the plant alive, and approached the receivers to ask if he could purchase some of the fixtures and fittings. As much of it was going to be dumped or recycled, they were happy to sell to him, and many items have been incorporated into the design of Black Slab Records. Others are available for sale alongside the vinyl and clothing.

The shop is named in honour of the steelworks; black steel slabs is what they produced. Thousands of singles are stored in beautiful steel drawers painted green. When Mark obtained them, each drawer contained 3000 negatives. The counter and walls are made from recycled wood from the steelworks, and the shop also uses light fixtures, clocks and hat stands from the plant. Displayed on the wall are pictures and photographs of the steelworks in its prime which are thought-provoking and moving. The shop attracts many ex-steelworkers, who presume that Mark worked at the plant.

There is one album that does particularly well at Black Slab Records: *Steeltown*, the 1984 album by Scottish rockers Big Country.

Bug Vinyl   *The shop with the best view*
11, Ladygate, Beverley, East Yorkshire HU17 8BH
01482 887293
nh52bug@yahoo.co.uk; @bugvinylrecords
Thursday-Saturday 9.30-6pm Established 2016
Stock: Vinyl, Pre-owned

Driving into Beverley in May on the road from York, the grass verges are full of beautiful yellow flowers. Just before the town you pass the racecourse on one side of the road and a stunning pond on the other. I was delayed a few minutes as I waited for hundreds of cows to cross the road.

Like the town, Bug Vinyl is an undiscovered gem. Overlooked by the tower of the stunning St Mary's church, it has the best view of any record shop I have visited.

Neil Harris has spent his career opening shops on behalf of others. He worked for Diesel, Toys "R" Us and Staples, where his job was to find suitable locations to open new shops. Taking redundancy from Staples gave him the opportunity to find a location for himself. He found a perfect setting in a lane just off the market square in a building that had previously been an independent craft beer shop.

The town has a large Tesco. It was bad news for the independent beer shop when the superstore embraced a greater selection of craft beer. With lower prices due to supermarket buying power, the writing was on the wall for the craft beer shop. It was a scenario played out many times for independent record shops during the last 25 years, as supermarkets used the incentive of selling cheap CDs to entice shoppers into the store. Fortunately for record shops (if not for independent off-licences) the supermarkets have moved on to other consumer goods to attract shoppers.

This is a delightful shop to visit. With a distinctive red brick exterior, it is painted black with a window box full of flowers above the shop's sign. The shop spans two floors with ancient wooden beams confirming the impression that you are buying vinyl in a historic location. The stand out feature is a counter that looks like a giant radio. Housed on top is a record deck where Neil sits to play the vinyl. Although some distance from other record shops, it is worth making the extra effort to visit Bug Vinyl.

Crash Records

35 The Headrow, Leeds, West Yorkshire LS1 6PU
0113 2436743
crashrecords.co.uk; crash_records@hotmail.com; @Crash_Records
Monday-Saturday 9.30-6pm Sunday 11am-4pm
Established 1985. Stock: Vinyl, CD, Pre-owned, Merchandise, In-stores, Tickets

Crash Records is owned by ex-Sony sales rep Ian De-Whytell. It opened originally in Woodhouse Lane before moving to a prime shopping location on The Headrow in Leeds city centre. Ian is an avid supporter of Leeds United. One of his first musical introductions was when his parents bought him "Back Home" by England's 1970 World Cup squad. The record was constantly on the record player along with the B-side "Cinnamon Stick". The first record Ian bought with his own money was "School's Out" by Alice Cooper and, many years later when he became a sales rep for Sony, he was delighted to be introduced to Alice backstage at Birmingham NEC.

Ian obtained his first album, *Ziggy Stardust* by David Bowie, in a most unusual way. Leeds had a record shop called Scene And Heard, owned by Len Lyons, and each Saturday in the *Yorkshire Evening Post* they ran a competition called Len's Ten. The paper would print the 10 best-selling singles in Len's shop, and the reader was invited to guess what the following week's Top 10 would be. Young Ian sent his entry on a postcard and correctly predicted nine out of 10. He was thrilled not only to see his name printed in the paper but to receive a record token to spend at Len's where he obtained his beloved *Ziggy Stardust* album, which he still plays more than 40 years later. Len's Ten became an obsession with young Ian and over the next two years he won the competition 15 times, rapidly expanding his record collection in the process.

After leaving school Ian worked at the Leeds Permanent Building Society. Although he enjoyed the work he found himself looking at the clock, longing for his lunch break which he invariably spent trawling around the record shops of Leeds, spending his wages on an ever-expanding record collection.

One of his favourite shops was Virgin, where he landed the job of assistant manager. He had some fabulous times at Virgin but nothing to top the drama of the day Motorhead turned up for a personal appearance in the shop.

Leeds city centre could be an intimidating place on Saturday afternoons in the 1980s. Gangs of punks, skinheads, mods and rockers would roam the city and often clash. On the day Motorhead showed up Leeds United were playing Manchester United, fans were drinking in the city pubs in advance of the game, and the atmosphere was like a tinderbox. Ian was beginning to think this was the worst timed personal appearance in the history of personal appearances. The event was held on the first floor and by the time Lemmy and the boys arrived, the queue was jam-packed up the stairs, out of the shop and halfway around the block. Lemmy was swigging from a bottle of Jack Daniels and Ian was sent outside to check on the crowd. The atmosphere was tense as the queue was moving so slowly, not helped by many fans copying their hero and swigging alcoholic drinks. The band was quite happy to take time talking to each fan, not realising they had another five hundred to see. Soon a heavy police presence surrounded the crowd and Ian was pulled aside by the commanding officer and told that unless he sorted the situation out, the police would arrest him. Ian did his best to placate the crowd and got Motorhead to speed up the signing to a pace that was sufficient for him to avoid being arrested.

Jumping ship in the 1980s, Ian took a job at Virgin's rival HMV. He found the move to be quite a culture shock. HMV were far more professional and proactive than Virgin. Everything at HMV was target-based and there was pressure all the time to increase sales.

In the 1980s HMV expanded quickly. Ian was given a pay rise and sent to work as an assistant manager in Manchester in an even bigger store. The shop would buy vast quantities of newly-released singles and Ian and co-buyer Derek would often have heated debates on how many copies of a new release they should purchase. Ian was a big fan of Elvis Costello who, under the pseudonym The Imposter, released "Pills and Soap", a single which was an attack on the changes in British society brought on by Thatcherism, brought out to coincide with the run-up to the 1983 UK general election.

Derek was cautious, but Ian was confident the record would shift vast quantities. As usual, Derek was right, and after the election, which Margaret Thatcher won easily, nobody was interested in buying the record, leaving the shop with a lot of stock. One lunchtime Elvis Costello himself came into the shop, and started browsing through the LP racks. Ian asked the singer if he would sign a few singles - not mentioning that this was as a last resort to get rid of them. Elvis obliged, and what was once an overstocked item sold out in the next few hours.

Here was an object lesson in the importance of getting records signed as a way to generate sales. When a young Mancunian band started receiving praise from the media, Ian contacted Rough Trade, the band's label, to request some signed copies of the band's forthcoming album. Rough Trade obliged and sent 50 autographed copies of the Smiths debut album. Ian now wishes he had bought a few for himself, as they are probably worth a fortune now. He did keep one copy, which is framed and takes pride of place above his fireplace.

Ian went on to manage his own store in Hull before securing a job as a sales rep at Sony. Ian is full of praise for the way that Sony looked after their staff. He recalls works outings to see Bruce Springsteen and getting the best seats in the house for Rolling Stones concerts, plus a football trip to Wembley to see England beat Holland 4–1.

The highlight of the Sony years was when he attended the first Michael Jackson concert at Roundhay Park in Leeds. There was a special backstage area for Sony staff and guests, and before the start of the gig the legendary Epic PR man Jonathan Morrish wandered over to say that Michael was keen to have some children dancing with him on stage for the encore. So it was that towards the end of the show in front of 70,000 fans, Ian's 12-year-old sister Rachel and half a dozen other volunteers were ushered through to the backstage area. Ian remembers Michael Jackson coming on stage for the encore holding his little sister's hand. There wasn't a prouder big brother in the world at that moment.

Sony often ran competitions among the sales team. One of these was that whoever exceeded their target by the highest percentage on the new Midnight Oil album *Diesel and Dust* would win a holiday in Australia. Ian was determined to win. To say that he exaggerated the sales potential of the album was an understatement and shop buyers in his area were given the firm impression that this album would be the Australian *Sgt. Pepper*. Ian won the competition by a mile, achieving sales 1,400% over budget. The second-best performance was from a rep who gained a 500% improvement. Ian was called into head office, expecting to receive his prize. Instead he received a serious telling off from his bosses who felt that to win by that margin he must have oversold the album (which he had) and that Sony were soon likely to be inundated with shops wishing to return unsold copies (which they were). Ian was gutted and felt that it was just an excuse to avoid the expense of sending him to Australia.

The Midnight Oil album sold below expectations, although it did produce the Top 10 single "Beds are Burning". For the next two years Ian would visit his customers and hear the familiar cry "When am I going to get my returns note for this Midnight Oil album?" It did teach Ian a valuable lesson; not to oversell an album, as it certainly strained his relationship with a few of his customers.

After 12 years at Sony, Ian took voluntary redundancy. He released a Leeds United greatest hits CD as a joint venture with his friend Kevin Smith - a resounding success which sold around 20,000 copies - before buying Crash Records from his old friend Steve Mulhaire.

Crash was an exciting new challenge. He had called on the shop every week when he was a Sony rep, so it was exciting to be able to implement his ideas to improve sales. He was lucky insofar as in 1987 Leeds had three great independent record shops all vying for trade: Way Ahead, Jumbo and Crash. Within a few weeks of Ian purchasing the shop, Way Ahead closed, leaving Crash and Jumbo to pick up the extra business. This included gig ticket sales, which have since proved to be vitally important to the ongoing success of the two remaining independent retailers in Leeds.

He credits his long-serving manager Paul Hodgson for being a great buyer who instinctively knows what will sell in the shop, and the fact that over the last few years they have doubled the space given over to vinyl and are looking to allocate even more.

A few years ago, Crash had a basement sales area dedicated to dance music, and in the early years of his time at the shop this was probably the most profitable area of the business, but that started to decline and was gradually closed. In its heyday, it attracted many of the local DJs and several of the Leeds United team. The most frequent football-playing visitor to the shop was Rio Ferdinand. Rio used to park his Ferrari outside the front door, blissfully unconcerned about parking tickets, and head downstairs for his regular fix of music.

Leeds is a university city and the shop is popular with students. Ian has found that when they move away from home for the first time they like to check out the cool bars, and the cool shops, and thus tend to embrace independent rather than mainstream record shops. The gig tickets which the shop sells not only bring customers into the shop, but also give Crash a presence on all the advertising by the local music venues.

In 2015 Elliot Smaje, who owned the record shop Wall Of Sound in Huddersfield, moved his vast vinyl stock into the basement of Crash, giving vinyl fans another reason to visit this wonderful record shop.

Earworm Records

1 Powells Yard, Goodramgate, York, North Yorkshire YO1 7LS
01904 627488
earwormrecords.co.uk; earwormrecordsyork@gmail.com; @EarwormRecords
Monday-Saturday 10am-6pm
Established 2013. Stock: Vinyl, CD, Pre-owned, Tickets, T-Shirts

Specialising in house, techno, disco, hip hop, indie, soul, dub and reggae, Earworm Records manages to cram a lot of stock into this historic building, yet still looks neat and tidy. If you do not know where this tiny shop co-owned by local DJs Paul Jackson and Richard Clark is located, it is a challenge to find. Walk down Goodramgate until you arrive at the Snikleway Inn, and then turn down the little alley. There is a little green sign pointing the way to Earworm Records. Keep walking until you see the green park bench which is stationed outside the shop, by which time you will be hearing the music that let's you know you have arrived. So many people have trekked around York trying to find them that the owners have made a video, posted on the shop's Facebook page, with a step-by-step guide on how to locate the shop. Treat it like a treasure hunt. You are sure to be rewarded when you get there.

The shop is housed in a listed building originating in 1410 and featuring wooden beams from that period. Upstairs the shop sells pre-owned hi-fi equipment, but you need to be nimble to check it out. One of the ancient beams goes through two opposite walls and is three feet off the ground. To look at all the product you need to either go under it or climb over it. Even more awkward to view is another upstairs room, crammed full of second-hand retro record carrying cases. To access it you need to clamber under a door only four feet tall. If you are on the tall side, be prepared to crawl through.

Richard told me of the day a young man told him that his budget record player had broken. Richard showed him the range of second-hand hi-fi they stocked and explained that the sound quality would be far superior to playing vinyl on a budget player. He sold him a system for £200 and was thrilled when he received a phone call from the young man, thanking him for his recommendation. "I never knew vinyl could sound that good" was his memorable quote.

Over my 30 years of visiting record shops, staff have told me many tales of less than appealing customers, such as the man who kept a £10 note under his false teeth, which he removed before handing over the soggy note to pay for his purchase. Richard told me of a woman who came in to sell a collection of vinyl. Sweat was pouring down her brow and Richard was trying to work out if she was selling the vinyl to buy drugs or was just very ill. The woman removed one of her shoes, then her sock and proceeded to use it to wipe the sweat off her face. Richard was pleased to buy her collection though he hesitated when she held her hand out to shake on the deal. The second she was out the shop he went to the bathroom to give his hands a thorough scrubbing.

The owners have done a great job at Earworm. They started by selling off their own record collections, before stocking new dance-related vinyl. Most of their profits are ploughed back into expanding the range, so the shop now has a varied collection of stock appealing to all vinyl fans.

Grind And Groove Records *The night when hundreds of men were "in Knikkers"*
59b Cavendish Street, Keighley, West Yorkshire BD21 3RL
01535 609626
grindandgrooverecords.com
Tuesday-Saturday 10am-6pm Sunday 10am-5pm
Established 2017. Stock: Vinyl, Pre-owned, Art, Coffee

It is a scenic trip across the moors to visit Keighley, a town more associated with rugby league than record shops. Grind And Groove Records is a small emporium with a fascinating history, run by Gareth and Kerry Beck. It used to be a lady's hosiery shop called Corsets and upstairs to the side of the building was a nightclub called Knikkers.

On December 19, 1977, the Sex Pistols played Knikkers as part of their *Never Mind the Bans* tour. Locals tell of Sid Vicious throwing pints of beer off the balcony on to the street below. Nearly every male over 50 in the town claims to have been at the gig, although it is hard to imagine hundreds of Keighley's menfolk "in Knikkers" that night.

The shop has a fine collection of Sex Pistols vinyl and memorabilia and is highly recommended for fans of the band. The shop has a fabulous collection of second-hand vinyl and will clean your records.

Jumbo Records
1-3 Merrion Centre, Leeds, West Yorkshire LS2 8NG
0113 245 5570
jumborecords.co.uk; info@jumborecords.co.uk; @JumboRecords
Monday-Thursday 9.30am-5.30pm
Friday-Saturday 9am-5.30pm,
Sunday 11am-5pm
Established 1971
Stock: Vinyl, CD, Books, Exclusive Jumbo T-shirts, In-stores, Magazines, Tickets

Adam Gillison, manager of Jumbo Records describes the shop as "A place where people explore their passion for music and meet other people who share that passion. Hopefully people come here and get the sense of adventure and fun from music that we do."

Jumbo Records was established by Hunter Smith, who took the name and logo from his successful disco and DJ business called Jumbo Mobile Discotheque. In the early days, Jumbo mainly sold singles including the big hits of the day, imports and all the latest soul and reggae releases. People would call by to ask for the tunes they had heard on previous evenings, and DJs were encouraged to purchase their records in the store. By late 1973 a full-time member of staff was required to help serve the increasing flow of customers. Enter Trevor Senior, who still works in the shop, being the senior member of the team. Soon after, Hunter's partner Lornette joined the business to help at weekends.

A move to the Merrion Centre was completed in 1974 a couple of years before punk took off. Jumbo was in the right place at the right time. The shop broadened the range of genres it stocked, becoming the hip place in Leeds for recorded music.

In 1988, with more space required, they moved to the St Johns Centre, where they remained for almost 30 years. In 2014 Hunter and Lornette took a well-deserved retirement after having guided Jumbo through good times and bad. They left the business in good shape despite all the difficulties surrounding music retail in the early part of the millennium. They sold the shop to long-term customers Nick Fraser and Justinia Lewis and Jumbo began a new era, still guided by most of the staff who had worked so hard to maintain the shop's role in the Leeds music scene. In early 2017, that new era was consolidated by a move back to the Merrion Centre, the shop's current location.

The new shop is bigger and has a small stage for live performances and signings, and a seated area to relax and have a cup of coffee. There is a vast selection of vinyl and CDs that reflect the staff's wide musical interests, taking in rock, pop, indie, electronica, dance, reggae, country, soul, blues and folk music from around the world. The staff have a non-elitist approach, taking time for everyone, regardless of their musical tastes.

The shop prides itself on its connection to the local music scene, providing a focal point for new releases by local bands, as well as being a place where bands and promoters can advertise their gigs for free. It sells tickets for most of the local venues and many venues in the surrounding area. It is somewhere that a local band can walk in off the street with their home-produced CD or record and get it stocked without any grand media plan or marketing scheme behind it. For the shop's 45th anniversary in 2016, they teamed up with the Too Pure record label to release a 45rpm record of their own, featuring local bands Post War Glamour Girls and Menace Beach.

One of the secrets of surviving and prospering is creating links with other independent businesses. Jumbo shares ideas and skills with likeminded traders in Leeds and other record shops around the country. If all record shops keep doing that it should not only ensure that record shops continue in their role, but also that they can contribute to regenerating growth in the country's town centres.

Nick and Justinia have a dedicated team running the shop, with manager Adam Gillison and assistant Matt Bradshaw looking after the day-to-day supervision, and an extended group that includes full-time staff members Jack, Sarah-Jane, Marko and Melissa along with part-timers Trevor and Sally (a voice of common sense for 30 years at Jumbo).

Loafers Vinyl & Coffee *Please call in and purchase a "George" mug*
Rustic Level, The Piece Hall, Halifax, West Yorkshire HX1 1RE
07960 532371
loafersvinyl.co.uk; loafersvinyl@gmail.com; @loafersvinyl
Monday-Saturday 10am-5pm Sunday 11am-4pm
Established 2017
Stock: Vinyl, Pre-owned, Art, Coffee, Cake, "George" mugs, In-stores

The Piece Hall in Halifax is one of the most impressive buildings in the UK. This Georgian Grade 1 listed structure was constructed in 1779 as a great northern cloth hall where traders met to buy and sell cloth and wool. These days it is home to more modern traders including Loafers Vinyl & Coffee.

In 2014 the Piece Hall had closed for a £19 million renovation. The building is operated by The Piece Hall Trust who, upon re-opening, were keen to fill it with artisan, boutique and independent businesses.

Having been made redundant after working for the same insurance company for more than 20 years, Mark Richardson was delighted to be accepted as one of the inaugural traders for when The Piece Hall re-opened on Yorkshire Day (August 1), 2017. I doubt there is a record shop anywhere in the world housed in such a beautiful, historic location. Two floors of shops surround a central square where you will often notice tour groups learning about its fascinating history.

Mark told me about his first day of business which was a triumph in more ways than one.

"I arrived at The Piece Hall where the crowds were massive. I had friends, family, my children and partner Sarah (soon to be my fiancée, unknown to her) and what seemed like the whole population of Yorkshire queuing to get in. It was a phenomenal day for the town, the county and all the new businesses opening their doors at 10am that morning. The Piece Hall was reborn, and all the hard work, sleepless nights, planning and effort proved to be worth it. The response was unbelievable. As I dropped the needle on 'Green Onions' by Booker T. & The M.G.s, The Piece Hall came alive again. Loafers became a mass throng of activity, where I can only describe it as like a 10-hour gig. People loved the place and so did we. I don't think I could have dreamt for a better first day.

Throughout the day, I met so many great people who commented on how impressed they were with the vibe in Loafers and the selection of records, the quality of the coffee and, of course, the artwork, which flew out of the door. That evening, I asked Sarah if she'd marry me one day and she said yes. I couldn't really think of a better day or place to put the ring on her finger. Fortunately, she said yes and a week later, agreed to join me in Loafers as my partner. I need her for many reasons but mainly for her brains, business acumen and ability to change the till roll when we're under pressure."

The opening weekend, however, was tinged with sadness, as Mark's grandad passed away at the age of 86 before getting the opportunity to visit the shop. The same day that he died, a man of 83 called George came into Loafers for the first time. He became a regular customer, returning every Tuesday for coffee and cake. He was a big fan of Simon & Garfunkel, so when he came in Mark would play the harmony duo's records for him. Over time, George became a fixture at The Piece Hall, gaining celebrity status. He became a good friend and joined Mark and his family for Christmas dinner last year as he did not have any family or children of his own.

In March 2018, the shop received the sad news that George had passed away. In his memory Mark worked with an artist friend designing a mug, with George's face on the front, which you can purchase in Loafers. All the proceeds go to Age UK. It's a wonderful way to remember such a lovely gentleman who is also pictured on the shop's limited-edition Record Store Day poster.

Loafers has already hosted some interesting events, including a coffee-tasting evening, beer and vinyl and a monthly open mic and poetry night.

"I'm living the dream and I love it," Mark says. "I know my grandad and George will be proudly looking down on our shop and its success."

Muse Music (Incorporating the Love Café)
38 Market Street, Hebden Bridge, West Yorkshire HX7 6AA.
0142 284 3496
musemusicandthelovecafe.co.uk Wednesday-Saturday 11am-6pm
Established 1997. Stock: Vinyl, CD, Coffee, Food

Is there a quirkier town than Hebden Bridge? Once known as "Trouser Town" for the garments produced in the mills, it now has many claims to fame. It is where Ed Sheeran spent his formative years. It is the home of the canal-based Centre of Alternative Technology. It has a clown workshop, a shop that sells sculptured soap, a barber with his own art gallery and a dog café. And it has been declared "the lesbian capital of the UK". Little wonder that *The Guardian* rated Hebden Bridge as the coolest place to live in the country.

It also boasts the highest proportion of independent shops per capita. No Starbucks or Costa coffee outlets here; just independent cafés. But no town can be hip and cool without an independent record shop and it is doubtful Hebden Bridge would have won the award if it wasn't the home of Muse Music and the Love Cafe.

The shop, owned by Sid Jones and his wife Valeen, is a haven for rock fans. Sid can chat for ages and is always keen to play his recommendations. It is amazing that the shop is still there at all. In 2012 the nearby River Calder burst its banks and the town was flooded. Sid and Valeen were forced to spend thousands on flood prevention as no insurance company would take them on to protect against possible flooding in the future.

Six months after the flood, the shop re-opened to enormous goodwill. Now known as Muse Music incorporating The Love Café, it had become a winning combination of record shop and artisan coffee house with a 1960s psychedelic twist, and enjoyed three years of excellent trading. While many people believed The Love Café was inspired by Sid and Valeen's devotion to each other, it was in fact named after the American group Love, led by Arthur Lee, whose 1960s classic *Forever Changes* can often be heard playing in the shop.

Then it all happened again. Unprecedented rainfall on Boxing Day 2015 wrecked many homes and business in the town. Sid and Valeen had no time to empty the shop, and everything was ruined. The couple thought that was the end of their dream, but they hadn't reckoned with the spirit of Hebden Bridge and the love of the music industry.

An internet campaign organised by a customer, Hazel Draper, encouraged collectors to donate records to the shop. It was a massive success and music fans all over the country sent them stock. Many record companies also donated stock free of charge. A Just Giving page was set up online, which raised £500. Mal Campbell, who books the bands at the world-famous Hebden Bridge Trades Club, reached out to all his contacts, with the help of local journalist Ben Myers and poet Adelle Stripe.

First to respond was former Smiths drummer Mike Joyce, who sent rare signed albums by his iconic band. Bjork sent records with a handwritten letter of support. The organisers received signed records from Tracey Thorn, Franz Ferdinand, Sparks, Hot Chip, Enter Shikari and Pete Wylie. Meanwhile, Sid received daily multiple deliveries as record companies such as Heavenly, Domino, Proper Music, One Little Indian, Snapper and rock magazine *Mojo* send aid packages of vinyl rarities. These were sold at a record fair in the town, which raised an incredible £5,000. "There was no way we could not open after that," Valeen said. After four months of drying out and repairs, the shop reopened in April 2016. The people of the town love the café, and Sid and Valeen love the town.

The shop has had problems with some less knowledgeable fans of the Who. One chap came in asking for the record with the line about that boy who "sure plays a mean trombone". Another, seeing the album title The Who *Live in Leeds* expressed his surprise at the discovery that the band came from Yorkshire... until it was pointed out to him that it was a live album, not a description of their place of residence.

The Love Café has established a reputation for excellent coffee. But despite all the love and goodwill, Sid and Valeen are still paying off the debts incurred by the floods. Do your bit and make a diversion when travelling up the M62 between Manchester and Leeds, even if it is only to stop for a coffee. I would be surprised if you did not leave with some music too.

P&C Music
6 Devonshire Place, Skipton Road, Harrogate, North Yorkshire, HG1 4AA
01423 504035
pomp-and-circumstance.co.uk; peter@pomp-and-circumstance.co.uk;@
PandCMusic
Tuesday-Saturday 9.30am-5.30pm Established 1994
Stock: Vinyl, CD, Pre-owned

Founded by an ex-mayor of Harrogate, P&C Music was originally named Pomp and Circumstance, after the set of marches written by Sir Edward Elgar. Everyone will know one of them, thanks to the words "Land of Hope and Glory" which were added to it, much to Elgar's annoyance.

Peter Robinson was a customer of Pomp and Circumstance, which sold classical, jazz, easy listening and nostalgia. He bought the business in May 2010, whereupon he changed the name to P&C, moved to new premises with a better window display and immediately diversified. All genres of music are now represented on vinyl, CD and even 78rpm discs. On that subject, ask Peter to play a 78rpm record on the original 1930s portable gramophone which he keeps in the shop. "Is this a wind-up?" asked one customer. "No," Peter said. "It's the real thing."

For Record Store Day 2017 he hired a vacant premises next door - formerly a barber shop, which was still displaying the original opening times and prices – to accommodate the throng of people who would arrive. Despite the long queue, the music playing, and the shop now being crammed full of records, he still had three people enquiring about a haircut.

One customer asked Peter if had got any Steps. Although the 1990s band, featuring H, Faye and the gang, had just released a new album, Peter explained that he did not have anything in stock. The customer looked puzzled before explaining that he could not reach the albums on the top shelf and was requesting something he could stand on in order to reach them.

Peter showed his customer service skills when an elderly woman wandered into the shop looking upset.

"I've just lost my husband," she said, looking tearful. Peter sat her down and was doing his best to comfort her in this moment of need, when an elderly chap wandered past.

The woman did a double-take. "Eric!" she said. "Where have you been? Why didn't you meet me where we arranged?" Her "lost" husband had ended up in the record shop, as she had probably guessed all along.

Peter's favourite classical tale involves an elderly vicar who had ordered a recording by the English composer William Krotch. After a few weeks, the CD that Peter had ordered for him had still not arrived and he was getting a little impatient. He asked Peter if he could "prod the Krotch to make it come quicker".

"As beauty is in the eye of the beholder, good music is in the ear of the listener," says Peter, who prides himself on tracking down records for customers, and displays a sign stating "We will order anything on vinyl or CD".

A visit to P&C Music might make you feel as if you are in an episode of the TV soap *Casualty*. The shop is located near to Harrogate's police station, fire station and hospital, so the sound of sirens is never far away. Ask Peter to play his miniature musical box shaped like an old radiogram. It plays the theme to "Love Story", composed by Francis Lai. It is utterly charming, and Peter is delighted to show it to customers, who always want to buy it. Unlike everything else in the shop, it is not for sale.

Record Café

45-47 North Parade, Bradford, West Yorkshire BD1 3JH
0127 472 3143
therecordcafe.co.uk; info@therecordcafe.co.uk; @TheRecordCafe
Monday-Thursday 11am-11pm
Friday-Saturday 11am-12midnight
Sunday 12noon-11pm
[The record shop is only open until 6pm each day]
Established 2014
Stock: Vinyl, Tickets, Coffee, Ale and Ham

It was a visit to the BBC6 Music Festival in Manchester in February 2014 that gave Keith Wildman a glimpse into what the modern-day record shop could be. Many of the UK's top vinyl record shops had stalls there. Keith came away from the event determined to open a unique record shop in his home town of Bradford. He decided to combine his love of food, drink and music and distil it down to vinyl records, real ale and charcuterie. Just nine months after he had the idea, The Record Café opened its doors on Bradford's North Parade, alongside a couple of like-minded businesses who'd been paving the way to turn back the tide of Bradford's retail decline.

The building is on two floors, with the ground floor bar concentrating on ale. They have four rotating cask beers and seven craft keg lines, three of which are permanent, and around 50 different bottled and canned beers from the UK and around the world. You won't find shots, alcopops, fruit ciders, vodka or industrial lager here. Instead, they stock real cider and a carefully curated selection of single malt whiskies for the connoisseur, plus a growing range of specially selected gins, as well as a small but quality wine list. You can combine your drink with the finest Spanish cured meats available. Cheese, olives, bread, oil, sherry and all things charcuterie are available.

The menus are a nice touch, as they are attached to original album sleeves. Don't expect all classics, though: mine was attached to *Non-Stop Bacharach* by the Sunset

Festival Orchestra (whatever happened to them?).

On other tables menus were attached to albums by Bryan Ferry, Simon & Garfunkel and - one that was very apt for a shop that sells charcuterie - the Cure. It got me thinking of other artists whose album covers would be suitable for such a record shop: the Meat Puppets, Meatloaf, Lambchop and Captain Beefheart all seem apt. I had no joy thinking of bands with cheese in their name. The nearest I could get were Edam & the Ants, the Cheeses & Mary Chain and the Brie Gees (maybe you can do better).

Upstairs is the record shop. It is tastefully designed with paintings, by a local artist, of famous British comedians such as Bob Monkhouse and Tommy Cooper on the wall.

There is a comfy chair and a vinyl deck for customers to sit and listen to records before they buy. Keith has picked up some interesting artefacts, and it is the only record shop I know of that has a hog's head on the wall. Although it is a vinyl shop, it makes an exception for local bands, who have their CDs and vinyl displayed on a separate table.

When it opened, the shop was an instant hit. Being the only vinyl, ham and ale store in the country, it soon received plenty of media attention. The shop was placed in the final three of *The Telegraph and Argus*'s hospitality and leisure business of the year at their Bradford Means Business Awards in 2015, and recently won Bradford CAMRA's Pub of the Season for autumn 2015.

Nearly every record shop I have visited will say that the best ever day's trading for them was the previous Record Store Day. For Keith, though, the best ever trading day was February 15, 2015, the day that his beloved Bradford City played Sunderland for a place in the quarter finals of the FA Cup. The shop is located close to the Bradford City football ground at Valley Parade and a signed picture of the team hangs in the bar. They were on a glorious cup run and had already beaten premiership giants Chelsea.

The shop was packed full of fans from the moment they opened and – once the game was over - until closing time. The atmosphere was fantastic, with both sets of fans mixing happily. This was, as Lou Reed eloquently puts it, Keith's "Perfect Day". Not only did the Record Café enjoy it best day's takings ever, Bradford City won the match 2-0. (Sadly for Keith, the team was knocked out by Reading in the next round.)

Thanks to the Record Café's unique combination of wares, there have been several bemused customers who have thought that the records are just there for show. Keith's greatest satisfaction is when people who come in for a pint leave with a bag full of albums.

Keith was inspired to open his own record shop by Record Store Day and BBC Radio 6 Music. People thought he was mad to open a vinyl, ham and ale store. His initial plan was to open in time for Record Store Day 2015 but, in the event, the shop opened five months earlier. So it was a bit of a tear-in-the-eye moment for Keith when Record Store Day eventually came around and they had people queuing outside.

Keith's favourite saying is "If it is worth doing, do it well". The cheese, the ham, the bread and the olives are all top of the range. Combining it with vinyl to browse through ensures that a visit to the Record Café is a memorable experience. In 2017 The Record Café was named Bradford Pub of the Year by CAMRA.

Record Collector *Customer gives Public Enemy a lift to an arena gig*
233-235 Fulwood Road, Sheffield, South Yorkshire S10 3BA
01142 668493
recordcollectorsheffield.co.uk; recordcollector.1978@yahoo.co.uk; @RCSheffield
Monday-Saturday 10am-6pm
Established 1978
Stock: Vinyl, CD, Pre-owned, In-stores

Barry Everard is the music man of Sheffield, responsible for giving many bands a helping hand in the early days of their fledgling careers. Def Leppard, ABC, Human League, Pulp, Richard Hawley, Comsat Angels and Gomez are just some of them. Music suggested by Barry was used in Sheffield's most famous film, *The Full Monty*.

Barry has had his ups and downs over the last few years. He has found it increasingly difficult to make a reasonable profit, and many times has felt it is time to call it a day. Then he gets a regular customer coming up, giving him a big hug, saying how much he loves the shop and making him promise never to close it. Moments like that have persuaded him to carry on serving the good people of Sheffield.

"It's more than just making a living," Barry says. "It's a calling, it's something we're almost driven to do, and we feel a deep responsibility of doing the job right." Even so,

Barry insists that shoppers must understand that record shops are not charities. He bemoans the fact that so many people come into the shop, check their mobile, then tell him that the app they have got shows they can buy the same CD 48p cheaper from an online retailer. Barry has thousands of items that he is selling cheaper, though it can be difficult to convince people that the internet is not always the better option. Amazon has done a fantastic job of giving the impression that it cannot be beaten on price.

Barry has a saying which he bases his business practices on:
Prices are vanity
Margins for sanity
Prices for show
Margins are dough.

To survive today, record shops must have a presence online. Record Collector is doing great business, selling collectable vinyl online. What's more, the resurgence of vinyl has had new customers beating a path to its door, so much so that the shop is now taking more money on vinyl than CDs.

Another change has been the return of students. Sheffield is a university city and for many years the students were the core customers for Barry. When downloading came along, students embraced the new technology and the numbers buying physical product from him dwindled to a trickle. Now the students are back, shopping in the store for vinyl.

Barry is having a great time recommending records for students who now shop there. Nothing beats introducing somebody to an artist, and the next time they come into the shop, they say that artist is fantastic and ask what else you have by them. Vinyl customers are less price-sensitive than people who buy CDs and are prepared to pay for what has become a premium, collectable product.

The shop has provided many moments of record store humour.

A customer purchases a record by the Specials. The next day he brings it back, complaining that he didn't receive his gift as promised by the sticker on the album bearing the legend "includes 'Free Nelson Mandela'."

Another disgruntled customer brings back "Le Peur", a record by the famous French rock star Johnny Hallyday, demanding a refund because he is "singing in froggie".

One of Barry's regular customers, a Roxy Music fan called Robin, was hospitalized after suffering a brain haemorrhage. As he started coming out of the coma, one of the doctors revived him by patting his face and asking him "What's your name?"

"Virginia Plain," Robin responded, quoting the lyrical sign-off from the end of Roxy Music's first hit. "Oh dear, he thinks he's Virginia Wade," one of the nurses said. Robin has since made a full recovery.

Barry is surprised that some people in Sheffield get confused between a classic soul singer and a type of crumpet. Twice in his retailing career he has been asked for records by Wilson Pikelet.

The shop celebrated its 33-and-a-third birthday recently. Two of Sheffield's favourite sons, Richard Hawley and Martin Simpson, both sang at an unforgettable party to celebrate the occasion.

Another celebrity, Johnny Marr, came into the shop and brought a pile of vinyl albums to the counter. "Are you Barry?" he asked. "Yes I am," Barry replied. "I understand you are something of a legend in these parts," Johnny said. For Barry, it is moments like that which make the constant struggle to keep going worthwhile.

Record Collector became the scene of a story that has passed into popular folklore, when Barry pulled off a coup by arranging for American rap crew Public Enemy to do an in-store signing before their gig supporting the Prodigy at Sheffield Arena in November 2015. Arriving somewhat later than expected at the shop to find a large crowd waiting to greet them, the band were happy to chat and sign copies of the new album, but were far from finished when their taxi arrived to pick them up at 6pm. When they eventually emerged from the shop to set off for the gig, the taxi had disappeared.

With the band due on stage at 7.30 there was no time to waste. Barry asked local photographer Kevin Wells, who had been among the fans who had come to get his CD signed, if he could give the band a lift to Sheffield Arena. With Chuck D in the passenger seat and Flava Fav together with two of the band's crew crammed in the back of his Ford Focus, Kevin set off. Although the traffic was bad, Kevin knew all the short cuts, so they were making good time. Even so, the band's phones were constantly ringing with cries of "Where the hell are you?" among the more printable enquiries from the other end.

Kevin put on a CD of Queen's "Bohemian Rhapsody" and was amazed to discover that Public Enemy were fans of the song. As the voices rose to an operatic crescendo, he found himself living a *Wayne's World* moment for real with Public Enemy headbanging and singing along to the song - a sight that he will never forget seeing in his rear-view mirror.

Lewis Hamilton would have been impressed by Kevin's driving. They reached Sheffield Arena in less than 20 minutes, only to be stopped by a security guard who didn't believe that Public Enemy would turn up to their own show crammed in to the back of a Ford Focus. The rappers were eventually let through and, thanks to Kevin, they made it on to the stage just in time. They invited him to be their guest of honour for the evening, but Kevin had another gig of his own to go to that night – he was due to take photos of Scouting For Girls at another venue.

The story was dramatised in an episode of the Sky Arts TV series *Urban Myths*, in which the *Life on Mars* star Philip Glenister played the part of Kevin in a comic re-telling of the tale.

Barry is happy to offer words of wisdom based on his 40 years of experience selling vinyl:

"The best bit of advice I can give any new record shop is to trust your own judgement. I am called Record Collector as that is what I am. The shop is an extension of what was once a hobby. I always believed in vinyl and over the years amassed vast quantities of it as I was convinced that in years to come my hunches would pay off. What I did not see coming was the internet. That turned many of my vinyl hunches that cost me pennies, extremely profitable.

In the early 1970s, David Bowie's self-titled first album on Deram could be found as deletions in Woolworths for 49p. I bought every copy I saw. The electronics retailer Tandy started stocking records for a while. Somehow, they would obtain RCA deletions which they would clear out at 29p. I would take quantity of anything interesting.

I was in South Wales and called into a shop in Swansea on the day of release of the limited-edition LP Live at the Padget Rooms, Penarth *from local rockers Man. I knew only 1,000 had been pressed, yet this shop seemed to have about half the stock. I bought a box lot for £1 each.*

In Sheffield we had a motor parts dealer selling deleted and overstock vinyl. A lot of it was on John Peel's Dandelion record label. Artists such as Gene Vincent, Kevin Coyne and Clifford T. Ward were on sale for 29p. I bought as much as I could. A few weeks later they cleared out what was left for 15p. It was time to have a second bite of the cherry.

Many vinyl fans in Manchester will recall Global Records. They were housed in a huge warehouse and would import vinyl from the USA. Prices were between 29p and 79p and you could pick up artists such as Neil Young, Frank Zappa, 13th Floor Elevators and thousands more. I was one of their best customers so would often be offered even lower prices.

Of course, you always think about the one that got away as opposed to the hundreds of brilliant deals I did. For me it was when Global offered me 200 Electric Prunes albums at 15p. At the time I was struggling for storage space so politely declined. I still cringe whenever I see copies being sold over the internet and the prices they are being sold for.

Then there was the day I lost a million — or, more accurately, failed to take advantage of an opportunity that would have made me a £1 million. I remember a day wasted checking out the branches of London's Harlequin Records. Every bargain rack in every store was full of this record featuring a cover where the band members' heads had been superimposed onto cats' bodies painted by a nine-year-old. Well over 1,000 copies at 50p each. No wonder that didn't sell, I thought, and left the lot. So, it seems, did everyone else. The title? Pussy Plays *by 1960s psychedelic band Pussy. Value now? £1,000 each.*

I was certain that one day picture discs would be highly collectable. Record companies would give away vast quantities to chart return shops so, as these shops had not paid any money for them, they would clear them out for around 50p. I would tour these shops each week buying what I thought would become collectable. It turned out to be a shrewd move as that 50p stock often sells for between £25 and £50.

Always put your customers first. Whatever bargains I bought I would always display in the shop and I would store any surplus in the belief it would one day be collectable. In the days of record store carnage that you highlighted in your first book, it was the vinyl that I had bought all those years ago that kept me going through those difficult times.

Don't just rely on the record companies for your stock. I have bought off record libraries, radio stations, businesses closing, wholesalers, etc. When you see clearance and sale lists being emailed to you, don't delete. Have a look and think, is there anything on this list that one day will be collectable?

This is how Record Collector has kept going through the tough times and thrived in the good. You can do it too if you go with your gut feeling."

One of the joys of visiting Record Collector is that Barry is a great raconteur and is always happy to have a chat and tell you some of his fabulous anecdotes, but please visit before it is too late. After 40 years of selling vinyl, retirement beckons for this retailing veteran. Before he closes the doors for the last time, it would be nice to think that his contribution to Sheffield music might be recognised by the music industry, the city of Sheffield and the country itself.

Record Junkee

7, Earl Street, Sheffield, South Yorkshire S14 PY
01142 759035
recordjunkee.co.uk; musicjunkee42@yahoo.co.uk
Established 2009
Stock: Vinyl, CD, Pre-owned, Books, Coffee, In-stores, Instruments, Turntables

Record Junkee is a jack-of-all trades shop. It carries an excellent selection of musical instruments and vast quantities of second-hand vinyl. And above the shop is the 150-capacity Record Junkee music venue. If visiting Sheffield, make this shop your last port of call so you can catch a live performance in the evening.

Record Revivals

6 Northway, Scarborough, North Yorkshire YO11 1JL
0172 335 1983
info@recordrevivals.co.uk
Tuesday-Saturday 10am-5pm
Stock: Vinyl, CD, Pre-owned, Merchandise
Established 1982

Record Revivals is housed in the beautiful art deco Stephen Joseph Theatre, originally a Rank Cinema. The theatre itself was formerly housed in a public library, later a boy's school and then, in 1988, their long-serving artistic director Alan Ayckbourn found them a permanent home. Richard Hawley fans will be aware of the building as he poses in front of it on the cover of his 2005 album *Coles Corner*.

The record shop was originally owned by Rod Emms, who was working as an insurance broker. The shop only opened three days a week, as Rod continued to combine his insurance work with selling records.

The best deal Rod ever did originated from his insurance work. Through his company Royal Insurance, Rod learned that the famous Cavern Club in Liverpool was being demolished. Rod shrewdly contacted the demolition team and did a deal to purchase some of the bricks. The result was that a huge pile of rubble was delivered to the shop. Rod numbered the individual items, then started selling them in the shop as Beatle Bricks for £5 each. You could argue that Beatle Bricks laid the foundations of the business.

In 2017, Rod retired and sold the business to Paul Ware who, after ten years working as a probation officer, felt he had served his debt to society. As a youngster Paul had worked at Golden Disc, a record shop in Oldham, since closed. He loved working there so much that he vowed to himself that one day he would own his own shop. While working in probation, Paul dipped his toe into gig promoting at a venue in the town called The Stage Door. It was here that he witnessed the power of music. He had been delighted to book one of his musical heroes, the Jamaican ska singer Desmond Dekker, famous for his number 1 single "The Israelites". His manager called Paul and explained that although they would be leaving straight after the gig, Desmond would need to rest in a B&B in the town for a few hours, as he had not been well. On the evening of the gig, Paul entered the dressing room to meet the band. There, slumped in a chair, sat Desmond, looking very poorly. Paul questioned the band on whether the gig should go ahead. They told him it would be OK. Paul took his place in the audience but was apprehensive about the gig, worrying whether this frail elderly gentleman was going to be able to make it through the show. What happened next left him open-mouthed. Desmond burst onto the stage and soon was jumping, dancing, moving and singing with great passion. The crowd went wild and it was a fantastic gig. For Paul it showed the power that music can have on the soul.

Paul remembers his first trading day vividly. He had decided to stock more vinyl, so to make more space he removed a large spinner rack full of easy listening and classical CDs, having decided to cut back on that sort of product. It was a tough job carrying the heavy spinner and its contents up the stairs to the top floor, which he was using for storage. The first customer came in and asked Paul if he had any Mario Lanza CDs. Paul remembered that he had noticed one on the spinner rack he had carried to the top floor. Up he went to bring it down, procuring a sale. Soon after a woman came in and asked for a Perry Como CD. Yet again Paul remembered that he had one on the spinner upstairs, so off he went again. The spinner lasted one day in the top room before he brought it down. It is a good lesson in stocking what your customers wish to buy. The shop stocks endless quirky items such as musical bow ties, Beatles lava lamps and, my favourite, a Luther Vandross clock. Before you leave, check out the Weird and Wonderful vinyl section which offers some oddball recordings.

Look out for Paul, as he is a DJ at festivals including Glastonbury and Womad, playing vintage R&B, jump blues, soul, funk and gospel on vinyl.

Revo Records *The former sock maker who can spin some great yarns*
26 Westgate, Halifax, West Yorkshire HX1 1DJ
01422 345789
nick@numptyville.com; @RevoRecordsHx
Monday-Saturday 9am-5.30pm
Sunday 11am-4pm
Established 1987
Stock: Vinyl, CD, Pre-owned, DVD, 7-inch

Disillusioned at working in a sock factory, Nick Simonet decided that he needed to pull his own socks up and find a job he enjoyed. He had always been a music fan and in the 1980s, when the media were giving favourable coverage to the CD, Nick began looking for finance to start his own music shop. He couldn't get a loan to purchase CD stock. But when he changed his request for a loan to buy a new car, the money was soon on its way.

He called the shop the Halifax CD Centre but as there was already a shop in the town called the Halifax CB Centre, selling CB radios, it was soon causing confusion amongst the delivery drivers and the buying public. It made sense to change the shop's name to Revo Records, particularly as he was buying so much second-hand vinyl. These were the days when many music fans were getting rid of vinyl and buying their collections all over again on CD.

Nick describes his thirty years in business as "10 years flying, 10 years surviving and 10 years hanging on." During one grim period, he reckons he was seeing more bailiffs than sales reps. At one point, it looked as if he could survive no longer, but then, just in the nick of time, he acquired a huge batch of DVDs. He held a DVD clearance sale which was so successful it enabled him to repay his creditors. Even today, the shop has a great selection of DVDs.

Thanks to the vinyl revival, the last few years of trading has been excellent, and Nick is confident he will never have to go back to work in the sock factory again.

Spinning Discs Sheffield

55 Chesterfield Road, Meersbrook, Sheffield, South Yorkshire S8 0RL
07521 450111
spinningdiscssheffield.co.uk; @Spinning_Discs
Thursday-Friday 12 Noon-7.30pm
Saturday 10.30am-5pm
Sunday 11am-3pm
Established 2015
Stock: Vinyl, Pre-owned, Coffee

Spinning Discs Sheffield is an independent record shop established to give music lovers in Sheffield a place to meet, relax, drink coffee and browse.

With its distinctive chipboard racks, this is the place to go if you have any old vinyl that crackles or pops. The shop has an original Keith Monks Record Cleaning Machine and will restore your vinyl for only £2.50.

The shop's owner, Martin Black works with rock as part of his day job in the construction industry, building bridges and roads. After work he sells rock (and other genres) in the shop.

Meersbrook has become a vibrant retail area. On Martin's side of the street more than 20 independent shops adjoin each other. The shop has positioned itself in the heart of this community, making itself a meeting place for the musically minded.

The shop is only open three days. Martin has a team of people who help on Thursday and Friday. If you call in of an evening or a weekend, you will meet one of the hardest workers in rock (and asphalt, brick, etc).

Vinyl Eddie

Tadcaster Road, York, North Yorkshire YO24 1LR
07975 899839
vinyleddie@hotmail.co.uk; @VinylEddie
Monday, Wednesday-Saturday 10am-6pm
Established 2014
Stock: Vinyl, Pre-owned

Eddie Parkinson's shop, Vinyl Eddie, is situated near the racecourse on the outskirts of York. The Fox and Roman Pub has kindly offered its nearby car park for use of the shop's customers. If travelling from the town centre, take the No.4 bus to the Cross Keys or the Nos.12, 13 and Coastliner buses, to the Holiday Inn. Vinyl Eddie, with its quaint blue frontage, is a few metres further along.

Most of the stock is second-hand, with a limited amount of new vinyl. Prices are low, with a 10% discount for students and an excellent three-vinyl-albums-for-£10 section. Check out the original vintage gig posters on the wall, from the days when you could see Genesis and Hawkwind for 50p. There is an excellent selection of 7-inch singles.

Vinyl Tap *International rock star mistaken for a motor vehicle*
42 John William St, Huddersfield, West Yorkshire HD1 1ER
01484 517720
vinyltap.co.uk; vinyltapshop@yahoo.co.uk; @vinyltaprecords
Monday-Saturday 9am-6pm
Sunday 11am-4pm
Established 1984
Stock: Vinyl, CD, Pre-owned, In-stores

Vinyl Tap is located opposite Huddersfield train station. The shop had long been off the media's radar, but that all changed on the day before Record Store Day in 2017, when Lauren Laverne broadcast her BBC 6 Music radio show live from the shop.

Vinyl Tap was started on a Huddersfield market by Elliot Smaje who now sells second-hand vinyl in the basement of Crash Records in Leeds. The current owner of Vinyl Tap, Tony Booth has taken it to the next level.

Upstairs it is a traditional record shop, selling new vinyl and CDs. The department is run by charismatic duo Matt Scholey and Marc Kershaw, the Ant and Dec of music retailing. Matt pestered his way into getting the job, calling in nearly every day to check if any vacancies had cropped up since he last asked 24 hours earlier. Marc already had a background of working in record retailing, having served at the defunct System Records, which originally traded at Hebden Bridge before moving to Bradford.

The highlight of Marc's time working at System Records was when DJ John Peel came in. He bought lots of vinyl from African artists, along with an album by a Bradford-based brass band. Marc queried the latter selection, and John pointed out that the brass band came from where his wife Shelia was born. Marc left System to help set up a new branch of Andy's Records in Halifax.

At that time, Andy's was the largest independent record chain in the UK, with more than 40 branches. It had been started by Andy Gray, who sold records on Felixstowe Pier in 1969. Over the years, it changed its name to suit changing trends, becoming Andy's Records & Video and then, during the CD boom, just Andy's.

At the start of the new millennium, like hundreds of independent shops, Andy's began to lose money and started closing shops. Eventually they called in the receivers and the final shops were closed on September 13, 2003. These days Andy Gray owns and runs the successful Beat Goes On reissue record label.

Like many ex-staff of Andy's, Marc has happy memories of working there. Andy Gray's brother Billy was the marketing director, and both came down to help open the new Halifax branch. Marc recalls them creating a strong team work ethic. Marc has always been keen on introducing the public to new music. When he started there, staff could play what they wanted in-store, but as time went on things changed. A new rule came in, dictating that between 11am and 2pm they had to play chart music and later the shops were sent playlists of titles they were required to play. For Marc, who was a big fan of funk, soul and jazz music – all of which the playlist lacked – it was time to move on.

Downstairs at Vinyl Tap you will find one of the largest collections of second-hand vinyl anywhere in the UK. There are more than 30,000 7-inch singles alone, along with tens of thousands of LPs and dozens of collectable albums. Any vinyl fan could spend hours in the shop's £1 vinyl room. The department is run by long-serving staff member JP. At the far end of the department is a full-size stage and the shop has put on free gigs featuring Hooton Tennis Club among others.

Vinyl Tap has an impressive website where you can listen to all the new music the shop recommends. One thing the boys regret is creating such an iconic logo - a giant tap with vinyl records pouring out of it - for the shop's signage. They have lost count of the number of people who have come in, walked past thousands of records, and asked for bathroom taps, kitchen taps or for plumbing to be done. Still not as bad, perhaps, as the person who came in and enquired "By any chance, do you stock records?"

Marc remembers the massive sale that never happened, back when he was working at System. One day near closing time a bunch of well-dressed, middle-aged men came in and started picking lots of stock out of the racks. One of them approached Marc at the counter and said, "You have got some cracking stuff here. Would you mind staying open a bit later and I will go and get a van?" Marc immediately asked the rest of the staff if they would work a bit longer, as they were expecting a mega-sale. These guys were going to buy so much that they needed a van to take it away. Ten minutes later, the man who had gone to get the van came back. Never has a team of record shop staff been so disappointed to see an international rock star walk through the doors.

It wasn't a motor vehicle that the man had gone to get: it was Van Morrison. the men who had been looking through the stock were Van's band. Although the staff never got the massive order they had hoped for, Van bought a lot of records and it gave them a great comic tale to tell people down the pub.

I have a lot of time for Van Morrison, about whom tales of visits to record shops abound. Barry at Record Collector in Sheffield recalled an occasion back in the late 1970s, when Van's record label Warner's threw a party in a posh London wine bar to celebrate the release of one of his albums. This was in the days before Van started wearing his distinctive hat, suit and shades, and he turned up wearing an old pair of jeans, a scruffy T-shirt and a jacket with patches on the elbows. The doorman stopped him from going in. "They're expecting me," Van said. "Just a minute then," said the doorman, before going into the bar and shouting: "Did anyone order a minicab?"

Vinyl Underground Records
3, Regent Street, Barnsley, South Yorkshire S70 2EG
01226 872232
vinylundergroundrecords@gmail.com; @Vinylundergroundrecords
Monday-Saturday 9am-5pm
Established 2017
Stock: Vinyl, Pre-owned

Vinyl Underground is easy to find. It is located near one of the most famous and beautiful buildings in Yorkshire, Barnsley Town Hall. The building, which dominates the skyline, was built in 1933 at a cost of £188,000, an enormous amount of money back then. George Orwell, in his book *The Road to Wigan Pier*, made the point that with so much poverty in the town, the money could have been put to better use. If you visit Vinyl Underground late on a winter afternoon, when it is dark, the fluorescent lights will be turned on in the spire of the Town Hall, giving off an eerie blue light. The spirit of Orwell is evoked, as local wags joke that the mayor is using his sunbed again.

Vinyl Underground is a welcome addition to a town that has suffered many record shop closures over the years. Owner Andrew Shaw opened Vox Pop, in Manchester's Northern Quarter in 1999. By the time he was forced to close in 2007, the number of record shops in Manchester had halved (from 20 to 10). Now, after a spell of working as a painter and decorator, Andrew is back thanks to the vinyl revival.

His sister-in-law Christine suggested that Barnsley would be perfect for a new record shop and offered to be a sleeping partner to help fund the project. Andrew had sold most of his stock but he remembered a friend who had the biggest collection he knew of. He got in touch and discovered that he wanted to sell his whole collection - 100,000 items in an all-or-nothing deal. Andrew raised the funds and a couple of weeks later, two huge, articulated trucks arrived in Barnsley with the 100,000 records.

Since the purchase Andrew has filtered 70,000 records into the shop. He is now adding them in at 1,000 per month, so at that rate, you have nearly three years to pay the shop a visit at the very least.

Wah Wah Records
15 Brook Street, Wakefield, West Yorkshire WF1 1QW
07763 660788
wahwahrecords@hotmail.co.uk; @wahwahrecord
Monday 9.30am-4.30pm
Tuesday 10am-4pm
Wednesday-Saturday 9.30am-4.30pm
Sunday 10am-3pm
Established 2014
Stock: Vinyl, Pre-owned, CD, Cassette, In-stores, Tickets

Wah Wah Records is owned by the husband and wife partnership of Alan and Gemma Nutton and is notable for the giant suitcases in which the shop's vinyl is held. It has one of the largest hip-hop sections in the North.

Alan's and Gemma's favourite characters include the man who first popped in just after they opened in 2014, to tell them that "Music is dead" and "It will never last". Almost every month since then he has returned to offer well-meaning advice about what the duo should sell instead of records. He has suggested tools, quality bedding and kids' toys.

Another favourite customer is the man who introduces himself as "Mr Jones from Wales" every time he pops in. He recently called in carrying an oversize bucket with about thirty bottles of shower gel inside. He informed them he was fed up with having half-bottles all over the house and was going to fix a tap onto the bucket and pour all his shower gels inside. "Should keep me going for a while," he kept saying.

ACKNOWLEDGEMENTS

This book would not have happened without the support of the following people: my good friend and editor David Sinclair for sorting out the wheat from the chaff; my son Ben for helping with the first edit and his constant support; Andrew Worsdale for helping to knock it into shape; Richard Allen for the great work he has done in helping to remove LVCR which has made a major contribution to the record shop revival; and James Weston for doing the sleeve.

My thanks also go to:
The many others who have supported me including Bob Lewis, Chris Lowe, David Stock at Music Sales, Ian Crockett, Jennifer Otter Bickerdike, Julia Weir, Kim Bayley, Lisa Redford, Michael Kurtz, Our Col, Pip Piper and Rachael Corcoran.

The people who have shaped my musical taste: the late John Peel, Johnnie Walker, Bob Harris and BBC 6 Music and to the many magnificent artists I distribute as part of my day job at Proper.

Alan Price for proofreading. Drew Hill, Malcolm Mills and all the wonderful team at Proper Music. You are a joy to work with.

My amazing Dad who makes me laugh each day, and my much-missed Mum for teaching me values, honesty and manners.

All the incredible record shop owners I have met over the years. Witnessing the record shop revival has been heartwarming. Long may it continue.

Kim Bayley, Megan Page and all at ERA.

Zahia Guidoum Castiblanque.

All the music fans who have continued to support their local record shop.

As Bon Jovi would say: Keep the Faith.

BIOGRAPHY

Graham Jones was born in Anfield, Liverpool.

After leaving school he worked in a factory making the flavour for cheese and onion crisps. Among his many claims to fame is his production of the first test batch of Worcester Sauce-flavoured crisps. Unfortunately, he misread the recipe adding 25 kilos of colouring instead of 25 grams. It was the best mistake he ever made. Forced as a result to seek alternative employment, he landed a job as an assistant at HMV.

He managed the Cherry Boys, a cult band from Liverpool that made Spinal Tap look mundane. He eventually found his vocation travelling around the country selling records, tapes and CDs to independent record shops, a job he has done for over 30 years.

One of the founders of Proper Music Distribution, Graham should be in the *Guinness World Records* for visiting more record shops than any other person. Following hundreds of record shop closures, and worried that record shops would go the way of stamp shops, coin shops and candlestick makers, he toured the UK to interview the owners and staff of 50 record shops and document their tales for his book *Last Shop Standing: Whatever Happened to Record Shops?*

The true story of Graham's time spent working in and around the world of independent record retailing was every bit as colourful, funny, strange, and occasionally as sad as any fictional yarn. In Last Shop Standing he amassed many extraordinary tales of the best shops he had done business with over the years and hilarious accounts of the worst. Blue Hippo Media produced an award-winning documentary film based on his book.

Over the years Graham has collected a vast number of funny stories and anecdotes. He related the best of them in his second book *Strange Requests and Comic Tales from Record Shops.*

For the last five years he has been writing *The Vinyl Revival and the Shops That Made it Happen*, a guide to independent record shops in the UK that sell new vinyl. The project took longer than expected due to so many new record shops opening.

Graham has given more than 100 talks at music and book shops and festivals, and is guaranteed to have an audience in hysterics with his tales from the crazy world of record retailing. He has appeared on many TV shows and BBC radio stations talking about record shops.

Graham lives in Petersfield, Hampshire.

He can be contacted via the website www.lastshopstanding.com; by email at graham@lastshopstanding.co.uk; and on Twitter @revival_vinyl

Introducing
Friels Vintage Cider

• Award winning medium dry vintage cider, crafted with a blend of traditional eating apple varieties including Red Falstaff, Katy and Windsor.

• Friels is made in a limited batch with the first press of the juiciest apples from each season's harvest of our Herefordshire and Worcestershire orchards.

• Official cider of Record Store Day 2018

Pure Refreshment

iHaveit Buy Sell Collect and Value Music

iHaveit was launched in 2018, it is a **Music Trading** platform like eBay but just for music.

iHaveit also includes a full **Music Collecting** module that lists, stores, catalogues, displays and reports on your collection, with lots of search and view choices

Once captured in iHaveit you can see the estimated **financial value** of your Vinyl, CD's and cassette collection

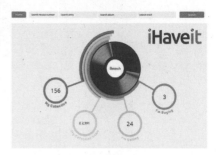

Sell, Buy, Collect and Value Music

Free to use at www.ihaveit.io

iHaveit can help you **buy** rare music with thousands of rare items for sale. You can also **sell** your music. iHaveit only charge a 6% seller commission fee on sold items

Music Trading Company
GIFT Certificate
www.iHaveit.io/shares

GIFT
Certificate

Own a Music
Trading Company

£25

£25

This gift certificate is valued at £25 and is redeemable at UK Independent Record Stores
* Conditions apply

To learn more or to buy shares go to www.ihaveit.io/shares